the COASTAL LIVING® COOKBOOK

the ultimate recipe collection for people who love the coast

the COASTAL LIVING® COOKBOOK

the ultimate recipe collection for people who love the coast

Oxmoor House®

Library of Congress Catalog Number: 2003113679

ISBN: 0-8487-2828-9

Printed in the United States of America

Second Printing 2004

To order additional publications, call
1-800-765-6400.

For more books to enrich your life, visit
oxmoorhouse.com

Coastal Living®

Editor-in-Chief: Kay A. Fuston

Art Director: Lane W. Gregory

Executive Editor: Jennifer Chappell

Managing Editor: Vicki J. Weathers

Senior Editors: Jeff Book, Susan Haynes,
Cathy Still Johnson, Steve Millburg

Food and Entertaining Editor: Julia Dowling Rutland

Features Writers: Sarah Brueggemann, Paige Porter

Assistant Homes Editor: Lacey N. Howard

Assistant Art Director: Craig Hyde

Photography Coordinator: Susan E. Cox

Copy Chief: Susan Cullen Anderson

Assistant Copy Chief: Susan Emack Alison

Assistant Copy Editor: Katie Finley

Production Manager: Nicole L. Johnson

Production Assistant: Charly Porter Kusta

Online Editor: Rex Perry

Office Manager: Mamie Walling

Oxmoor House, Inc.

Editor-in-Chief: Nancy Fitzpatrick Wyatt

Executive Editor: Susan Carlisle Payne

Art Director: Cynthia Rose Cooper

Copy Chief: Allison Long Lowery

The Coastal Living® Cookbook

Editor: Julie Fisher Gunter

Copy Editor: Diane Rose

Senior Designer: Melissa Jones Clark

Editorial Assistant: Dawn Russell

Test Kitchens Director: Elizabeth Tyler Luckett

Test Kitchens Assistant Director: Julie Christopher

Recipe Editor: Gayle Sadler

Test Kitchens Staff: Kristi Carter, Nicole L. Faber,
Kathleen Phillips, Jan A. Smith, Elise Weis,
Kelley Self Wilton

Photographers: Ralph Anderson, Jim Bathie,
Tina Cornett, William Dickey, Brit Huckabay,
Becky Luigart-Stayner, Randy Mayor,
Art Meripol, Allen Rokach, Charles Walton IV

Photo Stylists: Cindy Manning Barr, Kay E. Clarke,
Melanie J. Clarke, Lydia DeGaris-Pursell,
Buffy Hargett, Ashley Johnson Wyatt

Director of Production: Phillip Lee

Production Manager: Theresa L. Beste

Production Assistant: Faye Porter Bonner

Publishing Systems Administrator: Rick Tucker

Contributors

Editorial Intern: Leigh-Ann Laney

Indexers: Mary Ann Laurens, McCharen Pratt

Primer Text: Jane Doerfer, Catherine Fallin,
Tom Horton, Karen MacNeil

Photographers: Matt Brown, Bruce Buck,
Langdon Clay, Wyatt Counts, Fran Gealer,
J. Savage Gibson, David Harp, Michael Jensen,
Deborah Whitlaw Llewellyn, Sylvia Martin,
Gary Moss, Howard Lee Puckett, Barth Tillotson,
Ben Van Hook

Stylists: Virginia Cravens Houston, Mary Lyn H.
Jenkins, Leslie Byars Simpson

Cover: *Romas and Goats (page 20), Spiced Shrimp Zapala (page 18)*
Back Cover: *Strawberry Shortcake with Mint Cream (page 262), Bouillabaisse à la Marseillaise (page 211)*

Easy Antipasto, page 104

contents

welcome

Consider how you eat and entertain at the beach. If you're like me, you focus on the basics, leaving time to relax and enjoy your surroundings. After all, most of us escape to the beach because we prefer the slower pace. We go for long, leisurely walks, dipping our toes in the water and relishing the warmth of the sun on our skin. We pare down our belongings and schedule our days by the tides.

Reflecting that laid-back lifestyle, **The *Coastal Living* Cookbook** expresses a casual food and entertaining philosophy that works whether you live or vacation on the coast—or just dream of being there. This book stays true to its namesake magazine, *Coastal Living,* by showcasing informal, no-hassle menus and delicious seafood in an easy-to-follow format with captivating photography.

And while it celebrates the bounty of the sea—shrimp, scallops, lobster, crabs, oysters, and a multitude of fish—it's distinctive from other "coastal" cookbooks because it contains more than seafood fare. Much like the magazine's food section, it encompasses a large number of nonseafood recipes featuring beef, chicken, and pork. This volume also goes beyond main courses, offering chapters highlighting appetizers and beverages, salads, side dishes, breads, and desserts.

Our menus incorporate not only a wide variety of recipes and entertaining ideas, but also a wealth of other information. You'll find wine-pairing suggestions for many recipes and helpful techniques and tips for selecting, storing, and preparing ingredients. Plus, you'll have access to signature recipes from chefs who have mastered regional delicacies, such as lobster stew by New England celebrity chef Todd English. But you won't need professional expertise to get similar results. We'll walk you through the recipes, one step at a time.

Once you've explored this book, you'll agree that it truly is "The Ultimate Recipe Collection for People Who Love the Coast." By fusing *Coastal Living* magazine favorites with a handful of new recipes that cater to the palates of sea and land lovers alike, we've created a timeless cookbook that you can come to again and again. So kick off your shoes, pour a glass of wine, and enjoy the carefree entertaining style of life on the coast. Cheers!

Kay A. Fuston

—Kay A. Fuston, Editor-in-Chief
Coastal Living magazine

Strawberry Shortcake, page 262

our favorite recipes

Our staff loves to make these recipes for their own families and friends. They're the best of the best, and we've gathered them for you here.

▲ Creamy Shrimp and Grits (page 47): This Southern plate features succulent shrimp sautéed in wine and piled onto garlic grits.

◄ Strawberry Shortcake (page 262): Judy Feagin, a former *Coastal Living* food editor, pronounced this the best ever. Here's why: Classic sweet biscuit base meets fresh berries laced with balsamic vinegar.

Frozen Tropical Slush (page 124): Mango, rum, and lime juice blend into this slushy drink of choice.

▼ Grilled Grouper with Chimichurri Sauce (page 82): Mild and meaty grouper fillet marinates in chimichurri, the popular Argentinean salsa; then it's grilled to flaky perfection.

Halibut with Dried Tomato-Basil Pesto (page 311): Planked fish is all the rage, and we agree, particularly in this dish where the cedar flavor smolders its way into the fish and marries well with the tangy tomato topping.

▼ Sangría Pops (page 255): We've found the perfect beach refreshment—for adults only. These pops quench your thirst and satisfy the sweet tooth.

▲ Roasted Rosemary-Garlic Sweet Potatoes (page 85): High-heat roasting brings out the natural goodness in these potatoes tossed with olive oil, garlic, and fresh rosemary.

Peanut Butter and Chocolate Chunk Cookies (page 256): What's not to love in a jumbo chocolate chip cookie flavored with peanut butter and packed with pecans and oats?

▲ Dungeness Crab Cakes with Orange-Butter Sauce (page 176): What's special about these cakes is the presence of pickled ginger, the coarse breadcrumb coating, and a buttery rich sauce to drizzle over the end result.

Turnip, Apple, and Cheddar Gratin (page 91): Slices of turnip, apple, and onion are layered in a skillet, sprinkled with herbs, covered with cheese, and baked to a golden finish.

Slaw with Feta Cheese (page 131): One *Coastal Living* staffer who doesn't eat slaw professed a changed palate with this recipe.

▼ Lobster Salad with Papaya and Maui Onion (page 76): Fried spaghetti strands and a sesame dressing highlight this exotic salad.

entertaining menus

georgia sea thrill

Nature's bounty commands attention at this floating sunset party that toasts the arrival of summer, but it's Alan and Kimberly Worthley's food that the guests find most spectacular. Alan and Kimberly's restaurant, Georgia Sea Grill, is one of the top dining spots on St. Simons Island. The cozy place offers a mix of mostly Atlantic seafood dishes served creatively and generously. This menu hints at how much the Worthleys like to entertain, especially on board one of their favorite local cruise ships, the Zapala.

menu

serves 12 or more

Mint Julep Iced Tea

Chilled Georgia Peach Soup with Raspberry Cream

Cruisin' Crab Dip   Toasted French bread with Casino Butter

Spiced Shrimp Zapala   Romas and Goats

Artichoke Cakes with Cajun Rémoulade

Pecan Tarts   Coconut-Buttermilk Pie

Mint Julep Iced Tea

"This is bourbon-drinking country," Alan says.

8   mint leaves
1   lemon, sliced
1   lime, sliced
1   cup bourbon
3   cups cold sweetened tea
Cubed or crushed ice

Combine first 3 ingredients in a 2-quart pitcher, pressing with the back of a spoon to crush mint. Stir in bourbon and tea. Add ice. Yield: 8 cups.

"Everyone feels like they've gone back in time when they step aboard the *Zapala*," Kimberly says. **"It couldn't be more fun."**

Chilled Georgia Peach Soup with Raspberry Cream

(shown on page 16)

2   quarts chopped fresh peaches
1   cup dry white wine
1   cup peach schnapps
½   cup sugar
1   teaspoon chopped fresh mint
½   teaspoon ground cinnamon
⅛   teaspoon ground nutmeg
2   cups half-and-half
Raspberry Cream
Garnish: raspberry puree*

Stir together first 7 ingredients in a saucepan. Cook over medium heat 15 minutes or until peaches are tender and liquid is reduced. Cool; process in a blender until smooth, stopping to scrape down sides. Cover and chill. Stir in half-and-half. Top each serving with Raspberry Cream. Garnish, if desired. Yield: 10 cups.

Raspberry Cream

¼   cup fresh or frozen raspberries, thawed
¼   cup heavy whipping cream
½   cup sour cream

Process raspberries in a blender until smooth. Pour puree through a wire-mesh strainer into a small bowl. Press against strainer with the back of a spoon; discard seeds. Beat whipping cream until stiff peaks form. Fold in raspberry puree and sour cream; stir well. Yield: 1 cup.
*Puree ¾ cup thawed berries in blender; strain.

The *Zapala* was built in 1913 by the New York Yacht Engine and Launch Company for stockbroker Joseph Cousins. She was later acquired by the John Adams Floating Theatre Company, a barge and tugboat troupe that traveled the Eastern Seaboard presenting dockside shows. That led to her biggest claim to fame: John's friend Edna Ferber reportedly got the idea for the book and subsequent musical *Show Boat* from the floating vaudeville productions. Eventually, though, the yacht-turned-stage was abandoned for 18 years in a boatyard until it was found and refurbished. Now it's operated by The Sea Island Yacht Club, which provides it for guests of The Cloister and rents it out for private parties.

Chilled Georgia Peach Soup
with Raspberry Cream, page 14

Cruisin' Crab Dip

2   (8-ounce) packages cream cheese,
     softened
1   (4.5-ounce) can chopped green chiles,
     drained
1   cup seeded and chopped tomato
1   small garlic clove, minced
¼   to ½ cup whipping cream
2   tablespoons fresh lemon juice
1   teaspoon Worcestershire sauce
1   teaspoon hot sauce
¼   teaspoon salt
¼   teaspoon ground red pepper
¼   teaspoon black pepper
1   pound fresh jumbo lump crabmeat,
     drained
Garnish: chopped fresh parsley

Combine first 11 ingredients in a large nonstick
skillet; place over low heat, and cook, stirring
constantly, until mixture is smooth and bubbly.
Gently fold in crabmeat. Spoon into serving
bowl, and garnish, if desired. Serve with French
bread slices toasted with Casino Butter. Yield:
6 cups.

Casino Butter

*"This is meant to be served generously,"
says Alan. "Use leftovers for grilled meats
or pasta—anything, really."*

1   pound unsalted butter, softened
3   tablespoons white wine
2   tablespoons fresh lemon juice
1   teaspoon hot sauce
¾   teaspoon salt
4   green onions, chopped
⅓   cup chopped red bell pepper
⅓   cup chopped fresh parsley

Pulse first 5 ingredients in a food processor
until combined. Add remaining ingredients;
process until well blended, stopping to scrape
down sides.

Spread mixture on French bread slices; bake
or grill until toasted. Cover and refrigerate or
freeze remaining butter. Yield: 2 cups.

Cruisin' Crab Dip

vine advice

Chef Alan Worthley suggests these complementary wines to serve guests:
• **Frog's Leap Chardonnay:** Notes Alan, "It's
tart, crisp, apple-y. And it doesn't get sweet
as it warms up."
• **Grgich Hills Fumé Blanc:** "This one's
herbaceous and fruity and not as tart as most
varieties. It's smoother, more subtle," he says.
• **Robert Stemmler Pinot Noir:** Alan likes this
light, fruity wine slightly chilled: "It's an
excellent red for a summer seafood picnic."

A golden-hued horizon—more kaleidoscope than sunset—provides a glorious backdrop for this early evening cruise.

Spiced Shrimp Zapala

1	cup olive oil
1	cup cider vinegar
½	cup tomato sauce
¼	cup chopped fresh parsley
3	tablespoons capers, chopped
2	tablespoons hot sauce
2	tablespoons Worcestershire sauce
2	teaspoons dry mustard
1	teaspoon salt
1	red bell pepper, sliced
1	yellow bell pepper, sliced
1	green bell pepper, sliced
½	red onion, sliced
3	pounds jumbo fresh shrimp, peeled and deveined

Combine first 13 ingredients; cover and chill.

Cook shrimp in boiling salted water to cover 3 to 5 minutes or until shrimp turn pink; drain.

Add shrimp to vinaigrette; cover and chill 2 to 3 hours. Drain or serve with a slotted spoon. Yield: 8 cups.

movable feast

Follow the Worthleys' tips on how to pack party-boat fare.

• **Keep Mint Julep Iced Tea** in gallon-size plastic jugs. Chill in ice chest. Transfer to a pitcher once on board.

• **Store Chilled Georgia Peach Soup** in large plastic containers. Keep Raspberry Cream and puree separate in small plastic containers. Chill in ice chest.

• **Spoon Cajun Rémoulade** into a zip-top plastic bag or plastic container. Chill in ice chest.

• **Pack Spiced Shrimp Zapala** in large zip-top plastic bags. Store in ice chest.

• **Serve Cruisin' Crab Dip, Romas and Goats, and Artichoke Cakes** at room temperature. Pack in large zip-top plastic bags.

• **Pretoast French bread slices** with Casino Butter; seal in large zip-top plastic bags.

• **Transport Pecan Tarts** easily in large plastic containers. **Slice the Coconut-Buttermilk Pie** before packing it in a plastic pie container.

"This is a contemporary take on the traditional shrimp cocktail," Kimberly says. For the most appealing presentation, leave tails on.

Spiced Shrimp Zapala

Romas and Goats

Romas and Goats

Alan suggests serving at room temperature.

1 cup Japanese breadcrumbs (Panko*)
1 cup freshly grated Parmesan cheese
¼ cup chopped fresh parsley
1 tablespoon fresh lemon juice
1 teaspoon minced garlic
⅓ cup butter, melted
11 ounces goat cheese, softened
½ teaspoon freshly ground pepper
¼ teaspoon salt
12 plum (Roma) tomatoes
Pesto

Stir together first 5 ingredients in a shallow dish. Stir in butter; set aside.

Combine goat cheese, pepper, and salt in a small bowl.

Cut tomatoes in half horizontally; trim a small amount from rounded edges, if necessary, so halves will stand upright. Remove seeds and pulp. Spoon about 2 teaspoons goat cheese mixture into each half.

Dip tomato halves, upside down, in breadcrumb mixture, coating generously. Place right side up on an ungreased baking sheet.

Bake at 400° for 15 to 18 minutes or until lightly browned. Transfer tomatoes to a serving platter. Drizzle with pesto. Yield: 2 dozen.

*Panko—large, coarse breadcrumbs typically used in Japanese cooking—can be found at Asian or international markets. Toasted fresh breadcrumbs can substitute.

Artichoke Cakes with Cajun Rémoulade

3 (14-ounce) cans artichoke hearts, drained and chopped
2 large eggs, lightly beaten
1 cup soft breadcrumbs, lightly packed
½ cup chopped red bell pepper
2 tablespoons chopped green onions
¾ cup mayonnaise
¼ cup whipping cream
2 tablespoons fresh lemon juice
2 teaspoons Dijon mustard
1 teaspoon salt
1 teaspoon Worcestershire sauce
Cajun Rémoulade

Squeeze liquid from artichokes, using paper towels, until artichokes are just slightly moist. Place artichokes in a medium bowl. Add eggs and next 3 ingredients.

Combine mayonnaise and next 5 ingredients in a separate bowl; stir well. Add mayonnaise mixture to artichoke mixture; stir gently until thoroughly combined. Cover and chill at least 2 hours.

Place a large, lightly oiled nonstick skillet over medium-high heat. Scoop artichoke mixture into 1½-inch balls; place in skillet, and flatten slightly. Cook 2 to 2½ minutes on each side or until golden and slightly set. Transfer to a lightly greased baking sheet.

Bake at 400° for 10 to 12 minutes or until done. Serve with Cajun Rémoulade. Yield: about 2 dozen.

Cajun Rémoulade

½ cup chopped celery
½ cup chopped green onions
2 tablespoons chopped fresh parsley
2 garlic cloves, chopped
1 cup mayonnaise
1 tablespoon paprika
2 tablespoons capers
2 tablespoons prepared horseradish
1 tablespoon Dijon mustard
1 tablespoon ketchup
1 tablespoon fresh lemon juice
1 tablespoon Worcestershire sauce
1 tablespoon cider vinegar
1 tablespoon hot sauce
½ teaspoon salt

Pulse first 4 ingredients in a food processor until finely chopped; drain well. Add remaining ingredients; pulse 3 or 4 times, stopping to scrape down sides. Yield: 2 cups.

"I got a Girl Scout badge for this recipe way back when," Kimberly says. **"It's based on my grandmother's chess pie."**

Pecan Tarts

2 (3-ounce) packages cream cheese, softened
⅔ cup unsalted butter, softened
2 cups all-purpose flour
Pinch salt
1 cup chopped pecans
3 large eggs, beaten
1 cup firmly packed dark brown sugar
¾ cup light corn syrup
2 tablespoons butter, melted
1 teaspoon vanilla extract
½ teaspoon salt

Beat cream cheese and ⅔ cup butter at medium speed with an electric mixer until blended. Add flour and pinch of salt; beat until combined. Divide dough in half. Flatten each half into a round disk about 1 inch thick. Wrap in heavy-duty plastic wrap; chill 1 hour.

Shape dough into 2-inch balls. Flatten balls, and place in 3-inch muffin cups, forming each into a shell. (Dough should form a lip above muffin cups.) Sprinkle pecans evenly in pastry shells.

Whisk together eggs and remaining 5 ingredients until blended. Carefully pour egg mixture evenly over pecans. (Pastries will be full.)

Bake at 350° for 30 to 35 minutes or until set. Yield: 12 tarts.

Coconut-Buttermilk Pie

"We get so many compliments on this pie," Kimberly says.

½ (15-ounce) package refrigerated piecrusts
2 cups flaked coconut
½ cup butter, melted
1½ cups sugar
2 tablespoons all-purpose flour
4 large eggs, beaten
½ cup buttermilk
1 teaspoon vanilla extract
1 cup (6 ounces) semisweet chocolate morsels

Fit piecrust into a 9-inch pieplate according to package directions; fold edges under, and crimp. Bake at 450° for 5 minutes.

Toast coconut at 325° for 5 to 10 minutes or until golden brown, stirring twice. Set aside.

Beat butter, sugar, and flour at medium speed with an electric mixer until blended; add eggs, buttermilk, and vanilla, beating well.

Stir in toasted coconut and chocolate morsels. Pour filling into prepared piecrust.

Bake at 325° for 30 minutes; shield edges with foil to prevent excessive browning. Bake 25 to 30 more minutes or until set. Yield: 1 (9-inch) pie.

Pecan Tart

surf, sand & salmon

Salmonfest is the ultimate indoor/outdoor banquet, hosted annually by Peter Magnani at his Northern California beach home. After loading up their plates, guests meander from house to beach—and back again for seconds. Throughout the party, the feast changes as friends and family arrive with more culinary delights in hand. Some even share their favorite beverages. For Peter and his wife, Lisa Wrenn, Salmonfest welcomes others to enjoy their tradition of casual entertaining.

menu

serves 18 to 20

Poached Salmon   Cucumber-Dill Sauce   Watercress Sauce   Aïoli

Oysters on the half shell   Cocktail Sauce   Mignonette Sauce

Roasted Potato Salad   Fresh Mozzarella-Tomato-Basil Salad   Caesar Salad

Brownies Filled with Caramel Candies   Candy Apple Creations

Proud host Peter Magnani displays a prized salmon, bound for the dinner table. Each year, he varies his recipe by adding a bit of this and that—always with delectable results.

Poached Salmon

2   medium onions, quartered
3   celery ribs with leaves, cut into 1-inch pieces
2   carrots, cut into 1-inch pieces
6   parsley sprigs
10 black peppercorns
2   bay leaves
1   teaspoon salt
3   cups water
3   (8-ounce) bottles clam juice
2   cups dry white wine
1   (8-pound) salmon, dressed
Garnishes: Cucumber slices, lemon slices, and sprigs of fresh dill
Cucumber-Dill Sauce, Watercress Sauce, Aïoli

Combine first 10 ingredients in a fish poacher or a large oval roasting pan. Bring to a boil. Cover, reduce heat, and simmer 30 minutes. Cool to room temperature; strain, reserving liquid. Discard solids. Return liquid to poacher.

Remove the head, tail, and fins from salmon. Wrap fish in cheesecloth; tie ends with string. Place fish in poaching liquid; add water to cover by 1 to 1½ inches. Cover and bring to a simmer; simmer 20 minutes. Remove from heat, leaving fish in liquid for 15 minutes. Remove fish from liquid. Cool. Cover and refrigerate 8 hours.

Remove cheesecloth. Remove and discard skin. Place fish on a platter, and garnish, if desired. Serve with Cucumber-Dill Sauce, Watercress Sauce, and Aïoli. Yield: 18 to 20 servings.

Peter and Lisa serve the salmon on a platter with thin slices of lemon and cucumber, topped off with fresh dill sprigs. Condiments include Cucumber-Dill Sauce, Watercress Sauce, and Aïoli.

Peter shucks heaps of briny Kumamoto oysters, purchased just hours earlier at a nearby oyster farm.

Cucumber-Dill Sauce

1   (8-ounce) container low-fat yogurt
1/3   cup mayonnaise
1/2   cup unpeeled, seeded, finely chopped cucumber
1/4   teaspoon salt
1/4   teaspoon dried dillweed

Place strainer in a 1-quart glass measuring cup. Line strainer with a coffee filter. Spoon yogurt into filter. Cover loosely with plastic wrap; refrigerate 12 hours. Spoon yogurt into a bowl; discard liquid.

Add mayonnaise and remaining ingredients; stir well. Cover and chill. Yield: 1 1/2 cups.

Watercress Sauce

1   bunch fresh watercress, stemmed and chopped (about 1 1/2 cups)
1   green onion, chopped
1   cup mayonnaise
1/2   cup whipping cream
1 1/2 tablespoons fresh lemon juice
1/8   teaspoon ground red pepper

Process all ingredients in a blender or food processor until smooth, stopping to scrape down sides; cover and chill. Yield: 2 cups.

Aïoli

10   garlic cloves
3   cups mayonnaise
1/2   cup extra-virgin olive oil

Chop garlic in a food processor. Add mayonnaise, and process until smooth. With processor running, pour oil through food chute in a slow, steady stream, blending until smooth. Yield: 4 cups.

Cocktail Sauce

2/3   cup ketchup
1/4   cup fresh lemon juice
3   tablespoons prepared horseradish
2   teaspoons Worcestershire sauce
1/4   teaspoon hot sauce

Combine all ingredients, stirring well. Cover and chill at least 2 hours. Serve with oysters on the half shell. Yield: 1 cup.

Mignonette Sauce

3/4   cup red wine vinegar
1/3   cup finely chopped shallots
1/2   teaspoon salt
2   tablespoons black peppercorns, crushed

Combine all ingredients, stirring well. Serve with oysters on the half shell. Yield: 1 cup.

Roasted Potato Salad

5   pounds new potatoes
1   bunch fresh sage (about 1/2 cup sage leaves)
1/2   cup extra-virgin olive oil, divided
1 1/4 teaspoons salt, divided
3/4   teaspoon pepper, divided
1/4   cup red wine vinegar
3   tablespoons finely chopped shallots
1   teaspoon fresh thyme leaves
Garnishes: fresh sage leaves, fresh thyme sprigs

Place potatoes and sage in a 15- x 10-inch jellyroll pan. Drizzle 1/4 cup olive oil over potatoes; toss gently.

Bake at 450° for 35 to 40 minutes or until potatoes are tender and browned, stirring every 15 minutes. Cool. Cut potatoes in half; sprinkle with 1 teaspoon salt and 1/2 teaspoon pepper. Place potatoes in a large serving bowl. Crumble roasted sage leaves over potatoes.

Whisk together remaining 1/4 cup oil, red wine vinegar, 1/4 teaspoon salt, 1/4 teaspoon pepper, shallots, and thyme; drizzle over potato salad. Toss gently. Garnish, if desired. Serve at room temperature. Serve with Aïoli, if desired. Yield: 15 servings.

vine advice

"In the wine category," Peter says, "we stick to reasonably priced California wines, our favorites being Robert Mondavi Coastal Cabernet, Villa Mt. Eden Chardonnay, as well as the Rodney Strong Cabernet. Another one we like a lot is Rabbit Ridge Zinfandel. We find these wines are a good value, easy to find, and appropriate for a casual event."

Roasted Potato Salad

Friends bring along favorite dishes, such as colorful Fresh Mozzarella-Tomato-Basil Salad, bursting with the flavors of fresh basil and coarsely ground pepper.

Fresh Mozzarella-Tomato-Basil Salad

½ pound fresh mozzarella cheese, drained
2 large red tomatoes, sliced
2 large yellow tomatoes, sliced
1 cup pear tomatoes, cut in half
½ teaspoon salt
3 tablespoons extra-virgin olive oil
Freshly ground pepper
½ cup shredded or chopped fresh basil
Garnish: fresh basil sprig

Slice cheese into ¼-inch slices. Alternate tomato and cheese slices on a platter; add pear tomato halves, and sprinkle with salt. Drizzle with olive oil. Cover and chill 4 hours. Just before serving, sprinkle with freshly ground pepper and basil. Garnish, if desired. Yield: 6 to 8 servings.

Caesar Salad

2 heads romaine lettuce
¾ cup olive oil
¼ cup red wine vinegar
1 teaspoon Worcestershire sauce
½ teaspoon salt
¼ teaspoon dry mustard
1 large garlic clove, crushed
1 lemon, cut in half
Freshly ground pepper
Freshly shaved Parmesan cheese
Garlic Crostini
1 (2-ounce) can anchovy fillets, drained

Wash lettuce under cold running water. Trim core, and separate stalk into leaves; discard wilted or discolored portions. Shake leaves to remove moisture. Place lettuce in a large zip-top plastic bag; chill at least 2 hours.

Combine oil and next 5 ingredients in a jar. Cover tightly, and shake vigorously. Set aside.

Cut coarse ribs from large leaves of lettuce and discard. Tear leaves into pieces, and place in a large salad bowl. Pour dressing over lettuce; toss gently.

Squeeze juice from lemon halves over salad; sprinkle with pepper, and shave cheese over salad. Top with Garlic Crostini and anchovies. Serve immediately. Yield: 6 to 8 servings.
Note: Double both salads if you're serving a big crowd.

Garlic Crostini

1 small French baguette, cut into ½-inch slices
1 cup butter, melted
4 garlic cloves, pressed
¾ cup grated Parmesan cheese

Arrange baguette slices in 2 (15- x 10-inch) jellyroll pans.

Combine butter and garlic, and drizzle over bread.

Bake at 250° for 1 hour or until golden brown, turning every 15 minutes. Sprinkle immediately with cheese; cool. Store in an airtight container in refrigerator. Yield: 6 to 8 servings.

Caesar Salad

salmonfest spirits

When it comes to beer, host Peter Magnani says, "Red Tail Ale and Lagunitas—both Northern California microbreweries—would be our favorites. We drink a lot of Pacifico beer from Mexico, and Sierra Nevada Pale Ale from California."

Brownies Filled with Caramel Candies

1   (21-ounce) package brownie mix
1   cup coarsely chopped walnuts,
    toasted
1/2 pound milk chocolate-covered caramel
    patties*

Prepare brownie mix according to package
directions for fudgy brownies, adding walnuts.
Spoon half of batter into a greased 13- x 9-inch
pan. Place caramel patties in an even layer over
batter. Spoon remaining batter over candies.
    Bake at 350° for 30 to 35 minutes or until
done. Cool on a wire rack. Cut into squares.
Yield: 2½ dozen.
*We tested with See's milk chocolate-covered
caramel patties. One (12-ounce) package of
chocolate-covered caramels could also be used
in this recipe.

Candy Apple Creations

8   Red Delicious apples
8   (6-inch) wooden twigs or craft sticks
2   (14-ounce) packages caramels
1/4 cup water
Decorations: chopped peanuts, white
    chocolate morsels, assorted candies,
    ribbon

Wash and dry apples. Insert wooden twigs or
craft sticks into stem end of apples; set aside.
    Combine caramels and water in a heavy
saucepan. Cook over low heat, stirring constantly, until caramels melt. Remove caramel
mixture from heat.
    Dip apples in caramel mixture, covering
apples completely. (Spoon caramel mixture
over bare spots, if necessary.) Scrape excess
caramel from bottoms of apples; roll apples
in chopped peanuts, white chocolate
morsels, or assorted candies. Decorate craft
sticks with ribbon, if desired. Place apples
on wax paper coated with vegetable cooking
spray. Store in refrigerator. Let stand at room
temperature 15 minutes before serving to
allow caramel to soften. Yield: 8 servings.
Note: Double or triple your candy apple-making
if your party's packed with kids.

Brownies Filled with Caramel Candies

grill crazy

Combine an Italian heritage with a Key West lifestyle and a passion for all things grilled, and you've got one grillmaster extraordinaire—Joe Famularo. A cookbook author and backyard barbecue champion, Famularo prides himself on his ease of outdoor entertaining, which stems from his native roots and easygoing Floridian way of life. Think Mediterranean-style celebrations on the patio, and you've got a taste of what Famularo is all about.

menu

serves 8

Spicy Gingered Shrimp

Sautéed Scallops on Lasagna Squares with Chili-Cream Sauce

Mutton Snapper with Italian Flavors

Herbed Portobello Mushrooms with Mascarpone

Corn on the Cob with Chive-Fennel Butter

Asparagus with Red-Onion-and-Orange Vinaigrette

Pineapple Slices with Honeydew Sauce

Spicy Gingered Shrimp

16 (12-inch) wooden skewers
16 unpeeled, large fresh shrimp
¼ cup rice vinegar
¼ cup frozen orange juice or lemonade
     concentrate, thawed
¼ cup diced onion
1 tablespoon grated fresh ginger
½ teaspoon dried crushed red pepper

Soak skewers in water 30 minutes.

Peel shrimp, leaving tails on; devein shrimp, if desired. Place shrimp in a shallow dish.

Process rice vinegar and remaining ingredients in a blender or food processor until smooth. Pour over shrimp. Cover and chill 30 minutes.

Remove shrimp from marinade, reserving marinade. Bring marinade to a boil; set aside. Thread 1 shrimp onto each skewer.

Coat food rack with vegetable cooking spray, and place on grill.

Grill, without grill lid, over high heat (400° to 500°) 2 minutes on each side, basting with reserved marinade. Serve immediately. Yield: 8 appetizer servings.

To add zing to his grilled recipes, Famularo uses a combination of sauces, marinades, and herb rubs. These can be made in advance, leaving extra time for entertaining.

Enjoying a Famularo-inspired meal only requires a few simple adornments:
a long table laden with bright flowers and yellow dishes,
informal flatware, and fine linens. All that remains is the seating
of friends and family to share in the family-style spread.

Sautéed Scallops on Lasagna Squares with Chili-Cream Sauce

16 (4- x 4-inch) fresh lasagna squares*
1½ pounds sea scallops
2½ tablespoons all-purpose flour, divided
1 tablespoon butter
2 teaspoons canola oil
1 teaspoon chili powder
½ teaspoon curry powder
¾ cup low-fat milk
Pinch of salt
¼ cup thinly sliced green onions
Soy sauce

Cook lasagna squares according to package directions; drain. Cover with plastic wrap, and keep warm.

Dredge scallops in 2 tablespoons flour.

Heat 1½ teaspoons butter and 1 teaspoon oil in a large skillet over medium-high heat 2 minutes. Add half of the scallops, and cook about 2 minutes on each side or until lightly browned. Remove scallops, and set aside. Repeat procedure with remaining butter, oil, and scallops. Remove scallops, and set aside, reserving drippings in skillet.

Whisk remaining ½ tablespoon flour, chili powder, and curry powder into drippings in skillet. Cook over medium heat, whisking constantly, 1 minute. Gradually whisk in milk. Continue cooking over medium heat, whisking constantly, until thickened and bubbly. Stir in salt and scallops, and cook 1 minute or until thoroughly heated.

Place 2 lasagna squares on individual plates; spoon scallops and sauce evenly over squares. Sprinkle each serving with green onions and a dash of soy sauce. Yield: 8 appetizer servings.

*Fresh pasta may be purchased in sheets at specialty food shops and cut into squares. Dry lasagna noodles may be substituted and cut into squares after cooking.

Sautéed Scallops on Lasagna Squares with Chili-Cream Sauce

Mutton Snapper with Italian Flavors

Herbed Portobello Mushrooms with Mascarpone

"The grill is to the outdoors what the fireplace is to the indoors—people naturally gravitate toward it," Joe says. So Joe capitalizes on that theory and grills the entire meal outdoors where guests can mingle and even lend a hand. It makes for a relaxed and fun evening.

Mutton Snapper with Italian Flavors

2   (3-pound) whole mutton snapper, dressed
1   cup fresh lemon juice
¼   cup chopped fresh basil
¼   cup chopped fresh Italian parsley
¼   cup chopped fresh oregano
¼   cup minced onion
¼   cup olive oil
4   large garlic cloves, minced
½   teaspoon salt
½   teaspoon freshly ground pepper
Garnishes: Italian parsley, fresh oregano,
    lemon wedges

Make 2 (½-inch-deep) diagonal cuts on each side of fish. Arrange fish in a large shallow dish.

Combine lemon juice and next 8 ingredients. Set aside half of mixture to serve as a sauce with fish. Brush inside of each fish with 1 tablespoon of lemon mixture. Pour remaining mixture over fish. Cover and chill 30 minutes, turning fish once.

Remove fish from marinade, reserving marinade; place fish in 2 lightly greased grill baskets.

Grill, covered with grill lid, over high heat (400° to 500°) 15 to 17 minutes on each side or until fish flakes with a fork, basting often with reserved marinade. Garnish, if desired. Serve immediately with reserved sauce. Yield: 8 servings.

Herbed Portobello Mushrooms with Mascarpone

8   large fresh portobello mushroom caps
1½   tablespoons fresh lemon juice
2   garlic cloves, minced
⅓   cup low-sodium, fat-free chicken broth
1   tablespoon minced fresh basil
1   tablespoon minced fresh oregano
¼   teaspoon freshly ground pepper
½   cup (4 ounces) mascarpone cheese
Garnish: Fresh basil sprig

Coat mushrooms with vegetable cooking spray; set aside.

Stir together lemon juice and garlic in a small saucepan; cook over medium heat 1 to 2 minutes. Stir in broth and next 3 ingredients; bring to a boil. Remove from heat.

Brush mushrooms with herb mixture, applying generously to the underside.

Divide mascarpone into 8 portions, and roll into balls.

Grill mushrooms, top side up, covered with grill lid, over high heat (400° to 500°) 5 to 7

grill tips

Famularo offers several tips for the best barbecue: For a more natural barbecue taste, avoid lighter fluid. To achieve a less bitter flavor and avoid burning, allow the charcoal to cook down and turn ashen. To prevent flare-ups that lead to burned food, trim excess fat and skin from cuts. Allow meat and poultry, especially thick cuts, to rest for about 5 minutes off the grill before serving.

minutes. Turn mushrooms, and top each with a cheese ball. Grill, covered with grill lid, 5 minutes. Garnish, if desired. Serve immediately. Yield: 8 servings.

Corn on the Cob with Chive-Fennel Butter

8   ears fresh corn with husks
2   tablespoons butter, melted
2   large garlic cloves, minced
2   teaspoons fresh chives, minced
1/4 teaspoon fennel seeds

Soak corn in cool water 15 minutes. Pull back husks; remove and discard silks. Drain corn, and pat dry.

Stir together butter and remaining 3 ingredients; brush onto each ear. Pull husks back over corn. Tie string around husks, if desired.

Grill, covered with grill lid, over high heat (400° to 500°) 8 to 10 minutes on each side. (Watch carefully to make sure husks do not catch fire.) Yield: 8 servings.

Note: Corn may be husked and wrapped in foil. Grill, covered with grill lid, over high heat (400° to 500°) 30 minutes, turning every 10 minutes.

Asparagus with Red-Onion-and-Orange Vinaigrette

2   pounds fresh asparagus
1/2 teaspoon salt
1/2 teaspoon freshly ground pepper
1   small celery heart with leaves, minced (about 1/4 cup)
1/4 cup minced red onion
1   tablespoon minced carrot
1   tablespoon minced fresh ginger
1   teaspoon grated orange rind
1/3 cup unsweetened apple juice
2   tablespoons rice vinegar
1   tablespoon honey

Snap off tough ends of asparagus; sprinkle with salt and pepper.

Grill asparagus, without grill lid, over high heat (400° to 500°) 2 to 4 minutes on each side.

Stir together celery and remaining ingredients; spoon over asparagus. Yield: 8 servings.

Note: If asparagus spears are larger than 1/2 inch in diameter, cook in boiling water 1 minute; drain. Plunge into ice water to stop the cooking process; drain and pat dry. Grill as directed.

Pineapple Slices with Honeydew Sauce

1   ripe honeydew melon, peeled, seeded, and cubed
1/4 cup honeydew melon liqueur (we tested with Midori)
1/4 cup honey
1   pineapple, peeled and cored
1 1/2 tablespoons chopped fresh mint
Garnishes: fresh mint sprigs, fresh raspberries

Process first 3 ingredients in a food processor until smooth, stopping once to scrape down sides. Transfer to a bowl. Cover and chill 2 hours.

Cut pineapple in half lengthwise. Cut each half into 4 wedges.

Grill, covered with grill lid, over high heat (400° to 500°) about 5 minutes on each side, or until lightly browned.

Pour honeydew mixture into 8 chilled bowls; sprinkle with chopped mint. Arrange pineapple over honeydew mixture. Garnish, if desired. Serve immediately. Yield: 8 servings.

Recipes adapted from The Joy of Healthy Grilling and The Joy of Healthy Pasta, both by Joe Famularo (Barron's, 1998).

Corn on the Cob with Chive-Fennel Butter

Pineapple Slices with Honeydew Sauce

taste of the gulf

While gathering for a truly Southern spread featuring some of the Florida Panhandle's finest seafood, the Plowden family celebrates a dream come true at their beach house on St. George Island. For this weekend, Jerry Plowden has planned lunch from a favorite cookbook, A Taste of the Gulf Coast.

author Jessie Tirsch says she fell in love with the Gulf Coast when she visited New Orleans from New York over a decade ago—so much so that she relocated soon after. It was in New Orleans that she began writing cookbooks.

For several years, Tirsch traveled to coastal communities in Texas, Louisiana, Mississippi, Alabama, and Florida, visiting good cooks in their homes, writing down their recipes, their cooking tips, and their anecdotes about the area. She also photographed the people and places that most impressed her. The results are all found in *A Taste of the Gulf Coast: The Art and Soul of Southern Cooking.* The recipes that follow are from its pages.

menu

serves 6

Hot Cuban Black Bean Dip

Mr. Allen's All-Day Fish Chowder

Cortez Fish Cakes   Joan Canny's Avgolemono Sauce

Vandy's Butter-Braised Oysters   Miz Tolliver's Garlic Crabs

Irma Baker's Orange Pecan Pralines

With their tight-knit family, rich seafood, and glorious views, it's easy to understand why the Plowdens don't want to leave once they're here.

Hot Cuban Black Bean Dip

Hot Cuban Black Bean Dip

1   (15-ounce) can black beans, drained
1   cup (4 ounces) shredded sharp
     Cheddar cheese
1   small onion, diced
½   cup tomato sauce
1½ tablespoons lemon juice
½   teaspoon salt
½   teaspoon chili powder
½   teaspoon hot sauce
Dash of Worcestershire sauce (optional)
Garnish: assorted fresh hot chile peppers

Process first 9 ingredients in a food processor until smooth, stopping once to scrape down sides. Pour into a 1-quart microwave-safe bowl, and microwave at HIGH 3 to 4 minutes or until thoroughly heated, stirring once. Garnish, if desired. Serve with tortilla chips. Yield: 2 cups.
Note: Dip may be prepared a day ahead. Omit heating, and refrigerate. Before serving, microwave as directed.

Mr. Allen's All-Day Fish Chowder,
page 39

"When we cross the bridge from Apalachicola to St. George Island,"
Jerry says, "we throw all of our troubles in the water. We knew for a long time
that we wanted a home on the beach. We wanted a remote beach.
We found one on St. George."

The remote island, also known as The Forgotten Coast, has limited restaurants and grocery selections, but has plenty of oysters, shrimp, crabs, and all varieties of fish. Jerry picks up whatever looks best on her way in.

Mr. Allen's All-Day Fish Chowder

(shown on page 37)

3	fish bouillon cubes
6	cups boiling water
2	tablespoons all-purpose flour
2	tablespoons bacon drippings
4	large onions, chopped
1	large green bell pepper, chopped
2	celery ribs, chopped
4	garlic cloves, minced
4	cups diced red potatoes
1	(28-ounce) can whole tomatoes
2	(8-ounce) cans tomato sauce
3	bay leaves
1	tablespoon chopped fresh basil
1	tablespoon chopped fresh oregano
2	teaspoons chopped fresh rosemary
1	teaspoon salt
1/4	teaspoon freshly ground pepper
2	pounds grouper or red snapper fillets, cut into 1-inch chunks
1	tablespoon lemon juice
1	teaspoon prepared horseradish
1	to 2 dashes hot sauce

Garnish: fresh oregano sprigs

Stir together bouillon and water until bouillon dissolves. Set aside.

Whisk flour into hot bacon drippings; cook over medium heat, whisking constantly, 7 to 8 minutes or until caramel-colored. Stir in onion and next 3 ingredients. Cook over medium heat, stirring constantly, 15 to 20 minutes or until vegetables are tender. Stir in potato and reserved fish stock. Bring to a boil; reduce heat, and simmer 10 minutes. Stir in tomatoes and next 7 ingredients; cook 20 minutes. Stir in fish; cook 5 minutes or until fish flakes with a fork. Stir in lemon juice, horseradish, and hot sauce. Discard bay leaves. Garnish, if desired. Yield: 14 1/2 cups.

Cortez Fish Cakes

2	quarts water
2 1/2	pounds fresh tuna fillets, cut into chunks*
1	pound small Yukon gold potatoes, peeled and cut into 1/2-inch cubes
2	tablespoons unsalted butter, divided
1	small onion, diced
4	to 6 pepperoncini salad peppers, diced
1	tablespoon dried oregano
1	teaspoon salt
1	teaspoon dried thyme
1/4	teaspoon freshly ground pepper
1	tablespoon lemon juice
2	large eggs, lightly beaten
1 1/2	cups soft breadcrumbs
	Vegetable oil
	Joan Canny's Avgolemono Sauce

Garnish: fresh Italian parsley sprigs

Bring 2 quarts water to a boil in a Dutch oven; add fish. Cover, reduce heat, and simmer 5 to 7 minutes or until fish flakes with a fork. Drain.

Remove and discard any skin or bones from fish; flake. Set aside.

Cook potatoes in boiling water to cover in Dutch oven 20 minutes or until tender; drain and return to Dutch oven. Add 1 tablespoon butter. Mash with a potato masher until smooth; cool.

Melt remaining 1 tablespoon butter in a large skillet; add onion and pepperoncini pepper, and sauté 3 to 5 minutes. Stir in oregano and next 4 ingredients. Stir mixture into mashed potatoes. Fold in fish and eggs. Shape into 24 (2-inch) patties. Dredge in breadcrumbs, and place on a baking sheet. Cover and chill 2 hours.

Pour oil to depth of 1 inch into a Dutch oven; heat to 350°. Fry 4 fish cakes at a time, 3 to 4 minutes on each side or until golden brown. Drain on paper towels. Serve with Joan Canny's Avgolemono Sauce. Garnish, if desired. Yield: 24 appetizers.

*2 1/2 pounds other firm fish fillets may be substituted for tuna.

Joan Canny's Avgolemono Sauce

1 1/2	cups chicken broth
3	large eggs
1/3	cup fresh lemon juice
1	teaspoon cornstarch
1/4	teaspoon salt
1/4	teaspoon ground white pepper

Bring broth to a boil in a small saucepan.

Whisk together eggs, lemon juice, and cornstarch until frothy. Gradually whisk about one-fourth of hot broth into egg mixture; whisk into remaining hot broth. Cook over low heat, whisking constantly, 2 minutes or until thickened and mixture coats a spoon. Stir in salt and pepper. Serve immediately, or refrigerate up to 2 days. Yield: 1 2/3 cups.

Miz Tolliver's Garlic Crabs

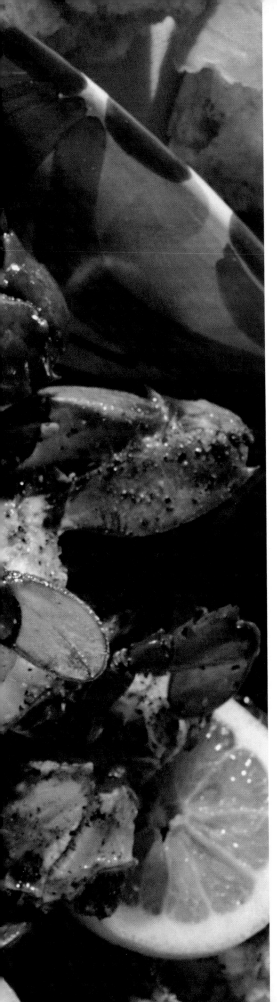

Vandy's Butter-Braised Oysters

1¼ cups unsalted butter
1 cup all-purpose flour
3 tablespoons minced fresh cilantro
1 tablespoon garlic powder
1 tablespoon ground white pepper
2 to 3 teaspoons salt
¼ teaspoon freshly ground pepper
2 (12-ounce) containers fresh oysters, drained
Tartar sauce

Microwave butter in a 2-cup glass measuring cup at HIGH 1 to 1½ minutes or until melted. Skim off any white froth from top of butter. Strain off clear, yellow butter, discarding milk solid sediment; set 1 cup clarified butter aside.

Stir together flour and next 5 ingredients in a small bowl. Dredge oysters in flour mixture, shaking off excess.

Heat clarified butter in a large heavy skillet over medium-high heat. Add oysters, in batches, and cook 2 to 3 minutes or until golden, turning once. Serve with tartar sauce. Yield: 4 to 6 appetizer servings.

Miz Tolliver's Garlic Crabs

8 live large hard-shell crabs*
4 large garlic cloves, minced
1½ teaspoons salt
1 teaspoon freshly ground pepper
¾ cup unsalted butter, cut into pieces
Garnish: lemon slices

Place live crabs on ice until almost immobilized. Pry up and pull off apron from undersides of crabs. Lift off, and discard top shells. Pull out and discard the feathery gills beneath top shells. Reserve orange fat, and discard stomach masses.

Place crabs, cleaned side up, in a single layer in a roasting pan. Sprinkle with garlic, salt, pepper, and reserved fat; dot with butter.

Bake, covered, at 300° for 35 to 40 minutes. Garnish, if desired. Serve with French bread. Yield: 4 servings.

*You may ask your local seafood market to clean the live crabs for you.

Note: We prepared 1½ times the recipe to yield 6 servings.

Irma Baker's Orange Pecan Pralines

Irma Baker's Orange Pecan Pralines

2½ cups sugar, divided
1 (12-ounce) can evaporated milk
1 teaspoon salt
2 cups pecan halves
2 tablespoons grated orange rind

Cook ½ cup sugar in a small heavy saucepan over medium heat, stirring constantly, 5 to 10 minutes or until sugar dissolves and turns a light caramel color.

Bring remaining 2 cups sugar, milk, and salt to a boil in a large heavy saucepan. Gradually stir boiling mixture into hot caramelized sugar. Cook over medium heat, stirring constantly, until a candy thermometer registers 235° (soft ball stage). Remove from heat; cool 5 minutes.

Beat with a wooden spoon until mixture just begins to thicken. Stir in pecans and orange rind. Drop by tablespoonfuls onto wax paper; let stand until firm. Store in an airtight container. Yield: 3 dozen.

From A Taste of the Gulf Coast: The Art and Soul of Southern Cooking *by Jessie Tirsch. © 1997 by Jessie Tirsch. All rights reserved. Reproduced here by permission of Wiley Publishing, Inc.*

marsh creek memoirs *Chef Christopher*

Hastings remembers childhood summers on Pawleys Island, South Carolina, hauling in baskets of the day's fresh-caught bounty. Tradition is important to Christopher and wife, Idie, as they prepare a menu that reflects their Southern roots and begin to pass along this Lowcountry legacy to their sons.

menu

serves 6 to 8

Clam and Corn Fritters   Deviled Crab

Baked Sheepshead on Hoppin' John or *Seafood Perlou*

Creamy Shrimp and Grits

Hot and Hot Fish Club Tomato Salad

Lemon-Buttermilk Tart

Clam and Corn Fritters

1	pound fresh littleneck clams in shells, scrubbed*
1	cup all-purpose flour
1	teaspoon baking powder
1	teaspoon salt
1	teaspoon freshly ground black pepper
½	teaspoon ground red pepper
1¼	cups fresh corn kernels (about 2 ears)
1	red bell pepper, diced
1	yellow bell pepper, diced
1	poblano chile pepper, diced
1	bunch green onions, sliced (about 1 cup)
6	egg whites
2	quarts peanut oil

Open clam shells; remove meat. Coarsely chop, and drain.

Combine flour and next 4 ingredients in a large bowl. Stir in corn and next 4 ingredients. Fold in clams. Whisk egg whites in a separate bowl until stiff peaks form; fold into clam mixture.

Pour oil to depth of 2 inches into a 4-quart Dutch oven; heat to 360°. Carefully drop batter by tablespoonfuls into oil; fry 1 to 1½ minutes on each side or until golden brown, turning with a slotted spoon. Drain on paper towels. Serve immediately. Yield: about 3 dozen.

*You may substitute ¼ cup drained, diced canned clams for fresh.

This weekend, there's no such thing as leftovers. Picnickers nibble on ever-present platters of food as unconsciously as brushing aside windswept hair. As high tide recedes, a gentle current pulls Christopher and his boys down Salt Marsh Creek. It's a relaxing ride after a morning of shucking corn.

Clam and Corn Fritters

Deviled Crab

Deviled Crab

6 large eggs, lightly beaten
1½ cups chopped green onions
2 tablespoons grated lemon rind
⅓ cup fresh lemon juice
¼ teaspoon ground nutmeg
1 pound fresh lump crabmeat, drained
1½ cups butter, melted and divided
5 cups soft breadcrumbs, divided
1 cup chopped fresh parsley
½ teaspoon salt
¼ teaspoon freshly ground pepper

Combine first 6 ingredients in a large bowl. Add 1 cup melted butter, 4 cups breadcrumbs, and next 3 ingredients. Spoon crabmeat mixture into 10 baking shells or individual baking dishes.

Top servings evenly with remaining 1 cup breadcrumbs; drizzle evenly with remaining ½ cup melted butter.

Bake, uncovered, at 400° for 20 minutes or until thoroughly heated.

Broil 5½ inches from heat 3 minutes or until golden brown. Serve immediately. Yield: 10 servings.

Baked Sheepshead on Hoppin' John

Baked Sheepshead on Hoppin' John

Sheepshead is a local game fish. You can substitute any firm white fish.

8   (6-ounce) sheepshead or grouper fillets (about 1 to 1½ inches thick)
½   teaspoon salt
½   teaspoon freshly ground pepper
Lemon-Herb Butter, softened
Hoppin' John
Garnish: fresh chives

Sprinkle fish with salt and pepper; spread 2 tablespoons Lemon-Herb Butter on each fillet. Place fish on a lightly greased jellyroll pan. Bake at 400° for 10 to 12 minutes or until fish flakes easily with a fork. Serve over Hoppin' John. Garnish, if desired. Yield: 8 servings.

Lemon-Herb Butter

If you make the butter ahead of time, let it stand at room temperature to soften before using.

1   cup butter, softened
1   tablespoon grated lemon rind
¼   cup fresh lemon juice
2   tablespoons chopped fresh parsley
1   tablespoon minced shallots
1   tablespoon chopped fresh chives
¼   teaspoon freshly ground pepper

Combine all ingredients, whisking well. Cover and chill. Yield: about 1⅓ cups.

Hoppin' John

6   bacon slices, chopped
1   large onion, chopped
4   cups fresh field peas, shelled
8   sprigs fresh thyme
1   tablespoon salt
4   cups hot cooked basmati rice
4   cups seeded, diced tomatoes
¼   cup Basil Pesto
1   teaspoon salt
½   teaspoon freshly ground pepper

Cook bacon in a Dutch oven over medium heat until crisp. Add onion; sauté 7 minutes or until tender.

Add peas, thyme, and 1 tablespoon salt. Add water to cover. Bring to a boil; cover, reduce heat, and simmer 30 minutes or until peas are tender. Drain.

Combine pea mixture and remaining ingredients. Yield: about 12 cups.

Basil Pesto

If you make pesto ahead, keep it stored, tightly covered, in the refrigerator.

1   garlic clove
1   tablespoon pine nuts, toasted
2   cups tightly packed fresh basil
½   cup olive oil
3   tablespoons freshly grated Parmesan cheese
¼   teaspoon salt

Combine garlic and pine nuts in a food processor; process until finely chopped. Add basil; process until finely chopped. With processor running, pour oil through food chute in a slow, steady stream. Add cheese and salt; process until smooth. Cover and chill. Yield: about 1 cup.
Note: You can substitute prepared, refrigerated pesto for Basil Pesto.

vine advice

Christopher selected these wines as seafood accompaniments:

- **Chateau de la Ragotiere Muscadet**
- **Saintsbury Carneros Chardonnay**
- **La Famiglia di Robert Mondavi Pinot Grigio**

Seafood Perlou

"Seafood Perlou is developed from whatever fresh catch you have that day plus tomatoes, onion, and rice," says Christopher.

18	fresh littleneck clams in shells, scrubbed
18	fresh mussels, scrubbed and debearded
18	unpeeled, large fresh shrimp
½	pound fresh lump crabmeat
½	cup butter
1	teaspoon minced garlic
2	cups diced onion
½	cup chopped celery
½	cup chopped carrot
1	bay leaf
1	tablespoon chopped fresh thyme
¾	teaspoon salt
½	teaspoon freshly ground pepper
2	cups uncooked basmati rice
2	cups seeded, diced tomato
2	cups chicken broth
1	cup fish broth
1	pound frozen crawfish tails, thawed, rinsed, and drained
1	cup chopped fresh parsley

Discard opened or cracked clams and mussels. Peel shrimp, leaving tails intact; devein if desired. Drain crabmeat; remove any bits of shell. Set aside.

Melt butter in a Dutch oven over medium-high heat. Add garlic and next 7 ingredients; sauté 4 to 5 minutes or just until tender. Add rice and tomato; stir well. Add chicken and fish broths; bring to a boil. Cover, reduce heat, and simmer 12 minutes.

Add clams, and cook 5 minutes. Add mussels and shrimp; cook 5 minutes. Stir in crawfish; cook 5 to 7 more minutes or until clams and mussels have opened. Discard any unopened shells. Stir in crabmeat and parsley. Remove from heat, and let stand 2 minutes. Discard bay leaf. Serve immediately. Yield: 6 servings.

Creamy Shrimp and Grits

(shown on page 13)

2	tablespoons butter
2	garlic cloves, minced
1	tablespoon chopped fresh thyme
1	cup chicken broth
1	cup heavy whipping cream
1	cup water
1	cup stone-ground yellow grits
¼	teaspoon salt
¼	teaspoon freshly ground pepper
1	cup butter, divided
¼	cup finely chopped celery
¼	cup finely chopped green bell pepper
¼	cup finely chopped shallots
1	teaspoon chopped fresh thyme
2¾	pounds large fresh shrimp, peeled and deveined (about 64 shrimp)
8	ounces verjuice or dry white wine*
½	cup fresh lemon juice
½	cup finely chopped tomato
1	tablespoon chopped fresh parsley

Garnishes: julienned prosciutto, crumbled cooked bacon, chopped fresh chives

The first Hot and Hot Fish Club (namesake to Christopher's renowned restaurant in Birmingham, Alabama) was a men's club founded more than 150 years ago. Membership included Christopher's great-great-grandfather. Its name evoked the tradition of serving many steamed seafood courses, one after the other.

Melt 2 tablespoons butter in a large saucepan. Add garlic and 1 tablespoon thyme; sauté 1 minute. Add broth, whipping cream, and 1 cup water. Bring to a boil; whisk in grits. Reduce heat to low; cook 10 minutes or until done, stirring occasionally. Season with salt and pepper. Keep warm.

Melt 2 tablespoons butter in a large skillet. Add celery and next 3 ingredients; sauté 30 seconds. Add shrimp, and cook 7 minutes. Remove shrimp from skillet. Add verjuice, and cook 6 minutes over medium heat or until most of liquid has evaporated, stirring to loosen browned bits.

Reduce heat to low; whisk in remaining butter, 1 tablespoon at a time. Stir in lemon juice, tomato, and parsley. Serve over grits. Garnish, if desired. Yield: 8 servings.

Verjuice is an acidic, sour liquid made from grapes. It's used like lemon juice or wine to heighten flavor.

Christopher often visited Salt Marsh Creek (an inlet from the Atlantic running parallel to Pawleys Island) as a child to harvest clams, crab, and fish. "It came naturally and it was fun," he says. This lifestyle inspired Christopher's philosophy on food—local and fresh.

Hot and Hot Fish Club Tomato Salad

6   large red tomatoes
4   large yellow tomatoes
Balsamic Vinaigrette, divided
¾   cup cooked lima beans
2   cups cooked whole kernel corn
1   cup cherry tomatoes, halved
4   ounces thick-sliced smoked bacon
     (about 6 slices), cooked
Fried Okra
Chive Dressing

Wash, core, and slice red and yellow tomatoes. Drizzle tomato slices with ½ cup Balsamic Vinaigrette; set aside.

Combine beans and corn with remaining ½ cup Balsamic Vinaigrette.

Arrange tomato slices on a salad platter; add cherry tomatoes. Top with corn mixture. Top with bacon and Fried Okra. Dollop with desired amount of Chive Dressing. Yield: 6 servings.

Balsamic Vinaigrette

¾   cup olive oil
¼   cup balsamic vinegar
2   green onions, thinly sliced
6   fresh basil leaves, chopped
¼   teaspoon salt
¼   teaspoon freshly ground pepper

Combine all ingredients in a jar; cover tightly, and shake vigorously. Store in refrigerator. Yield: about 1 cup.

Fried Okra

1   pound small whole okra, stems
     trimmed
2   cups buttermilk
1   cup cornmeal
1   cup all-purpose flour
1   teaspoon salt
½   teaspoon freshly ground pepper
Vegetable oil
Salt

**Hot and Hot Fish Club
Tomato Salad**

The tomato salad Christopher derived from succotash uses Southern favorites—lima beans, bacon, corn, and okra. He prefers heirloom tomatoes, not hybridized or altered from their original form. "They are imperfect and often blemished," he says, "but it gets back to the flavors. Flavor is first, last, and always."

Combine okra and buttermilk in a large bowl; toss to coat. Combine cornmeal and next 3 ingredients in a medium bowl. Drain okra, discarding buttermilk. Toss okra in cornmeal mixture to coat. Pour oil to depth of 2 inches into a Dutch oven; heat to 350°. Fry okra, in batches, 4 minutes or until golden. Drain well on paper towels. Sprinkle with additional salt, if desired. Yield: 6 servings.

Chive Dressing

2   garlic cloves, minced
⅓   cup thinly sliced fresh chives
3   tablespoons fresh lemon juice
2   tablespoons egg substitute
¼   teaspoon salt
¼   teaspoon freshly ground pepper
1   cup olive oil
1   (8-ounce) container crème fraîche or sour cream

Combine first 6 ingredients in a small bowl. Gradually whisk in oil. Add crème fraîche. Cover and chill. Yield: about 2½ cups.

Lemon-Buttermilk Tart

½   (15-ounce) package refrigerated piecrusts
4   large eggs
1⅓ cups sugar
½   cup butter, melted
¼   cup buttermilk
1   tablespoon grated lemon rind
¼   cup fresh lemon juice
2   tablespoons cornmeal
Ground nutmeg
Garnish: sweetened whipped cream

Place piecrust in a 9-inch tart pan according to package directions. Bake at 400° for 9 to 11 minutes or until lightly browned.

Beat eggs and sugar in a large bowl until pale yellow. Stir in butter and next 4 ingredients. Pour mixture into prepared crust. Sprinkle lightly with nutmeg.

Bake at 325° for 12 to 15 minutes or until set. Cool before serving. Garnish, if desired. Yield: 1 (9-inch) tart.

Christopher likes adding the seeds scraped from a vanilla bean pod to homemade pastry dough. To simplify, we call for a prepared crust for this Lemon-Buttermilk Tart.

picnic in cool weather

Cookbook author Sarah Leah Chase has fallen in love several times in her life—with Nantucket, with food, with her family and friends. Here, she savors them all as she hosts a late-season picnic on a quiet beach. The recipes are meant to be made ahead and carried seaside, though they are equally delicious at home—maybe on a deck overlooking the water.

Sarah Leah Chase lives on Nantucket, where she has spent years cooking with local ingredients. She owned a specialty food shop and catering business and has written several cookbooks. The menu she shares mingles native bounty with tastes from travels to Tuscany.

Pappa al Pomodoro

menu

serves 8

Pappa al Pomodoro

Smoked Bluefish Pâté　*Tuscan White Beans with Sage*　*Baked Chianti Olives*

Lobster Frittata

Insalata da Delfina

Cranberry Oatmeal Cookies

Pappa al Pomodoro

Tuscan tomato soup celebrates the best of summer ripe tomatoes and good olive oil.

1　medium onion, diced
8　garlic cloves, minced
½　cup extra-virgin olive oil, divided
3　pounds tomatoes, peeled, seeded, and coarsely chopped*
½　cup coarsely chopped fresh basil
½　teaspoon dried crushed red pepper
Pinch of sugar
¾　cup dry white wine
5　cups vegetable broth
½　teaspoon coarse-grained sea salt
¼　teaspoon freshly ground black pepper
½　pound day-old Italian bread, broken into hunks

Sauté onion and garlic in ¼ cup hot oil in saucepan until tender. Stir in tomato and next 3 ingredients; bring to a boil. Reduce heat and simmer, stirring often, 15 to 20 minutes or until thickened. Stir in wine, broth, salt, and pepper; bring to a boil.

Reduce heat, and simmer 5 to 7 minutes. Stir in bread. Ladle into bowls, and drizzle evenly with remaining ¼ cup oil. Yield: 8 cups.
Note: *Soup can be made a day ahead and refrigerated; omit remaining ¼ cup oil. Cook over low heat, stirring occasionally, until heated. Serve as directed.*
*1 (28-ounce) and 1 (16-ounce) can whole tomatoes, chopped, may be substituted for 3 pounds fresh tomatoes.

Pappa al Pomodoro; Insalata da Delfina, page 55; and Lobster Frittata, page 55

Smoked Bluefish Pâté

Smoked Bluefish Pâté

1½ pounds smoked bluefish fillets,
    skinned
2   (8-ounce) packages cream cheese,
    softened
3   tablespoons lemon juice
2½ tablespoons cognac
⅛   teaspoon freshly ground pepper
1   medium-size red onion, minced
½   cup minced fresh dill
2   tablespoons capers
Garnishes: lemon wedges, fresh dill sprigs

Remove and discard dark meat from fish fillets.
Flake white meat, and set aside.

Beat cream cheese at medium speed with
an electric mixer until fluffy. Add lemon
juice, cognac, and pepper; beat until thoroughly blended. Stir in fish, onion, dill, and
capers. Pack into a 1-quart crock or bowl;
cover and chill 2 hours. Let stand at room
temperature 15 to 30 minutes to soften.
Garnish, if desired. Serve with crostini or
crackers. Yield: 4 cups.

Tuscan White Beans with Sage

1   pound dried navy beans
3   garlic cloves, halved
12   to 16 fresh sage leaves
½   cup extra-virgin olive oil
1½ teaspoons fine-grained sea salt
½   teaspoon freshly ground pepper
Garnish: fresh sage sprigs

Place beans in a Dutch oven; cover with water
2 inches above beans; let soak 8 hours. Drain.

Return beans to Dutch oven. Cover with
water 2 inches above beans. Add garlic; bring
to a boil. Cover, reduce heat, and simmer 1 to
1½ hours or until tender. Add sage, and cook 5
minutes. Remove from heat; drain. Remove and
discard sage leaves. Place beans in a bowl;
drizzle evenly with olive oil, and sprinkle with
salt and pepper. Serve warm or at room temperature. Garnish, if desired. Yield: 6 to 8 servings.
Note: To make ahead, cook beans until tender,
and refrigerate until ready to use. Cook over
medium heat, stirring occasionally, until
thoroughly heated. Add sage leaves, and
cook as directed.

Baked Chianti Olives

1   pound imported ripe olives
3   garlic cloves, thinly sliced
1½ teaspoons fennel seeds
3   to 4 fresh rosemary sprigs
¾   cup extra-virgin olive oil
Garnishes: fresh rosemary sprigs, fresh
    sage leaves

Arrange olives in a single layer in a 3-cup
shallow baking dish; top with garlic, fennel
seeds, and rosemary. Drizzle with olive oil.

Bake at 350° for 25 minutes. Serve warm or
at room temperature. Garnish, if desired. Yield:
10 to 12 servings.

Baked Chianti Olives

Lobster Frittata

Lobster Frittata

3   medium-size yellow squash (¾ pound)
2   red bell peppers
1   yellow bell pepper
1   medium-size red onion, peeled
2   garlic cloves, minced
3   tablespoons olive oil
6   large eggs
¼   cup whipping cream
3   tablespoons chopped fresh basil
1½ teaspoons fine-grained sea salt
1   teaspoon saffron threads
½   teaspoon freshly ground pepper
1   pound steamed lobster, cut into 1-inch
    pieces (about 2 [2¼-pound] lobsters)
2   (5-ounce) packages buttery garlic-and-
    herb spreadable cheese
2   cups (8 ounces) shredded Swiss cheese
Garnish: fresh parsley

Cut squash into ¼-inch-thick slices; cut bell peppers into ¼-inch strips. Cut onion in half lengthwise, and slice.

Sauté squash, bell peppers, onion, and garlic in 3 tablespoons hot oil in a large skillet 5 to 8 minutes or until crisp-tender.

Whisk together eggs and next 5 ingredients; stir in lobster, cheeses, and sautéed vegetables. Pour into a buttered 10-inch springform pan. Place pan on a baking sheet. Bake at 350° for 1 hour or until set. Let stand 10 minutes before serving. Garnish, if desired. Yield: 8 servings.

Insalata da Delfina

½   pound pancetta, diced
12 cups mixed baby salad greens
¾   cup walnut halves, toasted
⅓   cup extra-virgin olive oil
¼   teaspoon freshly ground pepper
⅛   teaspoon fine-grained sea salt
Parmesan cheese shavings
⅓   cup balsamic vinegar

Sauté pancetta in a small skillet 3 to 5 minutes or until crisp; drain.

Toss together pancetta, salad greens, and next 4 ingredients. Place on individual plates; top with shaved Parmesan cheese and drizzle evenly with vinegar. Yield: 8 servings.

Cranberry Oatmeal Cookies

These are perfect picnic cookies. They're megasized, chewy, and easy to stack and pack.

Cranberry Oatmeal Cookies

1½ cups unsalted butter, softened
1¾ cups firmly packed light brown sugar
2   large eggs
1½ tablespoons honey
2   teaspoons vanilla extract
½   teaspoon salt
2   cups all-purpose flour
1   (18-ounce) container uncooked regular
    oats
1   (12-ounce) package fresh cranberries,
    coarsely chopped
½   cup golden raisins
1   tablespoon grated orange rind
1¼ cups coarsely chopped walnuts

Beat butter and sugar at medium speed with an electric mixer until creamy. Add eggs and next 3 ingredients, beating until blended.

Gradually add flour and oats, beating at low speed until blended. Stir in cranberries, raisins, orange rind, and walnuts. Shape dough by ⅓ cupfuls into ½-inch-thick rounds on parchment paper-lined baking sheets.

Bake at 350° for 20 minutes or until lightly browned. Cool on wire racks. Yield: 2 dozen.

toe dipping

Hostess Skeeter Diehl's family gathers to whet an appetite for the water, to enjoy some good Southern cooking, and to wet some tiny toes in Alabama's Mobile Bay.

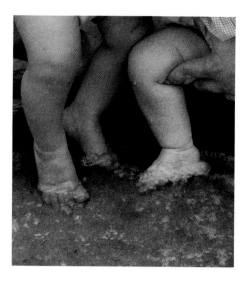

This toe dipping tradition dates to 1994, when Skeeter's first grandchild, Foster, was born in Savannah, Georgia. "Because Foster wasn't born near Mobile Bay, I thought the least I could do was dip that baby in the water and get the bay in his blood," recalls Skeeter. "I thought the dipping could be an initiation of sorts, one that would introduce Foster to the water that is such a huge part of our lives." So the family gathered at Skeeter's brother's house for the first dipping of the toes celebration. "We did a little dipping and served some grand food," recalls Skeeter. Three years later, another grandson, Mac, wet his toes in the bay. Today, Skeeter's friends and family have joined in the dipping fun, bringing their babies to the water and their empty stomachs to the pavilion outside Skeeter's Point Clear condominium.

menu

serves 12

Bay Cooler

Crabmeat Spread   Shrimp Sandwich with Pink Sauce

Roast Beef, Tomato, and Red Onion Sandwich with Peppery Balsamic Vinaigrette Sauce

Green Beans with Feta and Basil

Lemon-Buttermilk Ice Cream

Strawberry Cookies   Pistachio-White Chocolate Chip Cookies

Process maraschino cherries and limeade concentrate in a blender until smooth, stopping once to scrape down sides. Pour mixture into a large container. Stir in orange juice concentrate and remaining ingredients; cover, and freeze 8 hours, stirring occasionally. Let stand at room temperature 1 hour or until slushy. Yield: 12 cups.
*To reduce sweetness, substitute club soda for ginger ale.

Bay Cooler

1   (10-ounce) jar whole maraschino
     cherries, undrained
1   (12-ounce) can frozen limeade
     concentrate, thawed
1   (12-ounce) can frozen orange juice
     concentrate, thawed
1   (12-ounce) can frozen pink lemonade
     concentrate, thawed
6   cups ginger ale*
1½ cups light rum

Crabmeat Spread

1   pound fresh lump crabmeat
1   (3-ounce) jar capers, drained
3   tablespoons fresh lemon juice
2   to 3 tablespoons mayonnaise

Drain crabmeat, removing any bits of shell. Add remaining ingredients; toss gently. Cover and chill 30 minutes. Serve with assorted crackers. Yield: 2¼ cups.

Shrimp Sandwich with Pink Sauce, page 58

Shrimp Sandwich with Pink Sauce

(shown on page 57)

9	cups water		*Pink Sauce*	
3	pounds unpeeled, large fresh shrimp	1	large onion, quartered	
1	head romaine lettuce, torn	2	to 3 garlic cloves, crushed	
6	pita bread rounds, cut in half	1	cup mayonnaise	
¾	cup Pink Sauce	½	cup chili sauce	

9   cups water
3   pounds unpeeled, large fresh shrimp
1   head romaine lettuce, torn
6   pita bread rounds, cut in half
¾   cup Pink Sauce

Bring water to a boil; add shrimp, and cook 3 to 5 minutes or just until shrimp turn pink. Drain and rinse with cold water. Peel shrimp, and devein, if desired. Chill.

Place lettuce leaves in pita pockets; fill with shrimp. Drizzle with Pink Sauce. Yield: 12 sandwiches.

Pink Sauce

1   large onion, quartered
2   to 3 garlic cloves, crushed
1   cup mayonnaise
½   cup chili sauce
½   cup ketchup
½   cup vegetable oil
1   teaspoon freshly ground pepper
1   teaspoon paprika
3   tablespoons fresh lemon juice
2   tablespoons Worcestershire sauce
1   tablespoon water
2   teaspoons prepared horseradish
1   teaspoon prepared mustard

Process all ingredients in a blender until smooth, stopping once to scrape down sides. Chill 30 minutes. Yield: 4¼ cups.

Note: Leftover sauce may be used as a salad dressing or as a dip for boiled shrimp or crab claws.

Roast Beef, Tomato, and Red Onion Sandwich with Peppery Balsamic Vinaigrette Sauce

Peppery Balsamic Vinaigrette Sauce

3   (16-ounce) crusty French bread loaves,
      cut in half horizontally
Marinated Pepper-Crusted Beef Tenderloin,
      thinly sliced
2   medium-size red onions, thinly sliced
3 to 4 tomatoes, sliced
2 to 3 bunches arugula

Drizzle about 2 tablespoons Peppery Balsamic Vinaigrette Sauce on bottom half of each loaf of bread. Layer tenderloin slices, onion, tomato, and arugula over sauce; drizzle with remaining sauce. Cover with bread tops.

Cut each sandwich into 4 pieces. Yield: 12 servings.

Marinated Pepper-Crusted Beef Tenderloin

1   cup port
1   cup soy sauce
½   cup olive oil
1½   teaspoons freshly ground pepper
1   teaspoon dried thyme
½   teaspoon hot sauce
4   garlic cloves, crushed
1   bay leaf
1   (5- to 6-pound) beef tenderloin, trimmed
2   tablespoons coarsely ground pepper

Combine first 8 ingredients in a shallow dish or a large heavy-duty zip-top plastic bag. Place tenderloin in marinade. Cover or seal, turning to coat. Chill 8 hours, turning occasionally.

Remove beef from marinade, reserving marinade. Press pepper into beef. Place beef on a rack coated with vegetable cooking spray in a broiler pan.

Bring reserved marinade to a rolling boil in a small saucepan; reduce heat and simmer 3 minutes. Discard bay leaf.

Bake beef at 425°, basting 3 or 4 times with reserved marinade, for 45 to 55 minutes or until a meat thermometer inserted into thickest portion registers 145° (medium rare). Let stand 10 minutes. Yield: 12 servings.

Peppery Balsamic Vinaigrette Sauce

6   tablespoons mayonnaise
6   tablespoons olive oil
3   tablespoons balsamic vinegar
1   tablespoon freshly ground pepper

Combine all ingredients in a bowl, stirring until blended. Yield: 1¼ cups.

"I could live off the bay so long as it offered me seafood like this," Skeeter says. "There is nothing better than a plate full of shrimp and a bay full of barefoot babies."

Green Beans with Feta and Basil

3   pounds fresh green beans, trimmed
1/2 cup olive oil
3   tablespoons red wine vinegar
1 1/2 teaspoons Dijon mustard
3/4 teaspoon salt
1/4 to 1/2 teaspoon freshly ground pepper
1   (4-ounce) package feta cheese, crumbled
1/2 cup fresh basil leaves, chopped

Place beans in a steamer basket over boiling water. Cover and steam 4 minutes or until crisp-tender. Plunge in ice water to stop the cooking process. Drain.

Whisk together oil and next 4 ingredients in a large bowl. Add beans, feta, and basil; toss gently. Yield: 12 servings.

Lemon-Buttermilk Ice Cream

1   cup sugar
1   cup fresh lemon juice
3   cups light corn syrup
2   quarts buttermilk
1/2 teaspoon salt
4   teaspoons grated lemon rind
Garnishes: strawberries, fresh mint sprigs

Combine first 6 ingredients, and pour into the freezer container of a 6-quart hand-turned or electric freezer. Freeze according to manufacturer's instructions. Garnish each serving, if desired. Yield: 3 1/2 quarts.

Green Beans with
Feta and Basil

Strawberry Cookies

1/2 cup butter or margarine, softened
1/4 cup firmly packed brown sugar
1   large egg, separated
1   teaspoon vanilla extract
1   cup all-purpose flour
1/4 teaspoon salt
1   cup finely chopped pecans
1/3 cup strawberry preserves

Beat butter at medium speed with an electric mixer until creamy; gradually add sugar, beating well. Add egg yolk and vanilla, beating until blended. Combine flour and salt; add to butter mixture, beating at low speed until blended. Cover and chill 30 minutes.

Beat egg white lightly. Roll dough into 1/2-inch balls; dip into egg white and roll in pecans. Place cookies 1 inch apart on ungreased baking sheets.

Bake at 375° for 5 minutes. Remove from oven. Make an indentation in the top of each cookie using the handle of a wooden spoon. Bake 10 more minutes. Remove to wire racks to cool. Fill centers of cookies with about 1/2 teaspoon strawberry preserves. Yield: 3 dozen.

Pistachio-White Chocolate Chip Cookies

1 1/2 cups butter, softened
2   cups firmly packed brown sugar
2   large eggs
2   teaspoons vanilla extract
2 1/2 cups all-purpose flour
1/2 cup uncooked regular oats
1   teaspoon baking powder
1   teaspoon baking soda
1   (12-ounce) package white chocolate morsels
1 1/2 cups chopped pistachios

Beat butter and brown sugar at medium speed with an electric mixer until fluffy. Add eggs and vanilla, beating just until blended.

Combine flour and next 3 ingredients; gradually add to butter mixture, beating at low speed until blended. Stir in morsels and nuts. Drop by teaspoonfuls onto ungreased baking sheets.

Bake at 350° for 10 to 12 minutes or until lightly browned. Cool 2 minutes on baking sheets; remove to wire racks to cool completely. Yield: 6 dozen.

Recipes adapted from Bay Tables, *the cookbook of the Junior League of Mobile, Alabama, Inc. (1998).*

boca for brunch

Friends savor recipes from their successful Junior League cookbook at this South Florida gathering. Boca Raton is known for high style and pink buildings. Today's menu combines lively colors and spicy flavors, evoking the feel of this Coastal town.

menu

serves 8

Honeydew Mimosas   Florida Spritzer

Spiced Boca Nuts

Farmhouse Benedict   Stone Crab Claws with Mustard Sauce

Strawberry Streusel Muffins   Tropical Fruit with Mango Cream

Celestial Sugar Cookies with Royal Frosting

Best Friends Iced Coffee Frappé

A warm day beside the pool sets the tone for a cheerful brunch. "The mimosas look beautiful against the cobalt blue reflection of the pool," homeowner Michele Rochon says. "They say 'welcome'."

Honeydew Mimosas

This recipe can easily be doubled. Just be sure to make the mimosas in two batches. For best results, chill the melon overnight.

½   medium honeydew melon (about 4 cups), cubed
1   cup crushed ice
1   tablespoon sugar
1   (750-milliliter) bottle sparkling wine, chilled
Garnishes: lime wedges

Combine first 3 ingredients in a blender. Process until smooth. Pour mixture into a large pitcher; add sparkling wine. Pour into glasses. Garnish, if desired. Yield: 6 cups.

Florida Spritzer

1½ cups ruby red grapefruit juice
¼   cup sugar
1   (2-inch) cinnamon stick
Crushed ice
Ginger ale
Garnishes: grapefruit rind, cinnamon sticks

Combine first 3 ingredients in a saucepan. Bring to a boil over medium-high heat. Reduce heat, and simmer, uncovered, 5 minutes. Discard cinnamon stick. Chill grapefruit mixture thoroughly.

Fill 4 (8-ounce) glasses with crushed ice; add ⅓ cup grapefruit mixture to each. Fill glasses with ginger ale; stir gently. Garnish, if desired. Yield: 4 servings.

Honeydew Mimosas

Spiced Boca Nuts

Farmhouse Benedict

12 large eggs
12 squares warm Red Pepper Cornbread,
   halved horizontally
12 slices Canadian bacon, cooked
Rosemary Hollandaise
Garnishes: capers, finely chopped red bell
   pepper, lemon wedges, rosemary sprigs

Lightly grease a large saucepan. Add water to depth of 2 inches. Bring water to a boil; reduce heat, and maintain at a light simmer. Break eggs, 1 at a time, into a saucer; slip eggs, 1 at a time, into water, holding cup as close as possible to surface of water. (Cook eggs in batches to avoid overcrowding in pan.) Simmer 4 to 5 minutes or until done. Remove eggs with a slotted spoon. Trim edges, if desired.

   Stack 2 Red Pepper Cornbread halves on 12 individual serving plates; top each stack with 1 slice Canadian bacon, 1 poached egg, and about ¼ cup Rosemary Hollandaise. Garnish, if desired. Serve immediately. Yield: 12 servings.

Red Pepper Cornbread

1 tablespoon butter
½ cup chopped onion
½ cup minced shallots
2 cups cornmeal
1 cup all-purpose flour
1 tablespoon sugar
1 teaspoon baking powder
¾ teaspoon salt
½ teaspoon baking soda
½ cup butter, melted
1½ cups buttermilk
2 large eggs
1½ cups (6 ounces) shredded white Cheddar
   cheese
1 large roasted red bell pepper,
   chopped

Melt 1 tablespoon butter in a large skillet over medium-high heat. Add onion and shallots; sauté 5 minutes or until tender. Cool; set aside.

   Combine cornmeal and next 5 ingredients in a bowl. Set aside.

Spiced Boca Nuts

As guests await the buffet, they nibble on the not-to-be-missed Spiced Boca Nuts, a blend of mixed nuts infused with sweet and piquant flavors.

½ cup flaked coconut
¼ cup sugar
2 teaspoons curry powder
1 teaspoon salt
⅛ teaspoon ground red pepper
1 egg white
1 pound mixed nuts

Combine first 5 ingredients in a large bowl. Whisk egg white in a separate bowl 1 minute or until foamy. Stir nuts into egg white. Stir together coated nuts and coconut mixture. Spread in a single layer on a greased 15- x 10-inch jellyroll pan.

   Bake at 300° for 25 to 30 minutes or until golden brown. Cool in pan on a wire rack. (Nuts will crisp as they cool.) Yield: 4½ cups.
Note: Store in an airtight container at room temperature up to 2 weeks.

Farmhouse Benedict

Whisk together ½ cup butter, buttermilk, and eggs in a separate bowl. Stir in onion mixture, cheese, and roasted pepper.

Add cheese mixture to cornmeal mixture, stirring just until dry ingredients are moistened. Pour into a greased 13- x 9-inch pan.

Bake at 400° for 30 minutes or until a wooden pick inserted in center comes out clean. Cool on a wire rack. Yield: 12 servings.

Rosemary Hollandaise

¼ cup white wine vinegar
1 tablespoon fresh lemon juice
½ teaspoon pepper
½ cup hot water
6 egg yolks
1½ cups butter, cut into ½-inch pieces
1½ tablespoons chopped fresh rosemary

Combine first 3 ingredients in top of a double boiler. Cook over medium-high heat until reduced to 2 tablespoons; add ½ cup hot water. Whisk in egg yolks. Add about one-third of butter to egg mixture; cook over hot (not boiling) water, whisking constantly, until butter melts. Add another third of butter, stirring constantly. As sauce thickens, stir in remaining butter. Cook until temperature reaches 160°, stirring constantly. Stir in rosemary. Remove sauce from double boiler; serve immediately. Yield: 2½ cups.

Stone Crab Claws with Mustard Sauce

For appetizer servings, purchase 4 medium or 2 large cooked claws per person.

1 cup mayonnaise
½ cup spicy brown mustard
2 tablespoons light brown sugar
2 tablespoons dry sherry
1 tablespoon Worcestershire sauce
1 teaspoon dry mustard

Stir together all ingredients in a bowl until well blended. Cover and chill. Serve with stone crab claws. Yield: 1¾ cups.

Stone Crab Claws with Mustard Sauce

get crackin'

Every guest's favorite in this menu turns out to be the Stone Crab Claws with Mustard Sauce.
Unless you purchase claws cracked, you have to use a wooden mallet and strike the shell at the knuckle to avoid crushing the succulent meat. One swift stroke cracks the claw to expose the precious meat. "It's not an everyday indulgence," says league president Cindy Krebsbach, "but, oh, so South Florida."

With Key lime juice in the glaze, Strawberry Streusel Muffins are an instant South Florida success. "They just jump straight into your mouth," says Robin Deyo, cookbook chair.

Strawberry Streusel Muffins

1½ cups all-purpose flour
¼ cup sugar
¼ cup firmly packed light brown sugar
2 teaspoons baking powder
1 teaspoon ground cinnamon
¼ teaspoon salt
1 large egg, lightly beaten
½ cup butter, melted
½ cup half-and-half
1¼ cups thinly sliced fresh strawberries
2 teaspoons grated Key lime rind
Streusel Topping
Key Lime Glaze

Combine first 6 ingredients in a large bowl; make a well in center of mixture.

Stir together egg, butter, and half-and-half in a separate bowl. Add to flour mixture, stirring just until moistened. Gently fold in strawberries and Key lime rind. Spoon batter into paper-lined muffin pans, filling three-fourths full. Sprinkle each muffin with 1 tablespoon Streusel Topping.

Bake at 375° for 25 minutes or until muffins are golden brown and spring back when lightly touched in the center. Cool muffins in pans 10 minutes; remove from pans, and cool completely on a wire rack. Drizzle with Key Lime Glaze. Yield: 12 servings.

Streusel Topping

½ cup chopped pecans
½ cup firmly packed light brown sugar
¼ cup all-purpose flour
1 teaspoon ground cinnamon
1 teaspoon grated Key lime rind
2 tablespoons butter, melted

Combine all ingredients in a bowl; stir well until mixture is moistened and crumbly. Yield: 1 cup.

Key Lime Glaze

½ cup powdered sugar
1 tablespoon fresh Key lime juice
    (about 2 limes)

Stir together powdered sugar and lime juice in a small bowl until smooth. Yield: ¼ cup.

Tropical Fruit with Mango Cream

2 mangoes, peeled, seeded, and sliced
2 nectarines, sliced
3 kiwifruit, peeled and sliced
1 quart strawberries, sliced
1 pineapple, cored and sliced
1 honeydew melon, peeled and cubed
¾ cup fresh orange juice (about 2 large
    oranges)
Mango Cream
Garnish: fresh mint sprigs

Arrange first 6 ingredients on a serving platter. Drizzle with orange juice. Serve with Mango Cream. Garnish, if desired. Yield: 6 to 8 servings.

Mango Cream

1 mango, peeled and diced
¼ cup fresh orange juice
1 tablespoon kirsch (optional)
1 tablespoon fresh lemon juice
1 tablespoon sugar
1 cup whipping cream

Process first 4 ingredients in a blender 1 minute or until pureed. Pour puree into a small bowl; stir in sugar.

Beat whipping cream at medium speed with an electric mixer until soft peaks form. (Do not overbeat.) Fold whipped cream into mango puree, using a knife to swirl into a marbled effect. Yield: 3 cups.

Celestial Sugar Cookies with Royal Frosting

½ cup butter, softened
1 cup sugar
1 large egg
1 teaspoon vanilla extract
2⅓ cups all-purpose flour
2 teaspoons baking powder
¼ teaspoon salt
Royal Frosting

Beat butter at medium speed with an electric mixer until creamy. Gradually add sugar, beating well. Add egg and vanilla, beating well.

Combine flour, baking powder, and salt in a separate bowl; add to butter mixture, beating just until blended. Divide dough into 4 portions. Wrap each portion in plastic wrap, and chill at least 1 hour.

Roll each portion to ⅛-inch thickness between 2 sheets of wax paper. Cut with a 5-inch star-shaped cookie cutter. Place 1 inch apart on greased baking sheets.

Bake at 375° for 7 minutes or until edges lightly brown. Cool 3 minutes on baking sheets; carefully remove to wire racks, and cool completely. Spread or decoratively pipe Royal Frosting onto cookies. Yield: about 2 dozen.

Royal Frosting

3 cups sifted powdered sugar
⅓ cup butter, softened
3 tablespoons milk
1½ teaspoons vanilla extract

Combine all ingredients in a large mixing bowl; beat at low speed until blended. Yield: 2 cups.

Best Friends Iced Coffee Frappé

¼ cup instant coffee granules
½ cup chocolate syrup
¼ cup sugar
1½ cups boiling water
2 cups half-and-half
1 quart vanilla ice cream
2 cups ginger ale
Vanilla ice cream, optional

Stir together first 4 ingredients in a large pitcher; cool. Cover and chill at least 8 hours.

Stir together coffee mixture, half-and-half, and 1 quart ice cream in a punch bowl. Stir in ginger ale; ladle into glasses. Top with ice cream, if desired. Yield: about 10 cups.

Recipes adapted from Savor the Moment: Entertaining without Reservations, *published by the Junior League of Boca Raton, Inc. (1999).*

coastal sampling

Oregon cookbook authors Dan and Kathleen Taggart believe that wine enhances any dinner, especially those wines made from the abundant grapes of their rich region. Their menu pairs the fine foods and wines indigenous to the Northwest.

menu

serves 8

Rosemary-Sage Biscotti   *Curried Chicken in Lettuce Leaves*
Chateau Ste. Michelle Sauvignon Blanc

Northwest Clam Chowder with Oyster Mushrooms
Amity Vineyards Willamette Valley Pinot Blanc

Salmon Patties on Lightly Dressed Mixed Greens
Basil-Coated Grilled Sturgeon with Eggplant
Erath Vineyards Pinot Gris

Prune-and-Hazelnut Tart
Elk Cove Vineyards Late Harvest Riesling

Rosemary-Sage Biscotti

1¾ cups all-purpose flour
¼ cup cornmeal
2½ teaspoons baking powder
1 tablespoon sugar
¾ teaspoon salt
¼ teaspoon freshly ground pepper
2 tablespoons chopped fresh rosemary leaves
2 tablespoons chopped fresh sage leaves
3 large eggs
6 tablespoons olive oil
⅛ teaspoon hot sauce

Combine first 8 ingredients in a large bowl; make a well in center of mixture.

Beat eggs, oil, and hot sauce at medium speed with an electric mixer until blended. Pour liquids into dry ingredients, stirring just until moistened.

Turn dough out onto a lightly floured surface. Divide in half, and shape each portion into a 7- x 2-inch log. Place on a baking sheet lined with parchment paper.

Bake at 350° for 20 minutes or until lightly browned. Immediately remove to a cutting board.

Cut each log into ½-inch-thick slices with a serrated knife, using a gentle sawing motion; place slices on ungreased baking sheets.

Bake at 350° for 12 to 15 minutes; turn and bake 12 more minutes or until lightly browned. Remove to wire racks to cool. Yield: 2 dozen.

The Taggarts' expertise comes from 20 years spent sampling and relishing the Northwest's native foods and wines.

The Taggarts' beachside dinner begins with this savory biscotti flavored with zesty rosemary and sage. Dan and Kathleen serve the biscotti with a citrusy Sauvignon Blanc produced in Washington State. The wine's natural acidity partners well with the herbal biscotti.

Curried Chicken in Lettuce Leaves

6 medium-size dried shiitake mushrooms (about ½ ounce)
1 cup hot water
6 green onions
1¼ to 1½ pounds skinned and boned chicken thighs
¼ cup vegetable oil, divided
1 serrano chile pepper, minced
1½ tablespoons Thai curry paste
½ cup canned unsweetened coconut milk
3 tablespoons soy sauce
1 medium carrot, shredded
1 small Granny Smith apple, peeled and chopped
1 cup frozen sweet green peas
½ teaspoon freshly ground pepper
3 tablespoons cornstarch
3 tablespoons cold water
1 cup loosely packed fresh basil leaves, chopped
2 heads romaine lettuce

Soak mushrooms in 1 cup hot water 30 minutes; drain, reserving liquid. Rinse mushrooms in cold water; pat dry. Remove and discard stems; thinly slice tops. Pour reserved liquid through a fine wire-mesh strainer into a measuring cup; reserve ½ cup.

Slice green onions, separating green tops from white portions. Set aside.

Cut chicken into 1-inch cubes. Sauté chicken in 2 tablespoons hot oil in a large skillet 5 minutes or until done. Remove from pan; cool. Coarsely chop chicken. Set aside.

Sauté white portion of green onions and serrano pepper in remaining 2 tablespoons hot oil in a large skillet 1 minute; add mushroom liquid, curry paste, coconut milk, and soy sauce, and bring to a boil. Reduce heat, and simmer 3 minutes. Stir in mushrooms, carrot, and next 3 ingredients; simmer 3 minutes. Stir in chicken.

Whisk together cornstarch and 3 tablespoons cold water until smooth; stir into chicken mixture. Bring to a boil over medium heat, stirring constantly; boil, stirring constantly, 1 minute. Stir in basil and green onion tops. Serve over romaine lettuce leaves. Yield: 20 appetizer servings.

Curried Chicken in Lettuce Leaves

As the sun begins to set, guests gather in the kitchen to enjoy more Sauvignon Blanc, while the hosts serve spicy Curried Chicken in Lettuce Leaves, an Asian dish of chicken and vegetables spooned into romaine leaves.

Northwest Clam Chowder with Oyster Mushrooms

As the meal progresses to the dinner table, guests are offered a thick, steaming clam chowder topped with oyster mushrooms. With this course, the Taggarts serve a Pinot Blanc—a light, buttery, and crisp white wine that goes particularly well with clams.

3   pounds Manila, Pacific littleneck, Washington butter, or other small hard-shell clams
4   cups water
6   bacon slices, cut crosswise into ½-inch pieces
1   medium onion, diced
2   teaspoons chopped fresh thyme
1¼ pounds Yukon gold potatoes, peeled and cut into 1-inch cubes
2   cups half-and-half
1   teaspoon coarse salt
1   teaspoon freshly ground pepper
1   cup loosely packed fresh parsley leaves, chopped
4   ounces fresh oyster mushrooms, separated into pieces
Garnish: fresh oyster mushrooms

Wash clams thoroughly, discarding any opened shells; place in a stockpot. Add 4 cups water; cover and bring to a boil over medium-high heat. Cook 5 minutes or until shells open, discarding any unopened clams. Remove clams with a slotted spoon, and place in a large bowl. Cool. Remove clam meat from shell, reserving any juice. Coarsely chop clams, and set aside. Pour liquid through a wire-mesh strainer into a 4-cup liquid measuring cup, discarding solids. Reserve 3 cups liquid.

Cook bacon in a Dutch oven until crisp; remove bacon, reserving 2 tablespoons drippings in pan. Add onion and thyme, and sauté 5 minutes or until onion is tender. Add potato, 3 cups reserved clam liquid, half-and-half, salt, and pepper; bring to a boil. Cover, reduce heat, and simmer 7 minutes or until potato is tender. Stir in bacon, clams, parsley, and separated mushrooms; serve immediately. Garnish, if desired. Yield: 9 cups.

This sumptuous meal would be unfinished without a sampling of salmon, a hallmark of Northwest waters.

Salmon Patties on Lightly Dressed Mixed Greens

Kathleen uses salmon in this menu as the salad course, making salmon cakes that she serves on a bed of lightly dressed greens.

1   (1-pound) fresh salmon fillet
1   cup loosely packed fresh parsley leaves
4   green onions, cut into 1-inch pieces
1   tablespoon capers, rinsed and drained
1   large egg
⅔   cup cracker meal, divided
1   teaspoon dried dillweed
1   teaspoon Worcestershire sauce
½   teaspoon hot sauce
¼   teaspoon coarse salt
¼   teaspoon freshly ground pepper
2   tablespoons olive oil
2   teaspoons rice vinegar
1   teaspoon Dijon mustard
¼   cup extra-virgin olive oil
10 cups mixed salad greens
2   medium tomatoes, each cut into 12 wedges
Caper Tartar Sauce

Remove skin and bones from fillet; cut fish into 1-inch pieces. Set aside.

Pulse parsley in a food processor until minced; add green onions, capers, and salmon, and pulse 3 to 4 times or until mixture resembles ground beef. Add egg, 3 tablespoons cracker meal, dillweed, and next 4 ingredients; pulse 3 to 4 times or until blended. Shape mixture into 8 patties. Dredge patties in remaining cracker meal, shaking off excess crumbs.

Sauté patties in 2 tablespoons olive oil in a large skillet 3 minutes on each side or until golden brown. Remove from skillet; keep warm.

Whisk together vinegar, mustard, and ¼ cup olive oil; pour over salad greens and tomato, tossing gently. Serve salmon patties over salad with Caper Tartar Sauce. Yield: 8 servings.

Caper Tartar Sauce

½   cup loosely packed fresh parsley leaves, chopped
½   cup mayonnaise
1   tablespoon milk or buttermilk
1½ teaspoons sweet-hot mustard
1½ teaspoons capers, drained and coarsely chopped
¼   teaspoon dried dillweed
¼   teaspoon freshly ground pepper

Stir together all ingredients; cover and chill. Yield: about 1 cup.

{ vine advice

{ To accompany the salmon cake salad and
{ grilled sturgeon, the Taggarts serve a Pinot
{ Gris that hails from Oregon's Willamette
{ Valley. "Pinot Gris is a medium-bodied,
{ slightly citrusy wine," explains Dan. "Its
{ dry but fruity flavor is enhanced with lightly
{ flavored fish dishes."

Basil-Coated Grilled Sturgeon with Eggplant

Combine tomatoes and hot water to cover in a small bowl; let stand 30 minutes. Drain, and set aside.

Process olives and remaining 5 ingredients in a food processor until blended, stopping to scrape down sides. Add tomatoes; pulse 2 or 3 times. Yield: 1¾ cups.

Prune-and-Hazelnut Tart

For dessert, the Taggarts serve a late harvest Riesling whose concentrated flavors are a comfortable match with the intensely flavored tart.

½ cup hazelnuts
1   pound pitted prunes
¼ cup sugar
2   large eggs
1¼ cups crème fraîche
1   tablespoon grated orange rind
Pastry Tart Shell
Garnishes: sweetened whipped cream,
    chopped toasted hazelnuts

Bake ½ cup hazelnuts in a shallow pan at 350° for 15 minutes or until toasted. (The skins will be very dark.) Wrap nuts in a clean kitchen towel; let stand 20 minutes. Rub nuts briskly to loosen skins; discard skins. Chop nuts; set aside.

Bring prunes and water to cover to a boil in a nonaluminum saucepan over high heat; reduce heat, and simmer 30 minutes. Cool; drain.

Process sugar and next 3 ingredients in a food processor until blended.

Spread prunes in Pastry Tart Shell; sprinkle with hazelnuts. Pour crème fraîche filling over nuts. Place tart in a larger shallow pan.

Bake at 375° for 55 minutes or until set, shielding tart with aluminum foil after 40 minutes to prevent excessive browning. Cool on a wire rack. Garnish, if desired. Yield: 1 (10½-inch) tart.

Pastry Tart Shell

1¼ cups all-purpose flour
1   tablespoon sugar
⅛ teaspoon coarse salt
6   tablespoons very cold unsalted butter,
    cut into ½-inch cubes
3½ to 4 tablespoons ice water

The Columbia River's wild sturgeon is a delicacy native to the Northwest, available fresh during brief seasons in spring and autumn.

Basil-Coated Grilled Sturgeon with Eggplant

Kathleen serves the firm, lightly flavored fish with grilled eggplant and a tart tapenade of olives and sun-dried tomatoes.

6   tablespoons olive oil, divided
1   large sweet onion, halved and cut into
    ¼-inch slices
1   teaspoon coarse salt, divided
1   tablespoon sherry vinegar
2   cups fresh basil leaves, chopped
¾ teaspoon freshly ground pepper,
    divided
2   (1-inch-thick) sturgeon or swordfish
    steaks (about 1½ pounds)
1   medium eggplant, unpeeled and cut
    crosswise into 1-inch slices
Dried-Tomato Tapenade
Garnish: fresh basil sprigs

Heat 2 tablespoons olive oil in a large skillet over medium heat; add onion. Cover and cook 5 minutes. Uncover and sauté 10 minutes or until onion is lightly browned. Stir in ¼ teaspoon salt and vinegar. Set aside, and keep warm.

Stir together 2 tablespoons olive oil, basil, ¼ teaspoon salt, and ¼ teaspoon pepper. Spread mixture on both sides of fish.

Brush eggplant with remaining olive oil; sprinkle with remaining ½ teaspoon salt and ½ teaspoon pepper.

Grill fish and eggplant, covered with grill lid, over high heat (400° to 500°) 3 to 4 minutes on each side or until fish flakes with a fork and eggplant slices are done. Cut steaks in half. Serve with eggplant, onion, and Dried-Tomato Tapenade. Garnish, if desired. Yield: 4 servings.
Note: *We doubled the recipe to serve 8.*

Dried-Tomato Tapenade

¼ cup dried tomatoes
2   cups pitted kalamata olives
6   anchovy fillets, drained
2   large garlic cloves
2   tablespoons lemon juice
2   tablespoons extra-virgin olive oil
¼ teaspoon ground red pepper

Dessert features a slightly sweet Prune-and-Hazelnut Tart.
While recognized for its wines, the Willamette Valley also produces the
lion's share of hazelnuts harvested in the United States.

Prune-and-Hazelnut Tart

Process first 3 ingredients in a food processor until blended. Add butter, and pulse 8 to 10 times or until crumbly. Add water, and pulse 8 to 10 times or until dough holds together.

Turn dough out onto a lightly floured surface; shape into a ball. Place on plastic wrap; flatten slightly and wrap securely. Chill 30 minutes.

Roll pastry to ⅛-inch thickness on a lightly floured surface. Fit into a fluted 10½- x 3-inch-deep round tart pan; trim excess pastry along edges. Cover with plastic wrap, and chill 30 minutes. Freeze 30 additional minutes. Line pastry with aluminum foil; fill with pie weights or dried beans.

Bake at 375° for 17 minutes. Remove weights and foil; bake 8 more minutes. Cool on a wire rack. Yield: 1 (10½-inch) tart shell.
Recipes adapted from Northwest Food & Wine: Great Food to Serve with the Wines of Oregon & Washington *by Dan and Kathleen Taggart (Sasquatch Books, 2003).*

how to host a wine tasting

"For dinner parties," Dan Taggart says, "we often fall into the habit of serving only one or two different wines, generally a lighter (usually white) wine for the earlier courses, followed by a fuller (often red) wine for the main course." A small dinner party is an ideal setting if you really want to enjoy wine tasting informally. Here's what Dan suggests:

For up to eight diners, serve about one-half glass of a different wine with each course. (Use a clean glass for each wine.) Guests can experience the varied combinations of flavors and make up their minds about which pairings are most successful. Let everyone join in—assign each guest a variety to bring (such as Pinot Gris or Sauvignon Blanc), but let them select the vintage.

Sparkling wines are ideal for any course of the meal, not just with appetizers. Serve two or three varieties of sparkling wines with your meal.

livin' la vida aloha

Lisa Blades's dinner party invitations are local hot commodities. Known as one of Montecito, California's best and most laid-back entertainers, Lisa started her own business to help people successfully plan their special occasions—from intimate dinner parties to wedding receptions. But today is Lisa's day. She's invited close friends and family to a Hawaiian fête in her lush garden.

Lisa first went to the Hawaiian Islands 10 years ago, and has, over the years, brought home pieces of Hawaii. Her collection includes everything from fine linens to vintage hula-dancing dolls. She grows rows of red torch ginger that stand tall as Tiki torches amid the honeysuckle in her garden. Palm trees prop against the sky like parasols, and lush banana trees shade sculptural calla lilies. Just beyond the white flowers are Lisa's pride and joy—her pineapples.

Aloha Punch

menu

serves 6

Chi Chi   *Aloha Punch*

Lobster Salad with Papaya and Maui Onion   *Steamed Baby Bok Choy*

Coconut-Basmati Rice Bundles   *Ginger-Glazed Salmon Fillets*

Baby Pineapples Filled with Pineapple Sherbet

Chi Chi

3   cups crushed ice
1⅓ cups piña colada mix
¾   cup vodka
Garnishes: carambola (starfruit) slices, ornamental pineapples

Process first 3 ingredients in a blender until smooth, stopping to scrape down sides. Garnish, if desired. Serve immediately. Yield: 4 servings.

Aloha Punch

2   cups pineapple juice
1   cup strawberry juice
1   cup guava juice
1   cup pear nectar
1   cup orange carbonated beverage (we tested with Orangina)
Garnish: paper parasols

Stir together first 5 ingredients; serve over crushed ice. Garnish, if desired. Yield: 6 cups.

"A dinner party is a gift I give to people I care about. It's a time for me to bestow presents on them. The key to a good party is having the perfect mix of people and simple, fantastic food," says Lisa.

"There's something about food that frees people," says Lisa Blades, seated here at the head of her table. "I've found that the most stimulating conversations often occur over food. That's why I don't believe in tall centerpieces. Nothing should get in the way of eye contact or conversation."

Lobster Salad with Papaya and Maui Onion

Process all ingredients in a blender until smooth, stopping to scrape down sides. Yield: ¾ cup.

Steamed Baby Bok Choy

6   *heads baby bok choy, cut in half*
1   *teaspoon sesame oil*
¼   *cup dry white wine*
1   *tablespoon butter*
Pinch of salt

Sauté bok choy in hot oil in a large skillet over medium-high heat 1 minute or until wilted. Add remaining ingredients. Bring to a boil; cover, reduce heat, and simmer 1 minute or until tender. Yield: 6 servings.

Coconut-Basmati Rice Bundles

(shown on page 78)

2   *cups basmati rice*
4   *cups lite coconut milk*
1   *to 2 teaspoons green curry paste*
1   *teaspoon salt*
½   *teaspoon freshly ground pepper*
Ti leaves*
Black sesame seeds

Rinse rice in cold water until water is no longer cloudy; drain. Stir together rice and next 4 ingredients. Bring to a boil; cover, reduce heat, and simmer 15 minutes or until liquid is absorbed. Remove from heat; let stand, covered, 5 minutes.

Spoon about ½ cup rice onto center of each ti leaf; fold sides over rice, and roll up. Slice into 1½-inch lengths. Sprinkle with black sesame seeds. Serve with Ginger-Glazed Salmon Fillets. Yield: 6 servings.

*Ti leaves are used in Polynesia to wrap foods. Dried ti leaves, which must be soaked before using, can be found in some ethnic markets. Banana leaves may be substituted for ti leaves.

Lobster Salad with Papaya and Maui Onion

6   *(4-ounce) lobster tails, steamed*
2   *large Maui onions, thinly sliced**
1   *teaspoon canola oil*
1   *teaspoon brown sugar*
2   *teaspoons rice vinegar*
¼   *cup fresh orange juice*
Vegetable oil
30 *strands uncooked spaghetti*
1   *papaya, peeled and sliced*
1   *head Red Leaf lettuce*
Sesame-Miso Dressing
Garnishes: lobster tails, fresh chives

Cut shell of lobster tails lengthwise on the underside, using kitchen shears. Pry open tail segments; remove meat, reserving tails to use for garnish. Slice meat into ½-inch medallions. Cover and chill.

Sauté onion in hot canola oil in a large skillet over medium-high heat 10 to 15 minutes or until tender. Stir in brown sugar, rice vinegar, and orange juice. Cover and chill.

Pour vegetable oil to depth of 2 inches into a Dutch oven; heat to 375°. Deep-fry spaghetti, a few strands at a time, for 10 seconds or until golden. Drain on paper towels.

Arrange lobster medallions, onion, papaya, lettuce, and fried spaghetti; drizzle with Sesame-Miso Dressing. Garnish, if desired. Yield: 6 servings.

*Maui onions are from the Hawaiian island of the same name. Any sweet and mild onion can be substituted.

Sesame-Miso Dressing

2   *teaspoons sesame seeds*
½   *cup peanut oil*
¼   *cup fresh lemon juice*
1   *tablespoon lite soy sauce*
2   *teaspoons sesame oil*
1   *teaspoon rice vinegar*
1   *teaspoon miso paste*

countdown to the party

Here are some of Lisa's tips for getting ready.

• **Color schemes** and tones are essential. "Pick your flowers, linens, and serving pieces with care," she says. "I once threw a birthday party for a friend whose favorite color was red. I covered the table with thousands of red rose petals, put an enormous red cabbage rose at the head of each plate, tea lights on the tables, and red anthurium on the chocolate cake. It was simple yet incredibly elegant."

• Put thought into the **guest list**. "I find it's a necessity to invite an eclectic mix," says Lisa. "You need good storytellers, and you need good listeners." She also welcomes children to her parties "because they add life and keep things relaxed."

• Consider **invitations.** Lisa says they need to be sent out a month in advance, with even more notice during the holidays. "An invitation sets the tone," says Lisa. "If you're throwing a spring luncheon, you might want to send a hyacinth bulb, or send chopsticks for an Asian dinner party."

• **Flowers** can make as strong a statement as food and should complement the menu. "If it's a stately affair, I'll go for roses. If it's an Asian meal, I'll use orchids," says Lisa. The best centerpieces unite the guests. A trail of flowers stretching across the table gives a feeling of continuity, but a tall centerpiece can interrupt conversation.

• Don't be afraid to enlist the help of others—caterers, chefs, restaurants—to prepare the **menu.** But if you aim to do it alone, find recipes that allow for some advance preparation. "Often, you can chop vegetables or at least organize ingredients so that they are all right where you need them."

• Lisa prefers one long table at outdoor parties, round tables for intimate indoor dinner parties, and whimsical **children's tables.** "The children's tables are always the most fun," she says. "You want them to have enough activity at their table—via games or crayons or fun little toys—to keep them there throughout the meal."

• Don't forget to have a seasonal **covered location** if you're planning an outdoor event. "Either be comfortable with moving the party indoors, or have a backup plan such as a tent," says Lisa.

• "Conversation is the best music of all," she says. "But **music** livens up a party and serves as a great sound track for the mingling that precedes the meal." If it's a romantic dinner party, she might play Ella Fitzgerald. If it's a tapas party, she puts on Latin or samba music.

• Lisa is fond of **party favors**. "I often send guests home with bouquets of the flowers I've used on tables," she says. "And I always have favors for the children."

The right atmosphere masks any possible mistakes. Lisa says everyone can relax with a fun mix of people and wonderful food that's not overly complicated. And, she adds, "Don't be afraid to hire some help."

Ginger-Glazed Salmon Fillets;
Coconut-Basmati Rice Bundles,
page 76

Ginger-Glazed Salmon Fillets

¼ cup hoisin sauce
3 tablespoons minced fresh ginger
3 tablespoons honey
2 tablespoons Dijon mustard
2 tablespoons fresh lemon juice
½ teaspoon salt
6 (6- to 8-ounce) salmon fillets
Garnishes: ti leaves, purple basil leaves,
 fresh enoki mushrooms

Stir together first 6 ingredients. Place fillets on a lightly greased rack in a broiler pan; pat dry. Spoon ginger mixture over fillets. Bake at 450° for 8 minutes.

Broil 5½ inches from heat for 1 minute or until glaze begins to brown. Serve over Steamed Baby Bok Choy. Garnish, if desired. Yield: 6 servings.

"These are all such simple recipes, yet they're masterpieces on the plate," says Lisa's friend and guest chef, Gael Lecolley.

Baby Pineapples Filled with Pineapple Sherbet

6   baby pineapples*
1½ quarts pineapple sherbet
Garnishes: lemon zest, nectarine slices,
   mango slices

Cut tops from pineapples; reserve for garnish.
Cut and remove centers, leaving a 1-inch-thick
shell. Fill with pineapple sherbet. Garnish, if
desired. Yield: 6 servings.
*You can order baby pineapples from
friedas.com

one man is an island

Master of his own private South Carolina getaway, Ben Moise reigns as the king of coastal feasts. His rustic menu features a perfectly grilled grouper topped with chimichurri sauce and accompanied by various appetizers, side dishes, and desserts. All but the dip and the desserts share a common ingredient: garlic. Ben professes, "I think it's my favorite 'fruit'."

An island makes a tranquil escape for a man who loves the outdoors. Ben, whose primary residence is in Charleston, has spent 23 years as a conservation officer (game warden) for the South Carolina Department of Natural Resources. Moise Island, says its namesake, is "my walk-in Valium. The silence is so loud it's almost annoying."

menu

serves 12 to 14

Anne's Hot Sausage Dip

Moise Island Marinated Shrimp   *Crudités with Creamy Anchovy Dip*

Grilled Grouper with Chimichurri Sauce

Mixed Salad Greens with Garlic-Ginger Vinaigrette

Roasted Rosemary-Garlic Sweet Potatoes

Brown Sugar Bars   *Brownies with Fudge Icing*

Anne's Hot Sausage Dip

1   pound ground hot pork sausage
1   (10-ounce) can diced tomatoes and
    green chiles
1   (8-ounce) package cream cheese,
    softened
¾   cup (3 ounces) shredded sharp Cheddar
    cheese
Corn chips

Cook sausage in a large skillet, stirring until meat crumbles and is no longer pink; drain.

Drain diced tomatoes and green chiles, reserving ¼ cup liquid.

Stir together sausage, diced tomatoes and green chiles, reserved liquid, and cream cheese. Spoon into a lightly greased 1-quart baking dish; sprinkle with Cheddar cheese.

Bake at 350° for 20 to 25 minutes or until bubbly. Serve with corn chips. Yield: 10 to 12 appetizer servings.

Dinner is served at a long picnic table under a roofed shed that is otherwise open to the sea breezes. Hundreds of caps, brought by visitors over the years, hang overhead.

Moise Island Marinated Shrimp

Crudités with Creamy Anchovy Dip

1   cup mayonnaise
1   cup sour cream
1   tablespoon fresh lemon juice
2   garlic cloves, finely chopped
1   (2-ounce) can anchovy fillets, drained
     and finely chopped
1   hard-cooked egg, chopped
4   green onions, finely chopped
1   teaspoon coarsely ground pepper
1/2 teaspoon salt

Stir together all ingredients. Cover and chill 8 hours. Serve with fresh asparagus, carrots, celery, red and green bell pepper strips, and radishes. Yield: 3 cups.

Grilled Grouper with Chimichurri Sauce

1 1/2 teaspoons salt
1/2 cup water
2   cups finely chopped fresh parsley
1   cup seeded and chopped plum tomato
1   cup extra-virgin olive oil
1   cup white wine vinegar
1/4 cup chopped shallots
6   garlic cloves, finely chopped
1   tablespoon ground red pepper
1   teaspoon finely chopped fresh basil
1   teaspoon finely chopped fresh thyme
2   (3-pound) grouper fillets

Dissolve salt in 1/2 cup water.

Stir together parsley and next 8 ingredients in a large bowl; stir in salt water. Set aside 2 cups chimichurri sauce to serve with fish.

Place 1 grouper fillet, skin side down, on a sheet of heavy-duty plastic wrap in a 15- x 10-inch jellyroll pan. Spoon remaining sauce over fillet; top with remaining grouper fillet, flesh side down. Cover and chill 3 to 6 hours, turning occasionally.

Place grouper fillets, skin side down, on grill rack. Grill, covered with grill lid, over medium-high heat (350° to 400°) 30 to 40 minutes or until fish flakes with a fork. Serve with reserved sauce. Yield: 14 servings.

Moise Island Marinated Shrimp

2   tablespoons chopped fresh ginger
4   garlic cloves
1   tablespoon salt
3   pounds large fresh shrimp, steamed and
     peeled
1   tablespoon hot sauce
1   (12-ounce) bottle rice wine vinegar
Garnish: habanero peppers

Grind first 3 ingredients to a paste with a mortar and pestle. Combine ginger mixture with shrimp, hot sauce, and vinegar in a large heavy-duty zip-top plastic bag. Seal and chill at least 8 hours. Garnish, if desired. Yield: 12 appetizer servings.

vine advice

Dr. Tom Quattlebaum, a friend of Ben's and a passionate connoisseur of French vintages, loves wine so much he became part-owner of a wine importing business, New Castle Imports of Myrtle Beach, South Carolina. Here's what he selected for this autumn occasion.

- **For chatting and mingling:** Champagne Alfred Gratien Cuvée Brut Classique NV (nonvintage—blending wines of different vintages keeps the champagne consistent from year to year). Extended aging, typically four years, gives the products of this small champagne house a rich, rounded character with layers of fruit flavors and a crisp finish. Ben proclaims, "Too much of this would be just enough."
- **For the meal itself:** Château Calissanne Clos Victoire Blanc 1998. This blend of several grapes is aged for a year in oak barrels. The resulting white wine is smooth and complex, with just hints of herbs and spices—a perfect accompaniment to grouper and other delicately flavored fish.
- **For afterward:** Mas Amiel Cuvée Spéciale. A robust, fortified (alcohol-added) sweet wine aged 10 years, it's a French version of port that goes well with chocolate desserts.
- **The beverage selection also included two local beers.** The full-bodied Palmetto Amber, brewed by Palmetto Brewing Company, LLC of Charleston, came across as predominantly malty and slightly smoky, with just enough hops-derived bitterness to temper the malt's sweetness. Charleston Wheat, from Carolina Beer & Beverage Company, LLC of Mooresville, North Carolina, offered the light, refreshing taste of a typical wheat beer, but with more substance than most.

Mixed Salad Greens with Garlic-Ginger Vinaigrette

3   garlic cloves, chopped
1   tablespoon minced fresh ginger
½   teaspoon salt
½   teaspoon sugar
½   cup red wine
½   cup red wine vinegar
½   cup olive oil
12   cups gourmet mixed salad greens
1   head radicchio, separated into leaves
½   red onion, thinly sliced
1   cup cherry tomatoes
1   cucumber, sliced

Grind first 4 ingredients to a paste with a mortar and pestle. Whisk together garlic mixture, wine, vinegar, and oil. Let stand 2 to 3 hours to blend flavors.

Toss together salad greens and remaining 4 ingredients in a large bowl. Drizzle with vinaigrette; toss gently. Yield: 12 servings.
Note: *To make vinaigrette in a blender, process first 6 ingredients until smooth, stopping to scrape down sides. Turn blender on high; gradually add oil in a slow, steady stream until blended.*

**Roasted Rosemary-Garlic
Sweet Potatoes**

No matter how big the group, Ben always has time to enjoy his guests. His secrets aren't really that secret: Use familiar recipes. Make sure you have every ingredient and utensil that you'll need. Do as much as possible beforehand. (Everything on this menu was prepared in advance except the grouper.)

Roasted Rosemary-Garlic Sweet Potatoes

5   large sweet potatoes, peeled and cut into 1½-inch chunks (about 4½ pounds)
10 large garlic cloves, crushed
⅓   cup olive oil
1   tablespoon chopped fresh rosemary
1   teaspoon salt
½   teaspoon pepper
Garnish: fresh rosemary sprigs

Toss together sweet potato, garlic, and olive oil in a large, lightly greased roasting pan; sprinkle with chopped rosemary, salt, and pepper.

Bake, uncovered, at 450° for 30 to 35 minutes, stirring every 10 minutes, or until potato is tender and brown. Garnish, if desired. Yield: 10 servings.

Brown Sugar Bars

¾   cup butter, melted
1   cup firmly packed light brown sugar
1   large egg, lightly beaten
⅔   cup all-purpose flour
1   teaspoon baking powder
½   teaspoon salt
1   teaspoon vanilla extract
½   cup chopped pecans
Powdered sugar

Stir together butter and brown sugar. Add egg, stirring until blended.

Combine flour, baking powder, and salt; add to egg mixture, stirring well. Stir in vanilla and pecans. Pour mixture into a greased and floured 8-inch square pan.

Bake at 350° for 30 to 35 minutes or until set. Cool on a wire rack. Cut into squares, and sprinkle with powdered sugar. Yield: 16 squares.

Brownies with Fudge Icing

Brownies with Fudge Icing

2   (1-ounce) unsweetened chocolate baking squares
1   cup butter
4   large eggs
2   cups sugar
2   tablespoons vanilla extract
⅛   teaspoon salt
1   cup all-purpose flour
1   cup chopped pecans
Fudge Icing

Cook chocolate and butter in a heavy saucepan over low heat until melted, stirring occasionally. Remove from heat, and cool mixture slightly.

Beat eggs and next 3 ingredients at medium speed with an electric mixer until thick and pale (about 5 minutes). Fold one-third of chocolate mixture into egg mixture. Fold in remaining chocolate mixture, flour, and pecans. Pour batter into a greased and floured 13- x 9-inch pan.

Bake at 350° for 45 minutes. Pour warm Fudge Icing over hot brownies. Cool on a wire rack. Yield: 2 dozen.

Fudge Icing

¼   cup unsweetened cocoa
¼   cup butter
¼   cup milk
1   cup sugar
2   teaspoons vanilla extract

Bring first 4 ingredients to a boil over medium heat, whisking constantly; boil 1 minute or until sugar dissolves. Add vanilla, and beat 1 minute. Yield: 1 cup.

an english thanksgiving

Chef Todd English's fare may be nationwide, but his passion for cooking still simmers in his mother's harborside Maine kitchen. What Todd's mother Patty Breed finds most beautiful on this glorious fall morning is that Todd and family are home with her in Camden, Maine, for the holidays.

menu

serves 8

Open-Fire Caldron of Lobster Stew

Roast Turkey with Sausage-Clam Stuffing and Olive Gravy

Halibut Spoon Bread   Brussels Sprout Beignets with Bacon Aïoli

Six-Onion Roast with Goat Cheese Crema   Turnip, Apple, and Cheddar Gratin

Maple- and Ginger-Glazed Acorn Squash

Black Mission Fig Cake   Deep-Dish Apricot Pie

Todd makes his way to the shore with the caldron that welcomes lobster stew. He tastes and says, "Mmm. This is it. This is Maine, right here."

Open-Fire Caldron of Lobster Stew

We've transformed this campfire caldron recipe into something any home cook can do.

⅓ cup unsalted butter
3 leeks, chopped
3 carrots, chopped
3 celery ribs, chopped
2 shallots, sliced
1 pound shiitake or lobster mushrooms, sliced
3 parsnips, cut in half
1 gallon chicken broth
1 quart milk
½ cup brandy
5 sprigs fresh thyme
3 (1-pound) live lobsters
Salt and pepper to taste

Melt butter in a large Dutch oven over medium-high heat. Add leeks and next 4 ingredients; sauté 10 minutes or until tender. Add parsnips and next 4 ingredients; bring to a boil.

Plunge lobsters headfirst into boiling broth mixture; return to a boil. Reduce heat, and simmer 8 to 10 minutes or until lobsters are done. Remove lobsters, and cool. Remove arms and claws from lobsters; cut lobsters in half lengthwise. Remove intestinal vein, eyes, and antennae; discard.

Return broth mixture to a boil; reduce heat, and simmer, uncovered, 40 minutes or until mixture is reduced by half. Add salt and pepper to taste. Return lobster to broth, and cook until thoroughly heated.

Spoon broth mixture evenly into 6 large serving bowls; arrange lobster pieces in each. Serve with crusty bread. Yield: 6 servings.

Todd's food today will be much like his restaurant fare, which showcases Mediterranean flavors in bold, rustic style.

Roast Turkey with Sausage-Clam Stuffing and Olive Gravy

4   cups day-old bread cubes
1   pound Italian sausage
2   cups finely chopped onion
1½ cups chopped celery
3   large garlic cloves, minced
3   tablespoons chopped fresh thyme
1   tablespoon minced fresh sage
2   tablespoons Dijon mustard
⅔   cup minced fresh parsley
½   cup butter, melted
2   dozen littleneck clams, shucked
¼   teaspoon salt
¼   teaspoon pepper
2   (2½- to 3-pound) boneless, skinless
     turkey breast halves
½   teaspoon salt
½   teaspoon pepper
1   onion, coarsely chopped
2   carrots, coarsely chopped
2   celery ribs, coarsely chopped
8   quahogs or 1 dozen littleneck clams
½   cup dry white wine
½   cup chicken broth
1   teaspoon cornstarch
1   tablespoon water
¾   cup ripe olives
1   tablespoon chopped fresh rosemary

Place bread cubes on a baking sheet; bake at 325° for 15 to 18 minutes or until lightly browned. Transfer bread to a bowl; set aside.

Remove casings from sausage; discard. Cook sausage in a large skillet, stirring until meat crumbles and is no longer pink. Remove sausage, reserving drippings in skillet.

Sauté 2 cups onion and next 4 ingredients in drippings over medium-high heat 8 minutes or until tender; stir in sausage, mustard, and next 5 ingredients. Add to bread cubes, stirring until blended. Set aside.

Place turkey breast halves flat on heavy-duty plastic wrap, skin side down. Remove tendons, and trim fat. From center of each breast, slice horizontally through thickest part of each side almost to outer edge; flip breasts over. Pound breasts to flatten and create even thickness. Sprinkle each breast evenly with ½ teaspoon salt and pepper.

Roast Turkey with Sausage-Clam Stuffing and Olive Gravy

Spoon half of stuffing mixture over each breast, spreading to within 1 inch of edges. Fold in sides of breast over filling; roll up over filling. (Rolls should be 10 to 12 inches long.)

Tie rolls securely in several places with heavy string. Place coarsely chopped onion, carrot, and celery in a large roasting pan; nestle quahogs into vegetables. Place turkey rolls, seam side down, over vegetables.

Bake at 425° for 30 minutes. Reduce heat to 350°, and bake 50 more minutes or until a meat thermometer registers 170°. Remove turkey from pan; set aside.

Discard vegetables and quahogs, reserving drippings in pan. Place roasting pan on cooktop; add wine and chicken broth. Cook over medium heat, stirring constantly, 5 minutes or until liquid is reduced to ¾ cup. Combine cornstarch

> "My great-grandmother's family owned olive farms in Italy (hence the name of his first restaurant, Olives). She, like my mom and other family members, taught me about good food," says Todd.

Halibut Spoon Bread

Halibut Spoon Bread

½	pound unpeeled, large fresh shrimp
½	cup yellow stone-ground cornmeal
½	cup all-purpose flour
2½	teaspoons baking powder
½	teaspoon baking soda
1	teaspoon kosher salt
2	to 3 teaspoons chopped fresh basil
2	to 3 teaspoons chopped fresh parsley
¼	teaspoon chopped fresh thyme
3	medium eggs, separated
2	cups buttermilk
5	egg whites
⅛	teaspoon cream of tartar
1	tablespoon butter
1	(½-pound) halibut or grouper fillet

into cornmeal mixture; repeat procedure twice using remaining egg white mixture and cornmeal mixture.

Brown butter in a 10-inch cast-iron skillet over medium-high heat. Place fillet in center of skillet; pour batter over top.

Bake at 400° for 20 minutes; place shrimp on top, and cook 10 more minutes or until spoon bread is golden and shrimp turn pink. Serve immediately. Yield: 6 to 8 servings.

vine advice

For his holiday meal, Todd suggests a variety of reds and whites to accompany the menu's robust flavors.

● **Heitz Cellar Napa Valley Cabernet Sauvignon**—brimming with fruit but balanced with oak
● **McIlroy Cellars Chardonnay Aquarius Ranch Russian River Valley**—with hints of honey, vanilla, and citrus
● **Mount Langi Ghiran Billi Billi Creek Shiraz**—with rich plum and chocolate flavors from a blend of three Australian valleys' grapes
● **Martín Códax Albariño**—a medium- to full-bodied Spanish wine that's citrusy and similar to a Riesling; goes nicely with shellfish

and 1 tablespoon water, stirring until smooth; whisk into broth mixture. Bring to a boil over medium heat, stirring constantly. Boil, stirring constantly, 1 minute. Stir in olives and rosemary. Spoon gravy over sliced turkey. Yield: 12 servings.
Note: *The chef also roasted a whole turkey with skin and presented parts of it carved on the platter dribbled with olive gravy (shown above).*

Peel shrimp; devein, if desired. Set aside.

Combine cornmeal and next 7 ingredients in a large bowl. Stir together 3 egg yolks and buttermilk; add to dry ingredients, stirring just until moistened.

Beat 8 egg whites and cream of tartar at high speed with an electric mixer until stiff peaks form. Fold one-third egg white mixture

Brussels Sprout Beignets
with Bacon Aïoli

Brussels Sprout Beignets with Bacon Aïoli

1 pound Brussels sprouts
3 tablespoons olive oil
3 large garlic cloves, minced
¼ teaspoon dried crushed red pepper
1 cup all-purpose flour
1½ teaspoons baking powder
1 teaspoon kosher salt
½ teaspoon freshly ground black pepper
¾ cup milk
Vegetable oil
Salt (optional)
Bacon Aïoli

Chop ½ pound Brussels sprouts; cut remaining Brussels sprouts in half.

Sauté chopped Brussels sprouts in hot olive oil in a large skillet 7 minutes or until golden; add garlic and crushed red pepper. Sauté 30 seconds. Remove from heat; cool.

Combine flour and next 3 ingredients in a large bowl; whisk in milk. Stir in cooked and uncooked Brussels sprouts.

Pour vegetable oil to depth of 3 inches into a Dutch oven; heat to 375°. Drop batter by tablespoonfuls into hot oil. Fry beignets 2 minutes on each side or until golden. Drain well on paper towels. Sprinkle lightly with salt, if desired. Serve with Bacon Aïoli. Yield: 30 beignets.

Bacon Aïoli

5 bacon slices
1 garlic clove, chopped
⅓ cup egg substitute
2 tablespoons fresh lemon juice
½ cup vegetable oil

Cook bacon in a large skillet until crisp; remove bacon and drain on paper towels, reserving 1 tablespoon drippings in skillet. Crumble bacon.

Process reserved bacon drippings, garlic, egg substitute, and lemon juice in a food processor until smooth, stopping to scrape down sides. With processor running, pour oil through food chute in a slow, steady stream. Stir in bacon. Yield: ¾ cup.

"I've had the opportunity to sit at the ultimate chef's counter—my mom's kitchen," says Todd.

Six-Onion Roast with Goat Cheese Crema

10 ounces soft fresh goat cheese
3 tablespoons sour cream
2 tablespoons chopped fresh parsley
2 teaspoons chopped fresh mint
1 tablespoon chopped lemon zest
1 cup toasted ground walnuts, divided
1 garlic bulb, top removed
2 red onions, quartered, root ends intact
2 bunches green onions, trimmed, leaving 3 inches of green ends
½ pound cipollini, peeled*
½ pound red pearl onions, peeled
2 sweet onions, quartered, root ends intact
3 leeks, white part only, quartered lengthwise
½ cup olive oil
1 tablespoon fine-grained sea salt
1 tablespoon freshly ground pepper
Garnish: chopped fresh parsley

Combine first 5 ingredients in a small bowl, stirring until blended. Stir in ½ cup walnuts.

Toss together garlic and next 6 ingredients; drizzle with olive oil. Sprinkle with sea salt and pepper. Spoon mixture into a 3-quart baking pan.

Bake at 400° for 25 minutes, stirring once. Dollop goat cheese mixture over onion mixture; bake 20 minutes or until onions are tender.

Remove from oven; sprinkle with remaining walnuts. Garnish, if desired. Yield: 10 to 12 servings.

*Cipollini are bittersweet bulbs of the grape hyacinth. They look and taste like small onions. Shallots may be substituted.

Turnip, Apple, and Cheddar Gratin

1 large onion, cut into ¼-inch slices
2 tablespoons olive oil
1½ teaspoons butter
1 pound turnips, peeled and cut into ⅛-inch slices, divided
½ pound baking potatoes, peeled and cut into ⅛-inch slices, divided
½ pound Granny Smith apples, peeled and cut into ⅛-inch slices, divided
1 tablespoon chopped fresh rosemary
1 tablespoon chopped fresh thyme
¾ teaspoon fine-grained sea salt
¾ teaspoon freshly ground black pepper
1¼ cups (5 ounces) grated extra-sharp Cheddar cheese

Sauté onion in olive oil in a 10-inch cast-iron skillet over medium-high heat 5 minutes. Cover, reduce heat to medium-low, and cook 15 more minutes or until onion is tender, stirring often. Uncover and cook, stirring often, 5 to 10 more minutes or until browned. Remove onion from skillet.

Add butter to skillet. Layer half each of turnip, potato, and apple slices in skillet, overlapping slices; sprinkle with half each of onion, rosemary, thyme, salt, pepper, and cheese. Repeat procedure with remaining ingredients.

Bake, uncovered, at 400° for 40 to 45 minutes or until tender. Let stand 10 minutes before serving. Yield: 8 servings.

Maple- and Ginger-Glazed Acorn Squash

1   cup butter, softened and cut into chunks
2   tablespoons grated fresh ginger
2   tablespoons brown sugar
2   tablespoons maple syrup
2   medium acorn squash
½   cup fresh orange juice
2   tablespoons cider vinegar

Process first 4 ingredients in a food processor until blended.

Cut squash lengthwise into quarters. Scoop out seeds and membrane. Spread half of butter mixture on squash. Bake, uncovered, at 400° for 30 minutes.

Stir together remaining butter mixture, orange juice, and vinegar in a small saucepan. Cook over low heat until butter melts; brush on squash. Bake 15 minutes or until squash is tender and golden, basting occasionally with butter mixture. Yield: 8 servings.

Black Mission Fig Cake

1½ cups dried Black Mission figs
1   cup butter, softened
1½ cups sugar
1½ cups firmly packed brown sugar
4   large eggs
3   cups all-purpose flour
¼   teaspoon baking soda
¼   teaspoon salt
1   cup sour cream
1   teaspoon vanilla extract
2   tablespoons butter
2   tablespoons sugar
¼   teaspoon ground cinnamon
¼   teaspoon vanilla extract
Garnish: fresh figs

Cut figs in half; cover with hot water. Let stand 20 minutes; drain and set aside.

Beat 1 cup butter at medium speed with an electric mixer 2 minutes or until creamy; gradually add sugars, beating well. Add eggs, 1 at a time, beating until blended after each addition.

Combine flour, baking soda, and salt; add to butter mixture alternately with sour cream, beginning and ending with flour mixture. Beat at low speed until blended after each addition.

Maple- and Ginger-Glazed
Acorn Squash

Deep-Dish Apricot Pie

Deep-Dish Apricot Pie

To serve a crowd, double the recipe, including pastry, and spoon from the dish like a cobbler.

2   large eggs
1   cup firmly packed brown sugar
1   teaspoon vanilla extract
¼   cup whipping cream
3   tablespoons unsalted butter, melted
¾   teaspoon ground cinnamon
¼   teaspoon salt
1½ cups coarsely chopped walnuts
1½ cups dried apricots, cut into ½-inch
    pieces
1   cup fresh apricots, peeled, pitted, and
    sliced into quarters
Double-Crust Pastry

Whisk together first 3 ingredients in a large bowl. Whisk in cream and next 3 ingredients. Stir in walnuts and apricots.

Roll pastry to ⅛-inch thickness on a lightly floured surface. Fit into a 9-inch pieplate. Spoon apricot mixture into piecrust. Roll remaining pastry to ⅛-inch thickness. Place over filling; seal and crimp edges. Cut slits in top to allow steam to escape.

Bake at 375° for 1 hour, tenting if necessary. Cool on a wire rack. Yield: 1 (9-inch) pie. **Note:** ¾ cup dried apricots may be substituted for fresh. Add hot water to cover apricots; let stand 20 minutes. Drain apricots, and cut in half; use in addition to 1½ cups dried apricots.

Double-Crust Pastry

2   cups all-purpose flour
1   teaspoon salt
⅔   cup plus 2 tablespoons shortening
4   to 5 tablespoons ice water

Combine flour and salt; cut in shortening with a pastry blender until mixture is crumbly. Sprinkle ice water evenly over surface, and stir with a fork until dry ingredients are moistened. Shape into a ball; chill. Yield: enough pastry for bottom and top crusts of 1 (9-inch) pie.

"The thing about cooking is that you really put your heart and soul on the plate," says Todd. His dishes reflect his well-traveled life, with Italy his strongest magnet.

Stir in 1 teaspoon vanilla. Pour batter into a greased and floured 10-inch springform pan. Top with fig halves.

Bake at 300° for 1 hour and 50 minutes or until a wooden pick inserted in center comes out clean. Cool in pan on wire rack 10 minutes; remove from pan, and cool on rack.

Melt 2 tablespoons butter in a small saucepan over medium heat; add sugar and cinnamon, stirring until sugar dissolves. Stir in ¼ teaspoon vanilla. Brush over top of cake. Garnish, if desired. Yield: 1 (9-inch) cake. **Note:** *3 cups fresh figs can substitute for dried.*

coastal recipes

appetizers & beverages

Black Bean Dip

1   15-ounce can black beans, drained
1/4 cup olive oil
1 1/2 tablespoons ground cumin
1   tablespoon fresh lime juice
1/4 teaspoon salt
1/4 teaspoon freshly ground pepper
Dash of hot sauce
Garnish: toasted cumin seeds

Process first 7 ingredients in a blender or food processor until smooth. Garnish, if desired. Serve with raw vegetables. Yield: 1 1/3 cups.

Spinach-Vidalia Dip

1/4 cup butter or margarine
2   large Vidalia onions, chopped
1   (10-ounce) package frozen chopped spinach, thawed and well drained
1/2 (8-ounce) package cream cheese, softened
1/2 cup sour cream
1/2 cup shredded Parmesan cheese, divided
1/4 teaspoon salt
1   tablespoon Italian-seasoned breadcrumbs

Melt butter in a large skillet over medium-high heat. Add onion; sauté 20 minutes or until golden. Stir in spinach, cream cheese, sour cream, 1/4 cup Parmesan cheese, and salt. Spoon into an ungreased 1 1/2-quart shallow baking dish.

Combine remaining 1/4 cup Parmesan cheese and breadcrumbs. Sprinkle over spinach mixture.

Bake, uncovered, at 375° for 20 minutes or until golden. Serve with tortilla chips. Yield: 3 cups.

Guacamole

6   ripe avocados, peeled
1/3 cup fresh lime juice
2   large tomatoes, chopped
3   to 4 garlic cloves, minced
1   tablespoon chopped fresh cilantro
1/2 teaspoon salt
1/4 teaspoon pepper

Place avocados in a bowl; mash, leaving some small pieces. Stir in lime juice until blended. Stir in tomato and remaining ingredients. Cover tightly with plastic wrap; chill 30 minutes. Serve with tortilla chips. Yield: 4 cups.

Caribbean Guacamole

2   ripe avocados
1   papaya
1   tomato
1   red onion, quartered
2   green onions, diced
2   to 3 garlic cloves, minced
1/4 to 1/2 Scotch bonnet or habanero chile pepper, seeded and minced*
1/4 cup fresh lime juice
3   tablespoons minced fresh cilantro
1   tablespoon ground cumin
1   teaspoon hot sauce
1/4 teaspoon salt
1/4 teaspoon pepper
Garnishes: tomato rose, sliced cucumber

Peel avocado and papaya. Cut avocado, papaya, and tomato into chunks.

Process avocado, papaya, tomato, and next 10 ingredients in a food processor until finely chopped. Place in a bowl, and garnish, if desired. Serve with Party Plantain Chips (page 103) or tortilla chips. Yield: about 3 cups.
*2 to 3 jalapeño peppers may be substituted.
From the book The Sugar Mill Caribbean Cookbook, by Jinx and Jefferson Morgan © 1999. Reprinted with permission from The Harvard Common Press.

Hummus with Sun-Dried Tomatoes

Dried tomatoes paint this hummus a pretty red.

1   (7-ounce) jar dried tomatoes in oil
1   (15 1/2-ounce) can chickpeas (garbanzo beans), rinsed and drained
1   garlic clove, halved
1/2 cup mayonnaise
1/4 cup freshly grated Parmesan cheese
2   tablespoons fresh lemon juice
1/4 teaspoon dried basil
1/8 teaspoon ground red pepper

Drain tomatoes, reserving 3 tablespoons oil.

Process tomatoes, reserved oil, chickpeas, and remaining ingredients in a food processor until smooth, stopping to scrape down sides. Serve with olives and toasted pita bread. Yield: 2 1/2 cups.

summer shrimp salsa For a simple 10-minute snack, combine chopped cooked shrimp, black beans, and corn with minced garlic, chopped fresh cilantro, lime juice, ground cumin, and salt. Serve with blue corn chips.

Hummus with Sun-Dried Tomatoes

White Bean and Bacon Dip with Rosemary Pita Chips

White Bean and Bacon Dip with Rosemary Pita Chips

Homemade rosemary-flecked chips are a great complement to this garlicky dip, but store-bought pitas or bagel chips are a fine stand-in.

½ teaspoon dried crushed rosemary

¼ teaspoon salt

¼ teaspoon garlic powder

⅛ teaspoon freshly ground pepper

3 (6-inch) pita rounds, each cut into 8 wedges

2 applewood-smoked bacon slices, chopped (we tested with Nueske's)

4 garlic cloves, minced

⅓ cup chicken broth

1 (19-ounce) can cannellini beans or other white beans, drained

¼ cup chopped green onions

1 tablespoon fresh lemon juice

½ teaspoon hot sauce

⅛ teaspoon salt

⅛ teaspoon paprika

To prepare chips, combine first 4 ingredients. Arrange pita wedges in a single layer on a baking sheet. Lightly coat pita wedges with vegetable cooking spray; sprinkle evenly with rosemary mixture. Lightly recoat pita wedges with cooking spray.

Bake at 350° for 20 minutes or until golden.

To prepare dip, cook bacon in a small saucepan over medium heat until crisp. Remove bacon from pan with a slotted spoon; set aside. Add garlic to drippings in pan; sauté 1 minute. Add chicken broth and beans; bring to a boil. Reduce heat, and simmer, uncovered, 10 minutes.

Combine bean mixture, green onions, and remaining ingredients in a food processor, and process until smooth, stopping to scrape down sides. Spoon dip into a bowl; stir in 1 tablespoon bacon. Sprinkle dip with remaining bacon just before serving. Serve with pita chips. Yield: 1½ cups.

White Bean Relish

1   (16-ounce) can navy beans, rinsed and drained
1   cup diced tomato
3/4 cup sliced green onions
1/2 cup diced red bell pepper
1/2 cup diced celery
2   tablespoons chopped fresh cilantro or parsley
1   jalapeño pepper, seeded and chopped
1   garlic clove, pressed
1   (0.7-ounce) envelope Italian salad dressing mix
1/2 cup water
1/4 cup cider vinegar
1   tablespoon olive oil

Combine first 8 ingredients in a large bowl.

Combine salad dressing mix, water, vinegar, and oil in a jar. Cover jar tightly, and shake vigorously. Pour over bean mixture, tossing gently. Cover and chill; toss before serving. Serve with tortilla chips. Yield: 3 cups.

Onion-Cheese Dip

2   tablespoons butter or margarine
3   large Vidalia onions, coarsely chopped
1   garlic clove, minced
2   cups (8 ounces) shredded sharp Cheddar cheese
1/2 cup mayonnaise
1/2 cup sour cream
1/2 teaspoon salt
1/2 teaspoon pepper
1/2 teaspoon hot sauce

Melt butter in a large nonstick skillet over medium-high heat. Add onion and garlic; sauté 15 minutes or until onion is lightly browned. Reduce heat to medium. Stir in cheese and remaining ingredients. Cook 3 to 5 minutes or until cheese melts. Serve hot with tortilla chips. Yield: 3 1/2 cups.

Roasted Eggplant Spread on Crostini

3   medium eggplants, peeled and sliced 1/8 inch thick
2 1/2 teaspoons salt
1   French baguette, cut into 1/4-inch-thick slices
2   tablespoons extra-virgin olive oil
Freshly grated Parmesan cheese
10 large garlic cloves, peeled
2   tablespoons fresh lemon juice
3   tablespoons extra-virgin olive oil
1/4 teaspoon salt
1/4 teaspoon crushed red pepper
Garnish: roasted red bell pepper slices

Sprinkle eggplant slices with 2 1/2 teaspoons salt; let stand 30 minutes.

Brush baguette slices with 2 tablespoons olive oil, and place on baking sheets.

Bake at 450° for 6 to 8 minutes or until golden. Sprinkle with Parmesan cheese; bake 2 more minutes or until cheese melts. Set crostini aside.

Rinse eggplant, and place on well-oiled baking sheets; add garlic. Bake 25 minutes or until eggplant edges are crispy and garlic is tender. (Eggplant will be dark brown.) Cool slightly; chop eggplant and garlic.

Place eggplant mixture in a large bowl; stir in lemon juice and next 3 ingredients. Spoon onto crostini. Garnish, if desired. Yield: 2 cups.
—Louis Pappas Market Cafe
Tampa, Florida

Kalamata Olive Spread

1   (6-ounce) jar pitted kalamata olives, drained
1   (8-ounce) container sour cream
1   tablespoon dried dill
2   (8-ounce) packages cream cheese, softened
4   ounces crumbled feta cheese

Combine olives, sour cream, and dill in a food processor; pulse until well blended. Add cream cheese and feta; pulse until creamy. Serve with pita bread. Yield: about 3 cups.
—Louis Pappas Market Cafe
Tampa, Florida

Kalamata Olive Spread

Roasted Eggplant Spread on Crostini

Eggplant-Squash Caponata

Eggplant-Squash Caponata

Serve this colorful eggplant spread on crostini for an appetizer that's very accommodating. You can serve it as soon as you stir it up, or cover and chill it overnight.

1   small eggplant, peeled and cut into
     1-inch cubes (1 pound)
1   medium-size yellow squash, cubed
1   medium zucchini, cubed (½ pound)
1   green bell pepper, cut into thin strips
1   red bell pepper, cut into thin strips
1   yellow bell pepper, cut into thin strips
1   (8-ounce) package fresh mushrooms
1   medium onion, chopped
3   garlic cloves, pressed
1   tablespoon olive oil
1   (14½-ounce) can stewed tomatoes,
     undrained
1   (3-ounce) jar capers, drained
1   cup kalamata olives, pitted
1   tablespoon herbes de Provence
1   tablespoon dried basil
1   teaspoon salt
1   teaspoon dried thyme
1   teaspoon coarsely ground pepper
½   teaspoon ground cumin
Garnish: fresh basil

Toss together first 10 ingredients in a roasting pan. Bake at 400°, stirring occasionally, 40 minutes. Add tomatoes, and bake 10 more minutes. Spoon vegetables into a large bowl. Stir in capers and next 7 ingredients. Cool and serve at room temperature, or cover and chill 8 hours. Serve on crostini. Garnish, if desired. Yield: 4 cups.

—Caterer Sarah Aley
Tenants Harbor, Maine

Hot Cape Cod Dip

You can cook the cod a day ahead and chill it overnight, but stir up the base of the dip just before you're ready to serve it so it's hot for spooning into the chafing dish.

1   (1-pound) cod fillet
2   shallots, minced
3   tablespoons butter or margarine, melted
1   tablespoon all-purpose flour
¾   cup milk
½   cup whipping cream
2   tablespoons dry sherry
1   tablespoon fresh lemon juice
¾   teaspoon salt
½   teaspoon ground white pepper
¼   teaspoon freshly ground black pepper
¼   teaspoon Worcestershire sauce
Garnish: chopped fresh parsley

Pour water to depth of 2 inches into a large skillet; bring to a boil. Add fish, and return to a boil. Cover, reduce heat, and simmer 5 to 8 minutes or until fish flakes with a fork. Remove from skillet with a slotted spoon; cool slightly. Flake into bite-size pieces. Set aside.

Sauté shallots in butter in a heavy saucepan over medium-high heat 3 minutes or until tender; whisk in flour until smooth. Cook 1 minute, whisking constantly. Gradually whisk in milk; cook over medium heat, whisking constantly, until sauce is thickened and bubbly. Stir in whipping cream and next 6 ingredients.

Add fish; cook over low heat until thoroughly heated. Serve in a chafing dish. Garnish, if desired. Serve warm with assorted crackers. Yield: 2½ cups.

Note: Double the recipe to fill a chafing dish.

Smoked Salmon Spread

6   ounces thinly sliced smoked salmon
1   (8-ounce) package cream cheese, softened
8   green onions, sliced
1   to 1½ tablespoons fresh lemon juice
¼   teaspoon freshly ground pepper
¼   teaspoon hot sauce

Pulse all ingredients in a food processor until blended, stopping to scrape down sides. Cover and chill 2 hours. Spoon into Belgian endive leaves, or spread on crackers. Yield: 2 cups.

—Caroline Coleman Bailey
Tiburon, California

Creole Catfish Dip

4   (4-ounce) catfish fillets
1½   (8-ounce) packages cream cheese,
     softened
2   tablespoons mayonnaise
2   tablespoons Worcestershire sauce
1   tablespoon fresh lemon juice
1   teaspoon Creole seasoning
½   cup chopped green onions
1   (12-ounce) bottle chili sauce

Pour water to depth of 2 inches into a large skillet; bring to a boil. Add fish, and return to a boil. Cover, reduce heat, and simmer 5 to 8 minutes or until fish flakes with a fork. Remove from skillet with a slotted spoon; cool slightly. Flake into bite-size pieces.

Beat cream cheese and next 4 ingredients at medium speed with an electric mixer until smooth. Stir in ¼ cup green onions. Spread cheese mixture in an 8-inch bowl. Spread chili sauce over cheese mixture; top with flaked catfish and remaining onions. Serve immediately with crackers. Yield: 3½ cups.

Spicy Seafood Salsa

1   (1-pound) swordfish, amberjack, or
    grouper fillet
1   cup seeded, diced tomato
1/2   cup diced red bell pepper
1/2   cup diced yellow bell pepper
3   tablespoons chopped green onions
3   jalapeño peppers, seeded and finely
    chopped
3   tablespoons minced fresh cilantro
3   tablespoons fresh lime juice
2   tablespoons olive oil
1/4   teaspoon salt
1/4   teaspoon freshly ground pepper
1/4   teaspoon ground cumin

Pour water to depth of 2 inches into a large
skillet; bring to a boil. Add fish, and return to a
boil. Cover, reduce heat, and simmer 5 to 8
minutes or until fish flakes with a fork. Remove
from skillet with a slotted spoon; cool slightly.
Flake into bite-size pieces.

Stir together fish and remaining ingredients.
Cover and chill at least 1 hour. Serve with Party
Plantain Chips (page 103) or tortilla chips.
Yield: 4 cups.

Dorothy's Smoked Fish Spread

1   pound smoked fish, flaked
2/3   cup mayonnaise
1/2   cup pickle relish
1/4   cup prepared horseradish
1/4   cup finely chopped onion
1   teaspoon hot pepper sauce
1/4   teaspoon salt
1/4   teaspoon freshly ground pepper
1/2   teaspoon fresh lime juice

Stir together all ingredients. Cover and chill.
Serve with crackers or crostini. Yield: 3 cups.
From Keys Cuisine *by Linda Gassenheimer.*
© 1991 by Linda Gassenheimer. Used by
permission of Grove/Atlantic, Inc.

Spicy Seafood Salsa

Party Plantain Chips

Caribbean Salsa

Banana, peppers, ginger, and lime put the Caribbean spin on this salsa that's great paired with grilled meat.

1   large ripe banana, peeled and chopped
½   cup diced red bell pepper
½   cup diced green bell pepper
½   cup chopped fresh cilantro
3   green onions, diced
1   roasted jalapeño pepper*, chopped
2   tablespoons brown sugar
1   tablespoon minced fresh ginger
3   tablespoons fresh lime juice
1   tablespoon olive oil
¼   teaspoon salt
⅛   teaspoon pepper

Toss together all ingredients; cover and chill 2 hours. Yield: 2½ cups.

*To roast jalapeño, broil pepper on an aluminum foil-lined baking sheet 5½ inches from heat about 5 minutes or until pepper looks blistered. Place in a heavy-duty zip-top plastic bag; seal and let stand 10 minutes to loosen skin. Peel pepper; remove and discard seeds.

Corn Salsa

1   (15.25-ounce) can whole kernel corn, rinsed and drained
½   (4.5-ounce) can chopped green chiles, drained
½   (2¼-ounce) can sliced ripe olives, drained
1   small tomato, chopped
2   jalapeño peppers, seeded and diced
2½ tablespoons olive or vegetable oil
1½ tablespoons white vinegar
¼   teaspoon salt

Stir together all ingredients in a large bowl. Cover and chill, stirring often, at least 2 hours. Serve with flank steak or tortilla chips. Yield: 3 cups.

Add homemade flair to your dippers with these four easy recipes. Make any of them a day ahead, and store in an airtight container.

Garlicky Pita Chips

6   (6-inch) pita rounds
2   garlic cloves, pressed
¼   cup olive oil
½   teaspoon salt
½   teaspoon freshly ground pepper

Split pita rounds to make 12 rounds.
    Stir together garlic and oil; brush over insides of rounds. Sprinkle with salt and pepper. Stack pitas; cut stack into 6 wedges. Place wedges in a single layer on ungreased baking sheets; bake at 400° for 5 to 6 minutes or until crisp. Yield: 8 to 10 servings.

Margarita Chips

1½ teaspoons fine-grained sea salt
2   teaspoons grated lime rind
Vegetable oil
12 (6-inch) corn tortillas, each cut into 6 wedges

Combine salt and lime rind.
    Pour oil to depth of 2 inches into a Dutch oven; heat to 350°. Fry tortilla wedges in small batches in hot oil about 30 seconds or until golden. Drain on paper towels; sprinkle with lime salt. Yield: 8 to 10 servings.

Parmesan Won Ton Crisps

¼   cup butter or margarine, melted
20 won ton wrappers
½   cup freshly grated Parmesan cheese

Lightly brush 2 baking sheets with butter. Cut wrappers in half diagonally; place in a single layer on baking sheets. Brush wrappers with remaining butter; sprinkle with cheese.
    Bake at 375° for 5 to 6 minutes or until golden. Yield: 10 to 12 servings.

Party Plantain Chips

In Cuba, these treats are called mariquitas.

1½ teaspoons fine-grained sea salt
1½ teaspoons grated lime rind
Peanut oil
4   green plantains (about 1½ pounds)

Combine salt and lime rind; set aside.
    Pour oil to depth of 2 inches into a large Dutch oven; heat to 360°.
    Peel plantains; slice plantains lengthwise very thinly, using a mandoline.
    Fry plantain strips, 4 or 5 at a time, 30 seconds on each side or until golden. Drain on paper towels. Sprinkle with lime salt. Yield: 8 to 10 servings.

Left to right: Parmesan Won Ton Crisps, Garlicky Pita Chips, Margarita Chips

Black Bean and Mandarin Orange Salsa

1   (11-ounce) can mandarin oranges, undrained
2   (15-ounce) cans black beans, rinsed and drained
1   roasted red bell pepper from a jar, sliced
2   to 3 tablespoons chopped fresh cilantro
3   tablespoons olive oil
3   tablespoons red wine vinegar or balsamic vinegar
¼   teaspoon salt
¼   teaspoon pepper

Drain oranges, reserving ⅓ cup juice.

Combine oranges, beans, roasted red pepper, and cilantro in a large bowl.

Whisk together reserved orange juice, olive oil, and remaining ingredients; pour over orange mixture, tossing well. Serve with pork, chicken, or tortilla chips. Yield: 3 cups.

Plum Salsa

1   cup diced plum
½   cup diced honeydew
½   cup diced nectarine or peach
1   jalapeño pepper, seeded and finely chopped
2   tablespoons minced fresh mint
2   tablespoons lime juice
1   tablespoon honey

Stir together all ingredients; cover and chill 8 hours. Serve with poultry, pork, or fish. Yield: 1½ cups.

Dusty Olives

1½ pounds whole or pimiento-stuffed olives, drained
½   teaspoon smoked paprika
Olive oil

Place olives in a 1-quart decorative container. Dust with smoked paprika. Fill jar with olive oil. Yield: 10 appetizer servings.

—Steve Winston
The Spanish Table
Seattle, Washington

Fried Almonds

1   cup olive oil
1   pound Marcona or blanched almonds, skinned
Sea salt

Heat oil to 350°. Add almonds and cook, stirring constantly, until golden. Remove almonds with a slotted spoon. Drain on paper towels. Sprinkle with sea salt to taste. Yield: 2⅔ cups.

Marinated Manchego

1   pound manchego cheese, rind removed
12 arbequina or niçoise olives
4   to 6 fresh thyme sprigs
1   fresh rosemary sprig
Extra-virgin olive oil

Cut cheese into ¼-inch-thick wedges; arrange in a 1-quart jar. Add olives. Arrange thyme on outside edge of jar; place rosemary in center of jar. Fill jar with olive oil; cover. Allow to marinate in refrigerator for one week. Yield: 10 appetizer servings.

tomato stack This "no recipe" makes a colorful summer appetizer. Stack tomato, basil leaves, and fresh mozzarella slices; drizzle with olive oil, and sprinkle with salt and pepper.

Easy Antipasto

(shown on page 6)

Legendary winemaker Julio Gallo's granddaughter Caroline Coleman Bailey calls this appetizer sailboat-friendly fare, and suggests serving it with Gallo of Sonoma Chardonnay, which offers a hint of oak and a tinge of honey.

¾   pound thinly sliced Italian meats
¾   pound assorted cheeses
¾   pound assorted olives, drained
Marinated Tortellini
1   (10-ounce) jar pepperoncini salad peppers, drained
1   (8-ounce) container commercial hummus
1   (7-ounce) jar roasted red bell peppers, drained
1   (6-ounce) jar marinated artichoke hearts, drained

Arrange all ingredients on a platter or on small serving plates. Serve with French bread and assorted crackers. Yield: 12 appetizer servings.
Note: For this antipasto, Caroline selected a tomato-basil torte, Boschetto Italian cheese, fresh garlic-herb goat cheese, thinly sliced prosciutto, salami, and mortadella from her local market.

Marinated Tortellini

1   (9-ounce) package refrigerated cheese-filled tortellini
⅓   cup vegetable oil
2   tablespoons white wine vinegar
1   tablespoon water
½   teaspoon salt
½   teaspoon freshly ground pepper
1   garlic clove, crushed
1   tablespoon chopped fresh Italian parsley

Cook tortellini according to package directions; drain. Rinse with cold water; drain.

Whisk together vegetable oil and next 5 ingredients. Pour over tortellini; toss gently. Sprinkle with chopped parsley. Cover and chill. Yield: 12 appetizer servings.

Salmon Log

3 (6-ounce) cans skinless, boneless pink salmon, drained and flaked (we tested with Chicken of the Sea)
1 (8-ounce) package cream cheese, softened
1 tablespoon minced onion
1 tablespoon lemon juice
2 teaspoons prepared horseradish
¾ teaspoon salt
¼ teaspoon liquid smoke
½ cup finely chopped pecans, toasted
½ cup chopped fresh Italian parsley

Combine first 7 ingredients; cover and chill 4 hours. Shape salmon mixture into a 10-inch log. Combine pecans and parsley in a shallow dish; gently roll log in nut mixture. Wrap in plastic wrap, and chill until ready to serve. Serve with assorted crackers. Yield: 2¼ cups.

Shrimp Cakes

California chef Marc Dym originally prepared this recipe using abalone. We liked this shrimp version just as well.

1 pound peeled, deveined fresh shrimp
1 large egg, lightly beaten
¼ cup sour cream
2 tablespoons minced red bell pepper
2 tablespoons minced red onion
2 tablespoons minced seedless cucumber
1 tablespoon chopped fresh chives
2½ teaspoons grated orange rind
1½ teaspoons grated lemon rind
1 teaspoon grated lime rind
1 teaspoon salt
1 teaspoon ground coriander
1 teaspoon Old Bay seasoning
¼ teaspoon freshly ground white pepper
2 cups cornbread crumbs
2 tablespoons fresh orange juice
1 tablespoon fresh lime juice
1 tablespoon fresh lemon juice
2 cups Japanese breadcrumbs (Panko)
Canola oil

Place shrimp in a food processor and pulse until finely chopped. Transfer shrimp to a bowl; add egg and next 5 ingredients. Stir in orange rind and next 7 ingredients. Combine citrus juices. Slowly add juice until mixture is slightly wet but still holds together. Cover and chill at least 1 hour.

Form chilled mixture into 10 balls (golf ball size); lightly roll in Japanese breadcrumbs. Flatten balls to form ½-inch-thick patties.

Pour oil to depth of 1 inch into a cast-iron skillet; heat to 375°. Fry patties, in batches, 3 to 4 minutes on each side or until golden. Remove from skillet, and drain on paper towels.

Transfer to a baking sheet, and keep warm in a 200° oven. Repeat procedure with remaining patties. Yield: 10 cakes.
—*Executive Chef Marc L. Dym*
The Restaurant at Stevenswood Lodge
Mendocino, California

Crawfish-Eggplant Beignets with Rémoulade Sauce

Louisiana food writer Marcelle Bienvenu enjoys serving these savory beignets and mixing it up with her guests.

2 tablespoons vegetable oil
1 medium eggplant, peeled and chopped
½ cup chopped onion
¼ cup finely chopped celery
1½ teaspoons salt
¼ teaspoon ground red pepper
1 pound peeled crawfish tails, coarsely chopped
Vegetable oil
3 large eggs, lightly beaten
1½ cups milk
2 teaspoons baking powder
½ teaspoon ground red pepper
3 cups all-purpose flour
Rémoulade Sauce

Heat 2 tablespoons oil in a large skillet over medium-high heat. Add eggplant and next 4 ingredients; cook 7 minutes or until vegetables are tender, stirring occasionally. Add crawfish; cook 3 minutes. Remove from heat, and cool.

Pour oil to depth of 3 inches into a Dutch oven; heat to 360°.

Whisk together eggs and next 3 ingredients; whisk in flour just until moistened. Fold in eggplant mixture. Drop batter by heaping table-spoonfuls into hot oil. Fry beignets, a few at a time, 3 minutes or until golden, turning once. Drain on paper towels. Serve immediately with Rémoulade Sauce. Yield: 4 dozen.

Rémoulade Sauce

1 cup mayonnaise
½ cup finely chopped green onions
2 tablespoons chopped fresh parsley
2 tablespoons finely chopped celery
2 tablespoons Creole or whole-grain mustard
2 tablespoons ketchup
1 teaspoon paprika
1 teaspoon hot sauce
¼ teaspoon freshly ground pepper
3 garlic cloves, minced

Whisk together all ingredients. Cover and chill 1 hour. Yield: 1⅔ cups.

Crawfish-Eggplant Beignets with Rémoulade Sauce

vine advice

• **Salviano Orvieto Classico:** This dry, crisp, medium-bodied Italian white goes well with most everything—particularly Crawfish-Eggplant Beignets.

Codfish Fritters

8   ounces salt cod
2   green onions, minced
1   small tomato, peeled, seeded, and minced
½   to 1 Scotch bonnet or habanero chile
    pepper, seeded and minced
½   cup all-purpose flour
½   teaspoon baking powder
1   large egg, lightly beaten
¼   cup water
Vegetable oil

Soak cod in cold water to cover in the refrigerator for 12 hours, changing water at least 3 times.

Drain fish; remove and discard any skin and bones. Combine fish and water to cover in a small skillet; bring to a boil over medium heat. Reduce heat, and simmer, uncovered, 10 minutes or until fish flakes with a fork. Drain fish; cool and flake.

Combine cod and next 3 ingredients. Combine flour and baking powder in a separate bowl; add to cod mixture. Stir in egg and ¼ cup water just until blended.

Pour oil to depth of 3 inches into a heavy saucepan; heat to 350° to 375°. Drop cod mixture by teaspoonfuls into hot oil; cook 3 minutes or until golden, turning once. Drain on paper towels. Yield: 2 dozen fritters.

—Food Historian Jessica B. Harris
New York, New York

Crabettes

1   large egg
3   tablespoons mayonnaise
2   to 3 serrano chile peppers, finely chopped
2   tablespoons chopped fresh cilantro
1   teaspoon finely chopped fresh ginger
1   teaspoon chopped garlic
1   teaspoon hot sauce
1   teaspoon black soy sauce*
½   teaspoon Old Bay seasoning
½   teaspoon freshly ground pepper
1   pound fresh claw crabmeat
½   cup fine, dry breadcrumbs
Vegetable oil

Whisk together first 10 ingredients.

Drain and flake crabmeat, removing any bits of shell. Place in a large bowl. Pour egg mixture over crabmeat; toss gently. Add breadcrumbs; stir gently. Shape into 1½-inch patties.

Pour oil to depth of 1½ inches into a large skillet, and heat to 375°.

Add crab cakes; fry about 2 minutes on each side or until golden. Remove with a slotted spoon. Drain on paper towels. Yield: 5 servings.

*All-purpose soy sauce may be substituted for black soy sauce.

Fried Calamari with Roasted Garlic and Lime Aïoli

Use any leftover aïoli in place of mayo on your next po'boy or BLT.

1   (2.5-pound) package frozen, cleaned
    calamari (tubes and tentacles), thawed*
1½ cups all-purpose flour
1   teaspoon salt
1   teaspoon freshly ground pepper
Peanut oil
Roasted Garlic and Lime Aïoli

Cut calamari tubes into ¼-inch-thick rings; pat dry with paper towels. Combine flour, salt, and pepper in a shallow dish. Dredge rings and tentacles, in batches, in flour mixture.

Pour oil to depth of 2 inches into a Dutch oven; heat to 365°. Fry calamari, in batches, 2 minutes or until golden; drain on paper towels. Serve hot with Roasted Garlic and Lime Aïoli. Yield: 6 servings.

*You can use frozen and sliced calamari packaged without tentacles.

Roasted Garlic and Lime Aïoli

2   large garlic bulbs
2   teaspoons olive oil
1   cup mayonnaise
1   teaspoon grated lemon rind
2   tablespoons fresh lime juice
2   tablespoons chopped fresh cilantro
½   teaspoon salt
¼   teaspoon hot sauce

Peel outer skins from garlic bulbs, leaving cloves together. Cut off top quarter of each

the id of squid

• **When buying fresh squid (calamari),** choose small and whole seafood with an ocean-fresh fragrance. Allow about ½ pound per person. It should be refrigerated, airtight, no more than a day.

• **Frozen squid can be purchased clean** in a variety of forms: whole, tubes and tentacles, tubes only, and sliced tubes. Frozen squid thaws quickly under cold running water.

• **Squid meat consists mostly of fine muscle fibers** and no fat, accounting for its leanness (and toughness). It's low in calories and rich in protein and phosphorus, but it also has the distinction of being the seafood with the most cholesterol per serving.

• **Most often your fish market has cleaned its squid,** but if not, here's what to do: Make an incision lengthwise down the mantle (tubelike body), and remove the innards and transparent "pen" (cartilage) by gently scraping them out with a knife. Cut away the tentacles and pop out the small round bony piece called the "beak." Pull away and discard the fine, purplish skin from the mantle, and rinse. Discard everything but the mantle and tentacles.

• **Small squid are more tender** than large ones. To tenderize larger ones, pound cleaned flesh with a mallet until it's limp and satiny.

• **For best results, cook squid quickly** over high heat for 1 to 2 minutes (such as frying), or cook it 30 minutes or more (such as braising).

bulb. Place bulbs, cut side up, in center of a piece of heavy-duty aluminum foil. Drizzle 1 teaspoon oil over each bulb; fold foil over garlic, sealing tightly.

Bake at 425° for 45 minutes or until soft. Remove from oven; cool. Remove and discard garlic clove skins. Scoop out pulp; mash and stir until smooth.

Combine roasted garlic and remaining ingredients in a small bowl; stir well. Cover and chill 2 hours. Yield: 1¼ cups.

Fried Calamari with Roasted Garlic and Lime Aïoli

Newcomers usually approach calamari as they would onion rings, and after one bite of the fried loops, they're hooked.

Parmesan-Crusted Calamari Kabobs

Cooked properly—fast and hot—calamari moves beyond its rubber band reputation.

30 (6-inch) wooden skewers
1   pound cleaned calamari tubes (about 15)
½ cup freshly grated Parmesan cheese
½ cup Japanese breadcrumbs (Panko)*
2   tablespoons extra-virgin olive oil
½ teaspoon salt
½ teaspoon freshly ground pepper
1   large egg white, lightly beaten
Roasted Red Pepper and Basil Sauce

Soak wooden skewers in water for 30 minutes to prevent burning.

Slice tubes in half lengthwise. Thread onto skewers. Combine cheese and next 4 ingredients in a shallow dish. Brush egg white lightly over calamari; dredge in breadcrumb mixture.

Place skewers on a lightly greased rack in a broiler pan. Broil calamari 5½ inches from heat 2 to 4 minutes or until golden. Serve warm with Roasted Red Pepper and Basil Sauce. Yield: 2½ dozen.

Panko, or Japanese breadcrumbs, is available in Asian or gourmet grocery stores.

Roasted Red Pepper and Basil Sauce

Try this easy-to-make sauce over pasta or as a dip for breadsticks.

1   (7-ounce) jar roasted red bell peppers, drained
1   (8-ounce) can tomato sauce
¼ cup fresh basil leaves
¼ teaspoon freshly ground pepper
½ teaspoon balsamic vinegar

Place all ingredients in a food processor, and pulse several times until well blended. Place sauce in a small saucepan; cook over medium heat 5 minutes or until thoroughly heated. Yield: 1½ cups.

Shrimp Bruschetta with Tomatoes and Basil

Shrimp Bruschetta with Tomatoes and Basil

2   tablespoons olive oil
1   garlic clove, minced
¾ pound unpeeled, small fresh shrimp (about 36 shrimp)
2   plum tomatoes, seeded and chopped
2   tablespoons chopped fresh basil
1   to 2 tablespoons balsamic vinegar
⅛ teaspoon pepper
1   (8-ounce) French baguette, cut into ¼-inch-thick slices

Combine olive oil and garlic in a small bowl; set aside.

Peel shrimp, and devein, if desired; set aside.

Combine tomato and next 3 ingredients in a medium bowl; set aside.

Place shrimp on metal skewers. Grill shrimp, covered with grill lid, over medium-high heat (350° to 400°) 2 to 3 minutes on each side or until shrimp turn pink.

Brush garlic oil over bread slices. Grill bread slices 1 minute on each side or until golden.

Place bread slices on a large platter. Top with tomato mixture, using a slotted spoon. Place 1 shrimp on top of each slice. Yield: 12 servings.

Note: *If you use wooden skewers, be sure to soak them in water for 30 minutes to prevent them from burning on the grill.*

The crusty Italian appetizer bruschetta (pronounced broo-ske-ta)
is a simple party starter of grilled bread rubbed with garlic.
Enjoy it plain, or top it with just about anything.

Salmon Carpaccio with Wasabi

½ teaspoon wasabi powder
½ teaspoon water
1 tablespoon hot sesame oil
4 ounces very thinly sliced raw king salmon
Black and white sesame seeds
Garnishes: pickled ginger, sliced green onions
Won Ton Crisps

Combine wasabi powder and ½ teaspoon water; brush mixture onto a chilled large serving platter. Sprinkle with hot sesame oil.

Arrange sliced salmon on platter. Sprinkle with black and white sesame seeds. Garnish, if desired. Serve with Won Ton Crisps. Yield: 4 to 6 servings.

Won Ton Crisps

12 won ton wrappers, cut in half diagonally
Vegetable cooking spray

Place wrappers on a baking sheet, and spray lightly with cooking spray. Bake at 375° for 5 to 6 minutes or until golden. Yield: 2 dozen.

—Chef Jens Haagen Hansen
Jens' Restaurant
Anchorage, Alaska

Curried Cream Cheese and Chutney Party Sandwiches

1 (8-ounce) package cream cheese, softened
½ cup butter or margarine, softened
¼ cup whipping cream
2 teaspoons curry powder
1 small garlic clove, pressed
½ cup chutney, finely chopped
1½ cups pecans, finely chopped, toasted, and divided
1 (16-ounce) loaf very thinly sliced white bread
½ cup butter, softened

Beat cream cheese, ½ cup butter, and whipping cream at medium speed with an electric mixer until creamy. Add curry powder, garlic, chutney, and 1 cup pecans, beating until blended.

Spread cheese mixture on half of bread slices; cover with remaining bread slices. Trim

crusts, and cut sandwiches in half diagonally. Spread outside edges of bread with ½ cup butter, and roll in remaining chopped pecans. Serve immediately, or store, covered with damp paper towels, in an airtight container in refrigerator. Yield: 24 appetizer servings.

Note: Sandwiches may be frozen; thaw in refrigerator.
Recipe adapted from Cape Fear...Still Cooking.

Artichoke Leaves with Shrimp and Fennel

1½ teaspoons grated lemon zest
¼ cup fresh lemon juice
½ teaspoon salt
¼ teaspoon freshly ground pepper
¼ cup extra-virgin olive oil
½ cup diced red onion
¼ cup minced fresh oregano
1 small fennel bulb, thinly sliced
3 cups water
12 unpeeled, medium-size fresh shrimp
1 large artichoke
1 lemon, cut in half
1 tablespoon salt
3 tablespoons extra-virgin olive oil
Garnishes: fennel sprigs, fresh oregano

Whisk together first 4 ingredients until blended. Gradually whisk in ¼ cup olive oil. Stir in onion, ¼ cup oregano, and fennel. Set aside.

Bring 3 cups water to a boil; add shrimp and cook 3 to 5 minutes or until shrimp turn pink. Drain and rinse with cold water. Peel shrimp, and devein, if desired. Cut shrimp in half lengthwise. Set aside.

Cut off stem end so that artichoke will sit upright; place in a small saucepan. Squeeze cut lemon over artichoke. Add water to cover, salt, and 3 tablespoons olive oil; bring to a boil over medium heat. Cover, reduce heat, and simmer 20 to 30 minutes or until tender. Drain and cool.

Peel away leaves. Using a spoon, remove and discard thistle (choke) from the heart. Dice heart; add to vinaigrette.

Spoon vinaigrette on artichoke leaves; top with shrimp. Garnish, if desired. Yield: 2 dozen appetizer servings.

Anchovy Pinwheels

1 (2-ounce) can anchovy fillets, drained and minced
3 tablespoons butter, softened
1 garlic clove, minced
1 tablespoon minced fresh chives
1 tablespoon minced fresh parsley
1 (17.3-ounce) package frozen puff pastry sheets, thawed
1 egg yolk
1 tablespoon water
Freshly grated Parmesan cheese

Combine anchovies and next 4 ingredients; mix well, and set aside.

Roll each pastry sheet into a 12-inch square on a lightly floured surface. Cut pastry into 72 (2-inch) squares. For each square, cut a slit from each corner to within ¼ inch of center.

Spoon ¼ teaspoon anchovy filling into center of each square. Fold every other tip of slits toward center. (Tips will meet in center to form a pinwheel.) Press to seal.

Combine yolk and 1 tablespoon water. Brush pinwheels with egg wash; sprinkle with cheese. Bake at 375° for 10 to 12 minutes or until golden. Yield: 6 dozen.

Anchovy and White Bean Pizza

Anchovy and White Bean Pizza

1   (15.8-ounce) can great Northern beans,
    rinsed and drained
3   tablespoons olive oil
1   tablespoon fresh lemon juice
1   garlic clove, halved
⅛   teaspoon pepper
1   (12-inch) ready-made pizza crust (we
    tested with Mama Mary's Gourmet
    Pizza Crust)
½   red onion, sliced into thin rings
1   to 2 (2-ounce) cans anchovy fillets,
    drained
¼   cup shredded Parmesan cheese
1   tablespoon chopped fresh oregano
Freshly ground pepper
1   to 2 cups torn arugula (optional)

Combine first 5 ingredients in a food processor. Pulse until smooth. Spread bean mixture
evenly over crust. Top with red onion and next
4 ingredients. Bake at 450° for 12 to 15 minutes. Top with arugula, if desired. Yield:
1 (12-inch) pizza.

Beer-Battered Sardines with Wasabi Mayonnaise

½   cup all-purpose flour
½   cup cornstarch
½   teaspoon salt
½   cup beer
¼   cup butter, melted
2   egg yolks
Vegetable oil
16 fresh sardines, dressed
1½ tablespoons wasabi powder
1   tablespoon water
½   cup mayonnaise

Combine first 3 ingredients in a bowl. Add
beer, butter, and egg yolks, stirring batter until
smooth.

Pour oil to depth of 2 inches into a Dutch
oven; heat oil to 375°. Dip sardines into batter;
fry a few at a time 2 minutes or until golden.
Drain well.

Stir together wasabi powder and 1 tablespoon water; stir in mayonnaise. Serve with
sardines. Yield: 4 servings.

Beer-Battered Sardines with
Wasabi Mayonnaise

Red Snapper Seviche

1½ pounds red snapper fillets, skinned
1 cup fresh lime juice
½ cup fresh orange juice
4 plum tomatoes, seeded and diced
1 to 2 red chile peppers, seeded and minced
1 small red bell pepper, diced
⅓ cup chopped fresh cilantro
3 tablespoons minced red onion
3 tablespoons extra-virgin olive oil
3 tablespoons tomato juice
½ teaspoon fine-grained sea salt
½ teaspoon freshly ground pepper
Radicchio
Garnish: lime wedges

Cut red snapper into 1½- x ¼-inch strips. Place in a nonaluminum bowl. Add lime juice and orange juice; toss gently. Cover and refrigerate 2 to 3 hours or until fish is completely opaque. Drain and discard liquid.

Combine red snapper with plum tomato and next 8 ingredients; toss gently. Cover and chill 1 hour. Serve in radicchio-lined compotes. Garnish, if desired. Yield: 6 to 8 servings.

Barbecued Shrimp

5 pounds unpeeled, large fresh shrimp
1 celery bunch with leaves
4 garlic cloves, chopped
1 (2-ounce) jar cracked black pepper
2 to 3 teaspoons salt
1 to 2 tablespoons Worcestershire sauce
1 tablespoon hot sauce
6 lemons, cut into wedges
2 cups butter or margarine, cut into pieces

Place shrimp in a large roasting pan.

Cut celery into 4- to 6-inch lengths. Add celery and next 5 ingredients to shrimp. Squeeze lemon wedges over top, reserving wedges, and toss. Place reserved lemon wedges on top, and dot with butter.

Broil shrimp 5½ inches from heat, stirring often, 5 minutes or until shrimp just begin to turn pink. Reduce temperature to 350°, and bake, stirring often, 20 to 25 minutes or until shrimp turn pink. (Do not overcook.) Serve with French bread. Yield: 4 to 6 servings.

Shrimp in a Pickle

Shrimp in a Pickle

2½ quarts water
3 pounds unpeeled, large fresh shrimp
5 small red onions, sliced
8 bay leaves
1 (3-ounce) jar capers, drained
1 tablespoon sugar
¼ teaspoon salt
1 cup olive oil
½ cup red wine vinegar
½ cup tarragon vinegar
2 tablespoons fresh lemon juice
1 tablespoon Worcestershire sauce
½ teaspoon hot sauce

Bring 2½ quarts water to a boil; add shrimp, and cook 3 to 5 minutes or just until shrimp turn pink. Drain and rinse with cold water. Peel shrimp, leaving tails intact; devein, if desired.

Layer shrimp and next 3 ingredients in a large shallow dish.

Stir together sugar and remaining ingredients in a small bowl, and pour over shrimp mixture. Cover; chill 8 hours, turning occasionally. Drain before serving. Yield: 10 servings.
Recipe adapted from Cape Fear...Still Cooking.

Clams with Prosciutto and Thyme

3 pounds Manila or littleneck clams in shells, scrubbed
1 tablespoon olive oil
2 tablespoons butter
3 ounces prosciutto, diced
1 garlic clove, minced
¼ teaspoon dried crushed red pepper
½ cup dry white wine
2 strips lemon rind
1 tablespoon chopped fresh thyme
1 tablespoon chopped fresh parsley
Garnishes: lemon wedges, fresh herbs

Discard opened or cracked clams or any heavy ones (indicating they're filled with sand).

Heat oil and butter in a Dutch oven over medium heat. Add prosciutto; cook, stirring often, 5 minutes or until browned. Add garlic and red pepper; cook 2 minutes. Add wine, lemon rind, and thyme; bring to a boil. Add clams; cover and cook, stirring occasionally, 3 to 6 minutes or until clams open. Spoon into individual bowls. Sprinkle with parsley. Garnish, if desired. Yield: 6 servings.

—Judy Hawkins
Seattle, Washington

Clams with Prosciutto and Thyme

Mussels with Gorgonzola

3   pounds fresh mussels, scrubbed and
     debearded
½   cup dry white wine
½   cup unsalted butter, softened
⅓   pound Gorgonzola cheese (about 1 cup)
3   tablespoons chopped fresh parsley
¼   teaspoon salt
¼   teaspoon freshly ground pepper
½   to ⅔ cup fresh breadcrumbs

Discard opened, cracked, or heavy mussels.

Bring wine to a boil in a large skillet. Add mussels; cover and return to a boil. Boil 5 minutes. Immediately remove opened mussels with a slotted spoon. Continue cooking remaining mussels for 2 minutes; others may open. Discard any unopened mussels.

Beat butter and cheese at medium speed with an electric mixer until blended. Stir in parsley, salt, and pepper.

Spoon 1 tablespoon cheese mixture into each mussel. Sprinkle with breadcrumbs. Bake at 425° for 5 minutes or until cheese bubbles. Yield: 6 appetizer servings.

Recipe adapted from A Taste of New England, *published by the Junior League of Worcester, Massachusetts (1993).*

Barbecued Oysters with Pickled Ginger Mignonette Sauce

½   cup rice wine vinegar
¼   cup fresh lime juice
1½   tablespoons minced shallots
1   teaspoon freshly ground pepper
1   to 2 teaspoons minced pickled ginger
1   teaspoon soy sauce
36   fresh oysters in the shell

Whisk together first 6 ingredients in a small bowl. Set aside.

Scrub oysters with a stiff brush under running water. Insert an oyster knife into the hinged edge of each oyster; twist knife handle back and forth until top shell is loose. Slide oyster knife along the bottom of the top shell to detach muscle. Remove and discard top shell, keeping the oyster in the deeper bottom shell.

Spoon about 1 teaspoon sauce over each oyster.

Grill, without grill lid, over high heat (400° to 500°) 1 to 2 minutes or until sauce boils. Remove oysters from grill with tongs, being careful not to spill sauce. Serve immediately. Yield: 4 to 6 servings.

Grilled Grouper Wraps

1½   cups water
¾   cup teriyaki sauce
¼   cup sesame oil
¼   cup fresh lemon juice
2   tablespoons chopped fresh Italian
     parsley
1   tablespoon dried oregano
1   tablespoon chopped garlic
2   tablespoons prepared mustard
2   (8-ounce) cans sliced water chestnuts,
     rinsed and drained
16   bacon slices, cut in half
1   pound grouper, cut into 32 cubes

Combine first 8 ingredients in a 13- x 9-inch baking dish.

Place 1 water chestnut at end of each strip of bacon. Top with grouper cube and another water chestnut. Roll and secure with a wooden pick; place in marinade. Repeat process with remaining water chestnuts, bacon strips, and grouper cubes. Cover and chill 2 hours. Remove wraps, and discard marinade.

Grill, without grill lid, over medium-high heat (350° to 400°) about 15 minutes, turning often, until bacon is crisp and fish is cooked. Serve immediately. Yield: 32 wraps.

—Louis Pappas Market Cafe
Tampa, Florida

Mussels with Gorgonzola

Phyllo Sushi Rolls

2   cups water
1   cup uncooked short-grain rice
2   tablespoons seasoned rice vinegar
1   tablespoon sugar
1   teaspoon salt
1   (6-ounce) jar pickled ginger
¼   cup fresh lime juice
2   tablespoons soy sauce
1½ tablespoons dark sesame oil
1   (8-ounce) tuna steak (about 5 inches long)
8   sheets frozen phyllo pastry, thawed
8   sheets nori, cut into 7- x 6-inch rectangles*
Wasabi

Bring 2 cups water to a boil; stir in rice. Cover, reduce heat, and simmer 20 minutes or until liquid is absorbed and rice is tender. Stir in vinegar, sugar, and salt. Cover and chill thoroughly.

Drain pickled ginger, reserving ¼ cup juice. Set pickled ginger aside. Combine ginger juice and next 3 ingredients; stir well.

Cut tuna lengthwise into 8 strips; place strips in a heavy-duty zip-top plastic bag. Pour half the juice mixture over tuna, reserving remaining juice mixture. Seal bag. Chill 30 minutes.

Unfold phyllo; cover with plastic wrap and a damp towel to prevent drying. Fold 1 sheet of phyllo crosswise in half; spray phyllo with vegetable cooking spray. Place nori sheet on bottom edge of phyllo. Spoon 3 tablespoons rice mixture across 1 short end of nori. Place 1 strip of tuna on rice mixture. Spoon 3 tablespoons rice mixture over tuna. Roll up, tucking in phyllo while rolling. Place on a parchment paper-lined baking sheet. Repeat procedure with remaining phyllo, nori, rice mixture, and tuna.

Bake at 450° for 10 minutes or until golden. Cut each roll in half diagonally. Serve with remaining juice mixture, ginger, and wasabi. Yield: 8 servings.

*Nori is a paper-thin sheet of dried seaweed that is generally used for wrapping sushi and rice balls. It can be found in Japanese markets and some supermarkets.

Phyllo Sushi Rolls

Sardine Sandwiches

1   (8-ounce) container chive-and-onion cream cheese
¼   cup sour cream
1   teaspoon fresh dill
4   (2½- x 2½-inch) squares focaccia, split
2   (4.375-ounce) cans boneless, skinless sardines in olive oil
1   to 2 tablespoons capers, rinsed and drained
1   red onion, thinly sliced

Combine first 3 ingredients; spread on cut sides of focaccia. Arrange sardines, capers, and onion on cream cheese mixture on 4 squares of focaccia. Top with remaining focaccia. Yield: 4 sandwiches.

Note: In lieu of focaccia, you can use any kind of crusty bakery bread cut into squares.

Smoked Trout Turnovers with Horseradish Sauce

2   boneless smoked trout fillets, skinned, or
    1 (8-ounce) package smoked fillets
½   (8-ounce) package cream cheese,
    softened
1   tablespoon fresh lemon juice
⅛   teaspoon freshly ground pepper
2   tablespoons chopped fresh chives
¼   cup chopped pecans, toasted
1   large egg, lightly beaten
1   teaspoon water
1   (17.3-ounce) package frozen puff pastry
    sheets, thawed
Horseradish Sauce

Combine first 4 ingredients in a food processor; pulse until combined. Stir in chives and pecans; set aside.

Combine egg and 1 teaspoon water; set egg wash aside.

Roll 1 sheet of pastry into a 12-inch square on a lightly floured surface. Cut into 36 (2-inch) squares.

Spoon a level ½ teaspoon trout mixture into center of each square; brush edges of pastry with egg wash. Fold each square of pastry into a triangle; crimp with a fork to seal. Brush tops with egg wash. Place pastries on an ungreased baking sheet. Repeat procedure with remaining pastry and filling.

Bake at 425° for 10 to 12 minutes or until puffed and golden. Serve with Horseradish Sauce. Yield: about 6 dozen.

Horseradish Sauce

1   (8-ounce) container sour cream
½   cup mayonnaise
2   tablespoons prepared horseradish
¼   teaspoon salt
¼   teaspoon freshly ground pepper

Combine all ingredients. Cover and chill 1 hour. Yield: 1⅓ cups.

Smoked Chicken and Spinach Turnovers

Smoked Chicken and Spinach Turnovers

1   (10-ounce) package frozen chopped
    spinach, thawed
1   (17.3-ounce) package frozen puff pastry
    sheets, thawed
1   cup diced smoked or roasted chicken
1   (6.5-ounce) package garlic-and-herb
    spreadable cheese (we tested with
    Alouette)
1   egg yolk
1   tablespoon water

Drain spinach well, pressing between layers of paper towels. Set aside.

Unfold puff pastry on a lightly floured surface, and roll each sheet into an 11-inch square. Cut each square into 9 equal squares.

Stir together spinach, chicken, and cheese. Place about 1½ tablespoons spinach mixture in center of each pastry square. Stir together egg and water; brush on pastry edges, reserving remaining mixture. Fold squares in half diagonally to form triangles; crimp with a fork to seal. Brush tops with remaining egg wash, and place on a lightly greased baking sheet.

Bake at 425° for 15 minutes or until golden. Yield: 18 pastries.

Note: Unbaked sealed pastries may be covered and refrigerated up to 4 hours. Brush with remaining egg wash, and bake as directed.

—Chef/Owner Albert J. Bouchard III
Restaurant Bouchard
Newport, Rhode Island

Butternut Squash Empanadas

5   tablespoons olive oil, divided
1   medium butternut squash (about 2 pounds), peeled and cut into ¼-inch pieces
1   tablespoon dried thyme
½   teaspoon salt
½   teaspoon freshly ground pepper
7   tablespoons butter, divided
3   cups chopped onion
5¼ cups all-purpose flour, divided
1   cup milk
⅛   teaspoon ground nutmeg
1⅔ cups shortening
2   teaspoons salt
⅔   to ¾ cup ice water

Combine 3 tablespoons olive oil and next 4 ingredients in a large bowl; toss well. Spread squash in a 15- x 10-inch jellyroll pan coated with vegetable cooking spray. Bake at 450° for 15 minutes; stir squash, and bake 5 more minutes. Set aside.

Heat 3 tablespoons butter and remaining 2 tablespoons olive oil in a large skillet over medium heat until butter melts. Add onion, and cook 20 minutes or until caramelized, stirring often.

Melt remaining 4 tablespoons butter in a small heavy saucepan over low heat; whisk in ¼ cup flour until smooth. Cook 1 minute, whisking constantly. Gradually whisk in milk; cook over medium heat, whisking constantly, until sauce is thick and bubbly. Stir in nutmeg. Stir white sauce and squash into onion mixture. Let cool.

Combine remaining 5 cups flour, shortening, and 2 teaspoons salt using a fork or pastry blender until crumbly. (Mixture should have small lumps.) Sprinkle ⅔ cup ice water, 1 tablespoon at a time, evenly over surface; stir with a fork until dry ingredients are moistened. Shape into a ball; roll out dough to ⅛-inch thickness on a lightly floured surface. Cut dough into 4-inch circles. Place about 2 tablespoons squash filling in center of each dough circle. Moisten edges of dough with water. Fold dough over filling, and pinch to seal. Place on a foil-lined baking sheet.

Bake at 450° for 18 minutes or until golden. Yield: 2 dozen.

—Richard Visconte, Chef de Cuisine
Novato, California

Salmon Skin Fritters

Vegetable oil
1   (6-ounce) piece king salmon skin, scaled and washed (skin from about 1 side of salmon)
1   teaspoon sugar
½   teaspoon salt
½   cup all-purpose flour

Pour oil to depth of 1 inch into a large heavy skillet; heat to 375° over medium-high heat.

Slice salmon skin into 4- x ½-inch strips. Sprinkle with sugar and salt. Dredge strips in flour; fry in batches 2 to 3 minutes or until golden. Drain well. Yield: 8 appetizer servings.

Note: For extra flavor, add 1 tablespoon curry powder or Cajun seasoning to flour.

—Chef Jens Haagen Hansen
Jens' Restaurant
Anchorage, Alaska

Salmon Skin Fritters

Atlantic Smoked Salmon with Johnnycakes and Caviar

1   cup johnnycake cornmeal
½   teaspoon salt
1¼   cups milk
1   large egg, lightly beaten
2   tablespoons vegetable oil
1   pound smoked salmon, thinly sliced
1   (3.5-ounce) jar lumpfish or other black
     caviar
18   fresh Italian parsley sprigs
¾   cup crème fraîche or sour cream (optional)

Combine first 4 ingredients, stirring just until dry ingredients are moistened; stir in oil. Let batter stand 20 minutes.

Pour 1½ tablespoons batter for each johnnycake onto a hot, lightly greased griddle.

Cook johnnycakes until tops are covered with bubbles and edges look cooked; turn and cook on other side. Keep warm.

Top johnnycakes evenly with sliced salmon, black caviar, and a sprig of parsley. Serve with crème fraîche, if desired. Yield: 18 appetizer servings.

Note: *Johnnycake cornmeal can be ordered from Kenyon Corn Meal Company in Usquepaugh, Rhode Island. Look up kenyonsgristmill.com*

> —*Chef Christopher Freeman*
> *Toppers at the Wauwinet*
> *Nantucket, Massachusetts*

effortless appetizers to savor

These easy hors d'oeuvre ideas use ingredients you probably have in your pantry.

top cream cheese:

- Tomato chutney or hot pepper jelly
- Pesto sauce and chopped dried tomatoes
- Chili sauce, chopped cooked shrimp, and sliced green onions
- Mango chutney, sliced green onions, and toasted shredded coconut

dress up brie:

- Spread with honey; microwave at MEDIUM HIGH (70% power) 1 minute. Sprinkle with toasted chopped walnuts.
- Top with mango chutney; microwave at MEDIUM HIGH (70% power) 1 minute. Sprinkle with chopped cooked bacon.
- Score into pie-shaped wedges. Decorate each wedge with chopped dried fruit, toasted sesame seeds, and toasted sliced almonds.

stir up:

- Soft cream cheese, lump crabmeat, horseradish, salt, and pepper
- Cream cheese, chopped smoked salmon, horseradish, and chopped fresh dill
- Drained plain yogurt, diced seeded cucumber, sour cream, fresh lemon juice, chopped fresh dill, garlic, and salt

bake it:

- Spoon marinara sauce over feta cheese. Bake at 350° until bubbly; sprinkle with chopped fresh basil.
- Brush triangles of pita bread with melted butter. Sprinkle with garlic powder and Parmesan cheese, and bake at 350° until golden. Sprinkle with Italian seasoning.

can you top this?

Consider these bases for spreads:

- Water crackers
- Crostini (toasted baguette slices)
- Toasted focaccia or pita wedges
- Sliced ripe carambola (star fruit), apples, or pears

toss:

- Diced tomatoes, feta cheese, kalamata olives, salt, freshly ground pepper, olive oil, and red wine vinegar
- Fresh lump crabmeat, diced avocado, fresh lime juice, salt, and pepper

roll up:

- Spread salmon or crabmeat dip on a flour tortilla; roll up, and slice into pinwheels. Secure with wooden picks.
- Combine goat cheese, dried basil, and cracked pepper. Spread on thin strips of smoked salmon; roll up, and secure with wooden picks.

wrap:

- Wrap strips of prosciutto around chunks of honeydew or cantaloupe; secure with wooden picks. Drizzle with fresh lime juice.
- Wrap partially cooked slices of bacon around oysters or scallops; secure with wooden picks. Grill or broil until seafood is fully cooked.
- Sprinkle 8 ounces of cream cheese with garlic powder and fresh or dried dill; wrap in 4 ounces of refrigerated crescent dinner rolls. Bake at 350° until crust is golden.

drizzle:

- Drizzle goat cheese rounds with balsamic vinegar; sprinkle with herbes de Provence.
- Drizzle olive oil over grilled fish. Add fresh lemon juice, capers, and chopped fresh thyme.
- Drizzle a log of goat cheese with olive oil. Sprinkle heavily with cracked pepper.

- Sliced yellow squash or cucumber
- Celery stalks (with leaves attached for flair)

Sand-Pail Popcorn

1   (3.5-ounce) package butter-flavored
    microwave popcorn

Prepare popcorn according to package directions. Open carefully; pour into a clean sand pail. Yield: about 10 cups.

Cheese Popcorn: Add 1 (1.3-ounce) envelope cheese sauce mix. Toss well. Yield: about 10 cups.

Mexican Popcorn: Add 1 tablespoon taco seasoning mix. Toss well. Yield: about 10 cups.

Asian Popcorn: Add 1 (5-ounce) can chow mein noodles, 1 cup dry-roasted peanuts, and 1 teaspoon ground ginger. Yield: 11½ cups.

Blackberry Lemonade

3 cups fresh blackberries
7 cups water
¼ cup sugar
¼ cup sugar-free pink lemonade drink mix
  (we tested with part of a 1.9-ounce
  package of Crystal Light)
Garnishes: fresh mint sprigs, lemon slices

Process blackberries in a blender until smooth, stopping to scrape down sides. Pour through a fine wire-mesh strainer into a 2-quart pitcher, discarding solids; stir in 7 cups water, sugar, and drink mix. Serve over ice. Garnish, if desired. Yield: 8 cups.

Pink Lemonade

1¼ cups sugar
½ cup boiling water
4½ cups cold water
1½ cups fresh lemon juice
¾ cup maraschino cherry juice*

Combine sugar and boiling water, stirring until sugar dissolves. Stir in cold water, lemon juice, and cherry juice. Serve over ice. Yield: 7¼ cups.
*In testing, we used a portion of the juice from a 10-ounce jar of maraschino cherries, reserving the cherries for other uses.

Fruited Mint Tea

3 cups boiling water
4 regular-size tea bags
12 fresh mint sprigs
1 cup sugar
4 cups water
1 cup fresh orange juice
¼ cup fresh lemon juice

Pour boiling water over tea bags and mint sprigs; cover and let steep 5 minutes. Remove tea bags and mint, squeezing gently. Stir in sugar and remaining ingredients. Serve over ice. Yield: 8 cups.

Iced and Spiced Lemon Tea

6 lemon herbal tea bags
3 cinnamon-apple spice tea bags
2 (3-inch) cinnamon sticks
5 whole cloves
¼ cup honey
1 quart boiling water
2 cups water
2 cups ice cubes
1 lemon, sliced

Combine tea bags, cinnamon sticks, cloves, and honey in a large saucepan. Pour boiling water over tea bags; cover and let steep 8 hours. Using a slotted spoon, remove and discard tea bags, cinnamon, and cloves. Stir in 2 cups water, ice cubes, and lemon slices. Yield: 8 cups.
—Caterer Sarah Aley
Tenants Harbor, Maine

Watermelon Aqua Fresca

Watermelon Aqua Fresca

Food historian Jessica Harris describes this as "watermelon-scented water." The flavor doesn't overpower, but refreshes, especially on hot days.

6 cups seeded, cubed watermelon
8 cups water
½ cup sugar
½ cup fresh lime juice
Garnish: watermelon wedges

Process watermelon in a blender until smooth. Pour pureed melon into a large bowl; stir in 8 cups water, sugar, and lime juice. Cover and chill at least 8 hours. Stir; serve over ice in tall glasses. Garnish, if desired. Yield: 13 cups.

Lemon-Lime Slush

1 (12-ounce) can frozen lemonade, thawed and undiluted
1 (12-ounce) can frozen limeade, thawed and undiluted
6 cups crushed ice
5 cups lemon-lime soft drink, chilled (we tested with Seven-Up)
Garnishes: lemon slices, lime slices

Process half of the lemonade, limeade, and ice in a blender until smooth, stopping to scrape down sides. Pour mixture into a 4-quart plastic container. Repeat procedure with other half. Freeze until firm.
Remove from freezer 30 minutes before serving; break into chunks. Add soft drink; stir until slushy. Garnish, if desired. Yield: 10 cups.

Peach Melba Sipper

2 cups unsweetened frozen sliced peaches
1 cup fresh raspberries
1 (11.5-ounce) can peach nectar
¼ cup sugar
1 teaspoon vanilla extract
1 cup seltzer water, chilled

Process first 5 ingredients in a blender until smooth. Stir in seltzer. Yield: 5 cups.

Berry Refresher

2 cups halved fresh strawberries
1 (6-ounce) can orange juice concentrate, thawed
2 tablespoons powdered sugar
1 (8-ounce) container raspberry yogurt
10 ice cubes

Process all ingredients in a blender until smooth. Yield: 4 cups.

Pineapple-Apricot Cooler

2   cups ice cubes
1   (11.5-ounce) can apricot nectar, chilled
1   (8-ounce) can crushed pineapple, undrained and chilled
½   cup unsweetened pineapple juice
⅓   cup sour cream or plain yogurt
3   tablespoons sugar
¼   teaspoon coconut extract

Process all ingredients in a blender until smooth. Yield: 4 cups.

Frosty Cappuccino

2¼ cups strong coffee
1½ cups half-and-half
⅓   cup firmly packed light brown sugar
¼   teaspoon ground cinnamon
½   cup half-and-half
3   tablespoons bourbon

Combine first 4 ingredients; freeze in ice trays. Process frozen mixture with remaining ingredients in a blender until smooth. Yield: 5 cups.

Stanley's Mint Julep

2   cups water
¾   cup sugar
3   cups loosely packed fresh mint leaves
2   cups bourbon
Garnish: fresh mint

Combine 2 cups water and sugar in a saucepan over medium heat, stirring until sugar dissolves. Add mint; bring to a boil. Remove from heat; cover and steep 30 minutes. Pour mint syrup through a fine wire-mesh strainer lined with cheesecloth. Let cool. Combine syrup and bourbon. Pour into a sterilized bottle; cover tightly, and chill at least 1 month. Serve over ice. Garnish, if desired. Yield: 4 cups.

—Food Writer Marcelle Bienvenu
New Iberia, Louisiana

Scarlett O'Hara

3   cups cranberry juice
1   cup Southern Comfort
⅓   cup fresh lime juice
Garnish: fresh lime slices

Combine cranberry juice, Southern Comfort, and lime juice. Serve over crushed ice. Garnish, if desired. Yield: 4⅓ cups.

Barbados Punch

2   cups sugar
3   cups rum
1   cup cranberry-apple juice drink
1   cup fresh lime juice
1   cup fresh orange juice
1   cup passion fruit juice
1   cup pineapple juice
1   teaspoon bitters

Combine all ingredients; serve over crushed ice. Yield: 9 cups.

Patio Daddy-O Planter's Punch

1½ cups cracked ice or 6 ice cubes
4   ounces (½ cup) chilled pineapple juice
2   ounces (¼ cup) chilled orange juice
2   ounces (¼ cup) chilled fresh lime juice
2   ounces (¼ cup) dark rum
Grenadine
Garnishes: pineapple wedges, maraschino cherries, orange slices, lime slices, fresh mint

Fill a cocktail shaker with ice, and add juices and rum. Shake vigorously to blend.

Pour mixture into a tall glass. Top with a splash of grenadine. Garnish with a toothpick skewered with fruit, if desired. Yield: 1 serving.
From Atomic Cocktails © 1998 by Karen Brooks, Gideon Bosker, and Reed Darmon. Used with permission of Chronicle Books LLC, San Francisco. Visit ChronicleBooks.com

Stanley's Mint Julep

Peach Champagne Slush

3½ cups peeled, sliced fresh peaches
    (about 2 pounds)
2   cups pink champagne
⅓   cup sugar
½   cup peach schnapps

Process all ingredients in a blender until smooth. Pour into a shallow baking dish; freeze at least 3 hours. Let stand at room temperature 30 minutes before serving. Spoon into flutes to serve. Yield: 5 cups.

Frozen Tropical Slush

2½ cups ice cubes
1   cup peeled, cubed mango
1   cup guava nectar
½   cup light rum
2   tablespoons sugar
2   tablespoons frozen orange-tangerine juice
    concentrate, thawed
2   tablespoons fresh lime juice
½   teaspoon vanilla extract

Process all ingredients in a blender until smooth. Yield: 4½ cups.

Watermelon Daiquiri Slush

9   cups seeded, cubed watermelon
1   (10-ounce) can nonalcoholic frozen
    strawberry daiquiri mix, thawed
1   cup light rum
¼   cup fresh lime juice
¼   cup sugar

Freeze half the watermelon. Puree remaining watermelon with remaining ingredients in a blender until smooth. Pour half into a pitcher; add frozen melon to blender. Blend; stir into pitcher. Yield: 8 cups.

Sangría is Spanish in origin, named for its blood-red color. Made with red wine and fruit, Sangría is best served very cold, either over ice or well chilled.

Sangría

1   lime, cut into wedges
1   lemon, cut into wedges
1   orange, cut into wedges
1   Granny Smith apple, cored and cut into
    wedges
1   (750-milliliter) bottle dry red wine
1   (12-ounce) can lemon-lime soft drink
Garnishes: orange wedges and lime slices

Fill pitcher with citrus wedges; press fruit with the back of a spoon to release juice. Add apple wedges and wine. Chill until serving time. Just before serving, add lemon-lime soft drink. Serve over ice. Garnish, if desired. Yield: 12 cups.

—Steve Winston
The Spanish Table
Seattle, Washington

Sangría

island liqueur

Italy's famous limoncello is sunshine in a glass. Some say the intensely yellow *digestif* is the very essence of the famous Caprese lemons. Lemons grow large on the isle of Capri, and if you're fortunate enough to visit, you'll discover beautiful bottles of the elixir on display everywhere you turn.

Limoncello should be served icy-cold. It's great used in mixed drinks, splashed into desserts, or enjoyed as a late afternoon treat. The recipe is easy to make and a terrific gift idea.

Limoncello

10	lemons*
1	liter vodka
3	cups sugar
4	cups water

Using a coarse zester or vegetable peeler, remove just the yellow skin of the lemons. Avoid the bitter white flesh under the peel. Place the lemon peel in a large glass jar and add vodka.

Seal jar with a lid and let lemon flavor infuse for 1 week at room temperature. The mixture will turn a beautiful yellow color.

After 1 week, combine sugar and water; bring to a boil. Boil 15 minutes without stirring. Allow syrup to cool to room temperature.

Pour infused vodka through a strainer into the syrup. If you want pulp-free limoncello, pour the vodka mixture through a coffee filter.

Pour the filtered mixture into glass bottles and seal. You can store limoncello at room temperature, where it just gets better with age. Before serving, place bottle in the freezer and serve ice-cold. Yield: 9 cups.

Use ripe yellow lemons, rinsing them well before use.

salads

Summer Salad

1/3 cup extra-virgin olive oil
1/4 cup fresh lemon or lime juice
1 tablespoon Dijon or champagne mustard
1 tablespoon honey or sugar
1/4 teaspoon salt
1/4 teaspoon dry mustard
2 cups speckled leaf lettuce
2 cups torn Red Leaf lettuce
2 cups torn frisée or Bibb lettuce
2 oranges, peeled and sectioned
1/4 cup crumbled feta cheese (optional)

Whisk together first 6 ingredients until blended.

Arrange lettuces on a platter; top with orange sections. Drizzle with dressing; toss to coat. Sprinkle with cheese, if desired. Yield: 4 servings.

Endive-Arugula Salad

3 cups curly endive or frisée
3 cups arugula
1/2 cup olive oil
1/4 cup balsamic vinegar
2 tablespoons fresh lemon juice
2 hard-cooked eggs, cut into wedges
Freshly ground pepper

Combine endive and arugula; toss gently. Combine oil, vinegar, and lemon juice; drizzle over salad. Top with egg and sprinkle with pepper. Yield: 6 servings.

—*Cookbook Author Gideon Bosker*
Portland, Oregon

Italian Bread Salad

This popular salad, otherwise known as panzanella, makes the most of Italian bread. It's tossed with fresh produce, gutsy olives, and a tangy vinaigrette.

12 ounces country-style Italian bread, cut into 1-inch pieces (we tested with Ciabatta)
4 garlic cloves
1/2 cup fresh basil leaves
1 tablespoon fresh oregano leaves
1/2 teaspoon salt
1/2 teaspoon freshly ground pepper
3/4 cup extra-virgin olive oil
1/4 cup balsamic vinegar
6 tomatoes, seeded and coarsely chopped
2 zucchini, thinly sliced
1 large roasted yellow bell pepper, seeded and coarsely chopped
3/4 cup pitted kalamata olives
1/4 cup capers, drained

Divide bread evenly between 2 baking sheets.

Bake at 350° for 10 to 12 minutes or until toasted, stirring occasionally. Set aside to cool.

Combine garlic and next 4 ingredients in a food processor; pulse 5 to 6 times or just until chopped, stopping to scrape down sides. Add oil and vinegar, and pulse until combined.

Combine bread, tomato, and remaining ingredients in a large bowl; add vinaigrette, and toss well. Let salad stand, covered, at room temperature 30 minutes before serving. Yield: 8 to 10 servings.

Endive-Arugula Salad

Italian Bread Salad

Chop Salad with Corn, Snap Peas, and Bacon

Roasted Corn Salad

3   cups fresh corn kernels (about 6 ears)
2   tablespoons olive oil, divided
2   tablespoons white balsamic vinegar or white wine vinegar
1   tablespoon Dijon mustard
½   teaspoon salt
½   teaspoon pepper
1   large tomato, chopped
1   red or green bell pepper, chopped
6   green onions, chopped

Combine corn and 1 tablespoon oil on a lightly greased jellyroll pan.

Bake at 425° for 20 minutes or until browned, stirring occasionally.

Stir together remaining 1 tablespoon oil, vinegar, and next 3 ingredients in a medium bowl; add roasted corn, tomato, bell pepper, and green onions. Toss salad to coat. Yield: 4 servings.

Chop Salad with Corn, Snap Peas, and Bacon

1½ cups sugar snap peas, trimmed and cut in half diagonally
1½ cups fresh corn kernels (2 to 3 ears)
½   head romaine lettuce
1   cucumber, peeled, seeded, and diced
1   carrot, peeled and shredded
½   red bell pepper, diced
5   radishes, thinly sliced
3   green onions, sliced
6   cherry tomatoes, halved
1   cup basil leaves, cut into thin strips
Mustard Vinaigrette
½   cup grated Parmesan cheese
½   teaspoon kosher salt
¼   teaspoon freshly ground black pepper
12 bacon slices, cooked and crumbled

Cook peas in boiling water to cover for 1 to 2 minutes; immediately plunge peas into ice water to stop the cooking process. Cook corn in boiling water 2 minutes; immediately plunge corn into ice water to stop the cooking process. Drain peas and corn.

Chop lettuce into small pieces; place in a large bowl. Add peas, corn, cucumber, and next 6 ingredients; toss with Mustard Vinaigrette. Add cheese, salt, and pepper; toss gently. Mound salad on a large platter, and sprinkle with bacon. Yield: 8 servings.

Mustard Vinaigrette

2   tablespoons red wine vinegar
1   tablespoon fresh lemon juice
1   tablespoon Dijon mustard
2   teaspoons minced garlic
9   tablespoons olive oil
⅛   teaspoon kosher salt
⅛   teaspoon freshly ground pepper

Combine first 4 ingredients in a bowl. Whisk in oil; stir in salt and pepper. Yield: ¾ cup.
Recipe from Tom's Big Dinners *by Tom Douglas. © 2003 by Tom Douglas. Reprinted by permission of HarperCollins Publishers Inc.*

Tomato-Avocado Salad

3   medium avocados, peeled
1   to 2 tablespoons fresh lemon juice
3   medium tomatoes, cut into wedges
1   small red onion, sliced
2   tablespoons chopped fresh basil
⅓   cup olive oil
3   tablespoons red wine vinegar
½   teaspoon salt
½   teaspoon coarsely ground pepper
Bibb lettuce leaves

Cut avocados in half lengthwise; remove seeds. Cut into thin slices. Drizzle with lemon juice; toss gently.

Combine avocado, tomato, onion, and basil; toss gently. Drizzle with oil and vinegar; sprinkle with salt and pepper. Cover and chill. Serve over Bibb lettuce leaves. Yield: 12 servings.

—*Caroline Coleman Bailey*
Tiburon, California

Warm Chanterelle and Hazelnut Salad with Balsamic Syrup

1   cup hazelnuts
2   cups balsamic vinegar
3   tablespoons unsalted butter
5   cups sliced fresh chanterelle mushrooms
3   tablespoons minced shallots
1   tablespoon minced garlic
3   tablespoons minced fresh thyme
½   teaspoon salt
½   teaspoon freshly ground pepper

Bake hazelnuts in a shallow pan at 350°, stirring occasionally, 5 to 10 minutes or until toasted. Place hazelnuts in a colander; rub briskly to remove skins. Cool and chop.

Cook vinegar over low heat in a heavy saucepan, stirring occasionally, until reduced to 6 tablespoons (about 1 hour). Set aside.

Melt butter in a large skillet over medium-high heat; add mushrooms, and sauté until golden brown. Stir in shallots, garlic, thyme, and hazelnuts; sauté 30 seconds.

Spoon evenly onto individual serving plates. Drizzle with balsamic syrup, and sprinkle with salt and pepper. Serve immediately. Yield: 6 servings.

Asparagus, Roasted Beets, and Goat Cheese Salad

1 cheese slice in a 3-inch round cutter or ring mold; sprinkle with ¹⁄₂ teaspoon chives. Press chives into cheese; remove cutter. Transfer cheese to a serving plate. Repeat procedure with remaining cheese and chives.

Arrange asparagus spears evenly on top of cheese rounds. Top with beets and drizzle with remaining vinaigrette. Sprinkle cracked pepper and olive oil around rim of plate, if desired. Yield: 6 servings.

Small red beets may be substituted for golden beets.

—Chef Christopher Freeman
Toppers at the Wauwinet
Nantucket, Massachusetts

Four-Bean Marinated Salad

This familiar bean salad shows up often at potluck suppers and family reunions. It's a faithful make-ahead salad that tastes better the second day.

1   (16-ounce) can kidney beans, rinsed and drained
1   (15¹⁄₄-ounce) can lima beans, drained
1   (14.5-ounce) can cut green beans, drained
1   (14.5-ounce) can cut wax beans, drained
1   small green bell pepper, chopped
1   small onion, chopped
1   (2-ounce) jar diced pimiento, drained
³⁄₄ cup sugar
¹⁄₂ cup vegetable oil
¹⁄₂ cup white vinegar
¹⁄₂ teaspoon salt
¹⁄₂ teaspoon pepper

Combine first 7 ingredients in a large bowl.

Combine sugar and remaining ingredients in a small saucepan; bring to a boil over low heat, stirring until sugar dissolves. Pour hot vinegar mixture over bean mixture; stir gently. Cover and chill at least 4 hours. Serve with a slotted spoon. Yield: 10 servings.

Asparagus, Roasted Beets, and Goat Cheese Salad

9   small red beets (about 3 pounds)
9   small golden beets (about 3 pounds)*
1   cup olive oil
¹⁄₃ cup red wine vinegar
¹⁄₂ teaspoon salt, divided
¹⁄₂ teaspoon freshly ground pepper, divided
60 small asparagus spears
1   (11-ounce) log goat cheese
1   tablespoon chopped fresh chives
Garnishes: cracked pepper, olive oil

Roast beets in a single layer on a lightly greased baking sheet at 425° for 40 to 45 minutes or until tender, stirring every 15 minutes; cool.

Whisk together 1 cup oil, vinegar, ¹⁄₄ teaspoon salt, and ¹⁄₄ teaspoon pepper in a small bowl; set vinaigrette aside.

Peel beets; cut into wedges. Toss together red beets, ¹⁄₄ cup vinaigrette, ¹⁄₈ teaspoon salt, and ¹⁄₈ teaspoon pepper; set aside. In a separate bowl, toss together golden beets, ¹⁄₄ cup vinaigrette, remaining ¹⁄₈ teaspoon salt, and remaining ¹⁄₈ teaspoon pepper; set aside.

Cut top 3 inches from asparagus, and cook in boiling water to cover 1 to 2 minutes or until crisp-tender. Plunge into ice water to stop the cooking process; drain.

Combine asparagus and ¹⁄₂ cup vinaigrette; set aside.

Cut goat cheese into 6 equal slices. Place

Black Bean and Black-Eyed Pea Salad

You can top this salad with grilled or deli rotisserie chicken, leftover steak strips, or even canned albacore tuna.

1   teaspoon grated lime rind
½   cup fresh lime juice (about 4 limes)
¼   cup olive oil
1   teaspoon brown sugar
1   teaspoon chili powder
½   to 1 teaspoon salt
½   teaspoon ground cumin
1   (15-ounce) can black beans, rinsed and drained
1   (15.5-ounce) can black-eyed peas, rinsed and drained
1½ cups frozen whole kernel corn, thawed
½   small green bell pepper, chopped
⅓   cup chopped fresh cilantro
Romaine lettuce
2   large avocados, sliced
Garnishes: lime wedges, fresh cilantro sprigs

Whisk together first 7 ingredients in a large bowl. Add black beans and next 4 ingredients, tossing to coat. Cover and chill 30 minutes.

Serve over lettuce; arrange avocado slices around salad. Garnish, if desired. Yield: 6 servings.

Red Cabbage-Carrot Coleslaw

½   cup mayonnaise
¼   cup cider vinegar
1½ teaspoons salt
1½ teaspoons coarsely ground pepper
½   teaspoon sugar
4   cups shredded red cabbage
4   cups shredded carrots
1½ cups currants
¼   cup minced fresh chives
¼   cup minced fresh dill

Stir together first 5 ingredients in a large bowl. Add cabbage and remaining ingredients; toss well. Cover and chill. Yield: 6 to 8 servings.

—Caterer Sarah Aley
Tenants Harbor, Maine

Spinach Coleslaw

7½ cups shredded red cabbage
6   cups shredded green cabbage
8   ounces fresh spinach, torn into bite-size pieces
1   cup thinly sliced red onion
1   cup chopped green onions
½   cup chopped Italian parsley
1¼ cups mayonnaise
¼   cup Creole or coarse-grained mustard
1   teaspoon salt
¼   teaspoon freshly ground pepper

Combine first 6 ingredients in a large salad bowl. Combine mayonnaise, mustard, salt, and pepper in a small bowl; stir with a whisk. Add dressing mixture to slaw, and toss gently. Cover and chill at least 1 hour. Yield: 8 servings.

—Food Writer Marcelle Bienvenu
New Iberia, Louisiana

Spicy Slaw

1   teaspoon mustard seeds
1   teaspoon celery seeds
1   medium cabbage, finely shredded (about 3 pounds)
2   carrots, julienned
1   small red bell pepper, coarsely chopped
1   jalapeño pepper, sliced
2   garlic cloves, peeled
3   tablespoons cider vinegar
2   teaspoons salt
1   teaspoon sugar
⅛   teaspoon ground red pepper
¼   cup canola oil
2   tablespoons sour cream

Place mustard seeds and celery seeds in a mortar. Using a pestle, grind until coarse; set aside.

Combine cabbage and carrot in a large bowl; set aside.

Red Cabbage-Carrot Coleslaw

Combine ground seeds, red bell pepper, and next 6 ingredients in a food processor; process until smooth. With processor running, pour oil through food chute in a slow, steady stream. Add sour cream; pulse until smooth.

Pour dressing over cabbage and carrot, tossing well. Cover and chill 1 hour. Yield: 12 cups.

Slaw with Feta Cheese

²⁄₃ cup vegetable oil
¼ cup white vinegar
¼ cup water
1 garlic clove, pressed
2 teaspoons freshly ground pepper
1½ teaspoons salt
1 teaspoon dried Italian seasoning
1 medium head red cabbage, shredded
1 (4-ounce) package feta cheese, crumbled

Whisk together first 7 ingredients; pour dressing over cabbage. Toss gently. Sprinkle with feta cheese. Yield: 12 to 14 servings.

Seashell Salad

½ pound snow peas
1 (16-ounce) package uncooked small pasta shells
1 cup sliced celery
½ cup sliced green onions
1 red bell pepper, cut into thin strips
¼ cup shredded fresh basil
¾ cup vegetable oil
¼ cup white wine vinegar
1 teaspoon salt
½ teaspoon freshly ground pepper
1 garlic clove, minced

Cook snow peas in boiling salted water to cover 1 minute or until crisp-tender; drain. Plunge into ice water to stop the cooking process; drain and set aside.

Cook pasta according to package directions; drain. Rinse with cold water; drain. Stir together snow peas, pasta, and next 4 ingredients.

Whisk together vegetable oil and remaining ingredients. Pour over pasta mixture; toss gently. Cover and chill. Yield: 12 servings.

Confetti Orzo Salad

Confetti Orzo Salad

1½ cups uncooked orzo
1 carrot, chopped
1¼ cups chopped red, green, or yellow bell pepper
½ cup peeled, seeded, and chopped cucumber
¼ cup thinly sliced green onions
¼ cup chopped red onion
¼ cup chopped fresh parsley
½ teaspoon grated lemon rind
3 tablespoons lemon juice
2 tablespoons white wine vinegar
¾ teaspoon salt
⅛ teaspoon coarsely ground pepper
2 garlic cloves, minced
⅓ cup olive oil

Cook orzo according to package directions; drain. Rinse with cold water; drain. Combine orzo, carrot, and next 5 ingredients; set aside.

Combine lemon rind, lemon juice, vinegar, salt, coarsely ground pepper, and minced garlic. Gradually whisk in oil. Pour vinaigrette over orzo salad, tossing gently. Cover and keep chilled. Yield: 6 to 8 servings.

One can never have too many options for potato salad.

Horseradish Potato Salad

2½ pounds red potatoes
6 bacon slices, cooked and crumbled
4 hard-cooked eggs, chopped
3 green onions, sliced
¾ cup mayonnaise
¾ cup sour cream
6 tablespoons prepared horseradish
2 tablespoons chopped fresh parsley
1¼ teaspoons salt
¾ teaspoon freshly ground pepper

Cook potatoes in boiling water to cover 30 minutes or just until tender. Drain well, and cool slightly. Peel and cut potatoes into 1-inch cubes.

Combine potato and next 3 ingredients in a large bowl; toss gently. Combine mayonnaise and remaining ingredients. Spoon mayonnaise mixture over potato, tossing gently to coat. Cover and chill. Yield: 6 to 8 servings.

Shrimp and Potato Salad

1 pound red potatoes or Yukon gold potatoes
6 cups water
2 pounds unpeeled, medium-size fresh shrimp
½ cup finely chopped green onions
4 celery ribs, finely chopped
4 hard-cooked eggs
½ cup mayonnaise
2 tablespoons Creole mustard
1 teaspoon salt
2 teaspoons hot sauce
½ teaspoon pepper

Cook potatoes in boiling water to cover 25 minutes or until tender; drain and cool. Cut potatoes into 1-inch cubes. Set aside.

Bring 6 cups water to a boil in large saucepan; add shrimp, and cook 3 to 5 minutes or just until shrimp turn pink. Drain, and rinse with cold water.

Peel shrimp, and devein, if desired. Coarsely chop shrimp, if desired. Combine potato, shrimp, green onions, and celery in a large bowl. Chop egg whites and add to potato mixture. Mash egg yolks; stir in mayonnaise and remaining ingredients. Gently stir egg yolk mixture into potato salad. Cover and chill. Yield: 6 to 8 servings.

Mama's Wet Potato Salad

3½ pounds red potatoes, cut into ½-inch cubes
8 hard-cooked eggs, coarsely chopped
¼ cup minced celery
¼ cup finely chopped green onions
2 tablespoons chopped Italian parsley
1½ teaspoons salt
¼ teaspoon freshly ground pepper
Homemade Mayonnaise*

Boil potato in salted water to cover 10 minutes or until tender; drain and cool.

Combine potato, eggs, and remaining ingredients in a large bowl; toss gently. Yield: 10 servings.

*You may substitute prepared mayonnaise for the homemade version below.

Homemade Mayonnaise

1 large pasteurized egg or ¼ cup egg substitute
2 tablespoons fresh lemon juice
½ teaspoon salt
⅛ teaspoon freshly ground pepper
3 dashes hot sauce
1 cup vegetable oil

Combine first 5 ingredients in a food processor or blender; process 10 seconds. With processor running, pour oil through food chute in a slow, steady stream; process until blended. Cover and chill at least 1 hour. Yield: 1⅓ cups.
—Food Writer Marcelle Bienvenu
New Iberia, Louisiana

Lemon-Basil Potato Salad

2½ pounds small Yukon gold potatoes, cut into eighths*
¼ cup lemon juice
4 garlic cloves, minced
¾ cup chopped fresh basil
1 tablespoon Dijon mustard
1 teaspoon salt
½ teaspoon freshly ground pepper
⅔ cup olive oil
½ medium-size red onion, chopped
1 (10-ounce) package fresh spinach, cut into thin strips
10 thick bacon slices, cooked and crumbled

Arrange potato evenly on a lightly greased 15- x 10-inch jellyroll pan; coat potato with vegetable cooking spray.

Bake at 475° for 20 to 25 minutes or until tender and golden, stirring occasionally.

Whisk together lemon juice and next 5 ingredients; whisk in oil in a slow, steady stream. Gently toss potato and onion with ½ cup vinaigrette.

Arrange spinach in 6 bowls, and drizzle with remaining vinaigrette. Top with potato mixture; sprinkle with bacon. Yield: 6 servings.

*2½ pounds small new potatoes may be substituted.

Potato Cobb Salad

3 pounds Yukon gold potatoes
¾ teaspoon salt
1 (16-ounce) bottle olive oil-and-vinegar dressing, divided
8 cups mixed salad greens
2 large avocados
1 tablespoon fresh lemon juice
3 large tomatoes, seeded and diced
12 small green onions, sliced
2 cups (8 ounces) shredded sharp Cheddar cheese
4 ounces crumbled blue cheese
6 to 8 bacon slices, cooked and crumbled
Freshly ground pepper to taste

Potato Cobb Salad

Cook potatoes in boiling salted water to cover 30 minutes or until tender. Drain and cool slightly. Peel and cut into cubes.

Sprinkle potato evenly with ¾ teaspoon salt. Pour 1 cup dressing over potato; gently toss.

Reserve remaining dressing. Cover potato mixture; chill at least 2 hours or overnight.

Arrange salad greens evenly on a large serving platter. Peel and chop avocados; toss with lemon juice.

Arrange potato, avocado, tomato, and next 4 ingredients in rows over salad greens. Sprinkle with pepper. Serve with remaining dressing. Yield: 8 to 10 servings.

Grilled Shrimp and Bean Salad

Grilled Shrimp and Bean Salad

½ cup olive oil
¼ cup lemon juice
2 tablespoons balsamic vinegar
2 shallots, diced
4 large fresh basil leaves, thinly sliced
2 garlic cloves, minced
1 teaspoon salt
½ teaspoon pepper
4 ounces fresh green beans
1 pound tomatoes, chopped
1 green onion, thinly sliced
12 unpeeled, jumbo fresh shrimp
16 Belgian endive leaves
2 ounces goat cheese, crumbled
Garnishes: fresh basil sprigs, bean sprouts

Whisk together first 8 ingredients. Set vinaigrette aside.

Cook green beans in boiling water to cover 5 minutes or until crisp-tender; drain. Plunge into ice water to stop the cooking process; drain.

Toss together green beans, tomato, green onion, and ½ cup vinaigrette; cover and chill.

Peel shrimp, leaving tails intact, and devein, if desired. Brush with ¼ cup vinaigrette.

Grill in a lightly greased grill basket, covered with grill lid, over medium-high heat (350° to 400°) 10 minutes or until shrimp turn pink.

Arrange endive on 4 serving plates; top evenly with green bean mixture, and sprinkle with goat cheese. Top each with 3 shrimp. Drizzle shrimp with remaining vinaigrette. Garnish, if desired. Yield: 4 servings.

—Chef/Owner Albert J. Bouchard III
Restaurant Bouchard
Newport, Rhode Island

Southwestern Shrimp Caesar Salad

You'll need to buy about 2 pounds raw shrimp if you plan to cook it yourself.

1 (10-ounce) package torn romaine lettuce
1 red bell pepper, thinly sliced
1 yellow bell pepper, thinly sliced
1 pound peeled and deveined cooked medium shrimp*
¼ cup olive oil
2 tablespoons egg substitute
2 tablespoons cider vinegar
1 tablespoon fresh lemon juice
2 teaspoons minced chipotle peppers in adobo sauce
1 teaspoon Worcestershire sauce
1 teaspoon anchovy paste
¼ teaspoon salt
1 garlic clove
½ cup freshly grated Parmesan cheese
Chili Croutons

Combine first 4 ingredients in a large bowl. Set salad aside.

Process olive oil and next 8 ingredients in a blender until smooth, stopping to scrape down sides. Add cheese, and process until blended.

Just before serving, pour dressing over salad, tossing to coat. Divide salad among 4 individual serving plates. Sprinkle with Chili Croutons. Yield: 4 servings.

You may substitute 1 pound baked or grilled chicken breast slices for the shrimp, if desired.

Chili Croutons

2 cups commercial garlic-and-butter croutons
Olive oil-flavored cooking spray
1 teaspoon paprika
½ teaspoon chili powder
½ teaspoon ground cumin

Place croutons in a large heavy-duty zip-top plastic bag. Coat croutons with cooking spray. Combine paprika, chili powder, and cumin; sprinkle over croutons in bag. Shake bag to coat. Yield: 2 cups.

Marinated Shrimp and Cucumber Salad

2 quarts water
3 pounds unpeeled, large fresh shrimp
1 cucumber, sliced
½ red onion, sliced
1 cup vegetable oil
½ cup red wine vinegar
1 to 2 garlic cloves, pressed
½ teaspoon sugar
½ teaspoon salt
½ teaspoon ground coriander
½ teaspoon crushed red pepper flakes
½ teaspoon coarsely ground black pepper
½ (3-ounce) jar capers, drained
1½ teaspoons chopped fresh or ½ teaspoon dried basil
1½ teaspoons chopped fresh or ½ teaspoon dried oregano
1½ teaspoons olive oil
1½ teaspoons Worcestershire sauce
1½ teaspoons lemon juice

Bring 2 quarts water to a boil; add shrimp, and cook 3 to 5 minutes. Drain well; rinse with cold water. Peel shrimp, and devein, if desired.

Combine shrimp, cucumber, and onion in a large bowl; set aside.

Combine vegetable oil and next 7 ingredients in a large saucepan. Bring to a boil; reduce heat, and simmer 3 minutes. Let cool. Stir in capers and remaining ingredients. Pour over shrimp mixture; toss. Cover and chill 8 hours. Serve chilled. Yield: 6 to 8 appetizer servings.

Fiesta Shrimp Salad

6   cups water
1½ pounds unpeeled, large fresh shrimp
2   ripe avocados, peeled, seeded, and
    sliced
1   small red onion, cut in half and thinly
    sliced
1   small red bell pepper, cut into thin slices
¾   cup vegetable oil
⅓   cup fresh lime juice
2   tablespoons orange juice
2   fresh jalapeño peppers, seeded and
    minced
1   garlic clove, minced
2   tablespoons chopped fresh cilantro
½   teaspoon ground cumin
¼   teaspoon salt
¼   teaspoon freshly ground pepper
4   cups mixed salad greens
Garnish: fresh cilantro sprigs

Bring 6 cups water to a boil; add shrimp, and
cook 3 to 5 minutes or just until shrimp turn
pink. Drain and rinse with cold water. Chill
30 minutes.

Peel shrimp, leaving tails on, and devein,
if desired.

Toss together shrimp and next 3 ingredients.

Combine oil and next 8 ingredients in a jar;
cover tightly, and shake vigorously. Pour ½ cup
dressing over shrimp mixture, reserving remain-
der; toss gently. Cover and chill 30 minutes.

Serve shrimp salad on greens. Garnish, if
desired. Serve with reserved dressing. Yield:
4 servings.

effortless picnicking

Pack your favorite room-temperature pasta
salads, fruit and cheese, and a big blanket.
This is one no-fuss way to enjoy a simple
meal and a great view.

Thai Shrimp and Glass Noodle Salad

4   ounces glass noodles (bean threads)
½   cup fresh lime juice
¼   cup fish sauce
3   tablespoons vegetable oil
2   tablespoons rice vinegar
2   teaspoons sugar
1   pound peeled and deveined cooked
    shrimp*
1   large cucumber, halved lengthwise,
    seeded, and sliced
1   red bell pepper, cut into strips
½   cup thinly sliced green onions
½   cup shredded carrot
2   tablespoons fresh cilantro leaves

Soak noodles in hot water for 10 to 15 minutes or until tender; rinse and drain. Place in a bowl. (For easier serving, cut noodles into pieces with kitchen shears.) Combine lime juice and next 4 ingredients; pour over noodles, tossing to coat.

Stir in remaining ingredients, and toss salad until well blended. Cover and chill thoroughly. Yield: 4 servings.

*Start with about 2 pounds raw shrimp.

Marinated Shrimp and Fennel Salad

¼   cup extra-virgin olive oil, divided
¼   teaspoon kosher salt, divided
¼   teaspoon freshly ground pepper, divided
2   tablespoons chopped Italian parsley
2   tablespoons thinly sliced green onions
1   to 2 tablespoons coarsely chopped fresh
    cilantro
1   tablespoon fresh lemon juice
1   teaspoon chopped fresh jalapeño pepper
12 unpeeled, jumbo fresh shrimp
6   cups water
¼   cup vodka
1   medium-size fennel bulb, thinly sliced
2   tablespoons fresh lemon juice
Garnish: fresh cilantro sprigs

Stir together 2 tablespoons olive oil, ⅛ teaspoon kosher salt, ⅛ teaspoon pepper, and next 5 ingredients in a medium bowl. Set aside.

Peel shrimp, leaving tails intact; devein, if desired. Set aside. Bring water to a boil; dip shrimp in vodka, and add to boiling water. Cook

3 to 5 minutes or just until shrimp turn pink. Drain and plunge into ice water. Drain and pat dry with paper towels. Add shrimp to dressing mixture; toss well. Cover and chill 2 hours.

Combine fennel, remaining 2 tablespoons olive oil, salt, and pepper, and 2 tablespoons lemon juice; toss well. Cover and chill 2 hours.

To serve, spoon fennel mixture onto 2 individual serving plates. Arrange shrimp around fennel; drizzle remaining dressing mixture over shrimp. Garnish, if desired. Yield: 2 servings.

Shrimp Greek Salad

3   cups water
1   teaspoon Greek seasoning
1   pound unpeeled, jumbo fresh shrimp
1   head romaine lettuce
Greek Potato Salad
1   head iceberg lettuce, shredded
1   (16-ounce) jar sliced pickled beets
1   cucumber, peeled, seeded, and sliced
½   cup pitted kalamata olives
1   (8-ounce) package feta cheese, crumbled
1   (2-ounce) can anchovy fillets (optional)
½   cup red wine vinegar
½   cup olive oil

Bring water and Greek seasoning to a boil; add shrimp and cook 3 to 5 minutes or just until shrimp turn pink. Drain and rinse with cold water. Chill shrimp.

Peel shrimp, leaving tails on, if desired; devein, if desired.

Line a large platter with romaine leaves. Mound Greek Potato Salad in center. Arrange shrimp, iceberg lettuce, beets, and cucumber around potato salad. Sprinkle salad with olives and crumbled feta cheese. Top with anchovies, if desired. Drizzle with vinegar and oil just before serving. Yield: 6 to 8 servings.

Greek Potato Salad

2   pounds new potatoes
¼   cup olive oil
¼   cup red wine vinegar
3   tablespoons mayonnaise
½   teaspoon salt
½   teaspoon pepper
½   teaspoon dried oregano

Cook potatoes in boiling salted water to cover 25 minutes or until tender. Drain and cool slightly. Cut into 1-inch pieces.

Whisk together oil and remaining ingredients; toss with potato. Yield: about 5 cups.

Conch Salad

1   pound conch, finely chopped*
1   cup finely chopped celery
¾   cup finely chopped onion
¾   cup finely chopped red bell pepper
¾   cup finely chopped yellow bell pepper
¾   cup extra-virgin olive oil
¾   cup fresh lemon juice
½   cup fresh lime juice
½   teaspoon salt
½   teaspoon coarsely ground pepper
Garnish: chopped fresh parsley

Combine first 10 ingredients in a large bowl. Cover; chill 30 minutes. Garnish, if desired. Yield: 6 cups.
*Frozen and thawed conch or shrimp may be substituted.

—Louis Pappas Market Cafe
Tampa, Florida

Bailey's West Indies Salad

This salad may be assembled up to one day before serving.

1   medium-size sweet onion, diced
1   pound fresh lump crabmeat,
    drained
½   teaspoon salt
½   teaspoon pepper
½   cup vegetable oil
⅓   cup cider vinegar
½   cup ice water
Garnishes: leaf lettuce, lemon wedges,
    fresh Italian parsley sprigs

Place half of onion in a large bowl; top with crabmeat. Sprinkle with remaining onion, salt, and pepper. Pour oil, vinegar, and water over onion; cover and chill at least 2 hours. Toss before serving. Garnish, if desired. Yield: 6 servings.

Shrimp Greek Salad

Shrimp, Crabmeat, and Wild Rice Salad

2   (6-ounce) packages long-grain and wild
    rice mix (we tested with Uncle Ben's)
6   cups water
1½ pounds unpeeled, medium-size
    fresh shrimp
1   pound fresh lump crabmeat, drained
1   (14-ounce) can artichoke hearts,
    drained and halved
3   green onions, sliced
Fresh Herb Vinaigrette
1   tablespoon fresh lemon juice
3   heads Bibb lettuce
1   pound asparagus, steamed and
    chilled
3   small tomatoes, sliced
Garnish: lemon wedges, fresh oregano

Cook rice according to package directions,
omitting butter.

Bring 6 cups water to a boil in a Dutch oven.
Add shrimp; cook 3 to 5 minutes or just until
shrimp turn pink. Drain and rinse with cold
water. Peel shrimp, leaving a few tails intact for
garnish; devein, if desired.

Combine rice, shrimp, crabmeat, artichoke
hearts, and green onions in a large bowl. Add
Fresh Herb Vinaigrette; toss gently. Cover and
chill at least 2 hours. Drizzle with lemon juice.
Serve salad over Bibb lettuce leaves with
asparagus and tomato slices. Garnish, if
desired. Yield: 12 servings.

Fresh Herb Vinaigrette

½   cup olive oil
½   cup white wine vinegar
½   cup chopped fresh basil
2   to 3 tablespoons chopped fresh
    oregano
2   garlic cloves, minced
½   teaspoon seasoned salt
½   teaspoon sugar
½   teaspoon dried crushed red pepper

Combine all ingredients in a small bowl; stir
with a wire whisk. Yield: 1½ cups.

Marinated Crabmeat Salad

1   pound fresh lump crabmeat, drained
2   medium zucchini, diced
    (about 1 pound)
2   yellow squash, diced (about ¾ pound)
2   small red onions, diced
⅓   cup thinly sliced fresh basil
1   teaspoon Creole seasoning
1   teaspoon salt
½   teaspoon freshly ground pepper
¼   cup rice wine vinegar
½   cup extra-virgin olive oil
2   tablespoons fresh lemon juice
2   tablespoons hot sauce
24 red or yellow tomato slices (about
    6 medium tomatoes)
½   teaspoon salt
½   teaspoon freshly ground pepper
2   heads radicchio, separated into leaves
2   small heads Bibb lettuce, torn
1   red onion, thinly sliced and separated
    into rings

Stir together first 12 ingredients. Cover and
chill 30 minutes.

Arrange 3 tomato slices on each salad
plate. Sprinkle evenly with ½ teaspoon salt
and ½ teaspoon pepper. Arrange 1 or 2
radicchio leaves on each plate to form a cup.

Drain crabmeat mixture, reserving dressing.
Toss Bibb lettuce with ⅓ cup reserved dressing.
Divide lettuce among radicchio cups. Spoon
crabmeat salad over lettuce. Drizzle with
remaining dressing. Top each serving with onion
rings. Yield: 8 servings.

—Ralph Brennan/Chef Haley Gabel
Bacco
New Orleans, Louisiana

**Shrimp, Crabmeat, and
Wild Rice Salad**

Seared Tuna on Mixed Greens with Cilantro-Lime Vinaigrette

Seared Tuna on Mixed Greens with Cilantro-Lime Vinaigrette

3   to 4 tablespoons Southwest Seasoning
4   (6- to 8-ounce) tuna steaks, about
    1 inch thick
1   tablespoon olive oil
8   cups gourmet mixed salad greens
Cilantro-Lime Vinaigrette

Sprinkle Southwest Seasoning on tuna. Heat oil in a large nonstick skillet over medium-high heat. Add tuna; cook 3 to 5 minutes on each side or to desired degree of doneness.

Toss greens with desired amount of Cilantro-Lime Vinaigrette. Arrange greens on individual serving plates. Top with tuna, and drizzle with remaining vinaigrette. Yield: 4 servings.

Southwest Seasoning

2   tablespoons chili powder
2   tablespoons paprika
2   tablespoons ground cumin
2   tablespoons kosher salt*
1   tablespoon garlic powder
1   tablespoon ground coriander
2   teaspoons ground red pepper

Combine all ingredients. Store in an airtight container. Yield: ⅔ cup.

*If substituting regular salt, use 1 tablespoon.

Cilantro-Lime Vinaigrette

¼   cup fresh lime juice
2   tablespoons sugar
3   tablespoons rice wine vinegar
2   tablespoons olive oil
2   teaspoons finely chopped fresh
    cilantro
1   garlic clove, minced
1   shallot, minced
¼   teaspoon salt
¼   teaspoon coarsely ground pepper

Whisk together all ingredients until blended. Yield: ¾ cup.

White Bean and Tuna Salad with Warm Bacon Dressing

1   garlic clove, minced
¼   cup butter, melted
2   cups French bread cubes (¾ to 1 inch
    thick)
¼   cup grated Parmesan cheese
4   thick bacon slices
2   (8-ounce) tuna steaks
2   tablespoons vegetable oil
½   teaspoon salt, divided
½   teaspoon freshly ground pepper, divided
¼   cup cider vinegar
¼   cup chopped onion
2   tablespoons honey
2   tablespoons Dijon mustard
8   cups gourmet mixed salad greens
1   (19-ounce) can cannellini beans or other
    white beans, rinsed and drained
1   (4-ounce) package feta cheese, crumbled
Additional freshly ground pepper

Stir together garlic and butter; drizzle over bread cubes. Toss gently. Spread in a single layer on a lightly greased 15- x 10-inch jellyroll pan.

Bake bread cubes at 300° for 1 hour or until golden, stirring every 15 minutes. Sprinkle with cheese during last 15 minutes; cool. Set aside.

Cook bacon in a large skillet over medium heat until crisp; drain on paper towels, reserving ¼ cup bacon drippings. Coarsely crumble bacon; set aside.

Brush tuna steaks with oil; sprinkle evenly with ¼ teaspoon salt and ¼ teaspoon pepper.

Grill, covered with grill lid, over medium-high heat (350° to 400°) 3 to 5 minutes on each side or to desired degree of doneness. Cool fish and break into chunks.

Process reserved ¼ cup bacon drippings, remaining ¼ teaspoon salt and ¼ teaspoon pepper, cider vinegar, and next 3 ingredients in a blender or food processor until smooth, stopping to scrape down sides. Pour into a 1-cup glass measuring cup. Microwave at HIGH 30 to 45 seconds or until thoroughly heated.

Line salad plates with greens. Arrange tuna, bacon, beans, feta cheese, and croutons over lettuce. Drizzle with dressing; sprinkle with additional pepper. Serve immediately. Yield: 4 servings.

Fisherman's Salad

2 pounds fish fillets (salmon, halibut, swordfish, grouper, or other firm fish)
2 tablespoons olive oil
¾ teaspoon salt, divided
½ teaspoon freshly ground pepper, divided
⅔ cup mayonnaise
2 tablespoons fresh lemon juice
3 celery ribs, sliced
¼ cup minced onion
1 (2-ounce) jar diced pimiento, drained
2 tablespoons chopped fresh parsley
2 tablespoons capers, drained
Leaf lettuce
Garnish: tomato wedges

Brush fillets with olive oil; sprinkle with ½ teaspoon salt and ¼ teaspoon pepper, and place in a lightly greased grill basket.

Grill, covered with grill lid, over medium-high heat (350° to 400°) 8 to 10 minutes on each side or until fish flakes with a fork. Cool fish and flake.

Stir together mayonnaise, lemon juice, remaining ¼ teaspoon salt and ¼ teaspoon pepper in a large bowl; add fish, celery, and next 4 ingredients, tossing lightly. Cover and chill 30 minutes. Serve on lettuce-lined plates. Garnish, if desired. Yield: 6 servings.

Fried Oyster Salad

2 (12-ounce) containers fresh oysters, drained
2 egg whites, lightly beaten
1½ cups Italian-seasoned breadcrumbs
1½ cups vegetable oil
4 large fresh mushrooms, sliced
1 (10-ounce) package fresh spinach
Red Wine Vinaigrette
1 small red onion, thinly sliced
4 bacon slices, cooked and crumbled

Dip oysters in egg whites; dredge in breadcrumbs. Set aside.

Pour oil into a large heavy skillet; heat to 350°. Fry oysters, in batches, 1 minute on each side or until golden; drain on paper towels.

Arrange mushrooms evenly over spinach, and drizzle with half of Red Wine Vinaigrette. Top salad with oysters, onion slices, and bacon. Serve immediately with remaining vinaigrette. Yield: 6 servings.

Red Wine Vinaigrette

3 tablespoons Burgundy or other dry red wine
3 tablespoons red wine vinegar
1 tablespoon Dijon mustard
½ teaspoon sugar
½ teaspoon Worcestershire sauce
⅛ teaspoon pepper
¾ cup olive oil

Process first 6 ingredients in a blender until smooth. With blender running, add oil in a slow, steady stream. Yield: 1⅓ cups.

Grilled Sardines with Mesclun and Grilled Lime Vinaigrette

Using a grill basket is good insurance when grilling sardines.

16 fresh sardines, dressed
2 tablespoons olive oil
¼ teaspoon salt
½ teaspoon freshly ground pepper
6 cups gourmet mixed salad greens (mesclun) or baby lettuces
Grilled Lime Vinaigrette

Brush sardines lightly with oil. Sprinkle with salt and pepper. Grill, without grill lid, over medium-high heat (350° to 400°) 3 to 5 minutes on each side.

Divide greens evenly among 4 plates. Top with sardines. Serve with Grilled Lime Vinaigrette. Yield: 4 servings.

Grilled Lime Vinaigrette

2 large limes, halved
1 tablespoon minced fresh cilantro
1 garlic clove, minced
½ teaspoon salt
½ teaspoon freshly ground pepper
½ cup olive oil

Grill lime halves, cut side down, without grill lid, over medium-high heat (350° to 400°) 5 to 6 minutes.

Juice lime halves; reserve rind for garnish, if desired. Add remaining ingredients to lime juice. Cover tightly, and shake vigorously. Chill thoroughly. Yield: ¾ cup.

Chilled Lobster and Asparagus with Shallot-Tarragon Vinaigrette

4 quarts water
2 tablespoons salt
2 (1- to 1¼-pound) live lobsters
½ pound fresh asparagus
¼ cup olive oil
1½ tablespoons fresh lemon juice
1 tablespoon white wine vinegar
1 shallot, minced
¾ teaspoon chopped fresh tarragon
¾ teaspoon chopped fresh parsley
⅛ teaspoon salt
⅛ teaspoon freshly ground pepper
1 small head Bibb lettuce
Garnishes: fresh tarragon sprigs, lemon wedges

Bring 4 quarts water and salt to a boil in a large stockpot. Plunge lobsters, head first, into boiling water; return to a boil. Cover, reduce heat, and simmer 10 minutes; drain and cool.

Remove meat from claws and tails. Chill lobster meat.

Cook asparagus in boiling water to cover 3 minutes or until crisp-tender; drain. Plunge into ice water to stop the cooking process; drain and pat dry. Set aside.

Combine olive oil and next 7 ingredients in a jar; cover tightly, and shake vigorously.

Arrange lettuce leaves, lobster, and asparagus on plates; drizzle with dressing. Garnish, if desired. Yield: 2 servings.

Buckhead Diner Soft-Shell Crab Salad

1   cup French green beans
8   cups mixed baby lettuces
½   cup thinly sliced red bell pepper
½   cup thinly sliced yellow bell pepper
1½ cups all-purpose flour
¼   cup cornstarch
1   teaspoon garlic powder
1   teaspoon salt
1   teaspoon coarsely ground pepper
½   cup milk
½   cup buttermilk
8   soft-shell crabs, dressed
Vegetable oil
Red Wine Vinaigrette
Shallot-Dill Mayonnaise

Boil green beans in water to cover 2 minutes; drain. Plunge into ice water to stop the cooking process; drain again. Combine green beans, lettuces, and bell peppers; set aside.

Combine flour and next 4 ingredients in a shallow dish. Combine milk and buttermilk. Dredge crabs in flour mixture, and dip in milk mixture. Dredge in flour mixture again.

Pour oil to depth of 1 inch into a Dutch oven; heat to 350°. Fry crabs 1 to 1½ minutes on each side. Drain on paper towels. Cut crabs in half.

Toss together bean mixture and ½ cup Red Wine Vinaigrette; place on serving plates. Arrange 4 crab halves on each salad and dollop each with Shallot-Dill Mayonnaise. Serve immediately. Yield: 4 servings.

Red Wine Vinaigrette

⅓   cup red wine vinegar
1   garlic clove, coarsely chopped
2   tablespoons coarsely chopped shallots
½   teaspoon salt
½   teaspoon dried oregano
½   teaspoon dried basil
½   teaspoon stone-ground mustard
¼   teaspoon coarsely ground pepper
⅓   cup olive oil
⅓   cup vegetable oil

Process first 8 ingredients in a food processor or blender until blended. With processor running, add oils in a slow, steady stream; process until blended. Yield: 1 cup.

Shallot-Dill Mayonnaise

¾   cup mayonnaise
¼   cup finely chopped shallots
2   tablespoons chopped fresh dill
2   tablespoons fresh lemon juice
¼   teaspoon salt
¼   teaspoon coarsely ground pepper

Combine all ingredients. Cover and chill. Yield: 1 cup.

—Executive Chef Tony Pope
Buckhead Diner
Atlanta, Georgia

Seared Sea Scallops with Cucumber-Fennel Salad and Fennel Seed Vinaigrette

1   large cucumber
1   medium-size fennel bulb
3   tablespoons minced shallots, divided
1   tablespoon minced garlic, divided
1   tablespoon minced chives
¾   cup rice wine vinegar, divided
¼   cup extra-virgin olive oil
½   teaspoon salt, divided
½   teaspoon freshly ground pepper, divided
3   tablespoons fennel seeds
½   cup grapeseed or peanut oil
1   tablespoon fresh orange juice
6   (1-ounce) sea scallops
Salt and freshly ground pepper to taste
1   teaspoon olive oil
Garnish: fennel sprigs

Peel cucumber; cut in half lengthwise. Remove seeds, and thinly slice.

Trim and discard fennel bulb base. Trim stalks from bulb, discarding hard outside stalk. Cut bulb in half lengthwise, and cut crosswise into thin slices.

Stir together fennel, cucumber, 2 table-spoons shallots, ½ tablespoon garlic, chives, ½ cup rice wine vinegar, olive oil, ¼ teaspoon salt, and ¼ teaspoon pepper; let stand at room temperature 1 hour.

Place a small skillet over medium-high heat until hot; add fennel seeds, and cook, stirring constantly, 1½ minutes or until toasted. (Be careful not to burn seeds; they'll become bitter.)

Remove seeds from pan. Reduce heat to medium. Process seeds in a blender until ground; return to pan. Stir in ½ cup grape-seed oil. Remove from heat; cool to room temperature.

Whisk together fennel-infused oil, remaining tablespoon shallots, remaining ½ tablespoon garlic, remaining ¼ cup vinegar, remaining ¼ teaspoon salt, remaining ¼ teaspoon pepper, and orange juice; set aside.

Sprinkle scallops with salt and pepper to taste. Heat 1 teaspoon olive oil in skillet over high heat until very hot. Add scallops, and cook 2 minutes. Turn, and cook 1 minute.

Arrange salad on individual plates; top each with a scallop. Whisk vinaigrette, and drizzle over salads. Garnish, if desired, and serve immediately. Yield: 6 servings.

Crispy Smoked Quail Salad

Hickory chunks
1   cup peanut oil
2   tablespoons honey
2   tablespoons soy sauce or hoisin sauce
2   tablespoons bourbon
8   quail, breasts deboned
2   cups rice flour
½   teaspoon salt
¼   teaspoon freshly ground pepper
1½ cups water
Vegetable oil
8   cups gourmet salad greens
Bourbon Dressing
2   ripe pears, thinly sliced
Pickled Red Onion
½   cup thinly sliced celery hearts
Spiced Pecans

Soak wood chunks in water 1 hour.

Combine peanut oil and next 3 ingredients in a heavy-duty zip-top plastic bag; add quail. Seal and chill 1 hour, turning occasionally.

Remove quail from marinade, discarding marinade.

Prepare charcoal fire in smoker; let burn 15 to 20 minutes.

Drain wood chunks and place on coals. Place water pan in smoker; add water to depth of fill line.

Place quail on lower food rack; cover with smoker lid. Smoke 25 to 30 minutes. Let stand 30 minutes.

Stir together flour and next 3 ingredients in a small bowl just until blended.

Pour vegetable oil to a depth of 3 inches into a Dutch oven; heat oil to 375°.

Hold quail by legs, and dip into batter, coating thoroughly. Fry quail in batches in hot oil 2 to 3 minutes or until golden. Drain on paper towels.

Toss greens with ¼ cup Bourbon Dressing; place on individual serving plates. Top each with a quail; divide pear slices and remaining ingredients evenly among salads. Serve with remaining dressing. Yield: 8 servings.

Bourbon Dressing

2 cups chicken broth
1 tablespoon sugar
¼ cup chopped shallots
2 tablespoons molasses
2 tablespoons cider vinegar
2 tablespoons walnut vinegar or cider vinegar*
1 cup olive oil
½ teaspoon salt
½ teaspoon freshly ground pepper
1 to 2 tablespoons bourbon

Bring broth to a boil over high heat; boil about 20 minutes or until mixture is reduced to ½ cup.

Process broth, sugar, and next 4 ingredients in a blender until smooth, stopping to scrape down sides. Turn blender on high; gradually add oil in a slow, steady stream. Add salt, pepper, and bourbon. Yield: 1½ cups.

*Walnut vinegar can be found at Williams-Sonoma.

Pickled Red Onion

1 small red onion, thinly sliced
1 teaspoon pickling spice
1 cup cider vinegar

Combine all ingredients; cover and chill 8 hours. Yield: ½ cup.

Spiced Pecans

1 cup pecan halves
2 tablespoons sugar
2 tablespoons butter, melted
1 teaspoon salt
¼ teaspoon ground red pepper
2 teaspoons Worcestershire sauce

Stir together all ingredients; spread in a lightly greased 13- x 9-inch pan.

Bake at 350° for 10 to 12 minutes or until lightly toasted, stirring once. Yield: 1 cup.
Recipe adapted from The Food of New Orleans: Authentic Recipes from the Big Easy *by John DeMers (Periplus Editions, 1998).*

Crispy Smoked Quail Salad

surf & turf

Salmon and Mushroom Wellingtons with Cucumber Sauce

¼ cup chopped shallots
3 tablespoons butter, melted
¾ pound fresh mushrooms, coarsely chopped
2 garlic cloves, minced
3 tablespoons dry vermouth
2 teaspoons fresh thyme leaves
¾ teaspoon salt, divided
½ teaspoon freshly ground pepper, divided
6 (4- to 5-ounce) salmon fillets
1 (10-ounce) package frozen puff pastry shells, thawed
Cucumber Sauce
Garnish: fresh chives

Sauté shallots in butter in a large skillet over medium-high heat 2 minutes; add chopped mushrooms and garlic. Cook 5 minutes or until liquid evaporates. Add vermouth; cook until liquid evaporates. Remove from heat; stir in thyme, ¼ teaspoon salt, and ¼ teaspoon pepper.

Sprinkle fillets with remaining ½ teaspoon salt and ¼ teaspoon pepper. Cook fillets in a nonstick skillet over high heat 2 minutes on each side.

Roll each pastry shell into a 7-inch circle. Spread about ¼ cup mushroom mixture in center of each circle. Top with fillets. Wrap pastry over each fillet, tucking edges under fillet and pinching to seal. Place pastries, seam side down, on a rack in a broiler pan.

Bake at 450° for 15 minutes or until golden. Serve with Cucumber Sauce. Garnish, if desired. Yield: 6 servings.

Cucumber Sauce

1 (8-ounce) container sour cream
½ cup peeled, seeded, and chopped cucumber
1 teaspoon dried dillweed
Salt to taste
Freshly ground pepper to taste

Stir together all ingredients; cover and chill. Yield 1⅓ cups.

Mango-Glazed Salmon

1 (10-ounce) bottle mango nectar
2 tablespoons soy sauce
1 tablespoon minced fresh ginger
1 (3-inch) cinnamon stick
1 star anise
1 teaspoon rice vinegar
6 (6-ounce) salmon fillets (about 1 inch thick)

Stir together first 6 ingredients in a small saucepan. Bring to a boil; reduce heat, and simmer, uncovered, 25 minutes or until reduced to ¾ cup. Pour mango mixture through a wire-mesh strainer; discard solids. Return mango mixture to saucepan; keep warm.

Place salmon on a lightly greased rack in a broiler pan. Broil 5½ inches from heat 5 minutes. Brush fish with ⅓ cup mango mixture. Broil 3 more minutes or until fish flakes with a fork. Spoon remaining mango mixture evenly over fish. Yield: 6 servings.

—Judy Hawkins
Seattle, Washington

Gravlax with Honey-Dijon Sauce

1 (1½-pound) king salmon fillet, skin on
1 cup aquavit or vodka
1 cup sugar
1 cup kosher salt
2 tablespoons coarsely ground pepper
2 tablespoons dried dillweed
12 sprigs fresh dillweed
French bread slices, toasted
Honey-Dijon Sauce
Garnish: fresh dillweed sprigs

Remove pin bones from salmon with tweezers or needle-nose pliers. Rinse salmon with aquavit.

Combine sugar and next 3 ingredients. Pour half of sugar mixture into a 13- x 9-inch baking dish. Place salmon fillet over sugar mixture, skin side down; top with remaining sugar mixture and dillweed sprigs. Cover with plastic wrap. Place another 13- x 9-inch baking dish over plastic wrap. Fill with heavy cans. Chill 24 to 48 hours. Turn fillet every 12 hours, draining off any liquid that collects and replacing weights.

Rinse coating from salmon; pat dry. Slice thinly, starting at the tail. Serve on toasted French bread with Honey-Dijon Sauce. Garnish, if desired. Yield: 12 appetizer servings.

Honey-Dijon Sauce

¼ cup Dijon mustard
2 tablespoons chopped fresh dillweed
2 tablespoons honey

Combine all ingredients in a small bowl; cover and chill. Yield: ½ cup.

—Chef Jens Haagen Hansen
Jens' Restaurant
Anchorage, Alaska

Rich, succulent, and healthy, too, salmon has become one of America's most popular fish. It's an easy fish to prepare: A relatively high oil content makes it appropriate for poaching, grilling, baking, steaming, and broiling. Its distinctive flavor also blends well with a virtual melting pot of international ingredients.

Grilled Salmon with Nectarine-Onion Relish

4   (6-ounce) salmon fillets (about 1 inch
    thick)
½   teaspoon salt
½   teaspoon freshly ground pepper
Nectarine-Onion Relish
Garnish: fresh jalapeño peppers

Sprinkle salmon fillets with salt and pepper.
    Grill fillets, covered with grill lid, over
medium-high heat (350° to 400°) 5 minutes
on each side or until fish flakes with a fork.
Serve hot with Nectarine-Onion Relish.
Garnish, if desired. Yield: 4 servings.

Nectarine-Onion Relish

3   nectarines, coarsely chopped
1   large red bell pepper, coarsely chopped
1   red onion, coarsely chopped
¼   cup thinly sliced fresh basil
¼   cup white wine vinegar
½   teaspoon grated orange rind
¼   cup fresh orange juice
2   jalapeño peppers, seeded and minced
2   tablespoons fresh lime juice
2   teaspoons sugar
2   garlic cloves, minced
¼   teaspoon salt

Stir together all ingredients. Cover and chill
2 hours. Yield: 4 cups.

Poached King Salmon with Cucumber Beurre Blanc

Ask for a small king salmon at your fish market. If what's available is too large, use 10 (6- to 8-ounce) fillets and omit the head and tail for the poaching liquid.

1   (15- to 18-pound) whole king salmon, dressed
5   cups water
1¾   cups dry white wine
2   bay leaves
1   tablespoon white peppercorns
1   bunch parsley stems
1   small onion, thickly sliced
½   head fennel, thickly sliced
½   cup coarsely chopped celery
1   teaspoon salt
Cucumber Beurre Blanc
Peeled, chopped cucumber

Cut head and tail from salmon; set aside.

Cut salmon in half lengthwise; remove pin bones with tweezers or needle-nose pliers. Slice salmon crosswise into 2-inch pieces; cover and set aside.

Place head and tail in a 4-quart saucepan. Cover with 5 cups water; add wine and next 6 ingredients. Bring mixture to a boil. Reduce heat, and simmer 30 minutes. Pour mixture through a wire-mesh strainer into a bowl, discarding solids. Return liquid to pan. Stir salt into liquid.

Pour liquid into a fish poacher*; bring to a boil. Reduce heat, and simmer gently. Arrange fish on poacher insert, and place in liquid. Simmer 10 minutes; remove from heat, and let stand 5 minutes.

Remove salmon, and place on serving plates. Top with Cucumber Beurre Blanc and chopped cucumber. Serve with steamed fresh vegetables. Yield: 10 servings.

If you don't have a fish poacher, use a roasting pan large enough to hold the salmon in a single layer. Place salmon in gently simmering liquid with a metal spatula.

Cucumber Beurre Blanc

4   cups peeled, chopped cucumber
½   cup whipping cream
3   tablespoons fresh lemon juice
1   cup unsalted butter, cut into pieces
¼   teaspoon salt
⅛   teaspoon ground white pepper

Process cucumber in a food processor until liquefied. Strain and measure 1 cup cucumber liquid.

Combine cucumber liquid, cream, and lemon juice in a saucepan; bring mixture to a boil. Reduce heat, and simmer 25 to 30 minutes or until reduced to ½ cup.

Reduce heat to low; whisk in butter, 1 piece at a time. (Do not overheat or sauce will separate.) Stir in salt and ground white pepper. Yield: 1⅓ cups.

—*Chef Jens Haagen Hansen*
Jens' Restaurant
Anchorage, Alaska

Alder-Roasted Salmon with Dill and Cranberries

1   alder plank*
1   cup unsalted butter, softened
¼   cup chopped fresh dillweed
¼   cup dried cranberries, chopped
1   tablespoon fresh lemon juice
2   teaspoons crushed pink and green peppercorns
¼   teaspoon salt
6   (8-ounce) king salmon fillets, skin on

Soak plank in water to cover 1 hour; drain.

Combine butter and next 5 ingredients.

Preheat alder plank in a 400° oven. Place salmon, skin side down, on plank; cover with butter mixture.

Bake 10 to 15 minutes or until done. Yield: 6 servings.

We recommend a reusable alder plank with a trough cut in the center to hold juices. If using a flat disposable alder plank, place in a shallow baking pan to collect drippings.

Note: *See pages 309 and 312 for more information on planked fish.*

—*Chef Jens Haagen Hansen*
Jens' Restaurant
Anchorage, Alaska

vine advice

Salmon and Red Wine "If you have always drunk white wine with salmon, you've been missing something. Matched with the succulent richness of salmon, the earthiness of a great Pinot Noir is simply magical."

—*Wine Expert Karen MacNeil*

Pan-Sautéed Simple Salmon

Chef Mark Franz uses an old-fashioned European technique to create an easy but succulent salmon dish with crispy skin. (Be sure to use "pure" olive oil here, not extra-virgin olive oil, which burns more easily.)

4   (6-ounce) salmon fillets, skin on
1   teaspoon salt
½   teaspoon freshly ground pepper
Olive oil

Sprinkle salmon with salt and pepper.

Pour enough olive oil into a large skillet so that the oil will come up to about half the height of the fish. Heat oil; add fillets, skin side down, and cook 2 to 3 minutes on each side or to desired degree of doneness. Serve immediately. Yield: 4 servings.

—Chef Mark Franz
Farallon
San Francisco, California

Chili-Seared Salmon with Sweet Pepper Salsa

2   tablespoons chili powder
¼   teaspoon salt
⅛   teaspoon freshly ground pepper
4   (6-ounce) salmon fillets (about 1 inch thick)
2   teaspoons olive oil
Sweet Pepper Salsa

Combine chili powder, salt, and pepper; rub evenly over salmon fillets.

Heat oil in a nonstick skillet over medium-high heat; add salmon, cook 4 minutes on each side or to desired degree of doneness. Serve with Sweet Pepper Salsa. Yield: 4 servings.

coastal cuisine

Farallon, a San Francisco seafood house, first coined the phrase "coastal cuisine" to describe its cooking.

The idea of this concept is—at least as far as Farallon's chef and co-owner Mark Franz is concerned—magically compelling. **"The coast is a place with powerful meaning,"** he says. **"It symbolizes the connection between man, the land, and the sea."**

And when you enter the lavish restaurant, named for a small group of islands off the San Francisco coast, you feel that connection.

Sweet Pepper Salsa

4   plum tomatoes, seeded and julienned
2   fresh jalapeño peppers, seeded and minced
1   large yellow bell pepper, seeded and julienned
1   small red onion, julienned
2   tablespoons chopped fresh cilantro
2   tablespoons fresh lime juice
2   teaspoons cider vinegar
¼   teaspoon sugar
¼   teaspoon ground cumin
⅛   teaspoon salt
⅛   teaspoon ground red pepper

Stir together all ingredients. Let stand 30 minutes, stirring occasionally. Yield: 2⅔ cups.

Pinot Noir Poached Salmon

5   tablespoons butter, divided
3   garlic cloves, minced
2   carrots, chopped
1   onion, chopped
1   celery rib, chopped
1   (750-milliliter) bottle Pinot Noir
4   (6-ounce) salmon fillets
1   teaspoon sugar
¼   teaspoon salt
⅛   teaspoon freshly ground pepper

Melt 2 tablespoons butter in a 10-inch straight-sided skillet over medium heat. Add garlic and next 3 ingredients; sauté 15 minutes or until vegetables are tender and onion is lightly browned. Add wine; bring to a boil over high heat. Carefully place salmon in skillet. Cover, reduce heat to medium-low, and poach 5 minutes or until salmon flakes with a fork. Transfer salmon to a serving plate; cover with aluminum foil, and set aside.

Increase heat to high. Bring wine mixture to a boil; cook, uncovered, 10 minutes. Strain wine mixture through a wire-mesh strainer, discarding vegetables. Bring wine to a boil; cook over high heat 3 minutes or until reduced to ½ cup. Remove from heat, and whisk in remaining 3 tablespoons butter and remaining ingredients. Serve sauce over salmon. Yield: 4 servings.

Tuna with Tangy Onions

1   large onion, chopped
3   tablespoons olive oil, divided
½   cup red wine vinegar
½   teaspoon salt, divided
½   teaspoon pepper, divided
8   (¾-inch-thick) tuna steaks (about 2 pounds)
½   cup all-purpose flour

Sauté onion in 1 tablespoon hot oil in a large skillet over medium-high heat 5 minutes or until lightly browned. Add vinegar, ¼ teaspoon salt, and ¼ teaspoon pepper. Continue cooking until most of the liquid evaporates (about 2 minutes). Remove onion mixture from skillet; keep warm. Wipe skillet clean with a paper towel.

Sprinkle tuna with remaining ¼ teaspoon salt and remaining ¼ teaspoon pepper; dredge in flour. Heat 1 tablespoon oil in skillet over medium-high heat. Add 4 tuna steaks to skillet; cook 2 minutes on each side or to desired degree of doneness. Repeat procedure with remaining oil and tuna steaks. Serve with warm onion mixture. Yield: 8 servings.

Coriander Tuna with
Peppered Mayonnaise

Coriander Tuna with Peppered Mayonnaise

¼ cup mayonnaise

3 tablespoons milk

3 tablespoons sour cream

¼ teaspoon salt

1 teaspoon freshly ground pepper, divided

2 tablespoons coriander seeds

½ teaspoon salt

4 (6-ounce) tuna steaks (about ¾ inch thick)

2 tablespoons olive oil

Stir together first 4 ingredients and ½ teaspoon pepper; cover and chill.

Place coriander seeds in a small heavy-duty zip-top plastic bag, and seal. Crush seeds with a meat mallet or rolling pin.

Sprinkle ½ teaspoon salt and remaining ½ teaspoon pepper over tuna. Press crushed coriander seeds firmly onto both sides of tuna.

Cook tuna in hot oil in a large skillet over medium-high heat 3 to 4 minutes on each side or to desired degree of doneness. Serve with peppered mayonnaise. Yield: 4 servings.

Pan-Seared Tuna with Onion-Soy Vinaigrette and Vegetable Slaw

3 carrots

3 celery ribs

2 small cucumbers, seeded

½ cup rice vinegar

2 teaspoons vegetable oil, divided

¼ cup grated onion

¼ cup light soy sauce

Dash of pepper

4 (¾-inch-thick) tuna steaks (about 1½ pounds)

¼ teaspoon salt

¼ teaspoon coarsely ground pepper

Garnishes: red onion slices, celery leaves, lemon wedges

Cut carrots, celery, and cucumbers into thin 2-inch-long strips and place in a bowl.

Stir together rice vinegar, 1 teaspoon oil, and next 3 ingredients in a small bowl. Measure ½ cup vinaigrette mixture and toss with vegetables.

Brush tuna with remaining 1 teaspoon oil; sprinkle with salt and pepper. Place a large nonstick skillet over medium-high heat until hot. Add tuna, and cook 3 minutes on each side or to desired degree of doneness. Serve with vegetable slaw and drizzle with remaining vinaigrette. Garnish, if desired. Yield: 4 servings.

Adobo Tuna with Black-Eyed Pea Salad

⅓ cup fresh lime juice

½ teaspoon dried oregano

½ teaspoon ground cumin

¼ teaspoon salt

4 garlic cloves, minced

4 (½-inch-thick) tuna steaks (about 1½ pounds)

Black-Eyed Pea Salad

Garnishes: lime slices, fresh cilantro sprigs

Combine first 5 ingredients in a large heavy-duty zip-top plastic bag; add tuna. Seal; chill 1 hour, turning occasionally.

Remove tuna from plastic bag; discard marinade.

Place tuna on a lightly greased rack in a broiler pan. Broil 5½ inches from heat 4 minutes or to desired degree of doneness. (Do not turn.) Serve with Black-Eyed Pea Salad. Garnish, if desired. Yield: 4 servings.

Black-Eyed Pea Salad

3 tablespoons red wine vinegar

2 tablespoons olive oil

¼ teaspoon salt

¼ teaspoon pepper

2 (15.8-ounce) cans black-eyed peas, drained and rinsed

2 celery ribs, diced

¼ cup chopped fresh cilantro

¼ cup diced red bell pepper

¼ cup diced green bell pepper

¼ cup diced red onion

Stir together first 4 ingredients in a medium bowl; stir in black-eyed peas and remaining ingredients. Cover and chill at least 1 hour. Yield: 4 cups.

Olive Oil-Poached Mahimahi with Mediterranean Tomato Sauce

2½ cups olive oil

6 plum tomatoes, halved

1 fresh rosemary sprig

4 (6-ounce) mahimahi steaks

1 teaspoon kosher salt

½ teaspoon freshly ground pepper, divided

¾ cup pitted kalamata olives, quartered

1 tablespoon capers

2 teaspoons chopped fresh rosemary

1 teaspoon red wine vinegar

Garnish: fresh rosemary sprigs

Pour oil into an 8-inch straight-sided skillet. Heat over medium-low heat 8 minutes or until oil reaches 175° to 180°. Carefully add tomato halves and rosemary sprig. Cover and poach at a light simmer, adjusting heat as necessary, 10 minutes or until tomatoes are tender. (Keep heat on.) Remove tomatoes from skillet using a slotted spoon; place cut side down in a shallow dish. Cool 10 minutes; set aside.

Sprinkle fish with salt and ¼ teaspoon pepper. Carefully place in hot oil. Cover and poach 6 to 10 minutes or until fish flakes with a fork. Transfer to a serving platter; keep warm.

Remove skins from tomatoes; discard skins. Place tomatoes and any accumulated juices in a food processor; pulse 3 times or until coarsely chopped. Transfer tomato to a medium bowl, and stir in olives, capers, chopped rosemary, vinegar, and remaining ¼ teaspoon pepper. Serve over mahimahi. Garnish, if desired. Yield: 4 servings.

⟨ vine advice

"This Mediterranean mahimahi is a died-and-gone-to-heaven dinner with **Chianti**. The rosemary, tomato, olives, and heft of the fish dance with the spice and zest of Chianti," says Master Sommelier Andrea Immer.

Immer, author of *Great Wine Made Simple, Andrea Immer's Wine Buying Guide for Everyone,* and *Great Tastes Made Simple,* is one of only 10 women worldwide to receive the title of Master Sommelier. She is also the first woman named Best Sommelier in America.

Grilled Alaskan Halibut with Avocado-Lime Sauce

1   lime or lemon
1   large ripe avocado
¾   cup water
½   teaspoon sea salt, divided
½   teaspoon freshly ground pepper,
    divided
½   teaspoon ground cumin
⅓   cup loosely packed fresh cilantro
½   jalapeño pepper, unseeded
4   garlic cloves
4   (6-ounce) Alaskan halibut fillets (about
    1 inch thick)
2   teaspoons olive oil

Peel lime with a vegetable peeler, reserving green rind only; remove and discard pith. Cut lime into fourths, and place in a blender; add rind. Cut avocado in half, and scoop pulp into blender; add ¾ cup water, ¼ teaspoon salt, ¼ teaspoon pepper, cumin, and next 3 ingredients. Process until sauce is smooth, stopping once to scrape down sides.

Brush fish with oil, and sprinkle with remaining ¼ teaspoon salt and ¼ teaspoon pepper.

Grill, covered with grill lid, over high heat (400° to 500°) 5 minutes on each side or until fish flakes with a fork. Serve immediately with sauce. Yield: 4 servings.

—*Chef Nora Pouillon*
Restaurant Nora
Washington, D.C.

Pacific Halibut with Fava Beans and Shrimp

½   cup dry white wine
2   cups water
3   tablespoons green lentils
¾   teaspoon salt, divided
½   cup shelled fresh fava beans*
2   tablespoons olive oil, divided
1   shallot, minced
½   pound medium-size fresh shrimp, peeled
    and deveined
1   tomato, seeded and chopped
2   teaspoons chopped fresh cilantro
1   tablespoon unsalted butter
¼   teaspoon ground white pepper,
    divided
4   (7-ounce) halibut or grouper fillets
Saffron Beurre Blanc

Bring wine to a boil in a small saucepan. Reduce heat, and simmer 6 minutes or until reduced to 2 tablespoons. Pour reduced wine into a small bowl; set aside.

Bring 2 cups water, lentils, and ¼ teaspoon salt to a boil in a small saucepan. Reduce heat, and simmer, uncovered, 20 minutes. Add fava beans; simmer 5 minutes or until tender. Drain.

Heat 1 tablespoon oil in a medium skillet over medium-high heat. Add shallot; sauté 2 minutes. Add shrimp; sauté 3 to 4 minutes. Add lentils, fava beans, and tomato; sauté 2 minutes. Add reduced wine, cilantro, butter, ¼ teaspoon salt, and ⅛ teaspoon white pepper; stir until butter melts. Set aside, and keep warm.

Sprinkle fillets evenly with remaining ¼ teaspoon salt and ⅛ teaspoon white pepper.

Heat remaining 1 tablespoon oil in a large nonstick ovenproof skillet over high heat; add fillets, and sauté, skin side up, 2 minutes or until browned. Turn fillets, and bake, uncovered, at 350° for 8 minutes or until fish flakes with a fork.

To serve, spoon ¾ cup shrimp mixture in center of each plate. Top with a fillet; drizzle with 3 tablespoons Saffron Beurre Blanc. Yield: 4 servings.

Fava beans are available at most Middle Eastern markets, specialty stores, and farmers' markets. Lima beans may be substituted.

Saffron Beurre Blanc

1   cup dry white wine
2   shallots, coarsely chopped
1   bay leaf
1   thyme sprig
¼   cup heavy whipping cream
Pinch of saffron
½   cup cold unsalted butter, cut into pieces
⅛   to ¼ teaspoon salt
¼   teaspoon freshly ground pepper

Combine first 4 ingredients in a saucepan. Bring to a boil. Reduce heat, and simmer, uncovered, 15 minutes or until liquid is reduced to ⅓ cup.

Add cream and saffron; return to a boil. Reduce heat, and simmer, uncovered, 5 minutes or until liquid is reduced to ⅓ cup. Remove from heat. Whisk in cold butter, a few pieces at a time, stirring until smooth. Strain, discarding solids. Whisk in salt and pepper. Yield: ¾ cup.

Gaston's Trout Amandine

4   rainbow or brook trout, cleaned
2   tablespoons fresh lemon juice
Cracked pepper
½   cup butter or margarine, divided
1½ cups slivered almonds
¼   cup fresh lemon juice
2   tablespoons minced fresh parsley
Garnish: lemon slices

Brush trout with 2 tablespoons lemon juice, and sprinkle with cracked pepper.

Melt 2 tablespoons butter in a large nonstick skillet over medium-high heat; add 2 trout, and cook 6 to 8 minutes, turning once, or until fish flakes with a fork. Remove to a serving platter, and keep warm. Repeat procedure with 2 tablespoons butter and remaining trout. Wipe drippings from skillet with a paper towel.

Melt remaining ¼ cup butter in skillet; add almonds, and sauté until golden. Stir in ¼ cup lemon juice and parsley; pour over trout. Garnish, if desired. Yield: 4 servings.

Pacific Halibut with Fava Beans and Shrimp

Sweet Onion-Stuffed Trout

8   medium-size red potatoes, cubed
16   bacon slices, divided
4   baby Vidalia onions, sliced
1   cup whipping cream
2   tablespoons butter or margarine
2   teaspoons salt, divided
2   teaspoons pepper, divided
4   (12-ounce) butterflied trout
2   cups all-purpose flour
¼   cup olive oil
Vidalia Onion Sauce

Cook potato in boiling water to cover 10 minutes or until tender; drain.

Chop 8 bacon slices. Cook chopped bacon in a skillet over medium-high heat 10 minutes, stirring often; add onion, and sauté 10 minutes or until tender. Add potato to skillet, and mash with a fork. Stir in cream, butter, ½ teaspoon salt, and ½ teaspoon pepper; cook, stirring constantly, until thoroughly heated.

Sprinkle trout with ½ teaspoon salt and ½ teaspoon pepper. Spoon stuffing evenly onto 1 side of each trout; fold other side over stuffing. Wrap 2 bacon slices around each trout, securing with wooden picks.

Stir together flour, remaining 1 teaspoon salt, and remaining 1 teaspoon pepper in a shallow dish. Dredge fish in flour mixture.

Fry trout, 2 at a time, in hot oil in a skillet over medium-high heat 6 minutes on each side or until fish flakes with a fork. Serve with Vidalia Onion Sauce. Yield: 4 servings.

Vidalia Onion Sauce

2   baby Vidalia onions, sliced
1   tablespoon olive oil
2   cups whipping cream
¼   teaspoon salt
¼   teaspoon pepper

Sauté onion in a large skillet in hot oil over medium-high heat 10 minutes or until tender; stir in whipping cream. Reduce heat, and simmer 15 minutes or until liquid is reduced by half. Stir in salt and pepper. Yield: about 3 cups.

Executive Chef Robert J. Stricklin
Big Cedar Lodge
Ridgedale, Missouri

Cornmeal-Crusted Trout

2   bacon slices, chopped
2   tablespoons olive oil, divided
½   red onion, diced
½   green bell pepper, diced
3   garlic cloves, minced
¼   cup fresh or frozen whole kernel corn
2   cups crumbled cornbread
2   ounces lump crabmeat, drained
2   tablespoons chopped fresh cilantro
1   jalapeño pepper, seeded and chopped
1   large egg, lightly beaten
1   teaspoon salt, divided
1   teaspoon ground black pepper, divided
4   (12-ounce) butterflied trout
2   cups cornmeal
2   teaspoons ground red pepper
1   teaspoon salt
1   teaspoon garlic powder
8   bacon slices
Picante Aïoli

Cook chopped bacon in 1 tablespoon hot oil in a large skillet over medium-high heat 8 to 10 minutes. Stir in onion and next 3 ingredients, and sauté 5 minutes or until tender. Remove from heat; stir in cornbread, next 4 ingredients, ½ teaspoon salt, and ½ teaspoon pepper.

Sprinkle trout with remaining ½ teaspoon salt and remaining ½ teaspoon pepper. Spoon one-fourth of cornbread mixture on 1 side of each trout. Fold other side over stuffing. Stir together cornmeal and next 3 ingredients; dredge trout in mixture. Wrap 2 bacon slices around each trout, securing with wooden picks.

Fry trout, 2 at a time, in remaining 1 tablespoon hot oil 6 minutes on each side or until fish flakes with a fork. Serve immediately with Picante Aïoli. Yield: 4 servings.

Picante Aïoli

1   cup mayonnaise
⅓   cup picante sauce
3   garlic cloves, minced
¼   teaspoon salt
¼   teaspoon pepper

Stir together all ingredients. Cover and chill at least 30 minutes. Yield: 1⅓ cups.

Executive Chef Robert J. Stricklin
Big Cedar Lodge
Ridgedale, Missouri

Cedar Plank Fish with Citrus Horseradish Crust and Butter Sauce

1   cedar plank
½   cup grated fresh horseradish
1   teaspoon minced lemon rind
1   teaspoon minced orange rind
2   tablespoons fresh lemon juice
2   tablespoons fresh orange juice
1   tablespoon chopped fresh cilantro
½   teaspoon salt
2   teaspoons sugar
1   teaspoon olive oil
2   (10-ounce) trout fillets
2   teaspoons Creole seasoning (we tested with Emeril's Essence seasoning blend)
Butter Sauce
Garnish: citrus fruit slices

Soak plank in water to cover 1 hour; drain.

Stir together horseradish and next 7 ingredients in a small bowl.

Rub plank with olive oil. Place fillets on plank; sprinkle with Creole seasoning. Top each fillet with horseradish mixture.

Bake at 400° for 14 minutes or until fish flakes with a fork. Serve with Butter Sauce. Garnish, if desired. Yield: 2 servings.

Butter Sauce

¼   cup dry white wine
2   tablespoons fresh lemon juice
1   bay leaf
8   black peppercorns
½   teaspoon chopped fresh thyme
¼   cup whipping cream
1   cup cold butter, cut into 8 pieces
¼   teaspoon salt
¼   teaspoon pepper

Stir together first 5 ingredients in a small saucepan. Bring to a boil; reduce heat, and simmer 3 minutes, uncovered, or until mixture is reduced by half. Add whipping cream. Return to a boil; reduce heat, and simmer 3 minutes or until mixture is reduced by half. Remove from heat.

Whisk in butter, 1 tablespoon at a time, whisking until butter melts and sauce is thickened. Add salt and pepper. Pour mixture through a wire-mesh strainer into a bowl, discarding bay leaf and peppercorns. Yield: about 1¼ cups.

Note: See pages 309 and 312 for more information on planked fish.
Recipe from Louisiana Real and Rustic by Emeril Lagasse and Marcelle Bienvenu. © 1996 by Emeril Lagasse. Reprinted by permission of HarperCollins Publishers Inc.

Pan-Fried Roughy with Tomato-Basil Salsa

4   (6- to 8-ounce) orange roughy fillets
1   teaspoon salt
½   teaspoon pepper
1   cup yellow cornmeal
½   cup butter or margarine
2   tablespoons olive oil
1   sweet onion, chopped
1   large tomato, chopped
2   tablespoons lemon juice
2   tablespoons chopped fresh or
    2 teaspoons dried basil
½   teaspoon salt
¼   teaspoon pepper

Season fish with 1 teaspoon salt and ½ teaspoon pepper. Spread cornmeal in a shallow dish; dredge fish in cornmeal.

Melt butter in a large skillet over medium-high heat; add fish, in batches, and cook 3 to 4 minutes on each side or until fish flakes with a fork. Remove fish from skillet, and keep warm. Pour off drippings and wipe skillet clean with a paper towel.

Heat oil in large skillet over medium-high heat. Add onion, and sauté 4 minutes. Add tomato, and cook 3 minutes, stirring often. Drain liquid from skillet. Stir in lemon juice, basil, ½ teaspoon salt, and ¼ teaspoon pepper. Spoon salsa over fish. Yield: 4 servings.

Cajun-Baked Catfish

2   cups cornmeal
1   tablespoon pepper
2   teaspoons salt
8   (4-ounce) catfish fillets
2   tablespoons Cajun seasoning
1   to 2 teaspoons seasoned salt
¼   cup butter or margarine, melted
Garnish: lemon wedges

Combine first 3 ingredients. Dredge catfish fillets in cornmeal mixture; place fillets, skin side down, on a greased baking sheet.

Combine Cajun seasoning and seasoned salt; sprinkle over fillets. Drizzle with butter.

Bake at 400° for 30 minutes or until golden and fish flakes with a fork. Garnish, if desired. Yield: 4 servings.

Spicy Catfish with Vegetables and Basil Cream

3   tablespoons butter, divided
1   (16-ounce) package frozen whole kernel corn, thawed
1   medium onion, chopped
1   medium-size green bell pepper, chopped
1   medium-size red bell pepper, chopped
¾   teaspoon salt
¾   teaspoon pepper
½   cup all-purpose flour
¼   cup yellow cornmeal
1   tablespoon Creole seasoning
4   (6- to 8-ounce) catfish fillets
⅓   cup buttermilk
1   tablespoon vegetable oil
½   cup whipping cream
2   tablespoons chopped fresh basil
Garnish: fresh basil sprigs

Melt 2 tablespoons butter in a large skillet over medium-high heat. Add corn, onion, and bell peppers; sauté 6 to 8 minutes or until tender. Stir in salt and pepper; spoon onto a serving dish, and keep warm.

Combine flour, cornmeal, and Creole seasoning in a large shallow dish. Dip fillets in buttermilk, and dredge in flour mixture.

Melt remaining 1 tablespoon butter with oil in skillet over medium-high heat. Cook fillets, in batches, 2 to 3 minutes on each side or until golden. Remove and arrange over vegetables.

Add cream to skillet, stirring to loosen particles from bottom of skillet. Add chopped basil, and cook, stirring often, 1 to 2 minutes or until thickened. Serve sauce with fillets and vegetables. Garnish, if desired. Yield: 4 servings.

Rock's Fried Catfish with Creole Tartar Sauce

½ teaspoon salt
¼ teaspoon freshly ground black pepper
¼ teaspoon ground red pepper
1 cup milk
2 tablespoons prepared mustard
3 tablespoons fresh lemon juice
⅛ teaspoon hot sauce
1 pound catfish fillets, cut into 1- x 3-inch strips
Vegetable oil
2 cups fish-fry mix (we tested with Zatarain's)
1 tablespoon cornstarch
1 onion, thinly sliced
Creole Tartar Sauce

Place first 7 ingredients in a large heavy-duty zip-top plastic bag. Add fish; seal and shake gently. Chill 1 hour.

Pour oil to depth of ¾ inch into a large heavy-duty skillet; heat to 350°.

Combine fish-fry mix and cornstarch in a separate large heavy-duty zip-top plastic bag. Remove fish from milk mixture. Place in bag in batches, and shake to coat.

Fry fish, in batches, in hot oil 2 to 3 minutes on each side or until golden. Drain on paper towels. Separate onion slices into rings, and place over fish. Serve immediately with Creole Tartar Sauce. Yield: 4 servings.

Creole Tartar Sauce

1 cup mayonnaise
1 tablespoon chopped fresh parsley
1 tablespoon chopped green onions
1 tablespoon Creole or whole-grain mustard
1 teaspoon chopped garlic
½ teaspoon hot sauce
¼ teaspoon freshly ground pepper
⅛ teaspoon salt

Combine all ingredients in a small bowl; cover and chill at least 1 hour. Yield: 1⅓ cups.
—Food Writer Marcelle Bienvenu
New Iberia, Louisiana

Rock's Fried Catfish with Creole Tartar Sauce

Fried Lemon-Rosemary Catfish

1 large lemon
¼ cup milk
2 large eggs, beaten
2 tablespoons chopped fresh rosemary
2 tablespoons minced fresh garlic
4 (4- to 6-ounce) catfish fillets
2 cups yellow cornmeal
¼ cup extra-virgin olive oil
Garnishes: lemon slices, fresh rosemary sprigs

Grate lemon rind from lemon into a large bowl, avoiding the bitter pith. Squeeze lemon juice into bowl. Stir in milk and next 3 ingredients until blended.

Rinse fillets, and pat dry with paper towels. Add fillets to lemon mixture in bowl; cover and chill 1 hour.

Place cornmeal on a large plate or in a large shallow dish. Turn fillets in lemon mixture until thoroughly coated; dredge in cornmeal, coating evenly.

Cook fillets in hot oil in a large nonstick skillet over medium-high heat 4 minutes on each side or until browned. Remove from skillet. Garnish, if desired. Yield: 4 servings.

Fish and Chips

1   cup all-purpose flour
1   teaspoon salt
1   large egg, separated
¼   cup flat beer, at room temperature
¼   cup milk or water
2   pounds russet potatoes
Peanut oil or lard
2   pounds fish fillets such as haddock, cod,
      flounder, or sole
Malt vinegar
Salt

About 1 hour before you plan to fry the fish, make the batter. Combine flour and 1 teaspoon salt in a mixing bowl. In another bowl, stir together egg yolk, beer, and milk. Pour into dry ingredients, stirring (but not beating) mixture well with a wire whisk. Cover and chill 30 minutes.

Cut potatoes into 3- x ⅜-inch sticks and place them in a bowl. Cover with cold water, and stir to help remove excess starch.

Pour oil to depth of 3 or 4 inches into a stockpot or Dutch oven; place over medium-high heat, and heat to 375°. Preheat oven to 200°. Place a wire rack on a baking sheet and set it in the oven.

Drain potatoes well. Rinse them under running water, and lay them out on a cloth towel, patting them completely dry. When oil reaches 375°, fry potatoes, in batches, until thoroughly browned, 8 to 10 minutes. Do not crowd pot, and carefully maintain temperature at 375°. As they are finished, transfer potatoes to wire rack to drain and stay warm.

While the last batch of potatoes is frying, beat egg white to soft peaks, and gently but thoroughly fold it into the batter. Rinse fish fillets, and pat dry. Using tongs, drop several pieces of fish into the batter; then transfer to hot oil. Each batch will take about 4 minutes. Maintain the heat at 375°. Serve hot, and pass malt vinegar and salt. Yield: 4 servings.
Excerpted from The Fearless Frying Cookbook. *Recipes © 1997 by John Martin Taylor. Illustrations © 1997 by Peter Alsberg. Used by permission of Workman Publishing Co., Inc., New York. All Rights Reserved.*

Southern Fried Fish and Hush Puppies

Peanut oil
1½   cups stone-ground corn flour*
2   teaspoons salt, divided
½   teaspoon freshly ground black pepper
¼   teaspoon ground red pepper
1   large egg
2   cups buttermilk
1¾   cups stone-ground whole-grain
      cornmeal
½   cup minced onion
1   teaspoon baking powder
1   teaspoon baking soda
3   pounds small whole red snapper, dressed
      (may use fillets)
Garnishes: lemon wedges, fresh parsley sprigs

Pour oil to depth of 1½ inches into a stockpot or Dutch oven. Place it over medium-high heat, and heat to 375°. Preheat oven to 200°. Place wire racks on baking sheets, and set aside.

While oil is heating, prepare coating for the fish. In a wide bowl, mix corn flour, 1 teaspoon salt, black pepper, and red pepper.

Prepare hush puppy batter. Combine egg and buttermilk in a medium-size bowl. Stir in cornmeal until well blended. Stir in onion.

Place remaining 1 teaspoon salt, baking powder, and baking soda in a small bowl, and set both bowls aside while you fry the fish.

When oil reaches 375°, dip each fish or fillet in the seasoned corn flour, coating it all over but shaking off any excess. Carefully lower each piece into hot oil. Fill pot but do not crowd it; oil should bubble up around each piece of fish. Maintain temperature between 365° and 375°. Fry fish until golden, about 2 to 3 minutes on each side, depending on the size of the pieces. Set aside any remaining corn flour.

Remove fish from oil in the same order that the pieces were immersed, using a wire-mesh strainer, tongs, or any tool that will allow you to hold fish over the pot so excess oil can drain. Immediately place pieces on a wire rack, and place in the oven to keep warm.

Continue frying until all of the fish are done, always waiting for the oil to return to the proper temperature before adding more. Then proceed with frying the hush puppies.

Add reserved baking powder mixture to hush puppy batter and mix well. Add leftover seasoned corn flour (¼ to ½ cup) to the batter, a little at a time, until batter is thick enough to be spooned.

Make sure oil has returned to 375°, and then drop batter by spoonfuls into hot oil, using 2 teaspoons: one to scoop up the batter and the other to scrape it off and into the oil. Fry hush puppies until golden all over, about 3 minutes, carefully monitoring the temperature of the oil. Drain, and place on a wire rack.

Repeat procedure until all batter is fried. Serve fish and hush puppies immediately. Garnish, if desired. Yield: 3 dozen.
Corn flour is the finest grind of cornmeal; in Louisiana it's called "fish fry." If you can't find it, you can make your own by grinding cornmeal in a blender or food processor.
Excerpted from The Fearless Frying Cookbook. *Recipes © 1997 by John Martin Taylor. Illustrations © 1997 by Peter Alsberg. Used by permission of Workman Publishing Co., Inc., New York. All Rights Reserved.*

Stuffed Flounder

A light crabmeat stuffing laced with country ham sits neatly inside the flounder.

½   cup unsalted butter
1   medium onion, chopped
1   celery rib, chopped
⅓   cup chopped red bell pepper
4   slices white bread, torn into pieces
    (about 2 cups)
¾   cup finely diced cooked country ham
2   large eggs, lightly beaten
1   pound fresh lump crabmeat, drained
¼   teaspoon salt
¼   teaspoon freshly ground pepper
1   tablespoon chopped fresh parsley
1   tablespoon sherry
4   (¾- to 1-pound) whole flounders,
    dressed
2   tablespoons fresh lemon juice
Garnish: celery leaves

Melt butter in a large skillet over medium heat; set aside ¼ cup. Add onion, celery, and red bell pepper to skillet; sauté 5 minutes or until onion mixture is tender. Remove from heat. Add bread and next 7 ingredients; toss gently.

Make a slit down the center of the top of the fish to the backbone. Slide the knife blade along the backbone on each side of the cut to open the cavity. Spoon crab mixture into cavity. Place fish on a lightly greased rack of a broiler pan.

Combine reserved ¼ cup butter and lemon juice; pour over fish.

Bake at 350° for 30 to 35 minutes or until fish flakes with a fork. Garnish, if desired. Yield: 4 servings.
Recipe reprinted with permission from Hoppin' John's Lowcountry Cooking *by John Martin Taylor (Bantam Books, 1992).*

Sautéed Flounder with Balsamic Brown Butter

1½ tablespoons chopped fresh chives
1   teaspoon chopped fresh tarragon
1   teaspoon fresh thyme leaves
4   (7-ounce) flounder or sole fillets
½   teaspoon salt
½   teaspoon freshly ground pepper
½   cup all-purpose flour
3   tablespoons vegetable oil
¼   cup butter
¼   cup balsamic vinegar

Combine first 3 ingredients. Set aside.

Season fillets with salt and pepper. Dredge fillets in flour.

Sauté fillets in hot oil in a large skillet, over medium-high heat, 3 to 5 minutes on each side or until lightly browned and fish flakes with a fork. Remove to warm plates; set aside, and keep warm.

Melt butter in a small skillet over medium-high heat. Swirl pan by the handle until butter turns golden brown. Remove from heat; stir in balsamic vinegar. Spoon balsamic browned butter over fillets. Sprinkle with fresh herbs. Yield: 4 servings.
Recipe reprinted with permission from Great Fish, Quick *by Leslie Revsin (Doubleday, 1997).*

Flounder à la North Carolina

¼   cup unsalted butter, divided
3   to 4 medium onions, chopped
1¼ teaspoons salt, divided
¾   teaspoon freshly ground pepper, divided
2   pounds fresh spinach
2   tablespoons fresh lemon juice
4   (6- to 7-ounce) flounder fillets
¼   cup dry white wine
¼   cup fish stock*
2   tablespoons chopped fresh parsley
Garnish: lemon wedges

Melt 2 tablespoons butter in a large skillet over medium heat; add onions and sauté 2 minutes. Cover and cook over low heat, stirring occasionally, about 25 minutes or until onions are translucent. Stir in ½ teaspoon salt and ½ teaspoon pepper; keep warm.

Wash spinach in cold water and drain; remove stems and chop leaves. (Do not pat dry.)

Cook spinach in a large nonaluminum saucepan over medium-high heat, stirring constantly, until spinach comes to a boil. Cover, reduce heat, and cook 5 minutes or until tender. Drain spinach; stir in ½ teaspoon salt and lemon juice. Keep warm.

Sprinkle fillets with remaining ¼ teaspoon salt and ¼ teaspoon pepper.

Melt remaining 2 tablespoons butter in a large skillet over medium heat; add fillets, wine, and fish stock. Cook 6 minutes or until opaque on one side; turn and cook 5 more minutes or until fish flakes with a fork. Serve over spinach. Top with sautéed onions; sprinkle with chopped parsley. Garnish, if desired. Yield: 4 servings.
*Fish broth, made with a fish bouillon cube, or clam juice may be substituted for fish stock. Excerpted from Great American Seafood Cookbook. *Recipes © 1988 by Susan Hermann Loomis. Used by permission of Workman Publishing Co., Inc., New York. All Rights Reserved.*

Flounder Broiled with Olive Oil, Mustard, and Dill

4   (7-ounce) flounder or sole fillets
¼   large lemon
½   teaspoon salt
½   teaspoon freshly ground pepper
¼   cup olive oil
3   tablespoons Dijon mustard
2   tablespoons chopped fresh or 1 teaspoon
    dried dillweed

Place fillets in a lightly greased broiler pan. Squeeze lemon juice over fillets; season with salt and pepper.

Gradually whisk olive oil into mustard; stir in dillweed. Spread mustard mixture over fillets.

Broil 5½ inches from heat 6 to 10 minutes or until fish flakes with a fork. Serve with pan juices. Yield: 4 servings.
Recipe reprinted with permission from Great Fish, Quick *by Leslie Revsin (Doubleday, 1997).*

Flounder with a Warm Sauce of Capers, Olives, and Tomatoes

4   (8-ounce) flounder fillets
½   teaspoon salt
½   teaspoon freshly ground pepper
½   cup all-purpose flour
½   cup vegetable oil
Caper, Olive, and Tomato Sauce
Garnishes: capers, lemon wedges, plum
       tomato wedges, ripe olives

Sprinkle fillets evenly with salt and pepper;
dredge in flour.

Sauté fillets in hot oil in a large skillet 3 to
5 minutes on each side or until golden and fish
flakes with a fork. Remove fish and drain on
paper towels. Serve fish in a pool of warm
Caper, Olive, and Tomato Sauce. Garnish, if
desired. Yield: 4 servings.

Caper, Olive, and Tomato Sauce

¼   cup dried tomatoes
¼   cup pitted ripe olives
2   tablespoons chopped fresh parsley
1   tablespoon capers
½   cup olive oil
4   plum tomatoes, chopped

Process first 4 ingredients in a food processor
until coarsely chopped. With processor running,
pour oil through food chute in a slow, steady
stream. Add tomatoes, and pulse until blended.
Yield: 2 cups.
From Fish Talking by Pino Luongo, © 1994
by Giuseppe Luongo. Used by permission of
Clarkson Potter/Publishers, a division of
Random House, Inc.

Hickory-Grilled Redfish with Crawfish Maque Choux

Hickory chips
8   (8-ounce) redfish fillets
½   cup butter, melted
2½   tablespoons Creole seasoning
Crawfish Maque Choux
Garnish: sliced green onions

Soak hickory chips in water to cover 30 minutes; drain. Set aside.

Lightly brush fillets with butter; sprinkle
both sides with Creole seasoning.

Prepare fire; let burn 10 to 15 minutes.
Place hickory chips over hot coals. Coat grill
grate with vegetable cooking spray; place on
grill. Arrange fillets on grate. Grill fish, covered
with grill lid, over medium heat (300° to 350°)
6 to 8 minutes or until fish flakes with a fork,
turning and basting once with remaining butter.
Serve over Crawfish Maque Choux. Garnish, if
desired. Yield: 8 servings.

Crawfish Maque Choux

16   ears fresh corn
¼   cup butter
1   large onion, diced
3   red bell peppers, diced
3   green bell peppers, diced
3   jalapeño peppers, minced
1½   pounds frozen crawfish tails,
       thawed, rinsed, and drained
¾   cup whipping cream
2½   teaspoons Creole seasoning
½   teaspoon salt

Cut off tips of corn kernels into a bowl; scrape
milk and remaining pulp from cob with a knife.

Melt butter in a Dutch oven over medium
heat; add onion, and sauté 5 minutes or until
tender. Add bell peppers, jalapeño pepper, and
corn; cook, stirring constantly, 10 minutes. Stir
in remaining ingredients. Bring to a boil; cover,
reduce heat, and simmer 10 minutes, stirring
often. Uncover and simmer 5 minutes, stirring
occasionally. Yield: 12 cups.
—Ralph Brennan/Chef Haley Gabel
Bacco
New Orleans, Louisiana

Bundles with Sole

*Tender sole fillets and flavored butter balls
are wrapped and baked in crisp phyllo
packages.*

½   cup butter, softened
1   tablespoon fresh lemon juice
2   teaspoons chopped fresh thyme
2   teaspoons capers
½   teaspoon salt
½   teaspoon freshly ground pepper
4   (4- to 6-ounce) sole fillets
¼   teaspoon salt
¼   teaspoon freshly ground pepper
8   sheets frozen phyllo pastry, thawed
Gourmet salad greens, optional

Stir together first 6 ingredients. Cover and chill
until firm.

Sprinkle fish fillets evenly with ¼ teaspoon
salt and ¼ teaspoon pepper. Divide chilled
butter mixture into 4 portions; shape each
portion into a ball. Place 1 ball of butter
mixture at end of each fillet; carefully roll up
fillets, keeping butter inside.

Unfold phyllo; cover with plastic wrap and
a damp towel to prevent drying. Place 1 sheet
of phyllo on a flat surface. Spray half of
phyllo sheet with vegetable cooking spray.
Fold sheet in half crosswise; spray again.
Repeat procedure with a second sheet of
phyllo; stack the phyllo sheets.

Place 1 fillet in the middle of stacked phyllo
sheets. Gather corners of sheets together to
form a bundle. Twist slightly; tie bundle with
kitchen twine. Spray bundle with cooking spray.
Place bundle on rack of a lightly greased broiler
pan. Repeat procedure with remaining phyllo
sheets and fillets.

Bake at 450° for 15 minutes or until
golden. Serve immediately with gourmet
salad greens, if desired. Yield: 4 servings.

Sesame Fried Fish

1½ to 2 pounds small snapper fillets
½ teaspoon salt
½ teaspoon freshly ground pepper
½ cup all-purpose flour
¼ cup sesame seeds
2 large eggs
1 tablespoon sesame oil or chile sesame oil
Peanut oil
Hot sauce
Garnish: fresh cilantro sprigs

Pat fish dry and season with salt and pepper. Spread flour on a piece of wax paper. Place each fillet in flour and coat both sides well. Shake off any excess. Add sesame seeds to remaining flour, and mix well.

Beat eggs and sesame oil in a large shallow container. Dip each fillet in egg mixture, then in the flour-sesame mixture, coating it well, and place on a large platter. Place the platter of coated fish in refrigerator for 10 minutes.

Preheat oven to 200°. Place a wire rack on a baking sheet and set it in the oven. Place 4 ovenproof plates in oven to warm.

Pour peanut oil into a large heavy skillet or sauté pan to a depth of ½ inch. Heat oil over medium-high heat until it is very hot but not smoking (375°). Just as the surface begins to ripple, take fish out of the refrigerator and place as many in the pan as will fit without crowding, flesh side down.

Fry fish 3 minutes on each side or until golden. Transfer cooked pieces onto the wire rack to stay warm. Divide fish among warmed plates, and splash them with hot sauce. Garnish, if desired. Serve immediately. Yield: 4 servings.
Excerpted from The Fearless Frying Cookbook. *Recipes © 1997 by John Martin Taylor. Illustrations © 1997 by Peter Alsberg. Used by permission of Workman Publishing Co., Inc., New York. All Rights Reserved.*

Red Snapper à la Creole

6 (8-ounce) red snapper fillets, skinned
½ teaspoon salt
½ teaspoon freshly ground pepper
2 tablespoons olive oil
1 teaspoon unsalted butter
Creole Tomato Sauce
½ cup slivered fresh basil leaves

Sprinkle fillets with salt and pepper.

Heat oil and butter in a large skillet over medium heat; sauté fillets 2 to 3 minutes on each side or until fish flakes with a fork. Remove fish, and drain on paper towels; keep warm.

Add Creole Tomato Sauce to skillet. Stir to incorporate any fish juices or browned bits remaining in the skillet. Serve snapper fillets with a generous amount of sauce; top with slivered basil leaves. Yield: 6 servings.

Creole Tomato Sauce

1 bunch green onions, sliced
2 celery ribs, diced
1 medium onion, chopped
1 small red bell pepper, diced
¼ cup olive oil
3 garlic cloves, minced
½ cup chopped fresh parsley
1½ teaspoons chili powder
1 teaspoon lemon zest
1 (28-ounce) can crushed tomatoes
1 cup dry red wine
½ cup pimiento-stuffed green olives, sliced
2 tablespoons capers, drained
½ teaspoon freshly ground pepper
¼ teaspoon sea salt

Sauté first 4 ingredients in ¼ cup hot olive oil in a large skillet over medium heat 5 minutes or until tender. Add garlic and next 3 ingredients; sauté 2 minutes. Add tomatoes and remaining ingredients. Bring sauce to a boil, stirring occasionally. Reduce heat and simmer, stirring occasionally, for 30 to 40 minutes or until thickened. Yield: 6 cups.
—*Cookbook Author Sarah Leah Chase*
Barnstable, Massachusetts

Sesame Fried Fish

Blackened Red Snapper

The success of the blackening technique depends on having well-chilled fish and a very hot skillet. Prepare only in a well-ventilated area.

1   pound unsalted butter
½   cup fresh lemon juice
2   tablespoons dried thyme
2   tablespoons dried basil
1½   tablespoons coarsely ground black
      pepper
2   teaspoons dried crushed red pepper
1   teaspoon kosher salt
6   (8-ounce) red snapper fillets, skinned
Garnishes: chopped fresh parsley, lemon
      wedges

Melt butter in a saucepan over low heat. Stir in lemon juice and next 5 ingredients. Cook over low heat 10 minutes; pour into a shallow dish.

Dip fillets in butter mixture, coating thoroughly. Place fillets on a platter; cover and chill at least 1 hour. Set aside remaining butter mixture.

Heat a large cast-iron skillet over high heat until a drop of water sizzles in the skillet. Add 2 fillets, and cook 2 minutes on each side or until fish flakes with a fork. Repeat procedure with remaining fillets.

Reduce heat; add remaining butter mixture to skillet, and stir well. Drizzle butter mixture over each serving. Garnish, if desired. Yield: 6 servings.

—Cookbook Author Sarah Leah Chase
Barnstable, Massachusetts

Cod Poached in Tomato-Saffron Broth

2   tablespoons olive oil
1   small onion, diced
2   garlic cloves, minced
2   (14½-ounce) cans diced tomatoes,
      drained
2   cups dry white wine
2   cups clam juice
Pinch of saffron
¼   teaspoon salt
¼   teaspoon freshly ground pepper
4   (6-ounce) cod or sablefish fillets

Cod Poached in Tomato-Saffron Broth

Heat oil in a 10-inch straight-sided skillet over medium-high heat; cook onion 5 minutes or until softened. Add garlic and next 4 ingredients; cook, covered, over medium heat 10 minutes. Stir in salt and pepper. Add cod to skillet; reduce heat until wine mixture just simmers.

Cover and poach cod 5 to 7 minutes or until fish flakes with a fork. Serve in bowls with broth spooned over fish. Yield: 4 servings.

vine advice

"Marques de Caceres Rioja Rosado is so cheap it seems impossible, but it's delicious, and perfect with the saffron-garlic-seafood flavors in this poached cod recipe. Chin up, and don't snob out; drink what tastes expensive, not what costs expensive," says Master Sommelier Andrea Immer.

Long before fish tacos became a favorite in five-star restaurants, they were the belles of Baja California Sur. Rolled out like beach blankets on the sand, portable stands—also known as taquerías—continue to serve as culinary convocation centers for surfers. Born from Baja basics—fresh corn tortillas and the peninsula's surfeit of seafood—the recipe was too simple to keep secret.

Beer-Battered Fish Tacos with Baja Sauce

Beer-Battered Fish Tacos with Baja Sauce

1   pound firm white fish fillets, cut into 1½-inch pieces
1   (12-ounce) bottle Mexican beer
1   tablespoon Mexican seasoning (we tested with Via Nueva Pico de Gallo seasoning)
Vegetable oil
1   cup all-purpose flour
1   teaspoon salt
1   teaspoon sugar
½   teaspoon baking powder
1   cup Mexican beer
½   teaspoon hot sauce
12   fresh corn tortillas, warmed
1   lime, cut into wedges
¾   cup (3 ounces) shredded queso blanco or Monterey Jack cheese
3   cups shredded green cabbage
½   red onion, cut into strips (about ½ cup)
Baja Sauce

Place fish in a large heavy-duty zip-top plastic bag. Combine 12 ounces beer and Mexican seasoning in a bowl, stirring well. Pour beer mixture over fish; seal. Chill 2 to 3 hours.

Pour oil to depth of 1½ inches into a deep skillet or Dutch oven; heat to 360°.

Combine flour and next 3 ingredients in a medium bowl. Whisk in 1 cup beer and hot sauce. Drain fish, discarding marinade. Coat fish in batter.

Cook fish, in batches, in hot oil about 4 minutes or until done. Drain on paper towels.

Place 2 to 3 pieces of fish on each tortilla. Squeeze lime wedges over fish; top with remaining ingredients. Serve immediately. Yield: 4 to 6 servings.

Baja Sauce

½   cup sour cream
½   cup mayonnaise
2   teaspoons Mexican seasoning (we tested with Via Nueva Pico de Gallo seasoning)
1   small jalapeño pepper, seeded and diced
½   cup chopped fresh cilantro
¼   cup fresh lime juice

Combine all ingredients in a bowl; stir well. Yield: 1½ cups.

Hickory-Grilled Fish Tacos with Mango-Avocado Relish

Hickory-Grilled Fish Tacos with Mango-Avocado Relish

Hickory or alder wood chips
2   pounds firm white fish fillets
2   tablespoons olive oil
½   teaspoon salt
½   teaspoon freshly ground pepper
12   (6½-inch) flour or red chile tortillas
Mango-Avocado Relish
Garnishes: thinly sliced red onion, fresh cilantro leaves, lime wedges

Soak hickory chips in water to cover 30 minutes; drain. Wrap chips in heavy-duty aluminum foil; make several holes in foil. Set aside.

Brush fillets with oil; sprinkle with salt and pepper.

Light gas grill; place foil-wrapped chips directly on hot coals on one side. Coat grill grate on opposite side with vegetable cooking spray, and place on grill. Let grill preheat 10 to 15 minutes; turn off burner opposite wood chips. Arrange fillets on grate opposite wood chips, and grill, covered with grill lid, over medium heat (300° to 350°) 10 minutes on each side or until fish flakes with a fork.

Wrap flour tortillas in heavy-duty aluminum foil. Place on grill during last 5 minutes of cooking time to warm.

Serve immediately with Mango-Avocado Relish. Garnish, if desired. Yield: 6 servings.

Mango-Avocado Relish

2   avocados, chopped
1   mango, peeled, seeded, and chopped (about 1 cup)
½   cup chopped red bell pepper
½   cup chopped jicama
¼   cup fresh lime juice
2   tablespoons chopped fresh cilantro
1   teaspoon sugar
½   teaspoon salt
½   teaspoon ground cumin

Combine all ingredients in a large bowl, tossing to coat. Cover and chill. Yield: 2 cups.

Parsley-Crusted Cod with
Sauce Dijonnaise

Parsley-Crusted Cod with Sauce Dijonnaise

1   cup whipping cream
3   tablespoons Dijon mustard, divided
1/8 teaspoon salt
1/8 teaspoon pepper
4   (6-ounce) cod fillets
1/4 teaspoon salt
1/4 teaspoon pepper
1/4 cup soft breadcrumbs
1/4 cup chopped fresh parsley
2   garlic cloves, minced
2   tablespoons butter or margarine,
     melted
Steamed fresh asparagus spears
Garnishes: chopped fresh parsley, fresh
     parsley sprigs, whipped potatoes, fresh
     squash slices, pear-shaped red cherry
     tomatoes

Combine whipping cream, 2 tablespoons mustard, 1/8 teaspoon salt, and 1/8 teaspoon pepper in a small saucepan. Cook over medium heat, stirring constantly, 10 minutes or until slightly thickened. Remove from heat, and set aside.

Sprinkle fish with 1/4 teaspoon salt and 1/4 teaspoon pepper, and brush top with remaining 1 tablespoon mustard.

Stir together breadcrumbs, parsley, and garlic; press evenly onto fillet tops. Brush a 13- x 9-inch pan with melted butter; add fillets.

Bake at 425° for 10 minutes or until fish flakes with a fork. Serve with mustard sauce and steamed asparagus. Garnish, if desired. Yield: 4 servings.

—Chef/Owner Albert J. Bouchard III
Restaurant Bouchard
Newport, Rhode Island

Heavenly Broiled Grouper

2   pounds grouper fillets
1/2 cup grated Parmesan cheese
3   tablespoons chopped green onions
3   tablespoons mayonnaise
1   tablespoon butter or margarine, softened
1   garlic clove, pressed
1/4 teaspoon salt
Dash of hot sauce

Place fillets in a single layer in a lightly greased 13- x 9-inch pan. Stir together cheese and remaining ingredients; spread over fillets.

Broil 5 1/2 inches from heat 10 minutes or until lightly browned and fish flakes with a fork. Yield: 6 to 8 servings.

Grilled Herbed Grouper

1   (1 1/2-pound) grouper fillet
2   teaspoons olive oil
1/2 teaspoon salt
1/4 teaspoon pepper
1   cup fine, dry breadcrumbs
1/3 cup minced fresh parsley or 3 tablespoons
     dried parsley flakes
1   tablespoon minced fresh or 1 teaspoon
     dried basil
1   tablespoon minced fresh or 1 teaspoon
     dried thyme
Garnishes: fresh basil sprigs, fresh thyme
     sprigs, lemon slices

Brush fillet with oil; sprinkle with salt and pepper.

Stir together breadcrumbs and next 3 ingredients; press onto all sides of fillet. Place fillet in a lightly greased grill basket.

Grill fillet, covered with grill lid, over medium heat (300° to 350°) 7 to 8 minutes on each side or until fish flakes with a fork. Garnish, if desired. Yield: 3 to 4 servings.

Grouper Fingers

Cracker crumbs make a crisp coating for these fish fingers that kids will enjoy.

1 1/4 pounds grouper fillets (or any firm white
     fish)
1/2 cup all-purpose flour
1/2 teaspoon salt
1/4 teaspoon pepper
3   large eggs, lightly beaten
1 1/2 cups saltine cracker crumbs (about 30
     saltine crackers)
Vegetable oil
Tropical Tartar Sauce

Cut fish into 3- x 1/2-inch strips.

Combine flour, salt, and pepper. Dredge fish in flour mixture, shaking off excess. Dip in egg, and roll in cracker crumbs, shaking off excess crumbs. Place on a baking sheet. Cover and chill at least 1 hour.

Pour oil to depth of 2 inches into a Dutch oven. Heat to 375°. Fry fish fingers, in batches, in hot oil 2 minutes or until golden. Drain on paper towels. Serve immediately with Tropical Tartar Sauce. Yield: 6 servings.

Tropical Tartar Sauce

1 1/4 cups mayonnaise
3   tablespoons diced mango
2   tablespoons diced gherkin pickles
2   tablespoons lime juice
1   tablespoon diced onion
1   teaspoon gherkin pickle juice
1/2 teaspoon salt
1/4 teaspoon pepper

Combine all ingredients. Yield: 1 1/4 cups.

Alma's Striped Bass Seviche

1   pound striped bass or halibut, thinly
     sliced
1   red onion, halved and thinly sliced
2   Anaheim chiles, seeded and thinly sliced
2½ cups fresh grapefruit juice
1   cup fresh lime juice
½   cup dry sparkling wine
⅓   cup fresh lemon juice
1   tablespoon ground coriander
1   teaspoon ground cumin
½   teaspoon salt
½   teaspoon freshly ground pepper

Combine all ingredients in a stainless steel or
glass bowl. Cover and refrigerate 2 hours or
until fish is firm and opaque. Using a slotted
utensil, spoon into individual glasses. Serve
with crackers or crostini. Yield: 6 servings.
—Chef/Owner Johnny Alamilla
Alma Restaurant
San Francisco, California

Seafood lovers across the country are falling for the raw power of seviche, the cocktail of Nuevo Latino cuisine.

Seviche (pronounced "seh-VEE-chay" and also spelled ceviche and cebiche) is nothing new. While the raw food craze has just started sweeping across the United States, Latin Americans have been enjoying seviche for centuries. Cooks in kitchens from Central to South America prepare simple versions, bathing seafood in an acidic marinade such as lime juice or vinegar. This process cures the fish—firming its flesh and turning it opaque in the process.

In Mexico, every state has its own version. It's all about using the freshest fish and pairing each with the right seasonings. "The San Francisco Bay Area has an abundance of seafood and therefore a surplus of great sushi restaurants," says Chef Johnny Alamilla. "Some people can't handle 100 percent raw fish; seviche's the perfect alternative."

Many chefs serve seviche in martini glasses, elevating the seafood arrangements and surrounding them with such dipping tools as tostadas and corn tortillas.

While seviche is a refreshing creation, the fish isn't *really* cooked, so handling raw seafood must be done with care and caution. Buy the very best and freshest seafood from a reliable fish market, handle the seafood properly (keep it on ice in the refrigerator), and serve it the same day.

vine advice

When it comes to seviche, "no wine is ever in complete harmony with so much citrus and onion coming into play," says Virginia Philip, chef sommelier at The Breakers in Palm Beach, Florida. "However, wines with high acidity do adapt well. They are crisp and clean on the palate, enhancing flavors." Virginia selected these wines to accompany the following seviche recipes.
- **Alma's Striped Bass Seviche** Goldwater Dog Point Marlborough Sauvignon Blanc, New Zealand
- **Seviche de Veracruz** Gunderloch Riesling *Kabinett* Jean Baptiste, Germany

Seviche de Veracruz

Seviche de Veracruz

1	pound halibut or red snapper, cut into ¹⁄₂-inch cubes
¹⁄₂	cup fresh lime juice
1	small red onion, diced
2	tomatoes, seeded and diced
2	jalapeño peppers, seeded and finely chopped
¹⁄₂	cup loosely packed fresh oregano, chopped
¹⁄₂	cup small pitted black or green olives
¹⁄₂	cup fresh orange juice
¹⁄₂	cup tomato juice
¹⁄₄	cup extra-virgin olive oil
1	tablespoon fresh lime juice
1	teaspoon salt
¹⁄₂	teaspoon freshly ground pepper

Garnishes: olives, lettuce leaves, or tortilla chips

Combine fish and ¹⁄₂ cup lime juice in a stainless steel or glass bowl. Cover and refrigerate 30 minutes. (The fish will overcure and have a mushy texture if you exceed 30 minutes.) Drain and discard juice.

Stir in onion and next 10 ingredients. Cover and refrigerate 1 hour or overnight. Serve in chilled glasses or on lettuce-lined plates, and garnish, if desired. Yield: 4 to 6 servings.

—Mary Sue Milliken and Susan Feniger
Border Grill
Santa Monica, California

Beer-Boiled "Spot Prawns"

2   quarts beer
1   teaspoon dried thyme
1   teaspoon dried crushed red pepper
½   teaspoon whole cloves
½   teaspoon fennel seeds
2   bay leaves
2   pounds unpeeled, jumbo fresh shrimp or
    prawns
Ice cubes

Bring first 6 ingredients to a boil in a Dutch oven. Add shrimp, and cook 2 minutes or until shrimp turn pink. Drain. Discard bay leaves. Chill shrimp, and serve with cocktail sauce. Yield: 4 servings.

Note: To speed chilling time, toss shrimp with ice cubes.

© 1997 by Greg Atkinson. All rights reserved. Excerpted from In Season by permission of Sasquatch Books.

Shrimp and Sausage Pilau

1   pound unpeeled, large fresh shrimp
6   bacon slices
2   medium onions, chopped
2   garlic cloves, minced
1   (16-ounce) package kielbasa sausage,
    cut into 1-inch pieces
2   cups uncooked long-grain rice
1   (32-ounce) container chicken broth
½   teaspoon salt
½   teaspoon freshly ground pepper

Peel shrimp, leaving 6 or 8 with tails on; devein, if desired.

Cook bacon in a large Dutch oven until crisp; remove bacon, reserving 2 tablespoons drippings in pan. Drain bacon on paper towels; crumble and set aside.

Sauté 6 to 8 shrimp with tails on in hot bacon drippings 3 minutes or until shrimp turn pink. Remove from Dutch oven; set aside. Add onion and garlic; sauté 5 minutes or until tender. Add sausage, and cook 5 minutes or until sausage is browned. Add rice, and cook, stirring constantly, 3 to 4 minutes or until rice is coated with drippings. Stir in 2 cups chicken broth, salt, and pepper; bring to a boil, stirring

constantly. Cover, reduce heat, and simmer 10 minutes. Add 1 cup broth, and cook, covered, 15 minutes, adding additional broth, if necessary.

Arrange uncooked shrimp evenly over rice mixture in Dutch oven. Cover and cook 5 minutes; toss gently. Top with reserved shrimp with tails. Remove from heat; cover and let stand 5 minutes. Sprinkle with bacon. Yield: 6 to 8 servings.

Creole Shrimp Pot Pies

1   (11-ounce) package piecrust mix (we
    tested with Betty Crocker)
½   (5-ounce) jar sharp process cheese
    spread (we tested with Kraft Old English
    Cheese)
2½ teaspoons Creole seasoning, divided
½   cup ice water
10 plum tomatoes, halved and seeded
1   pound unpeeled, medium-size fresh shrimp
½   pound andouille sausage, thinly sliced
1   small onion, chopped
1   small green bell pepper, chopped
2   celery ribs, chopped
3   garlic cloves, minced
1   (6-ounce) can tomato paste
¼   teaspoon salt
¼   teaspoon freshly ground pepper

Combine piecrust mix, cheese spread, and 1 teaspoon Creole seasoning with a pastry blender until crumbly. Sprinkle ½ cup water, 1 tablespoon at a time, evenly over surface; stir with a fork until dry ingredients are moistened. Shape into a ball. Chill 30 minutes.

Place tomatoes, cut side down, on a 15- x 10-inch jellyroll pan lined with aluminum foil. Broil 5½ inches from heat 14 to 16 minutes or until skin is charred; cool. Remove and discard skins, reserving tomatoes and liquid; coarsely chop tomatoes. Set aside.

Peel shrimp; devein, if desired. Set aside.

Cook sausage and next 4 ingredients in a large nonstick skillet over medium-high heat 7 minutes. Stir in tomato paste. Stir in roasted tomato with liquid, remaining 1½ teaspoons Creole seasoning, salt, and pepper; bring just to a simmer. Add shrimp, and cook over medium heat just until shrimp turn pink.

(Do not overcook.) Spoon mixture evenly into 4 (1½- to 2-cup) ungreased ovenproof bowls.

Divide piecrust dough into 4 portions. Roll each portion into 6½-inch circles on a lightly floured surface. Place dough over bowls. (Dough should overlap bowl slightly.) Place bowls on a large baking sheet. Bake at 425° for 25 to 30 minutes or until pastry is golden. Yield: 4 servings.

Tequila Shrimp and Citrus

Tequila Shrimp and Citrus

1½ pounds unpeeled, large fresh shrimp
¼   cup tequila
2   tablespoons chopped fresh cilantro
2   tablespoons frozen orange juice
    concentrate, thawed
2   tablespoons fresh lime juice
2   garlic cloves, minced
1   jalapeño pepper, seeded and minced
½   teaspoon salt
1   red bell pepper, cut into 1-inch pieces
1   orange, cut into ½-inch wedges
1   lime, cut into ½-inch wedges

Peel shrimp, leaving tails intact, and devein, if desired.

Stir together tequila and next 6 ingredients in a large bowl. Add shrimp; cover and chill 30 minutes.

Alternately thread shrimp, bell pepper, and orange and lime wedges onto 8 (10- to 12-inch) skewers.

Grill, covered with grill lid, over medium-high heat (350° to 400°) 5 to 6 minutes on each side or until done. Yield: 4 servings.

Barbecued Shrimp

1½ cups Worcestershire sauce
2 to 3 tablespoons Creole seasoning
2 to 3 tablespoons cracked pepper
2 to 3 tablespoons freshly ground
   pepper
1 garlic clove, minced
3 pounds unpeeled, large or jumbo fresh
   shrimp, with heads on
4 lemons, cut in half
¼ cup water
1 pound butter, cut into pieces

Stir together first 5 ingredients.
   Place shrimp in a large Dutch oven; pour
Worcestershire sauce mixture over shrimp.

Squeeze lemons over shrimp mixture; add
squeezed lemon halves and ¼ cup water to
shrimp mixture. Bring to a boil over high heat,
stirring frequently; cook, uncovered, 6 minutes
or just until shrimp turn pink, stirring frequently.
Remove from heat. Gradually add butter, stirring until butter melts. Serve hot with crusty
French bread. Yield: 10 appetizer servings or
6 main-dish servings.
                    —Ralph Brennan/Chef Haley Gabel
                                              Bacco
                              New Orleans, Louisiana

Seafood Plateau

Seafood Plateau

7   cups water, divided
2   pounds unpeeled, large fresh shrimp
1   cup dry white wine
3   pounds fresh New Zealand green-lipped
     mussels, scrubbed and debearded
10   pounds crushed ice
3   pounds fresh oysters, opened in the half
     shell
2   pounds cooked crab claws, shells
     partially removed
Garnish: lemon wedges
Thai Peanut Sauce
Horseradish Cocktail Sauce
Creamy Mustard-Horseradish Sauce
Soy-Wasabi Sauce

Bring 6 cups water to a boil; add shrimp, and
cook 3 to 5 minutes or just until shrimp turn
pink. Drain and rinse with cold water; peel
shrimp, and devein, if desired, leaving tails
intact.

Bring 1 cup water and wine to a boil in a
Dutch oven. Add mussels; cover and return
to a boil. Boil 4 to 5 minutes. Immediately
remove open mussels with a slotted spoon.
Continue cooking remaining mussels 2 to 3
minutes; others may open. Discard any
unopened mussels.

Stack 3 graduated trays or pizza pans and
2 graduated cake pedestals, using the largest
tray as a base and ending with the smallest;
secure trays with floral clay. Mound trays with
ice. Arrange seafood over ice. Garnish, if
desired. Serve immediately with sauces. Yield:
12 appetizer servings.

Thai Peanut Sauce

1/2   cup chunky peanut butter
1/4   cup minced onion
1   small garlic clove, pressed
1/3   cup water
2   tablespoons soy sauce
1   tablespoon fresh lemon juice
1   tablespoon honey
1   teaspoon vegetable oil

Process all ingredients in a food processor
until smooth, stopping to scrape down sides.
Yield: 1 cup.

Horseradish Cocktail Sauce

2 (12-ounce) bottles cocktail sauce
1 tablespoon prepared horseradish

Stir together cocktail sauce and horseradish; cover and chill. Yield: 2 cups.

Creamy Mustard-Horseradish Sauce

1 (8-ounce) container light sour cream
2 tablespoons Dijon mustard
1 to 1½ tablespoons prepared horseradish

Stir together all ingredients; cover and chill. Yield: 1 cup.

Soy-Wasabi Sauce

¾ cup soy sauce
1 tablespoon wasabi powder

Stir together soy sauce and wasabi powder; cover and chill. Yield: ¾ cup.

—Food Stylist Susan Brown Draudt
La Canada, California

Coconut-Macadamia Nut Shrimp

2 cups all-purpose flour
½ cup ground macadamia nuts
1 (12-ounce) bottle beer, divided
2 egg yolks
2 tablespoons vegetable oil
2 tablespoons cream of coconut
1 teaspoon salt, divided
1 teaspoon freshly ground pepper, divided
18 unpeeled, jumbo fresh shrimp
1 tablespoon lime juice
1 garlic clove, minced
2 cups flaked coconut
Vegetable oil

Combine flour and macadamia nuts in a large bowl; make a well in center of flour mixture.

Combine half of beer, egg yolks, 2 tablespoons oil, and cream of coconut; add to dry ingredients, stirring just until moistened. Stir in remaining half of beer, ½ teaspoon salt, and ½ teaspoon pepper until smooth.

Peel shrimp, and devein, if desired, leaving tails intact. Combine remaining ½ teaspoon salt, remaining ½ teaspoon pepper, lime juice, and garlic in a large bowl; add shrimp, tossing to coat. Cover and chill 30 minutes.

Dip shrimp in batter; dredge in coconut.

Pour oil to depth of 2 inches into a Dutch oven; heat to 375°. Fry shrimp 6 to 8 minutes or until golden; drain. Yield: 6 servings.
From the book The Sugar Mill Caribbean Cookbook, *by Jinx and Jefferson Morgan © 1999. Reprinted with permission from The Harvard Common Press.*

Baked Italian Shrimp

Baked Italian Shrimp

⅔ cup fine, dry breadcrumbs
½ cup grated Parmesan cheese
¼ cup chopped fresh parsley
2 pounds unpeeled, large fresh shrimp
2 teaspoons minced fresh garlic
½ teaspoon seasoned salt
½ teaspoon freshly ground pepper
¼ cup olive oil

Combine breadcrumbs, cheese, and parsley in a shallow dish; set aside.

Peel shrimp, leaving tails intact, and devein, if desired. Place in a large bowl. Sprinkle shrimp with garlic, seasoned salt, and pepper. Drizzle with olive oil; toss gently.

Dredge shrimp in breadcrumb mixture. Arrange shrimp in an even layer on 2 greased 15- x 10-inch jellyroll pans.

Bake at 400° for 15 to 20 minutes, stirring twice. Yield: 12 servings.

—Caroline Coleman Bailey
Tiburon, California

Creamy Shrimp and Scallops Casserole

16 frozen phyllo pastry sheets, thawed
2½ pounds unpeeled, medium-size fresh shrimp
2 (10-ounce) packages frozen chopped spinach, thawed
5 tablespoons butter, divided
2 garlic cloves, minced
1 pound fresh bay scallops
1 (8-ounce) package cream cheese, softened
1 (8-ounce) container sour cream
⅓ cup shredded Parmesan cheese
1 teaspoon salt
½ teaspoon ground red pepper
¼ cup all-purpose flour
2 cups half-and-half

Cut phyllo sheets into 13- x 9-inch rectangles; reserve half of phyllo sheets, keeping covered with a damp towel to prevent drying out. Stack remaining 8 sheets in a lightly greased 13- x 9-inch baking dish, lightly coating each sheet with vegetable cooking spray.

Bake on lowest oven rack at 400° for 5 minutes or until lightly browned; set aside.

Peel shrimp, and devein, if desired.

Drain spinach well, pressing between paper towels.

Melt 1 tablespoon butter in a large skillet over medium heat; add garlic, and sauté 2 minutes. Add shrimp and scallops; cook 5 minutes or just until shrimp turn pink. Stir in cream cheese and next 4 ingredients until blended; remove from heat. Stir in spinach.

Melt remaining ¼ cup butter in a large saucepan over medium heat. Add flour, whisking constantly; cook, whisking constantly, 1 minute. Gradually add 2 cups half-and-half; cook, whisking constantly, 3 minutes or until thickened. Stir white sauce into shrimp mixture. Spoon into prepared baking dish.

Stack reserved phyllo sheets, coating each sheet with cooking spray. Roll up, jellyroll fashion, starting at long end, and cut into ¼-inch slices. Unroll each piece, and gently twist; arrange twists in a diamond pattern over casserole.

Bake at 400° for 14 minutes or until golden. Let stand 10 minutes. Yield: 8 servings.

Sesame-Crusted Scallops with Asian Vinaigrette

1¼ pounds sea scallops
¼ teaspoon salt
¼ teaspoon freshly ground pepper
⅓ cup sesame seeds
2 tablespoons peanut oil
1 medium-size red bell pepper, cut into thin strips
Leaf lettuce
3 green onions, sliced
Garnish: whole green onions
Asian Vinaigrette

Rinse scallops and pat dry; sprinkle with salt and pepper, and dredge in sesame seeds.

Heat 1 tablespoon oil in a large skillet over medium-high heat; add half of scallops, and cook 3 minutes on each side or until done. Repeat procedure with remaining scallops and oil.

Arrange red pepper strips and scallops over lettuce. Sprinkle with sliced green onions. Garnish, if desired. Serve with Asian Vinaigrette. Yield: 4 servings.

Asian Vinaigrette

¼ cup minced red onion
¼ cup rice wine vinegar
¼ cup peanut oil
3 tablespoons soy sauce
2½ tablespoons dark sesame oil
2 garlic cloves, minced
2 teaspoons sugar
2 teaspoons grated fresh ginger

Combine all ingredients in a jar; cover tightly. Shake vigorously. Yield: 1 cup.

Balsamic-Glazed Scallops

Balsamic-Glazed Scallops

2 cups water
1 tablespoon balsamic vinegar
½ teaspoon salt
1 cup uncooked long-grain rice
2 tablespoons all-purpose flour
½ teaspoon salt
¼ teaspoon pepper
2 pounds sea scallops
2 tablespoons olive oil
⅓ cup balsamic vinegar
3 tablespoons honey
1 teaspoon dried marjoram or oregano
Garnish: fresh chives with blossoms

Bring first 3 ingredients to a boil in a medium saucepan. Add rice; cover, reduce heat, and simmer 20 minutes or until water is absorbed and rice is tender. Remove from heat; set aside.

Combine flour, ½ teaspoon salt, and pepper in a pieplate; dredge scallops in flour mixture. Sauté scallops, in batches, in hot oil in a large nonstick skillet over medium-high heat 5 minutes. Remove scallops from skillet; set aside.

Add ⅓ cup vinegar, honey, and marjoram to skillet; bring to a boil. Reduce heat to medium, and cook 3 minutes. Add scallops, and cook 2 minutes or until thoroughly heated. Serve over rice. Garnish, if desired. Yield: 4 servings.

Shrimp and Scallops Mornay

1   cup butter or margarine, divided
¼   cup minced shallots
2   (8-ounce) packages fresh mushrooms, sliced
1   tablespoon lemon juice
1½   pounds unpeeled, large fresh shrimp
1½   pounds sea scallops
2½   cups half-and-half
⅓   cup all-purpose flour
⅔   cup grated Parmesan cheese
3   tablespoons dry sherry
1   teaspoon Dijon mustard
½   teaspoon salt
¼   teaspoon ground white pepper
Pinch of ground nutmeg
⅔   cup shredded Swiss cheese

Melt 6 tablespoons butter in a Dutch oven over low heat; add shallots, and sauté 1 minute. Increase heat to high. Add mushrooms and lemon juice, and sauté until mushrooms are just tender. Transfer to a bowl.

Peel shrimp; devein, if desired.

Melt 4 tablespoons butter in Dutch oven over medium heat; add shrimp, and sauté 3 to 5 minutes or just until shrimp turn pink. Add to mushroom mixture.

Bring scallops and half-and-half to a boil in a large saucepan over medium-high heat.

Reduce heat, and simmer, stirring often, 3 to 5 minutes or until scallops are opaque. Pour through a wire-mesh strainer into a small bowl; add scallops to mushroom mixture. Reserve half-and-half.

Drain any liquid from mushroom mixture. Add liquid to reserved half-and-half.

Melt remaining 6 tablespoons butter in Dutch oven over low heat; whisk in flour until smooth. Cook, whisking constantly, 1 minute. Gradually add half-and-half mixture; cook over medium heat, whisking constantly, until mixture is thickened and bubbly. Add Parmesan cheese and next 5 ingredients; cook, whisking constantly, 3 minutes or until cheese melts and sauce is smooth. Remove from heat; stir in mushroom mixture.

Spoon into 10 lightly greased shell-shaped baking dishes or individual serving bowls, and sprinkle evenly with shredded Swiss cheese.

Place on 2 (15- x 10-inch) jellyroll pans. Broil 5½ inches from heat 8 minutes or until Swiss cheese is golden and mixture is bubbly. Serve hot. Yield: 10 servings.
Note: *Mixture may be prepared a day ahead and chilled. Broil just before serving.*

Scallops in Coconut-Basil Sauce

2   (14-ounce) cans unsweetened coconut milk
¼   cup fresh lime juice
1   tablespoon grated fresh ginger
¼   teaspoon ground red pepper
2   pounds sea scallops
2   tablespoons chopped fresh basil
1   tablespoon fish sauce

Combine first 4 ingredients in a 12-inch straight-sided skillet; bring to a boil. Reduce heat to medium-low or until mixture simmers. Add scallops; cover and poach at a light simmer, adjusting heat as necessary, for 8 minutes or until scallops turn opaque.

Using a slotted spoon, remove scallops from skillet; place in a shallow dish or individual serving bowls. Cover with foil. Boil coconut-milk mixture over high heat, uncovered, 10 to 15 minutes or until reduced to 1½ cups. Stir in basil and fish sauce; spoon over scallops. Yield: 4 servings.

vine advice

Andrea Immer, master sommelier and dean of wine studies at The French Culinary Institute in New York City, selects wines to pair with Scallops in Coconut-Basil Sauce.

"Coconut milk has the lushness and tropical richness that begs for **California Chardonnay**. It's the flavor combo. **Gallo of Sonoma** is the best-tasting deal on the market, or go with **St. Francis** or **Cambria**."

Scallops in Coconut-Basil Sauce

Linguine with Bay Scallops

6   tablespoons butter or margarine, divided
1   pound bay scallops
1½ cups whipping cream
½   teaspoon salt
⅛   teaspoon ground nutmeg
⅛   teaspoon ground red pepper
1   cup freshly grated Parmesan cheese
⅓   cup chopped fresh or 1 tablespoon
    dried basil
⅓   cup chopped fresh chives
⅓   cup chopped fresh parsley
1   tablespoon grated lemon rind
16 ounces linguine, cooked

Melt 2 tablespoons butter in a Dutch oven; add scallops, and sauté 3 minutes. Remove with a slotted spoon; set aside.

Combine remaining 4 tablespoons butter, whipping cream, and next 3 ingredients in Dutch oven; bring to a boil over medium heat. Reduce heat, and simmer, whisking often, 15 minutes or until slightly reduced. Whisk in cheese and next 3 ingredients; simmer, whisking often, 5 minutes. Stir in scallops; simmer 1 minute. Stir in lemon rind; remove from heat.

Stir half of scallop mixture into hot cooked pasta; top with remaining scallop mixture. Yield: 6 servings.

Macadamia-Herb-Crusted Soft-Shell Crabs

½   cup fresh Italian parsley
¼   cup macadamia nuts
2   tablespoons fresh oregano
1   garlic clove
¾   cup fine, dry breadcrumbs
½   teaspoon salt
1   cup milk
2   large eggs
6   soft-shell crabs, dressed
1   cup all-purpose flour
2   tablespoons olive oil
½   cup dry white wine
¼   cup heavy whipping cream
2   tablespoons butter or margarine

Process first 4 ingredients in a food processor until finely chopped. (Do not overprocess

because nuts will become oily.) Stir in breadcrumbs and salt; set aside.

Combine milk and eggs.

Dredge crabs in flour; dip in milk mixture, and coat with nut mixture.

Sauté crabs in oil in a large skillet 2 to 3 minutes on each side. Remove and keep warm.

Add wine to skillet. Cook over medium-high heat until wine is reduced by half. Stir in whipping cream, and cook until hot and slightly thickened. Remove from heat, and stir in butter. Serve immediately with soft-shell crabs. Yield: 3 servings.

Soft-Shell Crabs with Asian Flavor

1   cup milk
2   large eggs
8   soft-shell crabs, dressed
¾   cup Oriental or chicken broth
2   tablespoons fresh lime juice
2   tablespoons tamari or soy sauce
1   tablespoon cornstarch
1   tablespoon chile garlic paste
1   teaspoon chopped fresh ginger
1   teaspoon sesame oil
½   cup all-purpose flour
¼   cup sesame seeds
½   teaspoon salt
¼   teaspoon pepper
¼   cup peanut oil
1   tablespoon chopped fresh cilantro
Hot cooked rice noodles or rice (optional)

Combine milk and eggs in a shallow dish. Add crabs, tossing to coat. Cover and chill 30 minutes.

Combine broth and next 6 ingredients; set aside. Combine flour and next 3 ingredients.

Drain crabs; dredge in flour mixture.

Sauté crabs in hot oil in a large skillet 2 minutes on each side or until done; drain on paper towels, discarding oil. Wipe skillet clean.

Add broth mixture to skillet; bring to a boil over medium-high heat. Boil 1 minute; stir in cilantro. Serve with crabs over cooked rice noodles, if desired. Yield: 8 appetizer servings or 4 main-dish servings.

Soft-Shell Crabs Bayou with Yellow Tomato Coulis

½   cup finely chopped green bell pepper
2   shallots, finely diced
1   garlic clove, minced
1   tablespoon olive oil
6   large yellow tomatoes, peeled, seeded,
    and chopped
½   teaspoon salt
¼   teaspoon ground black pepper
1½ tablespoons paprika
1   teaspoon salt
1   teaspoon garlic powder
1   teaspoon onion powder
1   teaspoon dried thyme
½   teaspoon ground white pepper
½   teaspoon ground red pepper
¼   teaspoon ground black pepper
8   soft-shell crabs, dressed
¼   cup butter or margarine, melted and
    divided
Hot cooked angel hair pasta

Sauté green pepper, shallots, and garlic in oil. Stir in tomato, salt, and pepper; cook 2 to 3 minutes. Set tomato coulis aside.

Combine paprika and next 7 ingredients. Brush crabs with 2 tablespoons melted butter, and coat with seasoning mixture.

Cook crabs in a hot nonstick skillet 1 to 2 minutes on each side or until done. Serve on pasta with tomato coulis. Drizzle with remaining butter. Yield: 4 servings.

Chilled Cracked Dungeness Crab with Sea Salt Butter and Ginger Mayonnaise

2   gallons water
2   lemons, thickly sliced
5   bay leaves
2   tablespoons sea salt
6   live Dungeness crabs (about 2½ pounds
      each)
Lemon wedges
Sea Salt Butter
Ginger Mayonnaise

Combine first 4 ingredients in an extra-large
kettle or soup pot; bring to a boil over high
heat. Add crabs to boiling water; cover and
boil 12 to 15 minutes or until crabs turn
bright red.

Rinse crabs quickly with cold water; drain
well, and cool. Remove top shell from crabs;
reserve for garnish, if desired. Clean crabs,
removing gray gills and mouth parts; break in
half. Cover and chill. Serve with lemon wedges,
Sea Salt Butter, and Ginger Mayonnaise. Yield:
6 servings.

Note: If you aren't sure the crabs are done,
pull off a top shell and look at the meat; it
should be white and opaque, not translucent.

Sea Salt Butter

1   cup unsalted butter, melted
2   tablespoons fresh lemon juice
      (about 1 lemon)
½   teaspoon sea salt

Combine all ingredients in a small bowl; stir
with a wire whisk. Yield: 1 cup.

Ginger Mayonnaise

1   cup mayonnaise
1   teaspoon grated fresh ginger
2   tablespoons fresh chives, sliced
      crosswise into ¼-inch pieces
¼   teaspoon sea salt
¼   teaspoon freshly ground pepper

Combine all ingredients in a small bowl; stir
with a wire whisk. Yield: 1 cup.
Recipe from Tom's Big Dinners *by Tom
Douglas. © 2003 by Tom Douglas. Reprinted
by permission of HarperCollins Publishers Inc.*

"If you only have one large pot, you can cook the
crabs in batches. Eating steamed crabs is delightfully messy.
Be sure to have crab crackers, cocktail forks, bowls for
the shells, a big stack of napkins, and lemon water
for cleaning your hands," says Chef Tom Douglas.

Sherried Crabmeat Pastries

¼   cup chopped shallots
¼   cup finely chopped red bell pepper
⅓   cup butter, melted
¼   cup all-purpose flour
¾   cup milk
1   pound fresh lump crabmeat, drained
¼   cup mayonnaise
2   tablespoons dry sherry
1   teaspoon Old Bay seasoning
½   teaspoon freshly ground pepper
5   dashes hot sauce
2   (15-ounce) packages refrigerated piecrusts
Fresh sage leaves

Cook shallots and red bell pepper in butter
in a large skillet over medium-high heat
until tender; whisk in flour. Cook 1 minute,
whisking constantly. Gradually whisk in
milk; cook, whisking constantly, until sauce
is thickened and bubbly. Stir in crabmeat
and next 5 ingredients. Remove from heat;
set aside.

Unfold 1 piecrust; cut crust in half.

Working with half of 1 crust, place sage
leaves on 1 side of pastry half; press sage into
pastry with a rolling pin. Carefully turn pastry
over. Place ⅓ cup crabmeat mixture on half of
pastry side without sage leaves. Brush edges of
pastry with water. Fold pastry over filling, and
pinch edges to seal. Trim sealed edges with a
pastry wheel or pizza cutter. Place on a baking
sheet lined with parchment paper. Repeat
procedure with remaining piecrust, sage, and
crabmeat mixture.

Bake at 425° for 20 minutes or until golden.
Yield: 8 servings.

We couldn't pick just one favorite crab cake, so we're giving you our top four.

Dungeness Crab Cakes with Orange-Butter Sauce

¼ cup milk
2 slices white bread
1 pound fresh Dungeness crabmeat
½ cup mayonnaise
1 large egg, lightly beaten
1½ tablespoons finely chopped red bell pepper
1½ tablespoons finely chopped green onions
1½ tablespoons finely chopped pickled ginger
½ teaspoon salt
¼ teaspoon freshly ground pepper
2 cups Japanese breadcrumbs (Panko)
½ cup vegetable oil
Orange-Butter Sauce
Garnishes: shredded fresh spinach, julienned red bell pepper, grated orange zest

Pour milk over bread in a small bowl.

Stir together crabmeat and next 7 ingredients in a medium bowl. Squeeze milk from bread, discarding excess milk. Add bread to crabmeat mixture, and toss gently.

Shape mixture into 8 patties; dredge in breadcrumbs. Press additional breadcrumbs onto each cake. Cover and chill at least 2 hours or overnight.

Heat ¼ cup oil in a large skillet over medium-high heat until hot; add 4 patties, and fry 3 to 4 minutes on each side or until golden. Repeat procedure with remaining oil and patties. Place crab cakes on a large baking sheet. Bake at 425° for 5 minutes.

Spoon Orange-Butter Sauce evenly onto serving plates. Place crab cakes over sauce. Garnish, if desired. Yield: 4 main-dish servings or 8 appetizer servings.

Note: Fresh lump crabmeat may be substituted for Dungeness crabmeat.

Dungeness Crab Cakes with Orange-Butter Sauce

Orange-Butter Sauce

¼ cup orange zest (about 3 oranges)
1½ cups fresh orange juice
1 teaspoon kosher salt
1 teaspoon freshly ground pepper
1 cup butter, chilled and cut into 1-inch pieces

Stir together first 4 ingredients in a nonaluminum saucepan; bring to a boil. Cook over medium-high heat 25 minutes or until mixture is reduced to ¼ cup. Remove from heat.

Gradually whisk butter into orange sauce. Serve immediately. Yield: 1½ cups.

—Chef Greg Atkinson
Bainbridge Island, Washington

Chesapeake Bay Crab Cakes

6 tablespoons mayonnaise, divided
1¼ teaspoons Old Bay seasoning, divided
1½ teaspoons dried parsley flakes
½ teaspoon Worcestershire sauce
⅛ teaspoon freshly ground pepper
4 saltine crackers, crushed
1 large egg
3 or 4 drops hot sauce
1 pound fresh lump crabmeat, drained
Paprika
Garnishes: fresh chives, lemon slices
Tartar Sauce

Stir together 3 tablespoons mayonnaise, ¾ teaspoon Old Bay seasoning, and next 6 ingredients in a medium bowl; gently stir in crabmeat. Shape into 12 patties. Place on a lightly greased baking sheet.

Stir together remaining 3 tablespoons mayonnaise and remaining ½ teaspoon Old Bay seasoning; spread evenly on crab cakes. Sprinkle with paprika.

Bake at 350° for 20 minutes or until lightly browned. (Do not overbake.) Garnish, if desired, and serve with Tartar Sauce. Yield: 12 crab cakes.

Tartar Sauce

1   cup mayonnaise
1½ tablespoons finely chopped fresh
       parsley
1½ tablespoons chopped capers
1   tablespoon sweet pickle relish
1   tablespoon chopped fresh chives
1   teaspoon Dijon mustard

Stir together all ingredients; cover and chill. Yield: 1 cup.

Eggplant Crab Cakes

2   pounds fresh lump crabmeat, divided
2   medium eggplants
1   teaspoon salt
1   cup water
1   medium onion, chopped
5   garlic cloves, chopped
2½ tablespoons olive oil, divided
⅓ cup dry white wine, divided
6   celery ribs, chopped
1   leek, chopped
1   tablespoon fresh thyme leaves
1   tablespoon fresh marjoram leaves
1   pickled pepperoncini pepper, diced
½ teaspoon salt
½ teaspoon pepper
1¼ cups soft breadcrumbs, divided*
½ cup grated Parmesan cheese
Garnishes: lemon wedges, fresh thyme sprigs,
       red pepper strips

Drain crabmeat, removing any bits of shell or cartilage; set aside.

Cut eggplants in half lengthwise and sprinkle with salt. Place eggplants, cut side down, in a 13- x 9-inch pan; add 1 cup water.

Bake, covered, at 400° for 40 minutes or until tender; set aside.

Sauté onion and garlic in 1 tablespoon hot oil in a large nonstick skillet 5 minutes or until tender. Add ¼ cup wine, celery, and next 3 ingredients. Bring to a boil, reduce heat, and simmer until liquid evaporates, stirring occasionally, about 10 to 12 minutes. Set aside.

Spoon pulp from eggplants, discarding peel. Pulse eggplant and vegetable mixture in a food processor 4 times or until coarsely chopped. (Do not overprocess.)

Heat 1½ teaspoons oil in a large skillet. Add 1 pound crabmeat and remaining wine; bring to a boil. Add eggplant mixture, pepperoncini, salt, and pepper, tossing gently. Remove from heat, and cool. Add 1 cup breadcrumbs and cheese; toss gently.

Shape into 8 (3½-inch) patties; dredge in remaining breadcrumbs.

Cook 4 patties in 1½ teaspoons hot oil in a large skillet 3 to 4 minutes per side, until golden brown. Repeat procedure with remaining oil and patties. Serve with remaining crabmeat. Garnish, if desired. Yield: 8 servings.

*Soft breadcrumbs are made by placing bread slices in a food processor or blender and processing. Store in an airtight container in the refrigerator for one week or up to six months in the freezer.

Recipe adapted from The Food of New Orleans: Authentic Recipes from the Big Easy by John DeMers (Periplus Editions, 1998).

Eggplant Crab Cakes

McClellanville Lump Crab Cakes with Whole-Grain Mustard Sauce

1 cup mayonnaise
1 egg white
3 tablespoons cracker meal
2 tablespoons fresh lemon juice
1/4 teaspoon dry mustard
1/4 teaspoon ground red pepper
1/4 teaspoon Old Bay seasoning
1 pound fresh lump crabmeat, drained
1 1/2 cups soft breadcrumbs
1/4 cup peanut oil
2 tablespoons unsalted butter, melted
Whole-Grain Mustard Sauce
Garnishes: lemon slices, chopped fresh parsley

Whisk together mayonnaise and egg white in a medium bowl; add next 5 ingredients. Stir in crabmeat.

Shape mixture into 6 (4-inch) patties. (Mixture will be very soft.) Carefully dredge patties in breadcrumbs; cover and chill at least 1 1/2 hours.

Cook crab cakes in hot oil and butter in a large skillet over medium-high heat 3 to 4 minutes on each side or until golden. Serve immediately with Whole-Grain Mustard Sauce. Garnish, if desired. Yield: 6 servings.

Whole-Grain Mustard Sauce

1/4 cup dry white wine
2 tablespoons brandy
1 cup whipping cream
1/4 cup whole-grain Dijon mustard
1 1/2 tablespoons fresh lemon juice
1/4 teaspoon salt
1/4 teaspoon freshly ground pepper

Stir together wine and brandy in a small nonaluminum saucepan; bring to a boil over medium-high heat. Boil 4 minutes or until mixture is reduced to 1 tablespoon. Add whipping cream; reduce heat to medium, and cook 6 to 8 minutes or until mixture thickens. Gradually stir in remaining ingredients; cook just until thoroughly heated. Keep warm. Yield: 1 cup.

—Chef Louis Osteen
Louis's at Pawleys
Pawleys Island, South Carolina

Crab Chops

2 tablespoons butter
2 tablespoons all-purpose flour
1/2 cup chopped green onions
1 teaspoon salt
1/4 teaspoon ground red pepper
1/4 teaspoon freshly ground black pepper
1/2 cup milk
1 large egg, lightly beaten
1 pound fresh lump crabmeat, drained
20 saltine crackers, finely crushed
1/2 cup fine, dry breadcrumbs
1 tablespoon Rustic Rub
1/4 cup butter, melted
1/4 cup vegetable oil
Garnishes: lemon wedges, fresh parsley sprigs

Melt 2 tablespoons butter in a heavy saucepan over low heat; whisk in flour until smooth. Cook 1 minute, whisking constantly. Stir in green onions and next 3 ingredients; cook 2 to 3 minutes, whisking constantly. Gradually whisk in milk; cook over medium heat, whisking constantly, until sauce is thickened and bubbly. Remove from heat.

Combine egg, crabmeat, and cracker crumbs; toss gently. Stir in white sauce. Shape into 6 patties (or chops).

Combine breadcrumbs and Rustic Rub in a shallow dish. Dredge patties in crumb mixture. Cover and chill 1 1/2 hours.

Cook crab chops in 1/4 cup melted butter and hot oil in a large skillet over medium-high heat 3 to 4 minutes on each side or until golden. Garnish, if desired. Yield: 6 servings.

Rustic Rub

1/4 cup paprika
3 tablespoons salt
3 tablespoons garlic powder
2 1/2 tablespoons freshly ground black pepper
1 1/2 tablespoons onion powder
1 1/2 tablespoons ground red pepper
1 tablespoon dried oregano
1 tablespoon dried thyme

Stir together all ingredients. Store in an airtight container up to 3 months. Yield: 1 cup.

—Food Writer Marcelle Bienvenu
New Iberia, Louisiana

Basic Steamed Clams

4 pounds clams in shells, scrubbed
1 cup water
1 cup dry white wine

Discard any open or cracked clams.

Bring water and wine to a boil in a stockpot. Add clams; cover and return to a boil. Boil 5 minutes. Immediately remove open clams with a slotted spoon. Continue cooking remaining clams 2 to 3 minutes; others may open. Discard any unopened clams, reserving clam broth. Serve immediately with broth, if desired. Yield: 6 servings.

Steamed Littleneck Clams with Champagne, Roma Tomatoes, and Scallions

72 littleneck clams in shells, scrubbed
1 tablespoon minced garlic
2 tablespoons olive oil
6 plum (Roma) tomatoes, peeled, seeded, and diced
2 cups champagne*
1 bunch scallions, sliced diagonally*
2 tablespoons chopped fresh Italian parsley
1/2 teaspoon cracked pepper

Discard any open or cracked clams.

Sauté garlic in hot olive oil in a Dutch oven over medium-high heat until tender. Add tomato, and sauté 1 minute. Add champagne; bring to a boil. Add clams; cover, reduce heat, and simmer 6 to 10 minutes or until clams open. With a slotted spoon, transfer clams, still in their shells, to a serving dish, discarding any unopened clams. Spoon cooking liquid over clams; sprinkle evenly with scallions, parsley, and pepper. Serve immediately. Yield: 6 servings.

*2 cups sparkling wine and 1 bunch green onions may be substituted.

—Chef Christopher Freeman
Toppers at the Wauwinet
Nantucket, Massachusetts

Steamed Littleneck Clams with Champagne, Roma Tomatoes, and Scallions

Broiled Clams with Herb Butter

1¼ cups unsalted butter, softened
25 saltine crackers, finely crushed
   (about ¾ cup)
1 egg yolk
1 garlic clove, minced
⅓ cup chopped fresh parsley
1 tablespoon chopped fresh thyme
1 tablespoon chopped fresh chives
¼ teaspoon salt
¼ teaspoon freshly ground pepper
¼ teaspoon hot sauce
36 large littleneck clams, scrubbed
Garnish: fresh thyme sprigs

Beat butter at medium speed with an electric mixer until fluffy. Add cracker crumbs, egg yolk, and garlic, beating until blended. Stir in parsley and next 5 ingredients. Place butter mixture on wax paper, and roll into a 14-inch, 1½-inch diameter log; chill 30 minutes or until firm.

Place clams in a single layer on a jellyroll pan. Bake clams at 350° for 10 minutes or until clams just begin to open. Open clams, and discard top shells. Loosen meat from bottom shell, and rinse in cold water. Drain and return clams in shells to jellyroll pan.

Cut butter log into ¼-inch-thick slices, and place 1 slice on each clam.

Broil 5½ inches from heat 5 minutes or until golden brown. Garnish, if desired. Yield: 6 servings.

—Chef/Owner Mark Gottwald
Ship's Inn
Nantucket, Massachusetts

Clam Cakes

1 pint shucked fresh clams*
1 cup crushed unsalted crackers
½ cup crushed round buttery crackers
4 green onions, minced
2 large eggs, lightly beaten
2 tablespoons all-purpose flour
2 tablespoons lemon juice
¼ teaspoon freshly ground pepper
¼ cup butter or margarine, divided
Tartar Sauce

Drain clams, reserving 2 tablespoons juice. Chop clams, and set aside.

Stir together clams, reserved clam juice, unsalted crackers, and next 6 ingredients; shape into 12 patties.

Melt 2 tablespoons butter in large skillet over medium-high heat; add 6 patties, and cook 3 to 4 minutes on each side or until golden. Repeat with remaining butter and patties. Serve hot with Tartar Sauce. Yield: 12 clam cakes.

2 (6.5-ounce) cans minced clams may be substituted for 1 pint shucked fresh clams. Drain clams, reserving 2 tablespoons juice.

Tartar Sauce

1 cup light mayonnaise
2 teaspoons Dijon mustard
2 green onions, minced
¼ cup chopped fresh dillweed
2 tablespoons chopped dill pickle
1 tablespoon capers, drained
1 tablespoon lemon juice
1 teaspoon Worcestershire sauce
¼ teaspoon freshly ground pepper

Whisk together mayonnaise and mustard. Stir in green onions and remaining ingredients. Cover and chill. Yield: 1¼ cups.

From Saltwater Seasonings: Good Food from Coastal Maine by Sarah Leah Chase. © 1992 by Sarah Leah Chase and Jonathan Chase. By permission of Little, Brown and Company, (Inc.)

Broiled Clams with Herb Butter

Broiled Oysters with Celery Cream and Virginia Ham

3   dozen fresh oysters in shells
Rock salt
1   cup heavy whipping cream
½   cup chopped fresh parsley sprigs
2   bay leaves
1   teaspoon grated lemon rind
2   tablespoons fresh lemon juice
½   teaspoon celery seeds
3   ounces Virginia ham, diced
3   celery stalks, finely chopped
¾   teaspoon freshly ground pepper
1½   cups peeled, chopped celery root
¼   cup heavy whipping cream
1   tablespoon unsalted butter
¼   teaspoon salt

Scrub oysters with a stiff brush under running water. Insert an oyster knife into the hinged edge of each oyster; twist knife handle back and forth until top shell is loose. Slide oyster knife along the bottom of the shell to detach muscle. Remove and discard top shell; drain and reserve 1 cup oyster liquor. Keep oysters in the deeper bottom shell. Arrange oysters over rock salt in a jellyroll pan; chill.

Combine 1 cup oyster liquor, 1 cup cream, and next 5 ingredients in a small saucepan. Bring to a boil; reduce heat, and simmer, uncovered, about 25 minutes or until thickened. Pour mixture through a wire-mesh strainer into a bowl. Stir in ham, celery, and pepper; set celery cream aside.

Cook celery root in boiling water to cover 10 minutes or until tender; drain. Place celery root, ¼ cup whipping cream, butter, and salt in a food processor. Process until smooth.

Place ½ teaspoon celery root puree under each reserved oyster in the shell. Top each with 1 teaspoon reserved celery cream. Broil 3 inches from heat 5 minutes or until bubbly. Serve immediately. Yield: 9 servings.

—Chef Bob Kinkead
Kinkead's
Washington, D.C.

Broiled Oysters with Celery Cream and Virginia Ham

Scalloped Oysters

½   cup butter or margarine
4½   cups crushed saltine crackers
2   (12-ounce) containers fresh oysters, undrained
¼   teaspoon salt
¼   teaspoon pepper
1   tablespoon chopped fresh parsley
1¼   cups half-and-half
Paprika

Melt butter in a skillet; add cracker crumbs, and cook, stirring constantly, until lightly browned.

Drain oysters, reserving ½ cup liquid. Place half of buttered crumbs in a lightly greased 2-quart baking dish; add oysters. Sprinkle with salt, pepper, parsley, and remaining cracker crumbs.

Combine reserved oyster liquid and half-and-half; pour over cracker crumbs. Sprinkle with paprika.

Bake, uncovered, at 350° for 35 to 40 minutes. Yield: 8 to 10 servings.

Roasted Oysters with Cilantro-Lime Dipping Sauce

¾ cup water
¼ cup sugar
½ cup chopped fresh cilantro
¼ cup chopped green onions
¼ cup dry white wine
¼ cup fresh lime juice
2 tablespoons fresh lemon juice
4 to 6 dozen fresh oysters, scrubbed

Stir together ¾ cup water and sugar in a small saucepan; bring to a boil, stirring until sugar dissolves. Cool. Stir in cilantro and next 4 ingredients. Set aside.

Place oysters on grill. Cook over medium-high heat (350° to 400°) 8 to 10 minutes or until shells open. (Shells will open about ¼ to ½ inch.) Remove from grill.

Pry open oysters using an oyster knife, discarding the empty half shells. Run knife under meat of oyster to release.

Arrange oysters on a platter, and serve with dipping sauce. Yield: 12 appetizer servings.

—Heloise
San Antonio, Texas

Southwest Fried Oysters

2 pints fresh select oysters, drained
2 cups buttermilk
1 cup all-purpose flour
½ cup yellow cornmeal
1 tablespoon paprika
1½ teaspoons garlic powder
1½ teaspoons chili powder
1½ teaspoons ground red pepper
1½ teaspoons dried oregano
½ teaspoon dried mustard
½ teaspoon salt
½ teaspoon ground black pepper
Vegetable oil

Combine oysters and buttermilk in a large shallow dish or heavy-duty zip-top plastic bag. Cover or seal, and chill at least 2 hours. Drain oysters well.

Combine flour, cornmeal, and next 8 ingredients. Dredge oysters in flour mixture, shaking off excess.

Pour oil to depth of 1 inch into a Dutch oven; heat to 370°. Fry oysters, in batches, 3 minutes or until golden. Drain on paper towels. Serve immediately. Yield: 4 to 6 servings.

Topless Oysters

Your guests have a choice of three sauces to spoon on these oysters.

2½ cups water
2 fresh kumquats
¼ cup fresh lime juice
1 teaspoon grated fresh ginger
¼ cup rice vinegar
1½ teaspoons lite soy sauce
1 shallot, minced
2 dozen fresh oysters in shells
Fresh Tomato Salsa
Lemon wedges

Bring 2½ cups water to a boil in a small saucepan. Reduce heat, and add kumquats; simmer 1 minute or until tender. Drain; let cool. Remove seeds, and cut kumquats into thin slices.

Combine kumquats, lime juice, and ginger, tossing gently to coat. Set aside.

Stir together vinegar, soy sauce, and shallot.

Scrub oyster shells, and open, discarding tops. Arrange shell bottoms (containing oysters) over crushed ice on a serving platter. Serve with kumquat sauce, vinegar sauce, Fresh Tomato Salsa, and lemon wedges. Yield: 4 to 6 servings.

Fresh Tomato Salsa

3 plum tomatoes, peeled, seeded, and diced
2 tablespoons chopped fresh cilantro
1 tablespoon minced onion
1 to 2 teaspoons minced jalapeño pepper
1 teaspoon fresh lime juice
⅛ teaspoon salt

Combine all ingredients in a small bowl. Yield: 1½ cups.

Steamed Mussels with Garlic and Herbs

2 pounds mussels, scrubbed and debearded
1 cup dry white wine
1 tablespoon olive oil
1 tablespoon fresh lemon juice
2 teaspoons chopped fresh thyme
8 sprigs fresh thyme
6 garlic cloves, minced
1 sprig fresh tarragon
1 bay leaf
2 tomatoes, peeled, seeded, and chopped (optional)
Garnishes: chopped fresh parsley, thyme sprigs

Discard opened or cracked mussels.

Combine wine and next 7 ingredients in a cataplana or a large skillet. Bring to a boil over medium-high heat; reduce heat, and simmer 10 minutes. Return mixture to a boil; add tomatoes, if desired, and mussels. Cook, covered, 5 minutes or until mussels open. Garnish, if desired. Serve with French bread. Yield: 3 servings.

Note: *A cataplana is a copper clamshell traditionally used for steaming in the oven; it can be used to steam mussels on the cooktop. Recipe adapted from* Classically Kiawah, *published by the Alternative Women's Group.*

Chilled Mussels with Tomato-Cognac Sauce

3 pounds mussels, scrubbed and debearded
1 cup white wine
½ cup water
¼ cup tomato paste
3 tablespoons Cognac
2 tablespoons fresh lemon juice
1 tablespoon dry sherry
1 small onion, minced
2 garlic cloves, minced
1½ cups mayonnaise
½ cup sour cream
2 to 3 tablespoons prepared horseradish

Discard opened or cracked mussels.

Bring wine to a boil in a large skillet. Add mussels; cover and return to a boil. Boil 5 minutes. Immediately remove opened mussels with a slotted spoon. Continue cooking remaining mussels for 2 minutes; other mussel shells may open. Discard any unopened mussels. Chill mussels.

Combine water and next 6 ingredients in a small saucepan. Cook over medium-low heat 15 minutes, stirring occasionally, until mixture is reduced to ¾ cup. Cool.

Add mayonnaise, sour cream, and horseradish to tomato paste mixture, stirring until blended; cover and chill at least 2 hours. Serve sauce with chilled mussels. Yield: 6 appetizer servings.

Mussels and Linguine with Garlic-Wine Sauce

3   pounds mussels, scrubbed and debearded
1   (9-ounce) package fresh linguine
⅓   cup butter, divided
4   garlic cloves, minced
4   green onions, sliced
2   tablespoons chopped fresh parsley
1½ cups dry white wine
½   teaspoon freshly ground pepper
¼   teaspoon salt
Garnishes: sliced green onions and chopped
    fresh parsley

Discard opened or cracked mussels.

Cook pasta according to package directions; drain well.

Melt 1 tablespoon butter in a large Dutch oven over medium heat. Add garlic and 4 green onions; sauté until tender. Add parsley and next 3 ingredients; bring to a boil. Add mussels; cover and cook over medium-high heat 5 minutes or until mussels open.

Immediately remove opened mussels with a slotted spoon. Continue cooking remaining mussels for 2 minutes; others may open. Discard any unopened mussels, reserving broth. Pour broth through a fine wire-mesh strainer, and discard any solids. Return broth to Dutch oven; bring to a boil.

Cook over high heat until mixture is reduced to

Mussels and Linguine with Garlic-Wine Sauce

¾ cup (about 6 minutes). Add remaining butter, and swirl in pan until melted. Return mussels to sauce and cook until thoroughly heated.

Serve over hot cooked pasta. Garnish, if desired. Yield: 4 servings.

Skillet-Roasted Mussels

2   dozen mussels, scrubbed and debearded
¼   teaspoon salt
¼   teaspoon pepper
2   tablespoons warm clarified butter*

Discard opened or cracked mussels.

Heat a large heavy skillet over high heat for

2 minutes; arrange mussels in a single layer, and cover. Turn heat off; let mussels stand 2 to 4 minutes or until mussels open. If mussels are slow to open, turn heat to high for 1 minute or until they open. Discard any unopened mussels.

Arrange mussels with the open sides up. Sprinkle with salt and pepper; drizzle with butter. Yield: 2 servings.
*To make clarified butter, melt ¼ cup butter over low heat. Skim white froth from top. Strain clear, yellow butterfat, leaving milk solids behind.

Paella

20 clams, scrubbed
20 mussels, scrubbed and debearded
¼ cup olive oil
10 chicken pieces (drumsticks or thighs)
2 to 3 garlic cloves, minced
1 large onion, chopped
1 pound chorizo sausage, cut into ½-inch
    slices
5 cups Bomba, Calasparra, or
    Valencia rice
2 tomatoes, finely chopped
1 (32-ounce) container chicken broth
¼ to ½ teaspoon saffron threads
½ cup dry white wine
½ pound green beans*
6 to 8 cups water
20 prawns, peeled if desired

Paella is Spain's ultimate comfort food. A broad, sizzling pan welcomes olive oil, then chicken, garlic, onion, chorizo, rice, and a host of meats or seafood. All ingredients cook in a single pan, producing a lively one-dish meal.

Discard opened, cracked, or heavy clams and mussels. Set aside.

Heat oil in a 17-inch paella pan. Add chicken and cook over medium coals, until chicken is golden and juices run clear. Add garlic and onion and cook until crisp-tender. Add chorizo and cook until thoroughly heated. Add rice and cook, stirring constantly, until grains are coated with oil. Add tomato, chicken broth, saffron threads, wine, and green beans. Bring to a slow boil. Cook 20 to 30 minutes, stirring occasionally.

Add additional water as needed. Add seafood and cook 15 more minutes, or until prawns turn pink and clams and mussels open. Yield: 10 servings.

*You may substitute 1½ cups frozen sweet peas for the green beans. Just add peas during the last 15 minutes of cooking.

—Steve Winston
The Spanish Table
Seattle, Washington

Paella

Fettuccine with Lobster and Shrimp in a Shallot and Wine Sauce

Have your local seafood department steam the lobster and shrimp while you shop, or call ahead and simply pick them up.

3 (6- to 8-ounce) lobster tails, steamed
½ cup butter or margarine
4 large shallots, diced
2 garlic cloves, minced
1½ cups dry white wine
3 tablespoons fresh lemon juice
1½ pounds peeled and deveined cooked shrimp
½ teaspoon fine-grained sea salt
½ teaspoon freshly ground pepper
12 ounces uncooked dried fettuccine
½ cup chopped fresh arugula
¼ cup chopped fresh parsley
¾ cup freshly grated Parmesan cheese

Cut shell of each lobster tail lengthwise on top and underside. Pry open tail segments. Remove meat and cut into bite-size pieces; set aside.

Melt butter in a large skillet over medium-high heat. Add shallots and garlic; sauté until tender. Add wine, and cook 3 minutes. Stir in lemon juice; reduce heat, and simmer 1 minute. Remove from heat. Add lobster and shrimp to shallot mixture; stir in salt and pepper. Cook over low heat until seafood is hot, stirring often.

Cook pasta according to package directions; drain and return to hot pan. Stir in arugula and parsley. Add seafood mixture; toss well. Sprinkle with cheese. Yield: 6 servings.

Boiled Lobster with Corn and New Potatoes

6 quarts water
4 teaspoons salt, divided
6 (1- to 2-pound) live lobsters
18 new potatoes, quartered
6 ears fresh corn
1½ cups butter, melted
3 lemons, halved
French baguette, sliced
Garnish: fresh Italian parsley sprigs

Bring 6 quarts water and 1 tablespoon salt to a boil in a large stockpot. Plunge 3 lobsters, head first, into boiling water; return to a boil. Cover, reduce heat, and simmer 10 minutes for the first pound and 3 minutes for each additional pound. Remove lobsters with tongs; set aside. Return water to a boil; repeat procedure with remaining lobsters.

Cook potato with remaining 1 teaspoon salt in boiling water to cover in a large Dutch oven 5 minutes. Add corn; cover and cook 5 more minutes or until potato is tender.

Arrange lobsters, potato, and corn on a serving platter. Serve with melted butter, lemon halves, and baguette slices. Garnish, if desired. Yield: 6 servings.

—Chef Christopher Freeman
Toppers at the Wauwinet
Nantucket, Massachusetts

Crawfish Boil

1½ gallons water
10 bay leaves
1 cup salt
¾ cup ground red pepper
¼ cup whole allspice
2 tablespoons mustard seeds
1 tablespoon coriander seeds
1 tablespoon dill seeds
1 tablespoon red bell pepper flakes
1 tablespoon black peppercorns
1 teaspoon whole cloves
4 celery ribs, quartered
3 medium onions, halved
3 garlic bulbs, halved crosswise
5 pounds fresh crawfish

Bring 1½ gallons water to a boil in a 19-quart stockpot over high heat. Add bay leaves and next 12 ingredients to water. Return to a rolling boil. Reduce heat to medium, and cook, uncovered, 30 minutes.

Add crawfish. Bring to a rolling boil over high heat; cook 5 minutes.

Remove stockpot from heat; let stand 30 minutes. (For spicier crawfish, let stand 45 minutes.)

Drain crawfish. Serve on large platters or newspaper. Yield: 5 servings.

Crawfish Étouffée

¼ cup butter or margarine
1 medium onion, chopped
2 celery ribs, chopped
1 medium-size green bell pepper, chopped
4 garlic cloves, minced
1 large shallot, chopped
¼ cup all-purpose flour
1 teaspoon salt
½ to 1 teaspoon ground red pepper
1 (14-ounce) can chicken broth
¼ cup chopped fresh parsley
¼ cup chopped fresh chives
2 pounds cooked, peeled crawfish tails*
Hot cooked rice
Garnishes: chopped fresh chives, ground red pepper

Melt butter in a large Dutch oven over medium-high heat. Add onion and next 4 ingredients; sauté 5 minutes or until tender. Add flour, salt, and red pepper; cook, stirring constantly, until caramel colored (about 10 minutes). Add broth and next 2 ingredients; cook, stirring constantly, 5 minutes or until thick and bubbly. Stir in crawfish; cook 5 minutes or until thoroughly heated. Serve with rice. Garnish, if desired. Yield: 4 to 6 servings.

*2 pounds frozen cooked crawfish tails, thawed and drained, may be substituted for fresh crawfish.

They're called mudbugs in Cajun country. And to capture the Louisiana flair, our Crawfish Boil presents them whole so you can peel and eat them at the table for traditional regional ambiance. A thick covering of newspaper is the tablecloth of choice.

Crawfish Risotto

¾ cup butter or margarine
1 medium onion, diced
1 poblano chile pepper, seeded and diced
4 garlic cloves, pressed
2 pounds uncooked Arborio rice
3 quarts chicken broth
2 pounds cooked, peeled crawfish tails*
2 cups (8 ounces) shredded Monterey Jack
    cheese with peppers
2 tablespoons Creole seasoning
Garnishes: shredded Parmesan cheese, fresh
    Italian parsley sprigs

Melt butter in a Dutch oven over medium heat; add onion, poblano chile, and garlic, and sauté until tender. Add rice, and cook, stirring constantly, 5 to 7 minutes. Add 1 cup chicken broth; cook, stirring constantly, until liquid is absorbed.

Repeat procedure with remaining broth, ½ cup at a time. (Cooking time is about 1 hour.) Stir in crawfish; cook, stirring constantly, 4 minutes. Add Monterey Jack cheese and Creole seasoning, stirring until cheese melts. Garnish, if desired. Yield: 12 servings.

*2 pounds cooked, peeled, medium-size shrimp may be substituted for crawfish.

—Chef Gus J. Martin
Dickie Brennan's Steakhouse
New Orleans, Louisiana

Calamari Marinara

1 (2.5-pound) package frozen, cleaned
    calamari (tubes and tentacles), thawed
2 tablespoons butter
3 garlic cloves, minced
½ cup diced onion
2 cups fish broth, clam juice, or chicken broth
1 (14.5-ounce) can crushed tomatoes
¼ cup chopped fresh parsley
¼ cup dry white wine
¾ teaspoon salt
¾ teaspoon freshly ground pepper
4 cups lightly packed fresh baby spinach
¼ cup sliced ripe olives
1 tablespoon pine nuts

Cut calamari tubes into ¼-inch-thick rings. Melt butter in a large skillet over medium-high heat. Add garlic and onion; sauté 3 minutes or until tender and lightly browned.

Add calamari rings and tentacles, broth, and next 5 ingredients. Bring to a boil; reduce heat, and simmer, uncovered, 30 minutes. Add spinach, olives, and pine nuts; simmer 8 minutes or until spinach wilts. Yield: 6 servings.

Calamari Curry

3 tablespoons peanut oil
1 onion, finely chopped
4 plum tomatoes, seeded and chopped
1 jalapeño pepper, seeded and minced
1 tablespoon grated fresh ginger
1 tablespoon minced garlic
1 tablespoon curry powder
2 teaspoons ground coriander
2 teaspoons grated lime rind
½ teaspoon freshly ground pepper
1 (14-ounce) can coconut milk
1½ cups fish or chicken broth
¼ cup chopped fresh cilantro
1 tablespoon light brown sugar
1 tablespoon fresh lime juice
½ teaspoon salt
1 (2.5-ounce) package frozen, cleaned
    calamari (tubes and tentacles), thawed
Hot cooked rice
Garnishes: chopped fresh mint, chopped
    fresh cilantro, toasted coconut

Heat oil in a Dutch oven over medium heat; add onion, and sauté 5 minutes. Add tomato and next 7 ingredients; sauté 4 minutes. Add coconut milk and next 5 ingredients; bring to a boil, reduce heat, and simmer 5 minutes.

Cut calamari into 1-inch pieces; add to curry sauce, and cook over medium heat 2 to 3 minutes or until calamari is opaque. Serve with rice. Garnish, if desired. Yield: 7 cups.

Salt and Pepper Squid with Asian Slaw

8 cups finely shredded cabbage
1 red bell pepper, cut into thin strips
½ cup chopped fresh cilantro
½ cup chopped fresh mint
2 green onions, diagonally sliced
3 tablespoons fresh lime juice
1¾ teaspoons salt, divided
1¾ teaspoons freshly ground pepper,
    divided
1 tablespoon sugar
2 tablespoons rice wine vinegar
1 tablespoon sesame oil
2 teaspoons garlic-chili sauce
1 teaspoon grated fresh ginger
1 (2.5-pound) package frozen, cleaned
    calamari (tubes and tentacles),
    thawed
1 tablespoon vegetable oil

Combine cabbage and next 4 ingredients in a large bowl; set aside.

Whisk together lime juice, ¼ teaspoon salt, ¼ teaspoon pepper, sugar, and next 4 ingredients; set aside.

Slice squid in half lengthwise. Score squid tubes with the tip of a knife in a diamond design; pat dry. Brush tubes and tentacles with oil, and sprinkle with remaining 1½ teaspoons salt and 1½ teaspoons pepper.

Coat grill grate with vegetable cooking spray. Place squid on grill, scored side down. Grill squid, covered with grill lid, over medium-high heat (350° to 400°) 1 minute on each side. Remove squid from grill, and cut into 1-inch pieces. Serve warm squid over cabbage slaw mixture, and drizzle with lime vinaigrette. Yield: 8 servings.

Note: You may broil squid 1 to 2 minutes on each side or until opaque.

vine advice

Master Sommelier Larry Stone of Rubicon restaurant in San Francisco offers these pairings:
• **Calamari Curry** Teruzzi e Puthod Vernaccia di San Gimignano 2001—"Light, crisp, and fruit-oriented, this wine has lots of interest on its own. But with a mildly spicy curry, it can really sing."
• **Calamari Marinara** Nozzole Chianti Classico 2000, Tuscany—"Even though the marinara sauce is made with white wine, I prefer to use a light red with acidity to match the fruity flavors of the tomatoes. Most Chianti Classico wines from good years will fill the bill nicely."

Grecian Skillet Rib Eyes

Grecian Skillet Rib Eyes

1½ teaspoons garlic powder
1½ teaspoons dried basil
1½ teaspoons dried oregano
½ teaspoon salt
½ teaspoon pepper
2 (1-inch-thick) rib-eye steaks (about 2 pounds)
1 tablespoon olive oil
1 tablespoon fresh lemon juice
¼ cup crumbled feta cheese
2 tablespoons pitted kalamata olives, sliced
Garnish: fresh oregano

Combine first 5 ingredients; rub onto both sides of steaks.

Pour oil into a large nonstick skillet; place over medium-high heat until hot. Add steaks, and cook 2 minutes on each side. Reduce heat to medium-low; cook 7 minutes on each side. Sprinkle with lemon juice; top with cheese and olives. Garnish, if desired. Yield: 2 to 4 servings.

Bistecca

This recipe uses thinly pounded steaks seasoned with traditional Italian flavors.

4 (1-inch-thick) chuck-eye steaks
½ teaspoon salt
¼ teaspoon pepper
½ cup olive oil
¼ cup balsamic vinegar
2 to 3 garlic cloves, chopped
1 to 2 teaspoons chopped fresh thyme

Place steaks between 2 sheets of heavy-duty plastic wrap; flatten to ½-inch thickness, using a meat mallet or rolling pin.

Sprinkle steaks evenly with salt and pepper.

Combine oil and remaining ingredients in a large shallow dish or heavy-duty zip-top plastic bag; add steaks. Cover or seal; chill 1 to 2 hours.

Remove steaks from marinade, discarding marinade.

Grill steaks, covered with grill lid, over medium-high heat (350° to 400°) 6 minutes on each side or until done. Yield: 4 servings.

Beef Filets with Stilton

4 (6-ounce) beef tenderloin filets
½ teaspoon salt
½ teaspoon freshly ground pepper
3 tablespoons butter or margarine, divided
⅔ cup dry red wine*
1 tablespoon chopped fresh or 1 teaspoon dried tarragon
4 ounces Stilton or other blue cheese, crumbled
Garnish: fresh tarragon sprigs

Rub filets with salt and pepper.

Melt 2 tablespoons butter in a large skillet over medium-high heat. Cook filets 6 minutes on each side or to desired degree of doneness. Remove from skillet; keep filets warm.

Add wine to skillet; bring to a simmer, and cook 2 to 3 minutes or until wine reduces by half. Stir in remaining 1 tablespoon butter. Add chopped tarragon. Remove from heat.

Arrange filets on a serving platter, and drizzle with wine reduction sauce. Sprinkle with crumbled cheese. Garnish, if desired. Yield: 4 servings.

*You can substitute beef broth for red wine, if desired.

Beef Tenderloin with Pebre Sauce

½ cup soy sauce
⅓ cup vegetable oil
1½ tablespoons brown sugar
1 tablespoon Dijon mustard
½ teaspoon garlic powder
1 (5- to 6-pound) beef tenderloin, trimmed
Pebre Sauce

Combine first 5 ingredients in a bowl. Place tenderloin in a shallow dish. Pour marinade over tenderloin; cover and marinate in refrigerator 8 hours, turning occasionally.

Remove tenderloin from marinade, discarding marinade. Place tenderloin on a lightly greased rack in a shallow roasting pan.

Bake at 400° for 45 to 60 minutes or until a meat thermometer inserted into thickest portion registers 145° (medium rare) or 160° (medium). Let stand 10 minutes before slicing. Serve with Pebre Sauce. Yield: 12 servings.

Pebre Sauce

4 jalapeño peppers, seeded and minced
¼ cup fresh lemon juice
1 tablespoon salt
¼ cup vegetable oil
2 tablespoons chopped fresh chives
2 tablespoons chopped fresh cilantro
2 tablespoons chopped fresh parsley
3 tablespoons white wine vinegar

Combine first 3 ingredients in a bowl. Cover and let stand 30 minutes; drain. Add oil and remaining ingredients. Yield: about ⅔ cup.

Beef Tenderloin in Wine Sauce

1 (3-pound) beef tenderloin
½ teaspoon salt
½ teaspoon pepper
½ cup butter or margarine
1 onion, thinly sliced
1 garlic clove, minced
1 (8-ounce) package sliced fresh mushrooms
½ cup dry red wine
1½ teaspoons Worcestershire sauce
1 teaspoon Italian seasoning
1 teaspoon hot sauce
1 cup beef broth
1 teaspoon all-purpose flour

Sprinkle beef with salt and pepper. Place in an aluminum foil-lined roasting pan.

Bake at 450° for 15 minutes.

Melt butter in a medium saucepan over medium heat. Add onion, garlic, and mushrooms. Cook, stirring often, 7 minutes. Stir in wine and next 3 ingredients. Whisk together beef broth and flour, and stir into wine mixture. Reduce heat, and simmer, stirring occasionally, 10 minutes or until onion is tender.

Remove beef from oven, and top with sauce. Bake beef 18 more minutes or to desired degree of doneness, basting once. Transfer beef to a serving platter, reserving sauce in pan. Let beef stand 10 minutes before slicing. Serve with wine sauce. Yield: 6 to 8 servings.

Veal Piccata

1   pound veal cutlets
1   teaspoon salt
½   teaspoon pepper
½   cup all-purpose flour
3   tablespoons butter
2   tablespoons olive oil
3   tablespoons lemon juice
2   garlic cloves, minced
3   tablespoons dry white wine
1   tablespoon chopped fresh parsley

Place veal between two sheets of plastic wrap or wax paper, and flatten to ¼-inch thickness, using a meat mallet or rolling pin.

Cut veal into 6 serving-size pieces. Pat veal dry. Rub salt and pepper on veal, and dredge in flour.

Heat butter and oil in a large skillet over medium-high heat. Add veal in 2 batches, and cook 1 to 2 minutes on each side. Remove veal to a warm platter; cover and keep warm. Drain drippings.

Add lemon juice, garlic, and white wine to skillet, stirring to loosen browned bits from bottom of skillet; cook over medium heat 1 to 2 minutes. To serve, spoon juices over veal; sprinkle with parsley. Yield: 4 servings.

Veal Marsala

1   teaspoon chopped fresh or dried
    rosemary
½   teaspoon salt
½   teaspoon freshly ground pepper
1   pound (¼-inch-thick) veal scaloppine
2   tablespoons olive oil
1   (8-ounce) package sliced fresh
    mushrooms
2   garlic cloves, minced
2   teaspoons cornstarch
1   teaspoon chicken bouillon granules
⅔   cup water
⅓   cup dry Marsala

Rub first 3 ingredients over veal. Heat oil in a large nonstick skillet over medium heat. Add half of veal; cook 2 minutes on each side or until lightly browned. Remove veal from skillet; keep warm. Repeat with remaining veal.

Add mushrooms and garlic to skillet; cook over medium-high heat, stirring constantly, 3 minutes or until tender.

Combine cornstarch and remaining ingredients; add to skillet. Cook, stirring constantly, 1 minute or until thick and bubbly. Serve over veal. Yield: 4 servings.

Garlic-Roasted Lamb with Oregano Pesto

1   (2-pound) rolled boneless leg of lamb
¼   cup Oregano Pesto
3   garlic cloves, sliced
¼   teaspoon salt
⅛   teaspoon pepper
1   whole garlic bulb

Unroll roast, and trim fat. Spread 1 tablespoon Oregano Pesto into the folds of the roast. Reroll roast, and secure at 1-inch intervals with heavy string. Make several ½-inch-deep slits in surface of roast; stuff garlic slices into slits. Cut 3 additional ½-inch-deep slits in surface of roast; stuff 1 teaspoon pesto into each slit. Spread remaining pesto over surface of roast, and sprinkle with salt and pepper. Place roast on a broiler pan; set aside.

Remove the white, papery skin of whole garlic bulb, making sure not to separate the cloves. Wrap the garlic bulb in aluminum foil.

Bake roast and garlic side by side at 325° for 45 minutes. Remove garlic from oven; set aside. Bake roast 40 more minutes or until a meat thermometer inserted into thickest portion registers 145° (medium rare). Let roast stand 10 minutes before slicing. Separate garlic bulb into cloves, and serve with roast. Yield: 6 servings.

Oregano Pesto

2½ cups torn spinach
2   cups fresh oregano leaves
1   cup fresh Italian parsley leaves
2   tablespoons grated fresh Parmesan
    cheese
2   tablespoons pistachio nuts
4   teaspoons lemon juice
¼   teaspoon salt
2   large garlic cloves
3   tablespoons extra-virgin olive oil

Process first 8 ingredients in a food processor until smooth. With processor running, pour oil through food chute in a slow, steady stream; process until blended. Spoon into a heavy-duty zip-top plastic bag; store in refrigerator. Yield: 1 cup.

Honey Mustard-Pecan Roasted Lamb

2   (1¼-pound) lamb rib roasts
    (8 ribs each)
2   tablespoons olive oil
¼   cup Dijon mustard
1   tablespoon honey
1   tablespoon molasses
2   small garlic cloves, minced
½   cup pecan halves, toasted
3   tablespoons soft breadcrumbs
    (homemade)
1   teaspoon fresh rosemary leaves

Trim exterior fat on lamb racks to ¼ inch; brown lamb racks, 1 rack at a time, in olive oil in a large skillet over medium-high heat.

Place lamb racks, fat side up, on a lightly greased rack in a roasting pan.

Combine mustard and next 3 ingredients in a small bowl, stirring well. Brush mustard mixture over both sides of lamb racks.

Process pecans, breadcrumbs, and rosemary in a food processor until pecans are finely chopped. Sprinkle lamb racks with pecan mixture.

Insert a meat thermometer into thickest portion of 1 rack, making sure it does not touch fat or bone.

Bake, uncovered, at 375° for 30 minutes or until thermometer registers 145° (medium rare) or 160° (medium). Let stand 10 minutes before slicing. Yield: 8 servings.

Lamb Chops with Mint Aïoli

Lamb Chops with Mint Aïoli

6   garlic cloves, minced
2   teaspoons dried summer savory
1   teaspoon salt
1   teaspoon pepper
16 (2-inch-thick) lamb rib chops
1   tablespoon olive oil
Mint Aïoli
Garnish: fresh mint sprigs

Combine first 4 ingredients, and rub evenly onto both sides of lamb chops.

Brown chops in hot oil in a large nonstick skillet over medium-high heat 2 to 3 minutes on each side. Arrange chops on a lightly greased rack in a broiler pan.

Bake chops at 350° for 35 to 40 minutes or until a meat thermometer inserted into thickest portion registers 145° (medium rare). Serve lamb with Mint Aïoli. Garnish, if desired. Yield: 6 to 8 servings.

Mint Aïoli

1   cup mayonnaise
¼   cup coarsely chopped fresh mint
4   garlic cloves, minced
1   teaspoon grated lemon rind
2   tablespoons fresh lemon juice
½   teaspoon salt
½   teaspoon pepper

Process all ingredients in a blender or food processor until smooth, stopping to scrape down sides. Yield: 1¼ cups.

Chicken in Lemon Marinade

This chicken dish gets its zing from lemon juice and Worcestershire sauce.

⅔ cup vegetable oil

½ cup lemon juice

1 tablespoon Worcestershire sauce

1 small onion, grated

1 teaspoon salt

1 teaspoon celery salt

1 teaspoon pepper

⅛ teaspoon hot sauce

6 skinned and boned chicken breast halves

Garnishes: lemon slices, lemon peel, fresh parsley

Process first 8 ingredients in a blender until smooth, stopping to scrape down sides. Reserve ¼ cup lemon mixture, and chill.

Place chicken in a shallow dish or zip-top plastic bag; pour remaining lemon mixture over chicken. Cover or seal, and chill 2 hours, turning chicken occasionally.

Remove chicken from marinade, discarding marinade; place chicken on a lightly greased rack in a broiler pan.

Broil 5½ inches from heat 11 to 12 minutes on each side or until tender, basting chicken often with reserved ¼ cup lemon mixture. Garnish, if desired. Yield: 6 servings.

Chicken with Artichokes

6 skinned and boned chicken breast halves

1 teaspoon paprika

½ teaspoon salt

½ teaspoon pepper

2 tablespoons butter or margarine, divided

1 (14-ounce) can artichoke hearts, drained and halved

2 green onions, chopped

⅔ cup water

¼ cup sherry

1 tablespoon cornstarch

1 teaspoon chicken bouillon granules

½ teaspoon dried rosemary

Sprinkle chicken with paprika, salt, and pepper.

Melt 1 tablespoon butter in a large nonstick skillet over medium-high heat; add chicken, and cook 5 minutes on each side or until lightly browned. Remove chicken, and set aside.

Melt remaining 1 tablespoon butter in same skillet over medium heat. Add artichoke hearts and green onions; sauté 1 minute.

Stir together ⅔ cup water and remaining ingredients; add to artichoke mixture. Return chicken to skillet. Bring to a boil, and cook, stirring constantly, 1 minute. Yield: 6 servings.

Salsa Chicken

4 large skinned and boned chicken breast halves

½ teaspoon pepper

1 tablespoon olive oil

3 cups mild salsa

¾ cup pimiento-stuffed olives, sliced and divided

½ cup currants

2 tablespoons honey

1 teaspoon ground cinnamon

½ teaspoon ground cumin

Hot cooked couscous

¼ cup sliced almonds, toasted

3 tablespoons chopped fresh cilantro

Garnish: fresh cilantro sprigs

Sprinkle chicken with pepper. Cook chicken in hot oil in a large skillet or Dutch oven over medium-high heat 5 minutes on each side or

Chicken in Lemon Marinade

Salsa Chicken

until chicken is done. Remove chicken from skillet, and keep warm.

Add salsa to skillet, stirring to loosen browned bits from bottom. Stir in ½ cup olives, currants, and next 3 ingredients. Bring to a boil; reduce heat, and simmer, uncovered, 10 minutes, stirring occasionally.

Prepare couscous according to package directions; keep warm.

Return chicken to skillet; cover and simmer 5 minutes. Place chicken on a bed of couscous. Spoon sauce over chicken. Sprinkle with toasted almonds, chopped cilantro, and remaining ¼ cup sliced olives. Garnish, if desired. Yield: 4 servings.

Chicken and Beef Fajitas

Chipotle seasoning contributes a smoky essence to the flavorful marinade for these fajitas.

2   tablespoons chili powder
2   teaspoons ground cumin
1   teaspoon brown sugar
1   teaspoon pepper
¼   teaspoon salt
¼   teaspoon garlic powder
¼   teaspoon chipotle seasoning (optional)
1   cup Italian dressing
6   skinned and boned chicken breast halves
4   pounds flank steak
20 (8-inch) flour tortillas, warmed
Toppings: sour cream, shredded lettuce, chopped tomato, shredded Cheddar cheese

Combine first 6 ingredients and, if desired, chipotle seasoning.

Stir together chili powder mixture and dressing. Pour half of marinade into a shallow dish or large heavy-duty zip-top plastic bag; add chicken. Cover or seal.

Pour remaining marinade into a separate shallow dish or large heavy-duty zip-top plastic bag; add beef. Cover or seal; chill chicken and beef 2 hours.

Remove chicken and beef from marinade, discarding marinade.

Grill, covered with grill lid, over medium heat (300° to 350°) about 15 minutes on each side or until chicken is done and beef is to desired degree of doneness.

Cut chicken and beef into strips. Serve in warmed flour tortillas with desired toppings. Yield: 8 to 10 servings.

Southwestern Chicken Bundles

4   skinned and boned chicken breast
    halves
1   (5.25-ounce) can whole green chiles,
    drained
4   (1-ounce) slices Monterey Jack cheese
    with peppers
1   large egg
2   tablespoons water
1   cup finely crushed tortilla chips
Salsa
Garnish: lime wedge

Place chicken between 2 sheets of heavy-duty
plastic wrap, and flatten to ⅛-inch thickness,
using a meat mallet or rolling pin. Top each
chicken breast with 1 green chile and 1 cheese
slice; roll up, securing with wooden picks.

Whisk together egg and 2 tablespoons water
in a shallow bowl. Dip chicken rolls in egg mixture; dredge in crushed chips. Place rolls in a
lightly greased 13- x 9-inch pan.

Bake at 375° for 30 to 35 minutes. Let
stand 5 minutes before slicing. Serve with
salsa. Garnish, if desired. Yield: 4 servings.

Parmesan Chicken Salad

4   skinned and boned chicken breast
    halves
½   teaspoon salt
½   teaspoon pepper
2   tablespoons vegetable oil
¾   cup shredded Parmesan cheese
¾   cup chopped pecans, toasted
½   cup finely chopped celery
3   green onions, chopped
¾   cup mayonnaise
2   tablespoons spicy brown mustard
1   garlic clove, pressed

Sprinkle chicken with salt and pepper. Cook
chicken in hot oil in a large skillet over medium-
high heat 4 to 6 minutes on each side or until
done; cool. Chop chicken.

Stir together chicken, cheese, and next
3 ingredients.

Stir together mayonnaise, mustard, and
garlic. Add to chicken salad; stir well. Cover
and chill at least 2 hours. Yield: 4½ cups.

Curried Chicken

*"The taste of this dish is first infused by
the curry marinade, second by the cooking
process, and third by the addition of whatever condiments the diner prefers," says
Food Historian Jessica Harris.*

3   tablespoons butter
1   large onion, minced
3   garlic cloves, minced
2   teaspoons minced fresh ginger
3   tablespoons hot curry powder
½   teaspoon dried crushed red pepper
½   cup cane or cider vinegar
3   pounds skinned and boned chicken
    breast halves, cut into ¼-inch strips
1   cup water
4   baking potatoes, peeled and cubed
Hot cooked rice
Tomato Chutney
Mommy's Watermelon Rind Pickles
Scallion-Cilantro Raita
Katchumber Salad
Onion Relish
Wortel Sambal
Garnishes: mango chutney, chopped roasted
    peanuts, raisins, flaked coconut, chopped
    green onions

Melt butter in a nonstick skillet over medium
heat. Add onion, garlic, and ginger; sauté 6
minutes or until tender. Add curry and red
pepper. Sauté 2 minutes. Stir in vinegar. Cool
10 minutes. Combine onion marinade and
chicken in a heavy-duty zip-top plastic bag;
seal and chill for 2 hours.

Combine chicken, marinade, and 1 cup
water in a large Dutch oven over medium-low
heat. Bring to a boil. Cover, reduce heat to low,
and simmer 20 minutes, stirring occasionally.
Add potato; bring to a boil. Cover, reduce heat
to low, and simmer 20 minutes or until potato
is tender. Serve over rice with desired condiments. Garnish, if desired. Yield: 4 to 6
servings.

Tomato Chutney

12 ripe tomatoes (about 3 pounds)
2   large onions, quartered
2   garlic cloves, minced
1   (1-inch) piece fresh ginger, peeled
½   habanero pepper
½   cup chopped fresh basil
1   cup firmly packed light brown sugar
½   cup raisins
1   cup white vinegar

Peel and slice tomatoes. Place tomato and next
5 ingredients in a food processor. Process 30
seconds or until mixture is smooth, stopping to
scrape down sides.

Place puree in a heavy saucepan; stir in
remaining ingredients. Bring to a boil over
medium heat. Reduce heat, and simmer,
stirring often, 2 to 2½ hours or until thickened.

Pack mixture into hot jars, filling to ½ inch
from top. Remove air bubbles; wipe jar rims.
Cover at once with metal lids, and screw on
bands. Process in boiling water bath 15
minutes. Yield: 4 (½-pint) jars.

Mommy's Watermelon Rind Pickles

*These pickles adhere to the Creole cooking
philosophy: Have enough to put some away.
"You don't waste that rind," Jessica says.
"It's the whole idea of using everything to
the fullest and at the peak of flavor."*

1   large watermelon, quartered
½   cup salt
2½ quarts water, divided
1¾ cups cider vinegar
½   cup balsamic vinegar
2   cups sugar
1   lemon, thinly sliced
2   (3-inch) cinnamon sticks
2   teaspoons cracked allspice
1   teaspoon whole cloves

Cut pulp from watermelon rind, leaving a small
amount of red pulp on rind. Reserve pulp for
another use. Cut rind into 1-inch cubes, and
place in a large bowl. Stir together salt and 2
quarts water. Pour over rind. Cover and chill 8
hours. Drain; rinse.

Combine rind with water to cover in a Dutch

Curried Chicken

Katchumber Salad

2   green bell peppers, coarsely chopped
2   tomatoes, coarsely chopped
1   onion, coarsely chopped
1   tablespoon minced fresh cilantro
2   tablespoons fresh lemon juice
¼   teaspoon freshly ground pepper

Combine first 5 ingredients; toss gently. Cover and chill 1 hour. Sprinkle with pepper; toss gently. Yield: 4½ cups.

Onion Relish

3   onions, chopped
1   hot green chile, seeded and coarsely chopped
1   teaspoon ground red pepper
2   teaspoons fresh lemon juice
¼   teaspoon salt

Combine all ingredients in a large bowl. Serve at room temperature. Yield: 4 cups.

Wortel Sambal

Sambals are condiments with many variations that often accompany Indian, Malaysian, and Indonesian foods, such as rice and curry dishes.

2   green cardamom pods
1   dried hot red chile
1   pound carrots, shredded
1½ cups sugar
1   garlic clove, minced
1   tablespoon minced fresh ginger
1   teaspoon sea salt
½   cup water
¾   cup distilled white vinegar

Remove seeds from cardamom pods, and discard pods. Combine cardamom seeds and chile in a spice mill or mortar and pestle; grind into a powder.

Combine cardamom mixture, carrot, and next 5 ingredients in a medium saucepan over medium-high heat. Bring to a boil, and cook, stirring occasionally, 30 minutes. Add vinegar; reduce heat, and simmer 30 more minutes or until thickened. Transfer mixture to a bowl; cover and chill at least 1 hour. Yield: 1½ cups.

"I like to have food people can handle," Food Historian Jessica Harris says. **"In my Curried Chicken, everything is already cut up. You can serve it with only a fork."**

oven. Bring to a boil; reduce heat, and simmer, uncovered, 10 minutes or until tender. Drain.

Combine remaining 2 cups water, vinegars, and remaining ingredients in Dutch oven or very large saucepan. Bring to a boil; reduce heat, and simmer, uncovered, 20 to 25 minutes or until mixture becomes a thin syrup. Add rind; simmer 5 to 6 minutes or until rind becomes translucent. Pack hot rind mixture into hot jars, distributing lemon and spices evenly and filling to within ½ inch from top. Remove air bubbles; wipe jar rims. Cover at once with metal lids, and screw on bands. Process in boiling water bath 20 minutes. Yield: 3 pints.

Scallion-Cilantro Raita

Raitas are yogurt-based condiments served to offset the spiciness of highly seasoned foods.

1   (8-ounce) container plain yogurt
2   scallions or green onions, minced
1½ tablespoons chopped fresh cilantro
½   teaspoon ground cumin
¼   teaspoon salt

Combine all ingredients, stirring well. Cover and chill 1 hour. Yield: 1 cup.

Asian-Glazed Cornish Hen

The Glazed Long Island Duck is complemented by **Cristom Pinot Noir Mount Jefferson Cuvée** from the Willamette Valley of Oregon. Another offering is **Fontodi Chianti Classico** from Italy's Chianti region. Its fruity, spicy flavor is well suited to bold-flavored foods such as duck.

Glazed Long Island Duck

2   (5½-pound) dressed ducks
2   teaspoons salt
2   teaspoons freshly ground pepper
12   shallots, peeled
10   garlic cloves, crushed
2   fresh rosemary sprigs
1   small lemon, cut in half
½   cup lemon marmalade
¼   cup firmly packed brown sugar
Garnishes: fresh rosemary sprigs, lemon
    slices, fresh berries

Remove giblets and necks from ducks; reserve for another use, if desired. Rinse ducks thoroughly under cold water, and pat dry with paper towels. Sprinkle cavities and skin with salt and pepper; fill cavities with shallots and next 3 ingredients. Prick skin with a meat fork. Tie ends of legs together with string; tuck wingtips under.

   Place ducks, breast side up, on a lightly greased rack in a broiler pan. Fill pan with hot water to depth of ½ inch.

   Bake, uncovered, at 450° for 45 minutes. Turn ducks over; bake 30 more minutes.

   Combine marmalade and brown sugar. Microwave at HIGH 2½ minutes. Turn ducks breast side up; brush with marmalade mixture. Insert a meat thermometer into thickest portion of thigh, without touching fat or bone. Bake 5 to 10 minutes or until thermometer registers 180°. Transfer ducks to a serving platter; let stand 10 minutes before serving. Garnish, if desired. Yield: 6 servings.

—Gideon Bosker
Portland, Oregon

Asian-Glazed Cornish Hens

¼   cup soy sauce
¼   cup teriyaki sauce
3   tablespoons honey
2   tablespoons lemon juice
1   tablespoon grated fresh ginger
1   teaspoon pepper
3   garlic cloves, minced
2   (1½-pound) Cornish hens
Garnishes: sugar snap peas, lemon slices

Combine first 7 ingredients; stir well. Pour half of marinade into a large heavy-duty zip-top plastic bag, reserving remaining marinade; add Cornish hens. Seal and marinate hens in refrigerator 1 hour.

   Remove hens from marinade; discard marinade. Tie ends of legs together, if desired, and place hens on a lightly greased rack in a roasting pan.

   Bake hens at 400° for 45 to 50 minutes or until done, basting occasionally with reserved marinade. Cover hens loosely with aluminum foil to prevent overbrowning, if necessary.

   Remove hens from oven; let stand 5 minutes. Garnish, if desired. Yield: 2 servings.

Glazed Long Island Duck

Rosemary Roasted Turkey

Avoid buying a prebasted turkey for this recipe. Prebasted turkeys include extra salt that fresh turkeys don't have.

1   (3/4-ounce) package fresh rosemary
    sprigs, divided
1/4 cup butter, softened
Grated rind from 1 large lemon (2 teaspoons)
1   (15- to 18-pound) turkey
1/4 cup salt
1   tablespoon pepper
1 1/2 tablespoons paprika
11 garlic cloves, crushed
2   lemons, quartered
2   onions, cut into wedges
1/4 cup butter, melted
2   cups dry white wine
1   cup orange juice
Garnish: fresh rosemary sprigs

Chop enough rosemary to equal 2 tablespoons; set aside remaining rosemary. Combine chopped rosemary, 1/4 cup softened butter, and lemon rind in a small bowl; stir well.

Remove and discard giblets and neck from turkey. Rinse turkey with cold water; pat dry. Loosen skin from turkey breast without totally detaching it. Carefully rub rosemary butter under skin.

Combine salt, pepper, and paprika; sprinkle turkey inside and out with mixture. Place 7 garlic cloves and all lemon quarters in body and neck cavities; stuff with onion wedges and all but 2 remaining rosemary sprigs.

Tucking wingtips under, place turkey, breast side up, in a large shallow roasting pan. Tie ends of legs together with string.

Bake, uncovered, at 325° for 30 minutes. Baste with melted butter; bake 30 more minutes.

Combine remaining 4 garlic cloves, 2 reserved rosemary sprigs, wine, and orange juice; pour into roasting pan.

Bake, uncovered, 3 to 3 1/2 more hours or until a meat thermometer inserted into thigh registers 180°, basting with pan juices every 30 minutes. If necessary, cover turkey loosely with aluminum foil to prevent overbrowning.

Transfer turkey to a serving platter. Cover with foil, and let stand 20 minutes before carving. Skim fat from pan drippings, and serve drippings with turkey. Garnish, if desired. Yield: 15 to 18 servings.

Herb-Peppered Pork Chops

4   (1 1/2-inch-thick) center-cut pork chops
    (about 3 1/4 pounds)
2   tablespoons vegetable oil, divided
2   garlic cloves, minced
2   teaspoons paprika
1 1/2 teaspoons dried thyme
1 1/2 teaspoons dried oregano
1   teaspoon black pepper
3/4 teaspoon salt
3/4 teaspoon ground cumin
3/4 teaspoon lemon pepper
1/2 teaspoon ground red pepper
1   (14-ounce) can chicken broth
1   tablespoon cornstarch
2   tablespoons water
1/4 teaspoon Worcestershire sauce
Garnish: fresh thyme sprigs

Brush chops with 1 tablespoon oil, and rub with garlic. Stir together paprika and next 7 ingredients in a small bowl. Rub over chops. Cover and chill 1 hour.

Heat remaining 1 tablespoon oil in a large ovenproof skillet over medium-high heat. Add chops, and cook 3 minutes on each side or until browned.

Bake chops in skillet, uncovered, at 350° for 20 to 25 minutes or until done. Remove chops from skillet; keep warm. Reserve drippings in skillet. Add broth to reserved drippings, stirring to loosen browned bits from bottom of skillet; bring to a boil. Cook until mixture is reduced to 1 cup (about 8 to 10 minutes); skim fat from broth.

Stir together cornstarch, water, and Worcestershire sauce. Gradually stir cornstarch mixture into broth; bring to a boil. Cook, stirring constantly, 1 minute. Serve with chops. Garnish, if desired. Yield: 4 servings.
Note: *If you're not sure your skillet handle is ovenproof, wrap the handle with aluminum foil as a safeguard.*

Cider Pork Chops

If you choose a thinner, less expensive chop, decrease the cooking time. Begin to check for doneness after 30 minutes.

1/2 cup all-purpose flour
1   teaspoon salt
1/4 teaspoon pepper
4   (1-inch-thick) bone-in pork chops
3   tablespoons butter or margarine, divided
4   Granny Smith apples, thinly sliced
1   cup raisins (optional)
1   cup firmly packed dark brown sugar
1   cup apple cider

Combine first 3 ingredients in a heavy-duty zip-top plastic bag; add chops. Seal and shake to coat. Remove chops, and set aside.

Melt 2 tablespoons butter in a large skillet; add chops, and cook 5 minutes on each side or until browned.

Grease a 13- x 9-inch baking dish with remaining 1 tablespoon butter. Place apples in dish; top with raisins, if desired, and sprinkle with brown sugar. Arrange chops over brown sugar, and drizzle with cider.

Bake at 350° for 1 hour or until pork chops are done. Yield: 4 servings.

Pork Medaillons in Mustard Sauce

If you don't have time to marinate the pork, it'll have plenty of flavor if you just brush or spoon on the mustard marinade and bake right away.

3   tablespoons olive oil
3   tablespoons coarse-grained mustard
3/4 teaspoon salt
3/4 teaspoon coarsely ground pepper
2   (1-pound) pork tenderloins
Mustard Sauce
Garnish: fresh rosemary sprigs

Combine first 4 ingredients in a large heavy-duty zip-top plastic bag. Add pork, tossing to coat; seal bag. Chill 8 hours, turning occasionally.

Place pork on a lightly greased rack in a broiler pan or shallow roasting pan. Bake,

Pork Medaillons in Mustard Sauce

uncovered, at 450° for 25 minutes or until a meat thermometer inserted into thickest portion registers 160°. Let stand 10 minutes before slicing. Slice and serve with Mustard Sauce. Garnish, if desired. Yield: 6 servings.

Mustard Sauce

2   cups heavy whipping cream
¼   cup coarse-grained mustard
¼   teaspoon salt
⅛   teaspoon ground white pepper

Bring whipping cream to a boil in a large skillet. Reduce heat to medium, and cook 12 minutes, stirring often. Stir in mustard, salt, and pepper, and cook 1 minute or until thickened. Yield: about 1½ cups.

Molasses Pork Tenderloin with Red Wine Sauce

1   cup reduced-sodium soy sauce
1¼ cups molasses
¼   cup fresh lemon juice
¼   cup olive oil
3   tablespoons minced fresh ginger
2   large garlic cloves, minced
3   (¾-pound) pork tenderloins
Red Wine Sauce (optional)

Combine first 6 ingredients in a shallow dish or heavy-duty zip-top plastic bag; add tenderloins. Cover or seal, and chill 8 hours.

Remove tenderloins from marinade, discarding marinade.

Grill tenderloins, covered with grill lid, over medium-high heat (350° to 400°) 20 minutes or until a meat thermometer inserted into thickest portion registers 160°, turning occasionally. Let stand 10 minutes before slicing. Serve with Red Wine Sauce, if desired. Yield: 8 servings.

Note: Tenderloins may be pan seared in a hot skillet to brown and then baked at 375° for 15 to 20 minutes.

Red Wine Sauce

½   small sweet onion, minced
2   tablespoons butter
½   cup dry red wine
1   (14-ounce) can beef broth
¼   cup water
2   tablespoons cornstarch

Sauté onion in butter in a large saucepan over medium-high heat 3 minutes or until browned. Add wine, and cook 3 minutes. Add beef broth; bring to a boil, and cook 5 minutes.

Stir together ¼ cup water and cornstarch; add to broth mixture and cook, stirring constantly, 1 minute or until mixture thickens. Remove from heat, and serve over tenderloin. Yield: about 1¼ cups.

Peppered Bacon-Wrapped Pork Tenderloin

¼ cup butter or margarine
¾ pound mushrooms, sliced
1 small onion, chopped
¼ cup chopped pecans, toasted
2 (¾-pound) pork tenderloins, trimmed
1 teaspoon salt
1 teaspoon ground black pepper
8 thick bacon slices
¼ cup firmly packed light brown sugar
1 teaspoon cracked black pepper

Melt butter in a large skillet over medium-high heat; add mushrooms and onion to skillet, and sauté 8 minutes or until tender. Stir in pecans; set aside.

Place pork between 2 sheets of plastic wrap; flatten to ¼-inch thickness, using a meat mallet or rolling pin. Sprinkle with salt and ground pepper.

Spread mushroom mixture evenly on 1 side of each tenderloin, leaving a ¼-inch border. Roll up jellyroll fashion, starting with 1 long end. Wrap 4 bacon slices around each tenderloin, and secure with wooden picks. Place tenderloins, seam sides down, on a lightly greased rack in a roasting pan. Rub evenly with sugar and cracked pepper.

Bake, uncovered, at 450° for 15 minutes. Reduce oven temperature to 400°.

Bake at 400° for 15 minutes or until a meat thermometer inserted into thickest portion registers 160°. Yield: 6 to 8 servings.

Grilled Pork Tenderloins with Rosemary Pesto

6 to 10 fresh rosemary sprigs
¼ cup chopped walnuts
2 tablespoons Creole mustard
3 garlic cloves, chopped
½ cup olive oil, divided
4 (½- to ¾-pound) pork tenderloins
⅛ teaspoon salt
⅛ teaspoon pepper
Garnish: fresh rosemary sprigs

Remove leaves from rosemary sprigs, and measure ¾ cup leaves. Soak rosemary stems in water; set aside.

Process rosemary leaves, walnuts, mustard, and garlic in a food processor until smooth, stopping to scrape down sides. With processor running, pour ¼ cup oil through food chute in a slow, steady stream; process until smooth. Set rosemary pesto aside.

Place tenderloins between 2 sheets of heavy-duty plastic wrap, and flatten to ½- to ¾-inch thickness, using a meat mallet or rolling pin. Spread pesto evenly over top of 2 tenderloins; place remaining tenderloins on top, and tie tenderloin pairs together with string. Rub remaining oil over pork; sprinkle with salt and pepper.

Prepare a hot fire by piling charcoal on 1 side of grill, leaving other side empty. (For gas grills, light only 1 side.) Remove rosemary stems from water; place on hot coals. Place grill grate on grill. Place pork over unlit side.

Grill, covered with grill lid, 1½ hours or until a meat thermometer inserted into thickest portion registers 160°. Let stand 10 minutes. Garnish, if desired. Yield: 10 to 12 servings.

Molasses-Coffee Glazed Ham

1 cup molasses
1 (12-ounce) jar apricot jam
¾ cup strong brewed coffee
2 tablespoons cider vinegar
1 tablespoon Dijon mustard
1 teaspoon salt
1 teaspoon vanilla extract
1 (8- to 9-pound) bone-in, fully cooked smoked ham half

Stir together first 7 ingredients until blended. Reserve 1 cup molasses-coffee sauce in a small bowl; set reserved sauce aside.

Trim ham, and, if desired, score in a diamond pattern. Place ham in a lightly greased 13- x 9-inch pan. Pour remaining molasses-coffee sauce evenly over ham.

Bake on lower oven rack at 350° for 2 hours or until a meat thermometer inserted into thickest portion registers 140°, basting with sauce in pan every 15 minutes. Cover loosely with lightly greased aluminum foil during the last 30 minutes to prevent excessive browning, if necessary.

Remove ham from baking pan; let stand at room temperature 30 minutes. Heat reserved molasses-coffee sauce, and serve with ham. Yield: 10 to 12 servings.

Baked Virginia Ham

1 (10- to 12-pound) uncooked country ham
Whole cloves
1 cup firmly packed light brown sugar
2 teaspoons dry mustard
½ cup fine, dry breadcrumbs
1 teaspoon paprika
1 quart ginger ale
Garnishes: Lady apples, kumquat fruit and leaves

Scrub ham in warm water with a stiff brush, and rinse well.

Place ham in a large aluminum stockpot. Cover with water; let stand 24 hours.

Drain ham, and rinse; return to stockpot. Add water to cover. Bring to a boil; reduce heat, and simmer, uncovered, 2 hours or until a meat thermometer inserted into thickest portion registers 140°, adding hot water as needed to keep ham covered. Remove from heat, and let stand 2 hours.

Drain ham; trim skin, leaving a thin layer of fat. Score fat on ham in a diamond design; stud with cloves.

Combine brown sugar and mustard; coat exposed portion of ham with sugar mixture and a thin layer of breadcrumbs. Sprinkle with paprika.

Bake, uncovered, at 325° for 30 minutes, basting with ginger ale every 5 minutes. Garnish, if desired. Serve with biscuits. Yield: 30 servings.

Recipe adapted from Cape Fear...Still Cooking.

soups & sandwiches

Oyster Stew

3 (12-ounce) containers fresh oysters, undrained
½ cup butter
6 shallots, minced
3 tablespoons all-purpose flour
3 pints half-and-half
1½ teaspoons salt
¾ teaspoon pepper
⅓ cup vermouth

Drain oysters, reserving ¾ cup liquid.

Melt butter in a skillet; add shallots, and sauté until tender. Whisk in flour; cook, whisking constantly, 1 minute. Gradually add reserved oyster liquid and half-and-half; cook over medium heat, whisking constantly, until thickened and bubbly. Add oysters, and cook 5 minutes or until done. Stir in salt, pepper, and vermouth. Serve immediately. Yield: 8 to 10 servings.

Fish Chowder

Just about any type of firm, mild white fish fillets will blend nicely into this chowder.

½ pound salt pork, cut into ¼-inch cubes
2 medium onions, chopped
3 large potatoes, peeled and cut into ½-inch cubes (about 5 cups)
4 cups water
1 cup dry white wine
2½ pounds fresh cod, haddock, or pollock fillets
1 (12-ounce) can evaporated milk
3 cups milk
½ teaspoon salt
1 teaspoon freshly ground pepper
½ cup minced fresh parsley
Paprika

Cook salt pork in a Dutch oven over medium heat until crisp; remove salt pork, reserving 2 tablespoons drippings in pan. Set salt pork aside.

Sauté onion in hot drippings over medium-high heat 5 minutes or until tender. Add potatoes, 4 cups water, and wine; bring to a boil. Reduce heat, and simmer, uncovered, 12 to 15 minutes or until potatoes are almost tender.

Arrange fillets over potatoes; cover and simmer 10 to 12 minutes or until fish flakes with a fork. Break fish into chunks. Add evaporated milk and next 3 ingredients; cook over medium heat just until thoroughly heated. Top each serving with reserved salt pork, parsley, and paprika. Serve with breadsticks or crackers. Yield: 16 cups.

—*Cookbook Author Sarah Leah Chase*
Barnstable, Massachusetts

Frogmore Stew

5 quarts water
¼ cup Old Bay seasoning
4 pounds small red potatoes
2 pounds kielbasa or hot smoked link sausage, cut into 1½-inch pieces
6 ears fresh corn, halved
4 pounds unpeeled, large fresh shrimp
Old Bay seasoning
Cocktail sauce

Bring 5 quarts water and ¼ cup Old Bay seasoning to a rolling boil in a large covered stockpot.

Add potatoes; return to a boil, and cook, uncovered, 10 minutes.

Add sausage and corn, and return to a boil. Cook 10 minutes or until potatoes are tender.

Add shrimp to stockpot; cook 3 to 4 minutes or until shrimp turn pink. Drain. Serve with Old Bay seasoning and cocktail sauce. Yield: 12 servings.

Whatever the ingredients, it's a take-your-shoes-off-and-relax kind of dish.

frogmore stew

When Frogmore Stew was first cooked in the 1960s, Frogmore was a little hamlet on St. Helena Island, near Beaufort, South Carolina. In the 1980s, however, the postal service abolished the name Frogmore. That changed the name of the popular dish to Lowcountry Boil or Beaufort Stew—except, of course, among the proud residents of Frogmore.

Richard Gay, whose family owns Gay Fish Company on St. Helena, created the dish in the early sixties. "I was on weekend duty in the National Guard," he says, "and I'd sometimes get a lot of shrimp, put it in a pot with sausage and corn, and boil it up. Within an hour, we could have a complete meal for 100 people. The boys teased me that since I was from Frogmore, we'd name it Frogmore Stew. We put out copies of the recipe at the seafood market dock and began selling the other ingredients as well."

At its most basic, the dish contains shrimp, seafood seasoning, smoked sausage, corn on the cob, and potatoes. But onions, crab, and butter are other frequent additions. "Every time I see someone else serve it, there are a couple of ingredients that I don't use," Richard says. He adds ½ pound of butter for every six people, and he prefers crab boil seasoning that comes in a bag.

Whatever the ingredients, it's a take-your-shoes-off-and-relax kind of dish. "People on vacation like it because you cook everything in one pot," Richard says. Beachgoers often serve it on heavy brown paper or newspaper for easy cleanup.

Frogmore Stew

Maine Clam Chowder

5 dozen medium-size steamer clams, scrubbed
3 cups water
½ cup butter or margarine
1 large onion, chopped
3 celery ribs, chopped
3 tablespoons all-purpose flour
3 large potatoes, peeled and cut into
   ½-inch cubes (2¼ pounds)
2 (12-ounce) cans evaporated milk
2 cups half-and-half
1 teaspoon salt
1 teaspoon freshly ground pepper
2 tablespoons minced fresh parsley
6 bacon slices, cooked and crumbled
Paprika

Discard any opened or cracked clams. Combine clams and 3 cups water in a large stockpot; bring to a boil. Cover and cook 8 to 10 minutes or until clams open, discarding any unopened clams. Remove clams with a slotted spoon; set aside. Pour liquid through a wire-mesh strainer into a large container, discarding debris. Set clam liquid aside.

Melt butter in a Dutch oven over medium heat; add onion and celery, and sauté 5 minutes or until tender. Whisk in flour; cook, whisking constantly, 1 minute. Gradually whisk in reserved clam liquid; cook over medium heat, whisking constantly, until thickened and bubbly. Add potatoes, reduce heat, and cook over low heat 15 to 20 minutes or until potatoes are tender.

Remove clams from shells, discarding shells. Peel membrane from clam necks and discard. Add clams, evaporated milk, and next 3 ingredients to potato mixture. Cook over medium-high heat until thoroughly heated. Top each serving with parsley, crumbled bacon, and a dash of paprika. Serve with French bread or crackers. Yield: 16 cups.

—*Cookbook Author Sarah Leah Chase*
Barnstable, Massachusetts

Lobster-and-Corn Chowder with Roasted Red Pepper Cream

Lobster-and-Corn Chowder with Roasted Red Pepper Cream

6 ears fresh corn, shucked
6 quarts water
1 tablespoon salt
3 (2- to 2½-pound) live lobsters
10 cups water
8 smoked bacon slices, chopped
1 large onion, chopped
1 pound new potatoes, quartered
1 cup milk
1 cup whipping cream
1½ teaspoons salt
1 teaspoon freshly ground pepper
½ cup shredded fresh basil
Roasted Red Pepper Cream

Coat food rack with vegetable cooking spray; place on grill over medium-high heat (350° to 400°). Place corn on rack, and cook 5 minutes on each side or until lightly browned. Cool; cut off kernels, and set aside, reserving cobs.

Bring 6 quarts water and 1 tablespoon salt to a boil in a large stockpot.

Plunge lobsters, headfirst, into boiling water; return to a boil. Cover, reduce heat, and simmer 10 minutes for the first pound and 3 minutes for each additional pound. Remove lobsters with tongs. Remove meat from claws and tails; set meat aside.

Place corn cobs and 10 cups water in a large stockpot. Bring to a boil over medium-high heat; cover, reduce heat, and simmer 1 hour. Discard corn cobs; pour liquid through a fine wire-mesh strainer into a large container, discarding solids. Set liquid aside.

Cook bacon in a large stockpot until crisp; remove bacon, reserving 2 tablespoons drippings in pan. Set bacon aside.

Sauté onion in hot drippings 5 minutes or until tender. Add reserved liquid and potatoes; bring to a boil. Reduce heat, and simmer 15 minutes or until potatoes are tender. Stir in corn, lobster meat, milk, and next 3 ingredients;

cook over medium heat 10 minutes or until mixture almost boils. Remove from heat; stir in basil. Top each serving with bacon and Roasted Red Pepper Cream. Serve with crackers, if desired. Yield: 16 cups.

Roasted Red Pepper Cream

1	large red bell pepper
1	large garlic clove, minced
½	teaspoon saffron threads
	Pinch ground red pepper
3	tablespoons olive oil
1½	tablespoons whipping cream
¼	teaspoon salt

Place bell pepper on an aluminum foil-lined baking sheet. Broil 5½ inches from heat 5 minutes on each side or until pepper looks blistered.

Place bell pepper in a heavy-duty zip-top plastic bag; seal and let stand 10 minutes to loosen skins. Peel pepper; remove and discard seeds.

Process pepper and next 3 ingredients in a food processor until smooth. With processor running, pour oil through food chute, processing until mixture thickens. Add whipping cream and salt; pulse 2 or 3 times. Yield: ⅔ cup.

—Cookbook Author Sarah Leah Chase
Barnstable, Massachusetts

Crab and Mushroom Bisque

½	cup butter, divided
½	cup chopped onion
½	cup chopped green bell pepper
2	green onions, finely chopped
¼	cup chopped fresh parsley
1	(8-ounce) package fresh mushrooms, chopped
¼	cup all-purpose flour
2	cups milk
1½	tablespoons Lemon Blend
1	teaspoon hot sauce
3	cups half-and-half
1	pound fresh lump crabmeat, drained
¼	cup dry sherry

Melt ¼ cup butter in a large saucepan over medium-high heat; add onion and next 4 ingredients. Cook, stirring often, 5 minutes or until tender. Remove from pan; set aside.

Melt remaining butter in same saucepan over low heat; add flour, stirring until smooth. Cook 1 minute, stirring constantly. Gradually stir in milk. Cook over medium heat, stirring constantly, until thickened and bubbly. Stir in onion mixture, Lemon Blend, hot sauce, and half-and-half. Bring to a boil, stirring often. Reduce heat; stir in crabmeat. Simmer, uncovered, 5 minutes, stirring often. Stir in sherry, and serve immediately. Yield: 9 cups.

Lemon Blend

3	tablespoons grated lemon rind
2	tablespoons kosher salt*
1	bay leaf
1	teaspoon celery seeds
1	teaspoon ground coriander
¼	teaspoon coarsely ground pepper

Combine all ingredients in a small food processor or coffee grinder. Process until finely and evenly chopped. Store in an airtight container. Yield: about ⅓ cup.

*If substituting regular salt, use half the amount (1 tablespoon).

Crab Bisque

Here's a quick and easy seafood soup using convenience products.

1	pound fresh lump crabmeat
1	(10¾-ounce) can cream of celery soup, undiluted
1	(10¾-ounce) can cream of mushroom soup, undiluted
1	(10¾-ounce) can tomato soup, undiluted
1	quart milk
½	cup dry sherry
2	tablespoons sugar
2	teaspoons freshly ground pepper
1	teaspoon salt
1	tablespoon Worcestershire sauce
5	drops hot sauce

Drain crabmeat, and remove any bits of shell. Set aside.

Stir together celery soup and remaining ingredients. Cook over medium heat, stirring

constantly, until mixture is thoroughly heated. Stir in crabmeat. Yield: 10 cups.
Recipe adapted from Cape Fear...Still Cooking.

Spicy Thai Lobster Soup

2	lobster tails, cooked*
1	tablespoon vegetable oil
1	to 1½ tablespoons Asian Blend
4	cups fish stock or chicken broth
1	tablespoon grated lime rind
⅓	cup uncooked long-grain rice
1	cup lite coconut milk
6	large mushrooms, sliced
2	green onions, chopped
1	Thai chile, halved
1	tablespoon chopped fresh cilantro
2	tablespoons fresh lime juice

Garnishes: fresh cilantro, lime wedges

Remove lobster meat from shell; slice and set meat aside.

Heat oil in a large saucepan over medium heat. Stir in Asian Blend; sauté 1 minute. Add broth and lime rind; bring to a boil. Stir in rice. Cover, reduce heat, and simmer 15 to 20 minutes.

Stir in coconut milk and mushrooms; cook, stirring occasionally, 5 minutes. Stir in lobster, green onions, chile, and cilantro; cook 3 to 5 minutes. Remove from heat, and stir in lime juice. Garnish, if desired. Yield: 4 servings.
¾ pound peeled and deveined shrimp may be substituted for lobster (1 pound if purchased in the shell).

Asian Blend

2	tablespoons ground ginger
2	tablespoons ground coriander
1	tablespoon ground turmeric
1	tablespoon ground cumin
2	teaspoons coarsely ground pepper
1	teaspoon ground cardamom
1	teaspoon ground fenugreek (optional)*

Combine all ingredients. Store in an airtight container. Yield: about ½ cup.
If fenugreek's not in your local grocery, try an international market or importer store.

Cooking a gumbo is like painting on a blank canvas—you can do anything you want with it.

rules of the roux

Let us walk you through the steps of making a rich brown roux, the necessary beginning for a great gumbo. A dark-colored roux gives gumbo its characteristic smoky, nutty taste.

- **A roux is nothing more than flour and fat.** The more delicious the fat, the better the roux. For example, duck fat or lard will impart more flavor than vegetable oil (but will be less healthy).

- **A heavy pot or cast-iron skillet is best for making a rich roux.** Heat the oil and stir in enough flour until it's the consistency of wet sand. For best results, cook a roux over low heat until it's the desired color (such as a copper penny). You can cook a roux at a higher temperature, but stir constantly and watch carefully—it burns easily. Once it turns a dark golden color, you've got seconds to get it just a wee bit darker; there's a fine line between ready and burned. Store roux in an airtight container in the refrigerator up to two weeks. Anytime you want gumbo, you're ahead of the game.

- **For a lower fat gumbo,** you can use a "dry" roux, which is simply flour that's been toasted in an oven until it's reached the desired color (a golden brown). The dry roux is then whisked into a liquid slurry, and the lumps are smoothed out before broth is added.

- **From the base of either a "wet" or "dry" roux,** you can create endless versions of gumbo by adding herbs and vegetables (such as corn, potatoes, beans, eggplant, cabbage, or squash). Most seafood can be used, as well as beef, poultry, and game. Remember to add delicate oysters and crabmeat at the end of cooking so they won't toughen or disintegrate. Cooking a gumbo is like painting on a blank canvas—you can do anything you want with it.

Shrimp and Sausage Gumbo

Shrimp and Sausage Gumbo

2   pounds unpeeled, large fresh shrimp
2   (32-ounce) containers chicken broth
1   pound andouille or smoked sausage, cut into ¼-inch slices
Vegetable oil
1   cup all-purpose flour
1   medium onion, chopped
1   green bell pepper, chopped
3   celery ribs, sliced
3   garlic cloves, minced
2   bay leaves
2   teaspoons Creole seasoning
½   teaspoon dried thyme
1   tablespoon Worcestershire sauce
2   to 3 teaspoons hot sauce
½   cup chopped green onions
Hot cooked rice

Peel shrimp, reserving shells, and devein, if desired. Set shrimp aside.

Combine shrimp shells and chicken broth in a large Dutch oven; bring to a boil. Reduce heat, and simmer, uncovered, 20 minutes. Pour mixture through a wire-mesh strainer into a bowl, discarding shells. Set broth aside; keep warm.

Cook sausage in Dutch oven over medium heat until browned. Remove sausage; set aside. Measure drippings, adding enough oil to measure ½ cup. Cook oil mixture and flour in Dutch oven over medium-low heat about 35 to 40 minutes, whisking constantly, until roux is chocolate colored.

Stir in onion and next 3 ingredients; cook 7 minutes or until vegetables are tender, stirring often. Gradually stir in warm broth; bring mixture to a boil. Stir in bay leaves and next 4 ingredients; reduce heat, and simmer, uncovered, 50 minutes, stirring occasionally.

Stir in shrimp, sausage, and green onions; cook 5 to 7 minutes or until shrimp turn pink. Discard bay leaves before serving. Serve over rice. Yield: 11 cups.

Duck and Oyster Gumbo

To save time on gumbo day, roast the ducks and make the stock a day ahead.

½ cup vegetable oil
1 cup all-purpose flour
2 celery ribs, chopped
2 medium onions, chopped
2 green bell peppers, chopped
3 garlic cloves, minced
8 cups Duck Stock
2 tablespoons tomato paste
1 tablespoon chopped fresh thyme
1 tablespoon chopped fresh oregano
1 tablespoon molasses
2 teaspoons hot sauce
1¼ teaspoons salt
½ teaspoon freshly ground black pepper
½ teaspoon ground red pepper
5 to 6 cups chopped duck meat
1 (12-ounce) container fresh oysters, drained
½ cup sliced fresh basil
Hot cooked rice
¼ cup chopped green onions

Cook oil and flour in a large Dutch oven over medium-low heat about 35 to 40 minutes, whisking constantly, until roux is chocolate colored.

Stir in celery, onion, and bell pepper; sauté 6 to 8 minutes. Add garlic; cook 2 minutes. Gradually stir in Duck Stock and next 8 ingredients; bring to a boil. Reduce heat, and simmer, uncovered, 1 hour, stirring occasionally.

Add duck meat; simmer 15 minutes. Remove from heat; stir in oysters and fresh basil. Let stand 5 minutes. Serve over rice. Sprinkle with green onions. Yield: 16 cups.

Duck Stock

2 (5-pound) dressed ducks
3 celery ribs, quartered
2 medium onions, quartered
1 green bell pepper, quartered
2 (32-ounce) containers chicken broth
2 quarts water
5 sprigs fresh thyme
2 bay leaves
1 teaspoon black peppercorns

Place ducks on a rack in a large roasting pan.

Bake at 350° until a meat thermometer inserted into thickest portion registers 180° (about 2 hours and 15 minutes). Cool completely. Remove meat from ducks, reserving bones. Chop meat, and set aside for gumbo.

Combine duck bones and remaining ingredients in a large Dutch oven; bring to a boil. Reduce heat, and simmer, uncovered, 1 hour. Skim fat and foam off top of stock after first 10 minutes of simmering. Pour stock through a wire-mesh strainer into a large bowl, discarding solids. Yield: 14 cups.

Note: Store stock in a tightly covered container in refrigerator up to 3 days, or freeze up to 3 months.

Shrimp-Crab Gumbo

1½ cups vegetable oil
2 cups all-purpose flour
9 (14-ounce) cans chicken broth
2½ cups chopped onion
1 cup chopped green onions
½ cup chopped celery
2 garlic cloves, chopped
1 (10-ounce) can diced tomatoes with green chiles
1 (8-ounce) can tomato sauce
3 pounds unpeeled, medium-size fresh shrimp
1 (16-ounce) container lump crabmeat
½ cup chopped fresh parsley
1 tablespoon filé powder (optional)
Hot cooked rice

Heat oil in a large stockpot over medium heat; gradually whisk in flour, and cook, whisking constantly, until roux is a dark mahogany color (about 30 minutes).

Stir in chicken broth and next 6 ingredients; bring to a boil. Reduce heat, and simmer, stirring occasionally, 3 hours.

Peel shrimp, and devein, if desired. Add shrimp to broth mixture; cook, stirring often, 15 minutes or just until shrimp turn pink. Stir in crabmeat and parsley. Remove from heat; stir in filé powder, if desired. Serve over rice. Yield: 20 cups.

Duck and Oyster Gumbo

Scallop and Vegetable Gumbo

6   bacon slices
2   tablespoons vegetable oil
1   cup all-purpose flour
5   celery ribs, chopped
2   medium onions, chopped
2   green bell peppers, chopped
2   garlic cloves, minced
2   (32-ounce) containers chicken broth
¾   cup fresh or frozen baby lima beans
2   bay leaves
1½   teaspoons chopped fresh thyme
1   teaspoon chopped fresh rosemary
1½   cups sliced fresh or frozen okra
1½   cups peeled, seeded, and chopped tomato
1   cup fresh or frozen yellow corn kernels
1   large potato, cubed
1   (8-ounce) package sliced fresh
      mushrooms
1   tablespoon butter, melted
2   pounds fresh bay scallops
1¾   teaspoons salt
½   teaspoon freshly ground pepper
1   to 2 teaspoons hot sauce
Hot cooked rice
Freshly ground pepper

Cook bacon in a Dutch oven until crisp; drain on paper towels, reserving drippings in pan. Crumble bacon, and set aside.

Add vegetable oil to pan drippings; whisk in flour. Cook over medium-low heat, stirring constantly, until roux is caramel colored (about 25 minutes). Add celery and next 3 ingredients; cook, stirring constantly, 10 minutes or until vegetables are tender.

Stir in broth and next 4 ingredients; bring to a boil. Reduce heat, and simmer, uncovered, 1 hour, stirring occasionally and skimming as necessary. Stir in okra and next 3 ingredients; bring to a boil. Reduce heat, and simmer, uncovered, 30 minutes.

Sauté mushrooms in butter in a large skillet over medium-high heat 3 to 4 minutes or until liquid evaporates. Add to broth mixture.

Add bacon, scallops, and next 3 ingredients to broth; bring to a boil. Reduce heat, and simmer, uncovered, 5 minutes or until scallops are done; discard bay leaves. Serve over rice. Sprinkle with pepper. Yield: 15 cups.

Mussel Soup with Saffron and Cream

Mussel Soup with Saffron and Cream

3   pounds fresh mussels, scrubbed and
      debearded
2   cups dry white wine
1   tablespoon chopped fresh garlic
2   tablespoons butter
2   tablespoons all-purpose flour
2   cups whipping cream
½   to 1 teaspoon saffron threads
¼   teaspoon salt
¼   teaspoon pepper
6   spinach or sorrel leaves, cut into thin
      strips

Discard opened, cracked, or heavy mussels.

Bring wine and garlic to a boil in a Dutch oven. Add mussels; cover and return to a boil. Boil 5 minutes. Immediately remove opened mussels with a slotted spoon. Continue cooking remaining mussels for 2 minutes; others may open. Discard any unopened mussels, reserving broth.

Remove mussels from shells; return mussels to broth, discarding shells.

Melt butter in a heavy saucepan over low heat; whisk in flour. Cook, whisking constantly, 1 minute. Gradually whisk in cream; cook over medium heat, whisking constantly, until thick and bubbly. Stir in reserved broth mixture, saffron, salt, and pepper; cook, stirring often, until thoroughly heated. Top with spinach or sorrel, and serve immediately. Yield: 7 cups.

Bouillabaisse à la Marseillaise

Bouillabaisse à la Marseillaise

1 cup sliced yellow onion (about 1 medium)
1 cup sliced leeks, white part only (1 large)
½ cup olive oil
2 to 3 cups chopped fresh tomatoes or
   1 (14½-ounce) can whole tomatoes,
   drained and chopped
4 garlic cloves, pressed
1½ quarts water
6 fresh parsley sprigs
1 bay leaf
½ teaspoon dried thyme
½ teaspoon fennel seeds
½ teaspoon saffron
1 (1- x 2-inch) strip of orange peel
4 cups fish stock or 4 (8-ounce) bottles
   clam juice
1 pound unpeeled, medium-size fresh shrimp
2 (1¼-pound) lobsters, cooked
1 pound firm-fleshed fish fillets (halibut,
   grouper, or cod)
½ pound littleneck clams, scrubbed
1 pound tender-fleshed fish fillets
   (flounder, snapper, or whiting)
½ pound mussels, scrubbed and debearded
½ pound sea scallops
½ pound crab claws
Rouille
French bread rounds, toasted
⅓ cup chopped fresh parsley

Sauté onion and leeks in hot oil in a large Dutch oven over medium-high heat 5 minutes or until tender. Stir in tomato and garlic, and cook 5 more minutes. Stir in 1½ quarts water and next 7 ingredients. Bring to a boil; reduce heat, and simmer, uncovered, 40 minutes, stirring occasionally. Strain broth, discarding solids. (Broth can be made up to this point one day ahead.)

Peel shrimp, leaving tails intact; devein, if desired. Chill.

Remove meat from lobster claws and tail; slice tail into medallions.

Bring broth to a boil. Add firm-fleshed fish and clams; boil, uncovered, 5 minutes. Add tender-fleshed fish, shrimp, mussels, and scallops; cook 3 minutes. Add lobster meat and crab claws; cook 2 to 3 minutes or until thoroughly heated and clam and mussel shells open.

a fine kettle of tips

• **Bouillabaisse requires a fair amount of effort to prepare.** We used bottled clam juice, which Julia Child offers as a substitute for fish stock, and made the broth a day ahead.

• **You can buy the lobster already steamed at the supermarket;** remove the shells and cut into pieces a day ahead.

• **Serve bouillabaisse** with a fork and spoon so diners can enjoy both fish and broth.

Spread Rouille on toasted French bread rounds; place in each of 8 individual soup bowls. Top with seafood and broth. Sprinkle each serving with parsley. Serve with additional French bread and Rouille. Yield: 6 to 8 servings.

Rouille

6 large garlic cloves, pressed
¼ teaspoon salt
18 large basil leaves (about ½ cup packed)
¾ cup soft breadcrumbs, lightly packed
2 to 3 tablespoons soup broth or milk
¼ cup plus 2 tablespoons egg substitute*
¾ cup olive oil
1 (4-ounce) jar diced pimientos, drained
4 drops hot sauce
Dash of freshly ground pepper

Place garlic in a mortar; add salt. Using a pestle, grind to a paste. Gradually add basil, and grind to a paste. Repeat procedure with breadcrumbs and broth.

Transfer mixture to blender; add egg substitute, and process until smooth. With blender running, add oil in a slow, steady stream, blending until thickened. Add pimientos, hot sauce, and pepper; process until smooth. Yield: 1½ cups.

Note: Make soft breadcrumbs by placing bread slices in a food processor or blender and processing. Store in an airtight container in the refrigerator for one week or in a freezer up to six months.

*Julia calls for 3 egg yolks in the traditional recipe; however, our Test Kitchens recommend replacing raw eggs with egg substitute. From The French Chef Cookbook by Julia Child, © 1968 by Julia Child. Used by permission of Alfred A. Knopf, a division of Random House, Inc. Recipe was originally published in Coastal Living magazine.

Harbourtown Scallop Soup with Chardonnay and Saffron

3 medium leeks
3 tablespoons unsalted butter, divided
1 red bell pepper, thinly sliced
4 cups fish stock*
1 cup Chardonnay or other dry white wine
1 cup whipping cream
½ teaspoon salt
¼ teaspoon pepper
Pinch of saffron threads
¼ pound fresh mushrooms, sliced
¾ pound swordfish steaks, cut into bite-size
   pieces
¾ pound bay scallops
Garnish: chopped fresh parsley

Remove roots, tough outer leaves, and tops from leeks, leaving 2 inches of dark leaves. Wash thoroughly; finely chop. Melt 2 tablespoons butter in a skillet over medium heat; add leeks. Cook 5 minutes or until tender, stirring constantly. Add sliced red pepper; cook 2 more minutes. Set aside.

Combine fish stock and wine in a 4-quart Dutch oven; bring to a boil. Cook, uncovered, 10 minutes or until reduced to about 4 cups. Add cream; cook 10 more minutes. Stir in salt, pepper, saffron, and reserved leek mixture; set aside.

Heat remaining 1 tablespoon butter in a skillet over medium heat; add mushrooms. Cook 3 minutes or just until tender, stirring constantly; set aside.

Bring fish stock mixture to a simmer; add swordfish. Cook, uncovered, 3 minutes. Add scallops; cook 3 more minutes. Stir in mushrooms. Garnish, if desired. Yield: 6½ cups.

*In place of fish stock, you can use fish bouillon cubes dissolved in water according to package directions.

Indeed, the broth is what separates a great cioppino from the ordinary.

Cioppino

Our cioppino uses ingredients native to the West Coast and is perfectly complemented by a loaf of sourdough bread to soak up the broth.

2   onions, diced
6   garlic cloves, chopped
1   green bell pepper, chopped
¼   cup olive oil
2   cups dry red wine
2   cups clam juice
1   (28-ounce) can diced tomatoes
1   (8-ounce) can tomato sauce
1   bay leaf
1   tablespoon sugar
1   tablespoon dried oregano
1   tablespoon dried basil
1   tablespoon ground black pepper
1   tablespoon dried crushed red pepper
1   teaspoon salt
¼   teaspoon dried thyme
1   tablespoon lemon juice
3   whole-cooked Dungeness crabs (about 6 pounds) or about 6 pounds lobster, steamed
1   pound Manila or littleneck clams, scrubbed
1   pound unpeeled, large fresh shrimp
3   pounds Pacific rockfish fillets or other firm white fish, cut into 1½-inch pieces
Garnish: chopped fresh parsley

Sauté first 3 ingredients in hot oil in a large stockpot until tender; stir in next 13 ingredients. Bring to a boil; cover, reduce heat, and simmer 1 hour. Let cool; cover and chill at least 12 hours.

Pry off apron or tail flap from crabs. Lift off top shell, saving cream-colored "crab butter" from inside the top shell, and discard shell. Pull out and discard feathery gills adhering to the body meat. Discard stomach mass, and break crab into left and right sections. Twist legs and claws from body. Cut each body section cross-wise into 2 pieces. Crack legs with a wooden mallet. Set body pieces, cracked claws, and "crab butter" aside.

Discard opened or cracked clams or heavy

cioppino

A San Francisco treat, cioppino (pronounced "chuh-PEEN-oh) is a savory stew made with freshly cracked Dungeness crab, shrimp, clams, and fish simmered in a spicy tomato sauce. This California classic can be traced back to the late 1800s, when Italian and Portuguese immigrant fishermen married their stew recipes to the seafood of the California coast. While at sea, a fisherman needed his meals to be inexpensive, easy, and quick. Home-canned tomatoes and other stew staples were stowed away for ready use. Over a hot fire, the catch of the day could be turned into a heart-warming, bread-sopping meal in minutes. All of the recipes were similar in their use of olive oil, tomatoes, garlic, and often a little wine with the freshly caught fish, but the end products varied as much as the fishermen's dialects.

There are still no strict rules for making this fisherman's stew. No matter how you make it—with fish or shellfish; with a thick or thin sauce that's tame or spicy; with red or white wine, little wine, lots of wine, or no wine; served with or without pasta—the result is this famed fish soup.

However, "in the end," as the Italian saying goes, "everything goes to the broth." The all-important broth makes or breaks a great cioppino. Slow simmering marries the tomatoes' sweetness and acid into a perfect balance with the flavorful juices from the sea. Dungeness crab season follows summer's tomato season, so canned tomatoes are commonly used.

Since the crab, clams, and shrimp are cooked in their shells, be sure to provide each diner with a bib and plenty of napkins for this finger fare. And pour up your choice of red or white wine to sip alongside.

ones (indicating they're filled with sand).

Warm chilled tomato broth in a large saucepan over medium heat, stirring occasionally, until thoroughly heated.

Place crab, clams, shrimp, and fish in a large stockpot. Pour warm tomato broth over seafood; bring to a boil. Reduce heat; simmer 10 to 12 minutes. Discard any clams that did not open during cooking. Garnish, if desired. Serve with sourdough bread. Yield: 10 servings.

Note: *Dungeness crab is typically sold precooked.*

—*Food Writer Jon Rowley*
Seattle, Washington

Shrimp-Feta Soup

1   pound unpeeled, jumbo fresh shrimp
1   tablespoon butter
2   tablespoons olive oil
1   medium onion, minced
1   to 2 garlic cloves, minced
1   cup dry white wine
1   (8-ounce) bottle clam juice
4   tomatoes, peeled and chopped
1   teaspoon salt
3/4   teaspoon dried oregano
1/2   teaspoon freshly ground pepper
1   (4-ounce) package feta cheese,
    crumbled*
1/4   cup chopped fresh parsley

Peel shrimp, and devein, if desired; set aside.

Melt butter with oil in a Dutch oven over medium heat. Add onion and garlic; sauté 5 minutes, stirring constantly.

Add wine and next 5 ingredients; bring to a boil. Reduce heat, and simmer 10 minutes or until thickened.

Stir in cheese, and simmer 10 minutes. Add shrimp, and cook 3 to 5 minutes or just until shrimp turn pink. Stir in parsley. Yield: 6 cups.

*1 (4-ounce) log goat cheese, crumbled, may be substituted.

Beer-Cheese Soup

1/4   cup butter or margarine
1/4   cup all-purpose flour
2   cups half-and-half
1   (12-ounce) can beer
1   (16-ounce) loaf pasteurized prepared
    cheese product, cubed
1   tablespoon Worcestershire sauce
1/4   teaspoon ground red pepper
1/4   teaspoon hot sauce
1/8   teaspoon salt
Ground red pepper

Melt butter in a Dutch oven or large saucepan over medium-low heat; add flour, stirring until smooth. Cook 1 minute, stirring constantly. Gradually add half-and-half and beer; cook over medium heat, stirring constantly with a wire whisk, until thickened.

Add cheese; cook over medium heat until cheese melts. Stir in Worcestershire sauce, 1/4 teaspoon red pepper, hot sauce, and salt. Ladle into bowls. Sprinkle with additional red pepper before serving. Yield: 5 cups.

Brie and Roasted Garlic Soup

Roasting the garlic makes a sweet and mellow base for this soup. Buttery Brie melts into the broth, making it rich, creamy, and in a class by itself.

2   large garlic bulbs
2   tablespoons olive oil
7   ounces Brie
2   celery ribs, finely chopped
1   medium onion, finely chopped
1   medium carrot, scraped and finely
    chopped
1/4   cup olive oil
1/4   cup all-purpose flour
6   cups chicken broth
1   teaspoon chopped fresh oregano
1   teaspoon chopped fresh parsley
1/2   teaspoon chopped fresh thyme
1/8   teaspoon ground white pepper

Peel outer skin from each garlic bulb, and discard. Cut off top one-third of each garlic bulb. Place garlic, cut side up, on an aluminum foil-lined baking sheet. Drizzle garlic with 2 tablespoons olive oil.

Bake, uncovered, at 350° for 1 hour or until garlic is soft. Remove from oven; cool 10 minutes. Squeeze pulp from each bulb into a bowl; set pulp aside.

Remove and discard rind from cheese; coarsely chop cheese, and set aside.

Sauté celery, onion, and carrot in 1/4 cup olive oil in a large saucepan over medium-high heat 10 minutes or until tender. Add flour, stirring until smooth. Cook 1 minute, stirring constantly. Gradually add chicken broth; bring to a boil, stirring often. Reduce heat, and simmer, uncovered, 15 minutes or until vegetables are tender, stirring often.

Process garlic pulp and 1 cup soup mixture in a food processor until smooth. Stir pureed mixture into remaining soup mixture; add oregano, parsley, and thyme. Bring to a simmer over medium-low heat. Add reserved Brie cheese, and cook, stirring constantly, until cheese melts. Stir in pepper. Yield: 6½ cups.

Sweet Corn Soup with Crab

Tom Noelke, chef/owner of Gulf Coast Grill in Macon, Georgia, simmers corn cobs with chicken broth for a wonderful depth of flavor.

6   ears fresh corn
1/3   cup diced salt pork
2   tablespoons butter or margarine
1/4   cup white cornmeal
2   celery ribs, diced
1   medium onion, diced
1   red bell pepper, diced
1   jalapeño pepper, diced
4¾   cups chicken broth
1   pound fresh lump crabmeat, drained
1   cup whipping cream
1/4   cup chopped fresh cilantro
1/2   teaspoon salt
1/4   teaspoon ground white pepper
Garnish: fresh cilantro sprigs

Cut corn from cobs to equal 3 cups kernels. Set corn kernels aside. Reserve 2 corn cobs.

Brown salt pork in a Dutch oven over medium heat; remove pork, and reserve for another use.

Add butter to pork drippings in Dutch oven over medium heat; whisk in cornmeal, and cook, whisking constantly, 1 minute. Add 3 cups corn kernels, celery, and next 3 ingredients; sauté 2 minutes.

Add broth and 2 corn cobs. Bring to a boil; reduce heat, and simmer 30 minutes. Remove and discard corn cobs. Stir in crabmeat and next 4 ingredients; cook until thoroughly heated. Garnish, if desired. Yield: 10½ cups.

Corn Soup with Chives

2 tablespoons unsalted butter
2 large white onions, chopped
2 cups fresh corn kernels (about 4 ears)
2 teaspoons sugar
2 (14-ounce) cans vegetable broth
2 cups heavy whipping cream
½ teaspoon salt
¼ teaspoon ground white pepper
¼ cup chopped fresh chives

Melt butter in a large skillet over medium heat; add onion, and sauté until tender. Stir in corn and sugar; cook, stirring occasionally, 12 minutes. Stir in broth; simmer, uncovered, 18 minutes. (Most of broth will evaporate.) Stir in cream, and simmer 5 minutes.

Transfer corn mixture to a blender; process until smooth. Pour mixture through a wire-mesh strainer into skillet, discarding solids. Stir in salt and white pepper. Reheat, if necessary. Pour into 4 serving bowls; sprinkle evenly with chives. Serve immediately. Yield: 4 cups.
Note: If you can't find canned vegetable broth, look for vegetable bouillon cubes. Reconstitute the cubes according to package instructions, and prepare soup recipe with 3½ cups broth.

Grilled Corn Soup with Cilantro and Ancho Chile Cream

Pureed grilled corn gives this soup a smoky essence.

8 ears fresh corn with husks
2 serrano chile peppers
4 cups chicken broth, undiluted
4 garlic cloves, minced
2 medium carrots, chopped
2 small onions, chopped
1 large celery rib, chopped
2 cups whipping cream
½ teaspoon salt
Cilantro Cream
Ancho Chile Cream

Soak corn in husks in water 15 minutes. Remove from water; grill corn in husks, covered with grill lid, over medium-high heat (350° to 400°) 15 to 20 minutes or until tender and slightly charred, turning occasionally. Let cool. Remove husks; cut corn kernels from cob, and set kernels aside.

Using rubber gloves, seed and mince chiles. Combine chiles, broth, and next 4 ingredients in a large saucepan. Bring to a boil; reduce heat, and simmer, uncovered, 10 minutes. Add corn to vegetable mixture, and simmer 10 minutes or until vegetables are tender. Let cool slightly.

Transfer half of corn mixture to an electric blender; process until smooth, stopping once to scrape down sides. Repeat procedure with remaining corn mixture. Return pureed mixture to pan; bring to a boil. Reduce heat; stir in whipping cream and salt. Cook until thoroughly heated.

To serve, ladle soup into individual serving bowls, and swirl Cilantro Cream and Ancho Chile Cream into each serving. Yield: 6 cups.

Cilantro Cream

5 large spinach leaves
2 cups water
1 cup loosely packed fresh cilantro leaves
3 tablespoons half-and-half
2 tablespoons sour cream

Wash and remove stems from spinach leaves. Bring water to a boil in a small saucepan. Add spinach, and cook 1 minute. Drain and rinse with cold water; drain. Press spinach between paper towels to remove excess moisture.

Place spinach, cilantro, and half-and-half in a blender; process until smooth, stopping once to scrape down sides. Place puree in a fine wire-mesh strainer over a small bowl; press with back of a spoon against sides of strainer to squeeze out liquid. Discard spinach and cilantro in strainer. Add sour cream to cream in bowl, stirring with a wire whisk until smooth. Yield: ⅓ cup.

Ancho Chile Cream

1 small dried ancho chile pepper
1 cup hot water
3 tablespoons half-and-half
2 tablespoons sour cream

Using rubber gloves, remove and discard stems and seeds from chile pepper. Wash chile in cold water; drain. Tear chile in half, and place in a small bowl; add hot water. Let stand 20 minutes; drain. Place chile and half-and-half in a blender; process until smooth, stopping once to scrape down sides.

Place puree in a fine wire-mesh strainer over a small bowl; press with back of a spoon against sides of strainer to squeeze out liquid. Discard chile pepper pulp in strainer. Add sour cream to cream in bowl, stirring well with a wire whisk. Yield: ¼ cup.

Chilled Roasted Pepper and Tomato Soup

This cold vegetable soup bears resemblance to gazpacho with roasted peppers adding a depth of flavor not associated with the traditional chilled tomato soup.

3 medium-size red bell peppers
2½ cups vegetable juice
2 garlic cloves, chopped
2 tablespoons vegetable oil
2 tablespoons cider vinegar
¼ teaspoon salt
¼ teaspoon freshly ground pepper
1 large avocado, chopped
1 cucumber, seeded and chopped
¼ red onion, chopped
2 tablespoons chopped fresh cilantro
1 jalapeño pepper, seeded and minced (optional)
Lime wedges (optional)

Broil peppers on an aluminum foil-lined baking sheet 5½ inches from heat about 5 minutes on each side or until peppers look blistered.

Place peppers in a heavy-duty zip-top plastic bag; seal and let stand 10 minutes to loosen skins. Peel peppers; remove and discard seeds.

Process peppers, vegetable juice, and next 5 ingredients until smooth; chill thoroughly.

Serve soup with avocado, next 3 ingredients, and, if desired, minced jalapeño and lime wedges. Yield: 4 cups.

Tomato-Basil Cream Soup

4 shallots, diced
1/2 pound leeks, chopped
1 celery rib, chopped
2 to 3 garlic cloves, pressed
2 tablespoons vegetable oil
2 (14 1/2-ounce) cans Italian-style tomatoes, undrained and chopped
1 tablespoon dried basil
2 (14-ounce) cans chicken broth
1/4 teaspoon salt
1 cup whipping cream
Garnishes: lemon slices, fresh basil sprigs

Cook first 4 ingredients in hot oil in a Dutch oven over low heat 10 minutes or until tender (do not brown). Add tomato and basil; cook over medium heat, stirring often, 10 minutes. Add broth and salt; bring to a boil. Reduce heat, and simmer, stirring occasionally, 1 hour. Cool.

Process half of mixture in a food processor or blender until smooth, stopping once to scrape down sides. Repeat procedure with remaining mixture.

Stir in whipping cream; cook, stirring constantly, until thoroughly heated (do not boil). Garnish, if desired. Yield: 6 1/2 cups.

Dilled Summer Soup

2 small leeks, sliced
2 tablespoons vegetable oil
1 1/2 pounds zucchini or yellow squash, sliced
3 cups chicken broth
1 cup half-and-half
1 (8-ounce) container sour cream
1/3 cup chopped fresh dill
1/2 teaspoon salt
Garnish: fresh dill sprigs

Sauté leeks in hot oil in a Dutch oven until tender. Add zucchini and broth. Bring to a boil; cover, reduce heat, and simmer 8 to 10 minutes or until zucchini is tender. Remove from heat; cool slightly.

Process mixture, in batches, in a blender until smooth, stopping to scrape down sides.

Stir in half-and-half and next 3 ingredients. Chill at least 3 hours. Garnish, if desired. Yield: 9 cups.

Cold Broccoli Soup

4 cups fresh broccoli florets
1/2 cup peeled, diced potato
1/2 cup sliced leeks
1 garlic clove, chopped
2 (14-ounce) cans chicken broth
1/2 teaspoon curry powder
1 (8-ounce) container sour cream
1/2 cup whipping cream
1/4 cup lemon juice
1/4 teaspoon salt
1/4 teaspoon pepper
Garnishes: steamed broccoli florets, cooked whole kernel corn, thin red bell pepper strips

Arrange broccoli in a steamer basket over boiling water. Cover and steam 5 minutes or until crisp-tender.

Bring potato and next 4 ingredients to a boil in a large saucepan over medium-high heat; reduce heat, and simmer 12 to 15 minutes or until potato is tender. Cool. Stir in broccoli, sour cream, and next 4 ingredients.

Process half of mixture in a blender until smooth, stopping once to scrape down sides; pour into a 1 1/2-quart container, and repeat procedure with remaining mixture. Chill. Garnish, if desired. Yield: 4 1/2 cups.

—Chef/Owner Albert J. Bouchard III
Restaurant Bouchard
Newport, Rhode Island

Cool as a Cucumber Soup with Shrimp

3 pounds English cucumbers
1/4 cup kosher salt or 2 tablespoons table salt
1 quart buttermilk
1/2 teaspoon freshly ground pepper
2/3 cup chopped fresh dillweed
3 tablespoons unsalted butter
1/2 cup finely minced shallots
1/2 pound medium-size fresh shrimp, peeled and cut into 1/2-inch pieces
1 cup dry vermouth
1 tablespoon red wine vinegar
1/2 cup diced tomato
1/2 cup razor red onions*
Garnish: dillweed sprigs

Peel cucumbers. Cut into 1/2-inch pieces; toss cucumber with salt, and transfer to a colander placed over a bowl. Cover and chill up to 8 hours.

Transfer cucumber to a food processor or blender, discarding all liquid. Puree until smooth, stopping to scrape down sides. Whisk in buttermilk, pepper, and dillweed. Pour mixture into a large bowl. Set aside.

Melt butter in a small skillet over medium heat. Add shallots, and cook 1 minute. Add shrimp, and cook 30 seconds. Add vermouth; bring to a boil, and immediately strain liquid into cucumber mixture. Place shrimp mixture in a bowl; cover and chill shrimp mixture and cucumber mixture.

Stir vinegar into cucumber mixture. Divide shrimp mixture evenly among individual soup bowls. Ladle soup over shrimp, and serve with diced tomato and razor red onions. Garnish, if desired. Yield: 8 cups.

*Razor red onions are red onions sliced paper-thin and tossed with a pinch of sugar and enough lemon juice to coat. Prepare 1 to 2 hours ahead, and toss occasionally until softened and pink.

From Not Afraid of Flavor: Recipes From Magnolia Grill by Ben and Karen Barker. Photographs by Ann Parks Hawthorne. © 2000 by Ben and Karen Barker. Used by permission of the University of North Carolina Press. http://www.uncpress.unc.edu/

Cantaloupe Soup

1 medium-size ripe cantaloupe, cubed
3 cups vanilla ice cream, softened
1/4 cup honey
1/2 (6-ounce) can frozen orange juice concentrate
1 1/2 cups ginger ale, chilled
Garnish: fresh mint leaves

Process first 4 ingredients in a large food processor until smooth; cover and chill at least 30 minutes. Gently stir in ginger ale just before serving. To serve, ladle soup into individual bowls. Garnish, if desired. Serve immediately. Yield: 8 1/2 cups.

Hawaiian Pineapple Gazpacho

1   cucumber, peeled, seeded, and chopped
1   cup chopped fresh pineapple
¼   cup chopped red bell pepper
¼   cup chopped yellow bell pepper
2   tablespoons chopped sweet onion
1   tablespoon chopped fresh Italian parsley
1   to 2 teaspoons minced jalapeño pepper
1   (6-ounce) can pineapple juice
⅛   teaspoon salt
Garnish: fresh Italian parsley

Combine all ingredients except garnish in a food processor; pulse 4 to 5 times or until finely chopped. Cover and chill 1 hour. Garnish, if desired. Yield: 2 cups.

Grand Marnier-Strawberry Soup

Crème fraîche has a tangy flavor that heightens the sweetness of the fresh strawberries in this soup.

1   cup whipping cream
2   tablespoons buttermilk
6   cups fresh strawberries, divided
1½ cups fresh orange juice
¼   cup Grand Marnier or other orange-flavored liqueur
3   tablespoons sugar

To make crème fraîche, combine whipping cream and buttermilk in a small saucepan; heat to 110°. Transfer to a small glass bowl; stir well. Cover and let stand at room temperature 6 to 12 hours or until thickened.

Reserve 6 strawberries for garnish; slice remaining strawberries.

Process half each of cream mixture, sliced strawberries, orange juice, liqueur, and sugar in a blender until smooth; pour into a bowl. Repeat procedure with remaining half of ingredients; stir well. Cover and chill 1 hour.

To serve, ladle soup into individual bowls; garnish with reserved strawberries. Yield: 6 cups.

Open-Faced Mexican Sandwiches

4   skinned and boned chicken breast halves
2   tablespoons chopped fresh cilantro
2   tablespoons vegetable oil
1   garlic clove, minced
2   teaspoons chili powder
¼   teaspoon ground red pepper
1   cup (4 ounces) shredded Mexican cheese blend
⅓   cup mayonnaise
4   (1-inch-thick) sourdough bread slices, lightly toasted
Orange-Black Bean Salsa

Place chicken between 2 sheets of heavy-duty plastic wrap, and flatten to ½-inch thickness using a meat mallet or rolling pin.

Stir together cilantro and next 4 ingredients. Spread on chicken.

Grill, covered with grill lid, over medium-high heat (350° to 400°) 8 to 10 minutes on each side or until chicken is done.

Stir together cheese and mayonnaise. Spread on bread slices. Place bread, cheese side up, on a baking sheet. Broil 5½ inches from heat 1 to 2 minutes or until cheese melts. Place chicken on bread, and serve with Orange-Black Bean Salsa. Yield: 4 servings.

Orange-Black Bean Salsa

1   navel orange
1   plum tomato
½   medium cucumber
1   avocado
⅓   cup chopped red onion
½   (15-ounce) can black beans, rinsed and drained
1½ tablespoons chopped fresh cilantro
1   tablespoon olive oil
1½ tablespoons lime juice
2   teaspoons red wine vinegar
⅛   teaspoon dried crushed red pepper
⅛   teaspoon salt

Peel and section orange. Dice tomato. Peel, seed, and dice cucumber and avocado. Combine orange, diced vegetables, onion, beans, and cilantro in a bowl.

Whisk together oil and remaining ingredients. Toss with orange mixture. Cover and chill. Yield: about 2 cups.

Open-Faced Mexican Sandwich

Open-Faced Summer Sandwiches

2   large tomatoes, cut into ½-inch-thick
    slices
1   teaspoon salt
½   teaspoon pepper
4   (1- to 1½-inch-thick) rustic bread slices
    or French bread slices
¼   cup olive oil
2   large sweet onions, cut into ½-inch-
    thick slices
½   cup mayonnaise
3   tablespoons pesto
1   cup sliced ripe olives
2½ tablespoons chopped fresh mint
    (optional)

Sprinkle tomato slices evenly with salt and
pepper; set aside.

Brush both sides of bread slices with oil.

Grill bread, without grill lid, over medium
heat (300° to 350°) 2 to 3 minutes on each
side or until lightly browned.

Grill onion, covered with grill lid, over high
heat (400° to 500°) 8 to 10 minutes on each
side or until tender and browned.

Stir together mayonnaise and pesto; spread
evenly on 1 side of each bread slice. Top with
tomato and onion slices; sprinkle with olives.
Sprinkle with mint, if desired. Yield: 4 servings.

Miniature Tomato Sandwiches

1   French baguette
¼   cup mayonnaise
1   (3-ounce) package cream cheese,
    softened
2   teaspoons chopped fresh basil
¼   teaspoon salt, divided
¼   teaspoon freshly ground pepper,
    divided
4   plum tomatoes, sliced

Cut baguette into 16 slices.

Stir together mayonnaise, cream cheese,
basil, ⅛ teaspoon salt, and ⅛ teaspoon
pepper; cover and chill up to 8 hours, if
desired.

Spread cheese mixture on baguette slices.
Top with tomato, and sprinkle with remaining
salt and pepper. Yield: 16 appetizer servings.

Miniature Tomato Sandwiches

Italian Club Sandwich

Italian Club Sandwich

½ (16-ounce) Italian bread loaf
¼ cup Italian dressing
⅓ cup shredded Parmesan cheese
½ cup mayonnaise
½ cup mustard
½ pound thinly sliced Genoa salami
½ pound thinly sliced mortadella ham
4 (1-ounce) provolone cheese slices
Romaine lettuce leaves
3 plum tomatoes, sliced
8 bacon slices, cooked and cut in half
Garnish: green olives

Cut bread diagonally into 12 (¼-inch-thick) slices; arrange on a baking sheet. Brush slices evenly with Italian dressing, and sprinkle with Parmesan cheese.

Bake at 375° for 5 to 6 minutes or until lightly toasted.

Spread untoasted sides of bread slices evenly with mayonnaise and mustard. Layer 4 bread slices, mayonnaise side up, with salami, mortadella ham, and provolone. Top with 4 bread slices, mayonnaise side up; layer with lettuce, tomato, and bacon. Top with remaining 4 bread slices, mayonnaise side down. Cut in half, and secure with wooden picks. Garnish, if desired. Yield: 4 servings.

French Market Sandwiches

¾ cup butter or margarine, softened
¼ cup Creole mustard
½ teaspoon poppy seeds
12 croissants, split
2 pounds deli ham, thinly sliced
12 (1-ounce) Swiss cheese slices

Stir together first 3 ingredients. Spread on cut sides of croissants. Top each bottom half evenly with ham and cheese. Top with remaining croissant halves. Place sandwiches on baking sheets.

Bake at 325° for 12 to 15 minutes or until cheese melts. Yield: 12 servings.

Focaccia Sandwich

Focaccia Sandwiches

1 (32-ounce) package frozen bread dough, thawed
½ cup pizza sauce
⅔ cup freshly grated Parmesan cheese
⅔ cup thinly sliced green onions
⅓ cup olive oil
½ pound thinly sliced hard salami
½ pound thinly sliced ham
½ pound thinly sliced mozzarella cheese
½ pound thinly sliced provolone cheese
6 plum tomatoes, thinly sliced
1 red onion, thinly sliced
1 green bell pepper, thinly sliced
1 (12-ounce) jar marinated artichoke hearts, drained
1 (2¼-ounce) can sliced ripe olives
1 (10-ounce) jar pepperoncini salad peppers, drained
1 (12-ounce) jar roasted red bell peppers, drained and sliced

Roll each loaf of dough into a 15- x 10-inch rectangle; fit each into a 15- x 10-inch jellyroll pan. Punch dough several times with the end of a wooden spoon. Spread pizza sauce evenly over dough; sprinkle with Parmesan cheese and green onions. Drizzle with oil.

Cover and let rise in a warm place (85°), free from drafts, 30 minutes or until doubled in bulk.

Bake at 450° for 10 to 12 minutes or until browned; cool. Cut each into 12 pieces.

Arrange salami and remaining ingredients on a tray; serve with focaccia. Yield: 12 servings.

best burger tips

- **For moist and juicy burgers,** avoid selecting finely ground beef for your hamburgers. Look for a coarse grind of meat.
- **Rescue hands from the messy mixing** of ground beef by combining ingredients in a heavy-duty zip-top plastic bag. Squeeze bag just until mixed.
- **For consistent sizes,** use a large spoon or ice cream scoop to measure meat.
- **Wet hands while forming burgers** in order to keep meat from sticking to your fingers.
- **Avoid heavily packing meat** into patties. Compacting meat produces a dense and solid burger.
- **Ground beef can be frozen** up to three months. Store in the refrigerator up to two days before use.

Jalapeño Cheeseburgers

2   pounds ground chuck
2   tablespoons grated onion
1½ teaspoons Greek seasoning
1   teaspoon salt
1   teaspoon pepper
1   (3-ounce) package cream cheese, softened
2   tablespoons minced pickled jalapeño pepper
4   hamburger buns
Toppings: lettuce leaves, red onion slices, tomato slices

Combine first 5 ingredients; shape into 8 thin patties.

Stir together cream cheese and jalapeño pepper; spoon evenly in center of 4 patties. (Do not spread to edges.) Top with remaining patties, pressing edges to seal. Cover and chill 30 minutes.

Grill patties, covered with grill lid, over medium-high heat (350° to 400°) 9 minutes on each side or until done. Serve on buns with desired toppings. Yield: 4 servings.

Mozzarella-Basil Burgers

½   cup mayonnaise
1   garlic clove, pressed
2   pounds lean ground beef
½   cup Italian-seasoned breadcrumbs
2   large eggs, lightly beaten
3   tablespoons ketchup
1   (8-ounce) package mozzarella cheese slices
8   hamburger buns
24 large fresh basil leaves
Toppings: tomato slices, red onion slices

Stir together mayonnaise and garlic; set aside.

Combine ground beef and next 3 ingredients. Shape into 8 patties.

Grill beef patties, covered with grill lid, over medium-high heat (350° to 400°) 5 minutes on each side or until done. Top each patty with a mozzarella cheese slice.

Place hamburger buns, cut sides down, on grill rack, and grill until lightly browned. Spread mayonnaise mixture on cut sides of buns; top each with 3 basil leaves, a beef patty, and desired toppings. Yield: 8 servings.

Grilled Portobello Burgers

6   large portobello mushroom caps
½   cup roasted garlic teriyaki sauce
6   (1-ounce) part-skim mozzarella cheese slices
¼   cup mayonnaise
6   sourdough buns, split

Combine mushroom caps and teriyaki sauce in a heavy-duty zip-top plastic bag; turn to coat. Seal. Let stand 20 minutes. Drain mushrooms, and discard marinade.

Grill mushrooms, covered with grill lid, over medium-high heat (350° to 400°) 2 minutes on each side.

Jalapeño Cheeseburger

Top with cheese, and grill 2 more minutes. Spread mayonnaise on cut sides of buns. Grill, cut sides down, 1 minute. Place mushrooms in buns, and serve. Yield: 6 servings.

Black Bean Burgers

3   (15-ounce) cans black beans, rinsed and drained
1½ cups uncooked regular oats
1   medium onion, diced
2   jalapeño peppers, seeded and diced
¾   cup chopped fresh cilantro
2   large eggs, lightly beaten
1   teaspoon salt
¼   cup all-purpose flour
¼   cup cornmeal
2   tablespoons vegetable oil
8   hamburger buns

Mash beans coarsely with a fork. Combine beans, oats, and next 5 ingredients. Shape into 8 patties. Stir together flour and cornmeal; dredge patties in flour mixture. Cook patties in hot oil in a large nonstick skillet over medium-high heat 5 minutes on each side or until lightly browned; drain on paper towels. Serve on buns. Yield: 8 servings.

Salmon Burgers

1   (8-ounce) package Italian-seasoned breadcrumbs
⅓   cup lemon juice
1   (8-ounce) carton egg substitute
2   (12-ounce) cans skinless, boneless pink salmon, undrained
1   teaspoon salt
1   teaspoon paprika
2   tablespoons vegetable oil
6   sourdough English muffins, split and toasted
Alfalfa sprouts

Combine first 6 ingredients; shape into 6 patties. Cook patties, in batches, in hot oil in a large nonstick skillet over medium heat 5 minutes on each side. Drain.

Serve on muffins with alfalfa sprouts. Yield: 6 servings.

Barbecue Pork Sandwiches

1   (1½-pound) package pork tenderloins
3   cups hot water
⅔   cup ketchup
3   tablespoons soy sauce
2   tablespoons hoisin sauce
2   tablespoons honey
2   tablespoons chili-garlic paste
6   hamburger buns

Place pork on a lightly greased rack in a broiler pan; add 3 cups hot water to pan (to prevent drippings from burning).

Stir together ketchup and next 4 ingredients; divide sauce in half. Reserve half of sauce to toss with cooked pork.

Bake pork at 475° for 15 minutes. Turn pork, and brush with remaining half of sauce; bake 15 more minutes or until a meat thermometer inserted into thickest portion registers 160°. Cool slightly. Coarsely chop pork, and toss with reserved half of sauce. Serve on buns. Yield: 6 servings.

Niçoise Sandwiches with Olive Mayonnaise

½   cup mayonnaise
¼   cup pitted kalamata olives, finely chopped
½   teaspoon anchovy paste
1   (12-ounce) can solid white tuna, drained and flaked
2   hard-cooked eggs, chopped
¼   cup chopped red onion
2   tablespoons olive oil
2   teaspoons white wine vinegar
½   teaspoon coarsely ground pepper
8   slices potato bread
1   cup loosely packed arugula or spinach leaves
8   tomato slices

Combine first 3 ingredients in a small bowl.

Combine tuna and next 5 ingredients in a medium bowl.

Spread mayonnaise mixture on one side of bread slices. Divide arugula evenly among 4 bread slices; top each with 2 tomato slices. Spread tuna mixture evenly over tomato slices; top with remaining 4 bread slices. Yield: 4 servings.

Open-Faced Crab Sandwiches

1   pound fresh crabmeat
1   cup (4 ounces) shredded Swiss cheese
¼   cup mayonnaise
1   tablespoon minced fresh chives
1   tablespoon lime juice
½   teaspoon salt
¼   teaspoon pepper
2   to 3 dashes hot sauce
2   tablespoons butter or margarine, softened
4   English muffins, split
Garnishes: lime wedges, fresh chives

Drain and flake crabmeat, removing any bits of shell. Stir together crabmeat, cheese, and next 6 ingredients. Set aside.

Spread butter evenly on cut sides of English muffin halves; top evenly with crabmeat mixture, and place on a baking sheet.

Broil 5½ inches from heat 2 to 3 minutes or until lightly browned. Garnish, if desired. Yield: 4 servings.

Rolled Vegetable Sandwiches

8   (6-inch) flour tortillas
1   (8-ounce) package cream cheese, softened
¼   pound fresh spinach, rinsed and drained
1   cucumber, cut into thin strips
1   (11-ounce) can whole kernel corn, drained
3   carrots, scraped and cut into thin strips
¼   teaspoon salt
¼   teaspoon pepper

Spread tortillas with cream cheese; top with spinach and next 3 ingredients. Sprinkle with salt and pepper; fold bottom third of each tortilla over filling, and roll up jellyroll fashion. Wrap sandwiches in heavy-duty aluminum foil; chill. Yield: 8 servings.

Double-Decker BLT

The humble BLT gets dressed up in this "big bite" sandwich.

Double-Decker BLTs

1   (16-ounce) French bread loaf
Olive oil-flavored cooking spray
Garlic-Basil Mayonnaise
8   lettuce leaves
4   small tomatoes, thinly sliced
16   bacon slices, cooked

Cut bread into 12 (½-inch-thick) slices. Coat 1 side of each slice with cooking spray. Toast coated side until golden brown.

Spread Garlic-Basil Mayonnaise on untoasted side of each bread slice; layer 4 slices with half of lettuce leaves, tomato, and bacon. Top with a second bread slice, remaining lettuce leaves, tomato, and bacon. Top with remaining 4 bread slices. Yield: 4 servings.

Garlic-Basil Mayonnaise

½   cup mayonnaise
1   tablespoon chopped fresh or 1 teaspoon dried basil
¼   teaspoon garlic salt
¼   teaspoon pepper

Combine all ingredients in a small bowl; cover and chill. Yield: ½ cup.

Crab Roll

Crab Rolls

2 pounds fresh lump crabmeat, drained
1/2 cup chopped celery
1/4 cup mayonnaise
2 to 3 tablespoons fresh lemon juice
1/2 teaspoon salt
1/2 teaspoon freshly ground pepper
8 soft unsliced buns*

Combine first 6 ingredients in a large bowl; toss gently. Split buns on top; fill with crabmeat mixture. Serve immediately. Yield: 8 servings.
*Hot dog buns may be substituted for unsliced buns.

Fried Grouper and Creamy Coleslaw Sandwich

1 cup all-purpose flour
1/4 cup cornstarch
1 tablespoon garlic powder
1/2 teaspoon freshly ground pepper
4 (4-ounce) grouper fillets
1/2 teaspoon salt
1/4 teaspoon freshly ground pepper
1/2 cup buttermilk
Canola oil
4 onion sandwich rolls, split
Creamy Coleslaw

Combine first 4 ingredients in a large shallow dish. Set aside.

Sprinkle fillets with salt and pepper. Dredge grouper in flour mixture; dip in buttermilk, and dredge in flour mixture again.

Pour oil to depth of 3 inches into a Dutch oven; heat to 350°. Fry fish 5 to 6 minutes or until golden; drain on paper towels. Serve on rolls with Creamy Coleslaw. Yield: 4 servings.

Creamy Coleslaw

1 (10-ounce) package finely shredded cabbage
1/2 carrot, shredded
1/4 cup sugar
1/4 teaspoon salt
1/8 teaspoon freshly ground pepper
1/4 cup mayonnaise
2 tablespoons milk
2 tablespoons buttermilk
1 1/2 tablespoons fresh lemon juice
1 tablespoon white vinegar

Combine shredded cabbage and carrot in a large bowl.

Whisk together sugar and remaining ingredients until blended; toss with cabbage mixture. Cover and chill coleslaw at least 2 hours. Yield: 4 cups.

Seared Sesame-Coated Salmon Sandwich with Wasabi Mayonnaise

1 garlic clove, minced
2 teaspoons minced ginger
2 tablespoons soy sauce
1 tablespoon rice wine vinegar
3 (6-ounce) salmon fillets
3 tablespoons sesame seeds
2 tablespoons vegetable oil
1 French baguette
Wasabi Mayonnaise
Spinach leaves
1 cucumber, thinly sliced lengthwise

Combine first 4 ingredients in a small bowl; brush mixture over salmon. Dredge salmon in sesame seeds.

Heat oil in a nonstick skillet over medium-high heat; add salmon, and cook 4 minutes on each side or to desired degree of doneness.

Split baguette lengthwise; toast, if desired.

Spread Wasabi Mayonnaise on bread; layer spinach, salmon, and cucumber. Cut into 4 pieces. Yield: 4 servings.

Wasabi Mayonnaise

3 to 4 teaspoons wasabi powder*
3 teaspoons water
1/2 cup mayonnaise

Combine wasabi powder and water to make a paste; stir into mayonnaise. Cover and chill at least 1 hour. Yield: 1/2 cup.
*Wasabi powder is available in Asian markets and some large supermarkets.

Open-Faced Chili-Seared Catfish Sandwich with Maque Choux

2 tablespoons chili powder
1/4 teaspoon salt
1/4 teaspoon freshly ground pepper
4 (6- to 8-ounce) catfish fillets
1 tablespoon vegetable oil
6 (3/4-inch-thick) French bread slices, toasted
Maque Choux

Combine chili powder, salt, and pepper; rub evenly over catfish fillets.

Heat oil in a nonstick skillet over medium-high heat; add catfish, and cook 4 minutes on each side or until fish flakes with a fork. Place on toasted French bread; top with Maque Choux. Serve immediately. Yield: 4 servings.

Maque Choux

6 ears fresh corn
1 tablespoon vegetable oil
1 tablespoon butter or margarine
1 large tomato, peeled, seeded, and chopped
1 small onion, chopped
1/2 green bell pepper, chopped
1 garlic clove, minced
1 teaspoon sugar
1/2 teaspoon salt
1/4 teaspoon freshly ground pepper
1/4 teaspoon hot sauce

Cut off tips of corn kernels into a bowl. Using a knife, scrape milk and remaining pulp from corn cobs into bowl. Combine oil and butter in a large skillet; heat until butter melts. Add corn, tomato, and remaining ingredients; cook, stirring constantly, 5 minutes. Cover, reduce heat, and simmer 20 minutes, stirring often. Yield: 4 cups.

Bacon, Lettuce, Tomato, and Tuna Sandwich

4   (4- to 6-ounce) tuna fillets
1   tablespoon olive oil
½   teaspoon salt
¼   teaspoon freshly ground pepper
1   loaf French bread
Olive oil-flavored cooking spray
Basil Mayonnaise
Bibb lettuce
8   basil leaves
2   to 3 medium tomatoes, sliced
8   bacon slices, cooked

Brush tuna fillets with olive oil; sprinkle with salt and pepper.

Grill, without grill lid, over medium heat (300° to 350°) 10 to 12 minutes or to desired degree of doneness, turning once.

Cut bread diagonally into 8 (¾-inch-thick) slices, reserving remaining bread for other uses. Coat slices with cooking spray. Grill or toast each side until golden.

Spread Basil Mayonnaise evenly on one side of each bread slice. Layer 4 bread slices with lettuce, basil, tuna, tomato, basil, and bacon; top with remaining bread slices. Yield: 4 servings.

Basil Mayonnaise

½   cup mayonnaise
2   tablespoons chopped fresh basil
1   teaspoon minced fresh garlic
¼   teaspoon freshly ground pepper

Process all ingredients in a blender or food processor until smooth, stopping once to scrape down sides. Yield: ½ cup.

Fish Burgers

1½ pounds cod or other white fish
1 large egg, lightly beaten
2 tablespoons mayonnaise
1 tablespoon prepared mustard
1 tablespoon butter or margarine, melted
1 teaspoon chopped fresh parsley
¾ teaspoon salt
½ teaspoon dry mustard
½ teaspoon freshly ground black pepper
¼ teaspoon garlic salt
⅛ teaspoon ground red pepper
¾ cup crushed cornflakes cereal
Vegetable oil
6 hamburger buns
Toppings: Red Leaf lettuce leaves, tomato slices, red onion slices
Jalapeño Tartar Sauce

Place fish in a lightly greased 13- x 9-inch baking dish; cover with aluminum foil.

Bake at 400° for 20 minutes or until fish flakes with a fork. Drain; cool and flake. Combine egg and next 9 ingredients in a large bowl. Stir in flaked fish. Shape into 6 patties; coat with crushed cereal. Place on paper towels; refrigerate 1 hour.

Pour oil to depth of ½ inch into a large heavy skillet. Fry patties in hot oil over medium heat about 2 minutes on each side or until golden. Drain on paper towels. Serve on buns with desired toppings and Jalapeño Tartar Sauce. Yield: 6 servings.

Jalapeño Tartar Sauce

1 cup mayonnaise
2 tablespoons pickle relish
1 tablespoon chopped fresh chives
1 tablespoon small capers, drained
1 teaspoon dried dillweed
1 jalapeño pepper, minced

Combine all ingredients; cover and chill. Yield: 1¼ cups.

Soft-Shell Po'boy

6 soft-shell crabs, dressed
1 cup milk
¾ cup all-purpose flour
1 teaspoon salt
½ teaspoon ground black pepper
¼ teaspoon ground red pepper
¼ cup peanut oil
6 French rolls, split
Rémoulade Sauce
Lettuce leaves
Tomato slices

Combine crabs and milk in a shallow dish. Cover and chill 1 hour; drain, discarding milk.

Combine flour and next 3 ingredients. Dredge crabs in flour mixture.

Sauté crabs, top side down, in hot oil in a large skillet 1 to 2 minutes on each side. Drain on paper towels. Place each crab on a French roll. Top with Rémoulade Sauce, lettuce, and tomato. Yield: 6 servings.

Rémoulade Sauce

1 cup mayonnaise
1 tablespoon Creole mustard
1 tablespoon chopped sweet pickle
1½ teaspoons chopped fresh or ½ teaspoon dried tarragon
1 teaspoon capers, rinsed and chopped
1 teaspoon lemon juice

Combine all ingredients; cover and chill. Yield: 1 cup.

Oyster Po'boy

1 (16-ounce) loaf French or Italian bread
1 pint shucked oysters, drained
¼ cup all-purpose flour
⅓ cup Dijon mustard
¼ cup corn flour or all-purpose flour
Vegetable oil
Tartar sauce
Lettuce leaves or shredded lettuce

Preheat oven to 200°. Place a wire rack on a baking sheet and put in the oven.

Split the bread lengthwise, and scoop out most of the fluffy center. Place the hollowed-out bread in the oven.

Pat the oysters dry. Put the all-purpose flour, mustard, and corn flour in separate shallow bowls or plates. Pour oil to a depth of about ½ inch in a deep skillet, sauté pan, or Dutch oven. Place over medium-high heat and bring the oil to 365°.

Using one hand to handle the food, dredge the oysters in the all-purpose flour, shaking off any extra. Then dip them in the mustard, and use a pastry brush to paint them evenly with a thin layer of mustard. Place the mustard-coated oysters in corn flour, and dust them all over. As each oyster is coated, set it aside on wax paper.

When the oil reaches 365°, add the oysters, using tongs, and fry until golden brown all over, about 1½ minutes on each side. Do not crowd the skillet. As they are done, transfer the oysters to the wire rack to keep warm and drain.

Remove the bread from the oven and spread both sides thickly with tartar sauce. Then line them with lettuce.

When all oysters have been fried, add them to the sandwiches and serve immediately. Yield: 4 servings.

Excerpted from The Fearless Frying Cookbook. *Recipes © 1997 by John Martin Taylor. Illustrations © 1997 by Peter Alsberg. Used by permission of Workman Publishing Co., Inc., New York. All Rights Reserved.*

side dishes

Oyster and Artichoke Gratin

2 cups fine, dry breadcrumbs
1 cup freshly grated Parmesan cheese
1/3 cup extra-virgin olive oil
3 tablespoons minced fresh parsley
2 (12-ounce) containers fresh
   oysters, undrained
2 (14-ounce) cans quartered artichoke
   hearts, drained
1/4 cup minced garlic
1 1/2 tablespoons cracked pepper
1/3 cup unsalted butter, cut into
   pieces
1/4 cup extra-virgin olive oil
Garnish: chopped fresh parsley

Stir together first 4 ingredients.
   Layer oysters, oyster liquid, and next 3
ingredients in 6 (1-cup) gratin dishes. Sprinkle
breadcrumb mixture over each; dot with butter.
Bake at 500° for 8 minutes or until thoroughly
heated and golden. Drizzle with 1/4 cup olive oil.
Let stand 5 minutes. Garnish, if desired. Yield:
6 to 8 servings.
Note: Haley prefers individual gratin dishes to
ensure a larger crispy portion for each serving;
however, gratin can be prepared as directed in
a shallow 2 1/2-quart casserole. Bake at 500°
for 10 minutes or until golden.

—Ralph Brennan/Chef Haley Gabel
Bacco
New Orleans, Louisiana

vine advice

Restaurateur Ralph Brennan pairs a dry
Italian white, Lacryma Christi del Vesuvio
Bianco, with his oyster gratin.

Vegetable Frittata

1 garlic bulb (about 9 cloves)
3 tablespoons olive oil, divided
4 small zucchini, sliced
1 pound asparagus spears, cut into 3-inch
   lengths
1 (1-pound) bunch Swiss chard
3 medium-size onions
3 tablespoons chopped fresh oregano
1 (4-ounce) jar sliced pimiento, drained
20 large eggs, beaten
2 1/4 teaspoons salt
1 1/4 teaspoons freshly ground pepper
4 cups shredded Parmesan cheese

Cut off and discard pointed tip of garlic bulb;
place bulb on a piece of foil. Drizzle with 1
tablespoon oil. Fold to seal.
   Bake at 350° for 40 minutes; cool. Squeeze
garlic pulp from bulb. Set pulp aside.
   Arrange zucchini in a steamer basket over
boiling water. Cover and steam 5 minutes or
until crisp-tender. Set aside.
   Arrange asparagus in steamer basket over
boiling water. Cover and steam 5 minutes or
until crisp-tender. Set aside.
   Remove and slice stalks from chard. Cut
leaves into 1-inch strips.
   Arrange chard stems and stalks in steamer
basket over boiling water. Cover and steam 3
minutes or until tender.
   Cut onions in half lengthwise; cut into very
thin wedges. Sauté onion in remaining 2 tablespoons oil in a large skillet over medium-high
heat 5 minutes or until tender. Add garlic pulp,
chard, zucchini, asparagus, oregano, and
pimiento; toss gently.
   Whisk together eggs, salt, and pepper.
   Layer half each of vegetable mixture, cheese,
and egg mixture; repeat procedure. Pour into a
lightly greased 12-inch ovenproof skillet.
   Bake at 325° for 55 minutes or until frittata
is set. Yield: 12 servings.

—Caroline Coleman Bailey
Tiburon, California

Vegetable Frittata

Chilled Asparagus with Caviar Mayonnaise

2   pounds asparagus
1   cup mayonnaise
1   (8-ounce) container sour cream
1   tablespoon fresh lemon juice
2   teaspoons prepared mustard
1   (2-ounce) jar salmon caviar, drained
1   (2-ounce) jar lumpfish caviar,
    drained
Garnish: chopped fresh parsley

Snap off tough ends of asparagus. Cook asparagus in boiling salted water to cover in a large saucepan 2 to 3 minutes or until crisp-tender; drain and plunge into ice water to stop the cooking process. Drain.

Combine mayonnaise and next 3 ingredients; spoon over asparagus. Sprinkle with caviars. Garnish, if desired. Yield: 10 servings.
Recipe adapted from Cape Fear...Still Cooking.

Lemon-Marinated Asparagus

½   cup fresh lemon juice
3   tablespoons olive oil
2   tablespoons sugar
¼   teaspoon salt
¼   teaspoon pepper
1   garlic clove, minced
1   (14-ounce) can quartered artichoke
    hearts, drained
1   (4-ounce) jar diced pimiento, drained
2   pounds fresh asparagus

Whisk together lemon juice and next 5 ingredients in a large bowl; add artichoke hearts and diced pimiento, and gently toss. Cover and chill 8 hours or overnight.

Snap off tough ends of asparagus. Cook asparagus in boiling salted water to cover 3 minutes or until crisp-tender.

Drain asparagus, and plunge into ice water to stop the cooking process. Place cooked asparagus in a large heavy-duty zip-top plastic bag, and store overnight in refrigerator, if desired.

Add asparagus to artichoke mixture, and gently toss. Cover and chill 2 hours. Yield: 10 servings.

Chilled Asparagus with Caviar Mayonnaise

Balsamic Asparagus

2   pounds fresh asparagus
¾   cup olive oil
1   tablespoon sugar
½   cup white balsamic vinegar
4   garlic cloves, minced
1   teaspoon red pepper flakes

Snap off tough ends of asparagus. Cook asparagus in boiling water to cover 3 minutes or until asparagus is crisp-tender; drain.

Plunge asparagus into ice water to stop the cooking process; drain. Arrange asparagus in a 13- x 9-inch baking dish.

Whisk together olive oil, sugar, balsamic vinegar, garlic, and red pepper flakes until well blended; pour over asparagus. Cover and chill 8 hours. Drain before serving. Yield: 6 to 8 servings.

Simple Roasted Asparagus

1   pound fresh asparagus
3   tablespoons olive oil
½   teaspoon sugar
¼   teaspoon salt
¼   teaspoon freshly ground pepper

Snap off tough ends of asparagus. Arrange asparagus in a 15- x 10-inch jellyroll pan. Drizzle with olive oil.

Broil 5½ inches from heat 4 minutes. Sprinkle with sugar, salt, and pepper. Yield: 3 to 4 servings.

Garlicky Green Beans

3   pounds fresh green beans, trimmed
6   garlic cloves
¼   cup olive oil
¼   cup balsamic vinegar
2   teaspoons salt
1   teaspoon freshly ground pepper

Cook beans and garlic in boiling salted water to cover 5 minutes or until crisp-tender; drain. Transfer beans to a serving bowl. Remove garlic cloves; mince. Whisk together minced garlic, oil, and remaining ingredients; drizzle over green beans, and toss gently. Yield: 6 servings.

—*Gideon Bosker*
Portland, Oregon

Marinated Green Beans

2   pounds fresh green beans, trimmed
1   small red onion, thinly sliced
½   cup vegetable oil
3   tablespoons white vinegar
1   tablespoon minced fresh parsley
1   teaspoon salt
1   teaspoon Dijon mustard
¼   teaspoon freshly ground pepper
1   garlic clove, minced

Cook beans in boiling water to cover 5 to 6 minutes or until crisp-tender; drain. Plunge into ice water to stop the cooking process; drain and set aside. Combine beans and onion; toss gently.

Combine oil and remaining ingredients in a jar; cover tightly, and shake vigorously. Pour over bean mixture; toss gently to coat. Cover and chill 2 hours. Yield: 8 servings.

Pan-Asian Vegetables

1   pound haricots verts or slender green
     beans
1   pound baby pattypan squash
1   tablespoon dark sesame oil
1   teaspoon sesame seeds, toasted
     (optional)

Cook beans and squash in boiling water to cover 5 minutes or until crisp-tender. Drain

Garlicky Green Beans

well. Toss with sesame oil; sprinkle with sesame seeds, if desired. Serve immediately. Yield: 6 servings.

Note: *Beans and squash may be prepared ahead. Plunge cooked vegetables into ice water to stop the cooking process. Drain well. Just before serving, steam vegetables until thoroughly heated; drain well, and proceed as directed.*

—*Judy Hawkins*
Seattle, Washington

Baby Vegetables with Honey and Lavender

1½ pounds assorted baby vegetables*
1 pound fresh asparagus spears
1 tablespoon unsalted butter
¼ cup honey
1 tablespoon dried lavender
½ teaspoon salt
¼ teaspoon freshly ground pepper

Trim baby vegetables, if necessary. Cook in boiling salted water to cover 5 to 7 minutes or until crisp-tender; drain. Plunge vegetables into ice water to stop the cooking process; drain and set aside.

Cut 4-inch tips from asparagus, discarding ends. Cook in boiling salted water to cover 3 to 4 minutes or until crisp-tender; drain. Plunge into ice water to stop the cooking process; drain and set aside.

Melt butter in a large skillet over medium heat; stir in honey, lavender, salt, and pepper. Add baby vegetables and asparagus; stir until coated. Cook until thoroughly heated. Yield: 4 servings.

*We tested with baby carrots, zucchini, yellow pattypan squash, and green pattypan squash.

Broccoli and Parsnips with Horseradish

1 pound fresh parsnips, peeled and cut into thin strips
1 pound fresh broccoli, cut into florets
3 tablespoons butter or margarine
2 tablespoons prepared horseradish
2 tablespoons fresh lemon juice
½ teaspoon salt
¼ cup chopped walnuts, toasted

Arrange parsnips in a steamer basket over boiling water. Cover and steam 8 minutes. Add broccoli; cover and steam 5 minutes. Place parsnips and broccoli in a large bowl.

Melt butter in a small saucepan over low heat. Cook 5 minutes or until lightly browned. Remove from heat. Stir in horseradish, lemon juice, and salt. Pour sauce over vegetables, tossing to coat. Sprinkle with walnuts. Serve immediately. Yield: 6 servings.

Broccoli Blue

2 pounds fresh broccoli
2 tablespoons butter
2 tablespoons all-purpose flour
1 (3-ounce) package cream cheese, softened
¾ cup crumbled blue cheese
1 (8-ounce) container sour cream
⅓ cup crushed round buttery crackers

Remove and discard broccoli leaves and tough ends of stalks; cut into bite-size pieces. Arrange broccoli in a steamer basket over boiling water. Cover and steam 5 minutes or until crisp-tender. Set broccoli aside, and keep warm.

Melt butter in a saucepan over low heat; add flour, stirring until smooth. Cook 1 minute, stirring constantly. Add cream cheese and blue cheese; cook, stirring constantly, until smooth. Add sour cream, and bring just to a boil. Remove from heat, and pour over broccoli; toss gently. Place broccoli mixture in a lightly greased 1-quart baking dish; sprinkle with cracker crumbs.

Bake, uncovered, at 350° for 30 minutes. Yield: 6 servings.

Oven-Blasted Broccoli

3 pounds fresh broccoli
¾ cup garlic-flavored olive oil
1 teaspoon salt
½ teaspoon pepper
¼ cup white balsamic vinegar

Cut florets from broccoli. Peel stalks, and cut diagonally into 1-inch pieces. Toss florets and stalk pieces with oil.

Place a 15- x 10-inch jellyroll pan in a 500° oven for 5 minutes; add broccoli in a single layer.

Bake at 500° for 10 minutes, stirring occasionally. Sprinkle with salt and pepper. Just before serving, drizzle with vinegar. Yield: 10 to 12 servings.

—Mauny Kaseburg
Seattle, Washington

Corn Pudding

6 ears fresh corn
4 large eggs
½ cup half-and-half
1½ teaspoons baking soda
⅓ cup butter or margarine
2 tablespoons sugar
2 tablespoons all-purpose flour
1 tablespoon butter or margarine, melted
¼ to ½ teaspoon salt
⅛ teaspoon pepper

Cut off tips of corn kernels into a large bowl using a knife; scrape milk and remaining pulp from corn cobs into bowl.

Whisk together eggs, half-and-half, and baking soda.

Melt ⅓ cup butter in a large saucepan over low heat; add sugar and flour, whisking until smooth. Remove from heat; gradually whisk in egg mixture until smooth. Stir in reserved corn; pour into a greased 1½-quart shallow baking dish.

Bake pudding at 350° for 40 to 45 minutes or until set. Drizzle with 1 tablespoon butter, and sprinkle evenly with salt and pepper.

Broil 5½ inches from heat 2 minutes or until golden. Let stand 5 minutes before serving. Yield: 6 servings.

Buttermilk Fried Corn

3 cups fresh corn kernels (about 6 ears)
2¼ cups buttermilk
1 cup all-purpose flour
1 cup cornmeal
1 teaspoon salt
1½ teaspoons pepper
Corn oil

Stir together corn and buttermilk; let stand 30 minutes. Drain.

Combine flour and next 3 ingredients in a large heavy-duty zip-top plastic bag. Add corn to flour mixture, a small amount at a time, and shake bag to coat.

Pour oil to depth of 1 inch into a Dutch oven; heat to 375°. Fry corn, in small batches, 2 minutes or until golden. Drain on paper towels. Serve hot. Yield: 3 cups.

Grilled Vegetables with Cilantro Butter

Sweet-and-Sour Onions

Grilled Vegetables with Cilantro Butter

4   ears fresh corn with husks
Cilantro Butter
4   medium tomatoes, halved
4   medium zucchini, cut into 1-inch-thick
    slices
1/2   teaspoon salt
1/2   teaspoon freshly ground pepper
Garnish: fresh cilantro

Soak corn in water to cover 1 hour. Peel back corn husks, leaving husks attached. Remove silks.

Spread Cilantro Butter evenly over corn, tomato halves, and zucchini; sprinkle vegetables with salt and pepper. Pull husks over corn, and twist ends tightly. Place tomato and zucchini in a grill basket.

Grill vegetables, covered with grill lid, over medium-high heat (350° to 400°) 10 to 15 minutes or until zucchini and tomato are tender, turning corn often. Grill corn 5 to 10 more minutes or until tender. (Husk edges will blacken.) Remove husks. Serve vegetables immediately. Garnish, if desired. Yield: 4 servings.

Cilantro Butter

1/2   cup butter or margarine, softened
1/4   cup minced fresh cilantro
4   garlic cloves, pressed

Stir together all ingredients. Yield: 1/2 cup.

Sweet-and-Sour Onions

2   pounds fresh white cocktail onions
2   tablespoons butter
1/4   cup firmly packed light brown sugar
1/3   cup balsamic vinegar
1/4   teaspoon salt

Cook onions in boiling water to cover 10 minutes; drain. Plunge into ice water to stop the cooking process; drain. Peel; set aside.

Cook butter and brown sugar in a saucepan over medium heat, whisking often, until butter melts. Whisk in vinegar and salt.

Add onions; bring to a boil. Reduce heat, and simmer, uncovered, 15 minutes or until thickened. Yield: 3 cups.

—Gideon Bosker
Portland, Oregon

Tricolor Peppers

2 large red bell peppers, cut into
  ¼-inch strips
2 large green bell peppers, cut into
  ¼-inch strips
2 large yellow bell peppers, cut into
  ¼-inch strips
¼ cup olive oil
6 garlic cloves, minced
¼ teaspoon salt
⅛ teaspoon freshly ground pepper
Chopped fresh parsley

Sauté bell peppers in hot oil in a large nonstick skillet over medium heat 10 minutes. Add garlic; sauté 5 minutes. Stir in salt and pepper; sprinkle with parsley. Yield: 6 servings.

—Gideon Bosker
Portland, Oregon

Grilled Peppers and Veggies

Cut vegetables into large pieces for easy management on the grill, or use a grill basket.

¾ cup olive oil
¼ cup red wine vinegar
1 tablespoon minced garlic
1 tablespoon chopped fresh rosemary
1 tablespoon chopped fresh basil
1 teaspoon fresh thyme leaves
1 teaspoon salt
½ teaspoon freshly ground pepper
1 yellow bell pepper
1 red bell pepper
1 green bell pepper
3 zucchini
2 large onions
1 eggplant

This colorful mix is great served hot off the grill or chilled and served the next day.

Combine first 8 ingredients in a large bowl.

Cut bell peppers into large pieces, discarding seeds and membranes. Cut zucchini in half crosswise; cut each piece in half lengthwise. Cut onions into large pieces. Slice eggplant into ½-inch slices. Add vegetables to marinade; toss to coat. Cover and chill 2 hours.

Remove vegetables from marinade, reserving marinade. Grill, without grill lid, over medium-high heat (350° to 400°) 10 to 12 minutes or until just tender, basting occasionally with reserved marinade. Serve warm or at room temperature. Yield: 6 to 8 servings.

Tricolor Peppers

Grilled Peppers and Veggies

Crispy Fried Potatoes

24   small red potatoes (about 2 pounds)
1/4   cup olive oil
1   tablespoon butter
1   slice onion
1/4   teaspoon salt

Cook potatoes in boiling salted water to cover 12 to 14 minutes or until tender. Drain; let cool.

Cut potatoes into quarters, leaving skin on or peeled, if desired.

Heat olive oil and butter until hot; add onion, and remove when it starts to turn golden. Discard onion. Add potato, and fry 6 to 8 minutes or until golden on each side, turning once. Remove potato from skillet; drain well on paper towels. Sprinkle with salt. Serve immediately. Yield: 8 servings.

—Gideon Bosker
Portland, Oregon

Potato Gratin in Garlic Cream

1   garlic bulb
1   quart whipping cream
⅓   cup all-purpose flour
3   pounds new potatoes, cut into ¼-inch-
    thick slices
2   teaspoons salt, divided
2   teaspoons freshly ground pepper,
    divided
½   teaspoon freshly ground nutmeg,
    divided (optional)
1   (7-ounce) container refrigerated shredded
    Parmesan cheese, divided

Cut off and discard pointed tip of garlic bulb;
place bulb on a piece of aluminum foil. Fold
foil to seal.

Bake at 400° for 1 hour. Cool. Squeeze
garlic pulp into a large bowl; stir in whipping
cream. Whisk in flour. Set aside.

Layer half of potato in a lightly greased
13- x 9-inch baking dish. Sprinkle with 1 teaspoon salt, 1 teaspoon pepper, ¼ teaspoon
nutmeg, and half of cheese. Repeat procedure
with remaining potato, salt, pepper, and nutmeg.
Place baking dish on a jellyroll pan. Pour
whipping cream mixture over potato.

Bake, covered, at 400° for 30 minutes.
Uncover; sprinkle with remaining half of
cheese. Bake 30 more minutes or until potato
is tender. Let stand 15 minutes before serving.
Yield: 12 servings.

—*Mauny Kaseburg*
Seattle, Washington

Potato-Stuffed Red Bell Peppers

4   large red bell peppers
4   cups frozen mashed potatoes (we tested
    with Ore-Ida)
1   cup half-and-half or milk
½   cup chopped fresh basil
½   (8-ounce) container chive-and-onion
    cream cheese
1   teaspoon salt
½   teaspoon pepper
Paprika

Cut tops off bell peppers, and remove
seeds. Prepare mashed potatoes with 1 cup

Potato-Stuffed Red Bell Peppers

half-and-half according to package directions. Stir in basil and next 3 ingredients;
spoon potato mixture into peppers. Place
peppers in a lightly greased 8-inch square
baking dish. Cover loosely with wax paper.
Microwave at HIGH 12 minutes. Sprinkle
with paprika before serving. Yield: 4 servings.

Corn, Okra, and Tomatoes

1 large onion, chopped (1½ cups)
1 large green bell pepper, chopped
2 garlic cloves, minced
¼ cup plus 2 tablespoons butter or
  margarine
2 cups chopped plum tomatoes
2½ cups fresh corn, cut from the cob
  (about 4 ears)
1 cup sliced fresh okra
1 teaspoon salt
½ teaspoon freshly ground pepper

Cook first 3 ingredients in butter in a skillet over medium-high heat, stirring constantly, until tender. Add tomato; bring to a boil. Reduce heat, and simmer, uncovered, 15 minutes. Add corn and remaining ingredients; bring to a boil. Reduce heat, and simmer 9 minutes or until corn is tender. Yield: 6 servings.

Hot Tomato Grits

2 bacon slices, chopped
2 (14-ounce) cans chicken broth
½ teaspoon salt
1 cup uncooked quick-cooking grits
2 large tomatoes, peeled and chopped
2 tablespoons canned chopped green
  chiles
1 cup (4 ounces) shredded Cheddar cheese
Garnishes: chopped tomato, cooked and
  crumbled bacon, shredded Cheddar
  cheese

Cook bacon in a heavy saucepan until crisp, reserving drippings in pan. Gradually add broth and salt; bring to a boil.

Stir in grits, tomato, and chiles; return to a boil, stirring often. Reduce heat, and simmer, stirring often, 15 to 20 minutes.

Stir in cheese; cover and let stand 5 minutes or until cheese melts. Garnish, if desired. Yield: 6 servings.

Tomato Basil Tart

½ (15-ounce) package refrigerated piecrusts
⅓ cup crushed round buttery crackers,
  divided
¾ cup grated Parmesan cheese
¾ cup mayonnaise
7 plum tomatoes, sliced
½ teaspoon salt
½ teaspoon freshly ground pepper
¼ cup fresh basil, thinly shredded
6 bacon slices, cooked and crumbled
Garnishes: fresh basil, sliced tomato

Fit piecrust into a 9-inch square tart pan according to package directions; trim edges. Prick crust with a fork.

Bake crust at 350° for 14 minutes or until lightly browned. Sprinkle half of cracker crumbs over crust.

Stir together cheese and mayonnaise. Dollop and then spread half of cheese filling over crumbs. Arrange tomato slices over filling, sprinkling evenly with salt and pepper. Add basil and crumbled bacon. Dollop and then spread remaining cheese filling on top. Sprinkle with remaining cracker crumbs.

Bake at 350° for 24 to 25 minutes or until browned. Garnish, if desired. Yield: 8 to 10 servings.

Note: A 9-inch pieplate may be substituted for a 9-inch square tart pan.

Recipe adapted from Cape Fear...Still Cooking.

Tomato Basil Tart

Herbed Rice and Orzo

Add chicken broth, water, and wild rice to saucepan; bring to a boil over medium heat. Cover, reduce heat, and simmer 10 minutes.

Stir in orzo, long-grain rice, and next 5 ingredients. Return to a boil; cover, reduce heat, and simmer 40 minutes or until moisture is absorbed and rice is tender. Remove from heat, and let stand 10 minutes. Remove and discard bay leaf. Garnish, if desired. Yield: 8 servings.

Stir-Fried Rice with Black-Eyed Peas and Shrimp

For this hoppin' John-style fried rice, we suggest buying already peeled and deveined cooked shrimp and cooking the rice a day ahead to save a little time.

2 tablespoons vegetable oil, divided
3 large eggs, lightly beaten
1 tablespoon dark sesame oil
1½ tablespoons minced fresh ginger
3 large garlic cloves, minced
1 cup cooked long-grain rice, chilled
1 cup cooked brown rice, chilled
4 green onions, chopped
½ pound peeled and deveined cooked shrimp
¾ cup cooked black-eyed peas
¼ cup chopped dry-roasted peanuts
¼ cup chopped fresh parsley
¼ cup chopped fresh cilantro
1 teaspoon freshly ground pepper

Heat 1 tablespoon vegetable oil in a wok or large nonstick skillet over medium-high heat.

Whisk together eggs and sesame oil in a small bowl. Pour egg mixture into wok and cook 1 to 2 minutes or until set; turn, using a large spatula, and cook 1 to 2 minutes more or until completely set and lightly browned. Remove egg from wok and cool slightly; thinly slice egg, and set aside.

Heat remaining 1 tablespoon vegetable oil in wok. Add ginger and garlic; stir-fry 1 minute. Add rices and green onions; stir-fry 2 minutes. Add sliced egg, shrimp, and remaining ingredients; stir-fry 2 minutes or until heated. Yield: 4 to 6 servings.

Coconut-Ginger Rice

1 (14-ounce) can unsweetened coconut milk
2¼ cups water
2 cups jasmine or basmati rice
4 slices peeled fresh ginger
Garnish: chopped fresh parsley

Combine coconut milk and 2¼ cups water in a heavy saucepan. Stir in rice and ginger. Bring mixture to a boil. Reduce heat; cover and simmer 20 minutes. Remove from heat. Fluff with a fork; cover and let stand 5 minutes. Remove ginger before serving. Garnish, if desired. Yield: 4 to 6 servings.

—Judy Hawkins
Seattle, Washington

Herbed Rice and Orzo

⅔ cup uncooked orzo
2 tablespoons vegetable oil
2 (14-ounce) cans chicken broth
½ cup water
⅔ cup uncooked wild rice
¾ cup uncooked long-grain rice
1 bay leaf
1 tablespoon chopped fresh or 1 teaspoon dried thyme
1 tablespoon chopped fresh or 1 teaspoon rubbed sage
1 teaspoon salt
¼ teaspoon ground white pepper
Garnish: Fresh sage

Lightly brown orzo in oil in a 3-quart saucepan over medium-high heat for 3 to 5 minutes, stirring often. Remove orzo from saucepan; set aside.

Savannah Red Rice and Shrimp

Savannah Red Rice and Shrimp

1   pound unpeeled, medium-size fresh
    shrimp
1/4 pound hot Italian sausage
1/3 cup chopped country ham (about
    2 ounces)
1/2 cup chopped onion
1/4 cup chopped green bell pepper
1   (14 1/2-ounce) can no-salt-added diced
    tomatoes, undrained
1   tablespoon tomato paste
1   cup low-sodium chicken broth
1   cup instant brown rice

Peel shrimp; devein, if desired. Set aside.

Remove and discard casings from sausage.
Cook sausage in a large skillet, stirring until it
crumbles and is no longer pink. Drain. Add
country ham, onion, and bell pepper; cook, stirring constantly, 2 minutes. Add tomatoes,
tomato paste, and broth. Bring to a boil; reduce
heat, and simmer 10 minutes. Cool slightly.

Process tomato mixture in a blender or food
processor 15 seconds or until smooth, stopping
once to scrape down sides.

Combine rice and tomato mixture. Spoon
into a greased 8-inch square baking dish.

Bake at 350°, covered, for 25 minutes.
Add shrimp, and bake, covered, 15 more
minutes or until rice is tender and shrimp
turn pink. Yield: 6 servings.

—Chef Elizabeth Terry
Elizabeth on 37th
Savannah, Georgia

Oyster-Cornbread Dressing

1/2 cup butter or margarine
2/3 cup chopped onion
1   cup chopped celery
2   teaspoons minced garlic
3   bay leaves
1   (12-ounce) container fresh oysters,
    undrained
1   cup chicken broth
1/2 cup chopped green onions
2   tablespoons minced fresh parsley
2   teaspoons salt
1   teaspoon pepper
1/2 teaspoon dried thyme
3   large eggs
1 1/2 cups milk
Cornbread

Melt butter in a large skillet over medium-high
heat; add onion, celery, garlic, and bay leaves;
sauté 5 minutes or until tender.

Drain oysters, reserving liquid; set oysters
aside. Add oyster liquid, broth, and green onions
to skillet; bring to a boil. Reduce heat, and
simmer 5 minutes, stirring occasionally; remove
from heat. Stir in oysters, parsley, salt, pepper,
and thyme. Remove and discard bay leaves.

Whisk together eggs and milk in a large
bowl; crumble cornbread into egg mixture.
Stir in oyster mixture; pour into a lightly
greased 2-quart baking dish.

Bake at 350° for 45 minutes or until lightly
browned. Yield: 8 to 10 servings.

Cornbread

2   tablespoons vegetable oil
1   cup all-purpose flour
1   cup yellow cornmeal
1   tablespoon baking powder
1   teaspoon salt
1   cup milk
1   large egg

Place oil in a 10-inch cast-iron skillet, tilting
pan to coat bottom evenly; heat in a 375° oven
10 minutes.

Combine flour, cornmeal, baking powder,
and salt in a bowl. Whisk together milk and
egg; add to flour mixture, stirring just until
dry ingredients are moistened.

Pour hot oil from skillet into batter; stir until
blended. Pour batter into skillet.

Bake at 375° for 20 minutes or until done.
Remove from skillet. Yield: 8 servings.

Crabmeat Stuffing

15 white bread slices
1   pound claw crabmeat
1   pound jumbo lump crabmeat
1   cup whipping cream
1/2 cup dry sherry
1 1/2 teaspoons Old Bay seasoning
1/8 teaspoon white pepper
1/8 teaspoon freshly ground black pepper
1/8 teaspoon ground red pepper
2   teaspoons hot sauce
1 1/2 teaspoons Dijon mustard
2   cups shredded provolone or Swiss
    cheese
3/4 cup minced celery
3/4 cup chopped green bell pepper
5   green onions, sliced
1   tablespoon vegetable oil
1/4 cup mayonnaise

Cut bread slices into 3/4-inch squares. Place in
a single layer on a baking sheet.

Bake at 350° for 10 minutes or until lightly
toasted. Set aside.

Drain crabmeat, removing any bits of shell;
set aside.

Bring whipping cream and sherry to a boil;
boil 5 minutes. Stir in Old Bay seasoning and
next 5 ingredients. Gradually add cheese, stirring until blended. Set aside.

Sauté celery, bell pepper, and green
onions in 1 tablespoon hot oil in a large
skillet over medium-high heat 5 minutes or
until crisp-tender.

Combine bread cubes, crabmeat, cheese
mixture, vegetables, and mayonnaise; toss
gently. Spoon stuffing into a greased 13-x 9-inch
baking dish.

Bake at 350° for 40 minutes or until
bubbly. Yield: 10 to 12 servings.

—Chef Larc Lindsey
Lark's Wood Grill
Hendersonville, North Carolina

breads

Baked French Toast Casserole

1   (16-ounce) French bread loaf
8   large eggs, lightly beaten
3   cups milk
2   tablespoons sugar
1   teaspoon vanilla extract
¼   teaspoon salt
¼   teaspoon ground cinnamon
¼   teaspoon ground nutmeg
1   cup firmly packed light brown sugar
1   cup chopped pecans
½   cup butter or margarine, softened
2   tablespoons light corn syrup
½   teaspoon ground cinnamon
½   teaspoon ground nutmeg

Butter a 13- x 9-inch baking dish. Cut bread into 20 equal slices. Arrange bread slices in 2 rows down length of dish, overlapping slices.

Combine eggs and next 6 ingredients; pour egg mixture over bread slices. Cover and chill overnight. Meanwhile, combine brown sugar and remaining 5 ingredients; cover and chill overnight.

Crumble sugar mixture over bread. Bake at 350° for 40 minutes or until browned. Yield: 10 servings.

Make-Ahead French Toast with Strawberry Sauce

1   (16-ounce) challah bread loaf, cubed*
1   (8-ounce) package cream cheese, cut into pieces
6   large eggs
4   cups half-and-half
½   cup butter or margarine, melted
¼   cup maple syrup
2   cups fresh strawberries, sliced
1   (12-ounce) jar strawberry preserves

Arrange half of challah bread in a lightly greased 13- x 9-inch pan. Sprinkle with cheese pieces, and top with remaining bread.

Whisk together eggs and next 3 ingredients; pour over bread mixture, pressing bread cubes to absorb egg mixture. Cover and chill 8 hours.

Bake, covered, at 350° for 25 minutes. Uncover and bake 20 more minutes.

Heat sliced strawberries and strawberry preserves in a saucepan over low heat, and serve over French toast. Yield: 10 servings.
*Challah is a rich egg bread with a light, airy texture. French bread may be substituted.

Blueberry-Stuffed French Toast Bake

Weekend guests will rave about this cream cheese- and berry-stuffed delight. The crowning touch is a drizzle of buttery blueberry sauce.

12   white bread slices
2   (8-ounce) packages cream cheese, cut into 1-inch cubes
2   cups fresh blueberries, divided
12   large eggs, lightly beaten
2   cups milk
⅓   cup maple syrup
1   cup sugar
2   tablespoons cornstarch
1   cup water
1   tablespoon butter

Trim crusts from bread slices; cut bread slices into 1-inch pieces. Place half of bread pieces in a buttered 13- x 9-inch baking dish. Layer cream cheese and 1 cup blueberries over bread; top with remaining bread pieces.

Combine eggs, milk, and syrup; pour over bread mixture. Cover and chill 8 hours.

Bake, covered, at 350° for 30 minutes. Uncover and bake 35 more minutes or until puffed and golden.

Combine sugar and cornstarch in a saucepan; gradually add water. Cook over medium-high heat, stirring constantly, 5 minutes or until thickened. Stir in remaining 1 cup blueberries; bring to a boil. Reduce heat, and simmer, uncovered, 10 minutes,

stirring occasionally. Add butter; stir until melted. Cut French toast into squares, and serve with blueberry sauce. Yield: 10 servings.

Easy Caramel-Chocolate Sticky Buns

1   (15-ounce) container coconut-pecan frosting
1   cup pecan halves
2   (10-ounce) cans refrigerated buttermilk biscuits
20   chocolate kisses, unwrapped

Spread frosting in a lightly greased 9-inch square pan. Arrange pecan halves over frosting.

Separate biscuits; flatten each to ¼-inch thickness. Place a chocolate kiss to 1 side of center of each biscuit. Fold biscuit in half, forming a semicircle; press edges gently to seal. Repeat procedure with remaining biscuits and chocolate kisses. Arrange biscuits over pecans, placing flat sides down.

Bake at 375° for 28 to 30 minutes or until lightly browned. Cool in pan on a wire rack 5 minutes; invert onto a serving plate, and serve immediately. Yield: 20 servings.

Easy Berry Pancakes

1   large egg, lightly beaten
⅔   cup milk
2   tablespoons vegetable oil
1   (5.5-ounce) package or 1¼ cups all-purpose baking mix
1   cup fresh blueberries or blackberries
Garnish: fresh berries

Stir together egg, milk, and oil; add to baking mix, stirring just until moistened. Stir in berries.

Pour about ¼ cup batter for each pancake onto a hot, lightly greased griddle. Cook pancakes until tops are covered with bubbles and edges look cooked; turn and cook other side. Serve warm with powdered sugar or maple syrup. Garnish, if desired. Yield: 9 pancakes.

Easy Berry Pancakes

Coffee Lovers' Coffee Cake

A buttery coffee crumb mixture makes a shortbreadlike crust for this easy snack cake.

2   cups all-purpose flour
2   teaspoons instant coffee granules
2   cups firmly packed light brown sugar
1   teaspoon ground cinnamon
½   teaspoon salt
½   cup butter or margarine, cut into
       pieces
1   (8-ounce) container sour cream
1   teaspoon baking soda
1   large egg, lightly beaten
¾   cup chopped pecans or walnuts

Combine flour and coffee granules in a large bowl. Add brown sugar, cinnamon, and salt; stir well. Cut in butter with a pastry blender until crumbly. Press half of crumb mixture into a 9-inch square pan; set aside.

Combine sour cream and baking soda, stirring well. Add to remaining crumb mixture, stirring just until dry ingredients are moistened. Add egg, stirring gently to combine. Pour sour cream mixture over crumb crust in pan; sprinkle with pecans.

Bake at 350° for 45 minutes. Yield: 1 (9-inch) coffee cake.

Old-Fashioned Buttermilk Drop Biscuits

Classic Cream Scones

2   cups all-purpose flour
¼   cup sugar
2   teaspoons baking powder
⅛   teaspoon salt
⅓   cup butter or margarine, cut into pieces
½   cup whipping cream
1   large egg
1½ teaspoons vanilla extract
1   egg white
1   teaspoon water
Sugar

Combine first 4 ingredients. Cut butter into flour mixture with a pastry blender until crumbly.

Whisk together cream, egg, and vanilla; add to flour mixture, stirring just until dry ingredients are moistened. Turn dough out onto a lightly floured surface. Pat dough to ½-inch thickness; cut with a 2½-inch round cutter, and place on baking sheets.

Whisk together egg white and 1 teaspoon water; brush egg wash over scones. Sprinkle scones with additional sugar.

Bake at 425° for 13 to 15 minutes or until lightly browned. Yield: 1 dozen.

Old-Fashioned Buttermilk Drop Biscuits

2   cups stone-ground flour*
1   tablespoon baking powder
½   teaspoon salt
½   teaspoon baking soda
⅓   cup butter or margarine, cut into pieces
⅔   cup buttermilk
1   tablespoon honey

Be careful not to overwork biscuit dough. A light touch will produce light biscuits.

Stir together first 4 ingredients in a large bowl. Cut butter into flour mixture with a pastry blender until crumbly; add buttermilk and honey, stirring until dry ingredients are moistened.

Drop dough by rounded tablespoonfuls onto a lightly greased baking sheet.

Bake at 400° for 15 to 20 minutes or until golden. Yield: 14 biscuits.

All-purpose flour may be substituted.

—Caterer Sarah Aley
Tenants Harbor, Maine

Butter Muffins

These bite-size quick breads will melt in your mouth.

Butter Muffins

2   cups self-rising flour
1   (8-ounce) container sour cream
1   cup butter or margarine, melted

Stir together all ingredients just until blended. Spoon batter into lightly greased miniature muffin pans, filling to the top.

Bake at 350° for 25 minutes or until lightly browned. Yield: 2½ dozen.
Note: *For Herbed Muffins, add a tablespoon or two of your favorite chopped herb to the batter.*

Cheese Muffins

We gave these muffins top marks for ease, taste, and versatility.

2   tablespoons butter or margarine, divided
½   cup chopped onion
1½   cups all-purpose baking mix
1   cup (4 ounces) shredded sharp American cheese, divided
1   large egg, lightly beaten
½   cup milk
1   tablespoon sesame seeds, toasted

Melt 1 tablespoon butter in a skillet over medium-high heat; add onion, and cook, stirring constantly, 3 minutes or until tender.

Combine onion, baking mix, and ½ cup cheese in a large bowl. Combine egg and milk; add to onion mixture, stirring just until moistened. Spoon into greased muffin pans, filling half full. Sprinkle with remaining ½ cup cheese and sesame seeds; dot with remaining 1 tablespoon butter.

Bake at 400° for 12 to 13 minutes or until golden. Remove muffins from pans immediately, and serve warm. Yield: 1 dozen.

Sunny Corn Muffins

2 ears fresh corn with husks
2 tablespoons butter or margarine
¼ cup finely chopped onion
1 cup all-purpose flour
1 cup yellow cornmeal
2 tablespoons sugar
1½ teaspoons baking powder
1 teaspoon salt
½ teaspoon baking soda
1 cup plus 2 tablespoons buttermilk
1 large egg
¼ cup butter or margarine, melted
1 cup (4 ounces) shredded Cheddar
   cheese
1 (4.5-ounce) can chopped green chiles,
   drained
¼ cup sunflower seed kernels

Remove husks from corn. Tear husks into
½-inch strips, and soak in hot water 15
minutes; drain. Cut corn kernels from cobs.

Melt 2 tablespoons butter in a large skillet
over medium-high heat; add corn and onion,
and sauté until tender. Set mixture aside.

Combine flour and next 5 ingredients in a
large bowl; make a well in center of mixture.

Stir together buttermilk, egg, and ¼ cup
butter; add to flour mixture, stirring just until
moistened. Stir in corn mixture, cheese, and
green chiles.

Arrange 4 husk strips across each lightly
greased muffin cup to resemble spokes, if
desired; spoon batter into cups, filling each
three-fourths full. Sprinkle with sunflower
seed kernels.

Bake at 375° for 20 to 25 minutes or until
muffins are golden (corn husks will become
dark brown). Remove from pans; cool on wire
racks. Yield: 1 dozen.

Sunny Corn Muffin

Roasted Red Pepper Bruschetta

1 (16-ounce) French bread loaf
Olive oil
1 medium onion, coarsely chopped
1 teaspoon sugar
2 tablespoons olive oil
1 (7-ounce) jar roasted red bell peppers,
   drained and cut into thin strips
1 (3- or 4-ounce) log goat cheese, crumbled
24 basil leaves

Cut bread into 24 diagonal slices; place on baking sheets. Brush with olive oil.

Broil bread slices 5½ inches from heat
1 minute on each side or until golden brown.
Set aside.

Cook onion and sugar in hot oil in a large
skillet over medium-low heat, stirring occasionally, 25 minutes. Cool.

Top bread evenly with onion mixture and
pepper strips. Sprinkle evenly with cheese, and
broil 1 minute or until cheese melts. Top with
basil leaves. Serve immediately. Yield: 2 dozen
appetizer servings.

Pumpkin Seed Focaccia

Pumpkin Seed Focaccia

1   (¼-ounce) envelope active dry yeast
1½ cups warm water (100° to 110°)
1   teaspoon extra-virgin olive oil
3½ to 3¾ cups unbleached all-purpose
    flour, divided
1   tablespoon wheat gluten*
1½ teaspoons fine-grained sea salt
½   cup hulled, unsalted pumpkin seeds,
    toasted*
1   large red tomato, thinly sliced
1   large yellow tomato, thinly sliced
1½ to 2 tablespoons dried oregano
¼   teaspoon fine-grained sea salt
¼   teaspoon freshly ground pepper
½   cup crumbled feta cheese
2   tablespoons extra-virgin olive oil

Stir together yeast and warm water in a large bowl; let stand 5 minutes.

Add 1 teaspoon olive oil, 1 cup flour, wheat gluten, and 1½ teaspoons sea salt; beat at medium speed with an electric mixer until well blended. Gradually stir in enough remaining flour to make a soft dough.

Turn dough out onto a well-floured surface, and knead until smooth and elastic (about 5 minutes). Place in a well-greased bowl, turning to grease top.

Cover and let rise in a warm place (85°), free from drafts, 45 minutes or until doubled in bulk.

Punch dough down. Knead pumpkin seeds into dough. Lightly grease hands, and pat dough evenly into a lightly greased 14-inch pizza pan. Arrange red and yellow tomato slices on top of dough, overlapping slices.

Combine oregano, ¼ teaspoon sea salt, and pepper; sprinkle over tomato. Sprinkle evenly with cheese, and drizzle with 2 tablespoons olive oil.

Bake at 400° for 35 minutes or until bottom of crust is browned. Let cool slightly; cut into wedges. Yield: 8 servings.

*Wheat gluten can be found in the baking section of grocery stores or in health food stores. Hulled, unsalted pumpkin seeds can be found in the natural foods section of grocery stores or in health food stores.

—Mary Ann Esposito
Durham, New Hampshire

Greek Bread

1   (8-ounce) package cream cheese,
    softened
2   tablespoons mayonnaise
2   teaspoons Greek seasoning
1   (16-ounce) French bread loaf
1   (4-ounce) package crumbled tomato-
    basil or plain feta cheese
1   (2¼-ounce) can sliced ripe olives,
    drained
½   cup drained, chopped pepperoncini
    salad peppers

Combine first 3 ingredients, stirring until smooth. Slice bread loaf in half lengthwise. Spread cream cheese mixture on cut sides of bread. Sprinkle feta cheese, olives, and peppers over cream cheese mixture. Place bread on an ungreased baking sheet.

Bake at 375° for 15 minutes or until thoroughly heated. Yield: 1 loaf.

Italian Cheese Breadsticks

Dip these pizza-flavored sticks into your favorite marinara sauce or ranch dressing.

1   (11-ounce) can refrigerated breadsticks
1   to 2 tablespoons olive oil
1½ teaspoons garlic powder
1   teaspoon dried Italian seasoning
1   cup (4 ounces) shredded mozzarella
    cheese

Unroll breadstick dough; twist breadsticks, and place 1 inch apart on a lightly greased aluminum foil-lined baking sheet. Brush breadsticks with oil.

Combine garlic powder and Italian seasoning; sprinkle over breadsticks.

Bake at 400° for 9 to 10 minutes or until golden. Sprinkle with cheese; bake 1 to 2 more minutes or until cheese melts. Serve immediately. Yield: 8 breadsticks.

desserts

Vanilla Custard Ice Cream

2   cups milk
1   vanilla bean, split
8   egg yolks
¾   cup sugar
¼   cup (2 ounces) vanilla extract
½   teaspoon salt
2   cups whipping cream
Garnishes: crumbled pralines, fresh mint sprigs

Cook milk in a heavy saucepan over medium heat, stirring often, just until bubbles appear; remove from heat. Add vanilla bean; cover and let stand 20 minutes. Remove and discard vanilla bean.

Combine yolks and next 3 ingredients in a large bowl; whisk until mixture is thick and pale. Gradually whisk in warm milk; return mixture to saucepan. Cook over very low heat, stirring constantly, 5 to 7 minutes or until mixture coats a spoon. Remove from heat; pour through a wire-mesh strainer into a bowl. Cool custard, stirring occasionally.

Stir in whipping cream; cover and chill at least 1 hour.

Pour custard into freezer container of a 4-quart hand-turned or electric freezer. Freeze according to manufacturer's instructions. Garnish, if desired. Yield: ½ gallon.

Lemon Ice Cream

You won't even need an ice cream freezer for this supereasy blend.

2   cups sugar
2   cups milk
2   cups half-and-half
2   teaspoons grated lemon rind
1   cup fresh lemon juice
6   drops yellow liquid food coloring
Garnish: fresh mint sprigs

Stir together first 6 ingredients in a large bowl. Pour into a 13- x 9-inch pan; cover and freeze

at least 2 hours. Break mixture into pieces. Process half of mixture in a food processor or blender until smooth. Remove from processor; set aside in freezer. Repeat procedure with remaining mixture. Return all of mixture to pan. Cover and freeze at least 4 hours or until firm. Garnish, if desired. Yield: 1½ quarts.

Fresh Lime Ice Cream

2½ cups sugar
6   cups half-and-half
1   tablespoon grated lime rind
¾   cup fresh lime juice (about 6 limes)
⅛   teaspoon salt

Combine all ingredients; pour into freezer container of a 4- or 5-quart electric freezer. Freeze according to manufacturer's instructions.

Pack freezer with additional ice and rock salt, and let stand 1 hour before serving. Yield: 2½ quarts.

Orange Ice Cream: Substitute orange rind and fresh orange juice for lime rind and juice.

Mocha Ice Cream

1   (8-ounce) package semisweet chocolate baking squares, coarsely chopped
¼   cup strong brewed coffee
2   cups whipping cream
1   cup half-and-half
¾   cup sugar, divided
3   tablespoons instant coffee granules
4   egg yolks

Microwave chocolate in a 1-quart microwave-safe bowl at HIGH 1½ minutes or until melted, stirring twice; stir in coffee. Set mixture aside.

Bring whipping cream, half-and-half, ½ cup sugar, and coffee granules to a boil in a heavy saucepan over medium-high heat, stirring until sugar and coffee granules dissolve. Beat yolks and remaining ¼ cup sugar at high speed with an electric mixer until thick and pale. With

mixer at low speed, gradually pour hot cream mixture into yolk mixture; return to saucepan.

Cook over medium heat, stirring constantly, 6 to 8 minutes or until mixture thickens and coats a spoon. Remove from heat; stir in chocolate mixture. Cover and chill 2 hours.

Pour chilled custard into freezer container of a 2- or 4-quart hand-turned or electric freezer. Freeze according to manufacturer's instructions.

Pack freezer with additional ice and rock salt, and let stand 1 hour before serving. Yield: 5 cups.

Peanut Butter Ice Cream

1½ quarts half-and-half
1   (12-ounce) jar chunky peanut butter (about 1¼ cups)
6   large eggs
2   cups sugar
1   (14-ounce) can sweetened condensed milk
1   cup milk, divided
1   tablespoon vanilla extract
2   tablespoons all-purpose flour

Stir together half-and-half, peanut butter, and eggs in a Dutch oven. Cook over medium-low heat, whisking constantly, 25 minutes or until a thermometer registers 160°. Whisk in sugar, condensed milk, ¾ cup milk, and vanilla.

Combine remaining ¼ cup milk and flour in a small bowl; stir until smooth. Whisk into hot mixture; cook until sugar dissolves. Let cool.

Pour custard into freezer container of a 5-quart hand-turned or electric freezer. Freeze according to manufacturer's instructions.

Pack freezer with additional ice and rock salt, and let stand 1 hour before serving. Yield: 1 gallon.

Dip into this collection of our favorite homemade ice creams.

ice cream bowl

Here's a fun idea for serving homemade or store-bought ice cream to guests. Pick several flavors or just one. Make scoops the night before your party, and arrange them on a foil-lined jellyroll pan. Cover loosely, and freeze overnight. Just before serving, pile scoops in a trifle bowl or other glass serving bowl. Have a serving spoon, stack of bowls, spoons, and assorted toppings at the ready. Let guests know what ice cream flavors you're serving so they can build their own dessert.

Mocha Ice Cream; Pecan-Caramel Crunch Ice Cream, page 250; Peanut Butter Ice Cream

homemade hints

- **Skip the skim milk;** whole milk or cream makes a richer dessert.
- **Use fresh, ripe fruit for the best flavor.** Sweeten fruit before adding it to your custard to keep fruit soft. Mashed fruit distributes throughout ice cream more evenly.
- **Fill the canister two-thirds full** or to the fill line so the ice cream has room to expand as it freezes.
- **Use crushed ice and plenty of rock salt** so the custard will freeze. (But too much salt may cause ice crystals to form.)
- **If using a hand-turned freezer, start cranking slowly** for an even temperature; speed up as ice cream freezes.
- **For thicker, richer ice cream, take out the dasher,** pack down the ice cream with a spoon, and replace the lid. Then place foil over the hole in the top, and put the canister back in the container. Repack with ice and salt, using more salt this time. Wrap newspaper or a towel around the top, and let stand for about 1 hour.
- **Seal leftovers tightly,** and store them in your freezer no longer than 1 week.

Pecan-Caramel Crunch Ice Cream

(shown on page 249)

1 cup chopped pecans
¾ cup quick-cooking oats
¼ cup all-purpose flour
¼ cup firmly packed light brown sugar
¼ cup butter, melted
2 cups firmly packed light brown sugar
3 cups milk
1 (12-ounce) can evaporated milk
½ teaspoon salt
4 egg yolks
4 cups whipping cream
1 (14-ounce) can sweetened condensed milk
2 tablespoons vanilla extract
1 (16-ounce) bottle caramel topping

Stir together first 5 ingredients; spread in a thin layer on a baking sheet. Bake at 350° for 15 minutes. Cool completely on a wire rack. Process oat mixture in a food processor until finely chopped; set aside.

Stir together 2 cups brown sugar and next 3 ingredients in a large saucepan over low heat, and simmer, stirring often, 1 minute. (Do not boil.)

Beat egg yolks until thick and lemon-colored. Gradually stir 1 cup hot brown sugar mixture into yolks. Add egg yolk mixture to remaining hot mixture; cook, stirring constantly, over low heat 2 minutes or until mixture begins to thicken. Remove pan from heat; stir in cream, condensed milk, and vanilla. Let cool to room temperature.

Pour mixture into freezer container of a 5- or 6-quart hand-turned or electric freezer. Freeze according to manufacturer's instructions 5 to 7 minutes or until partially frozen. Layer top of ice cream evenly with oat mixture and caramel topping. Freeze according to manufacturer's instructions 10 to 15 more minutes or until mixture is frozen. Pack freezer with additional ice and rock salt, and let stand 1 hour before serving. (If desired, remove mixture from freezer container, and place in another container. Return to freezer, and freeze 8 hours or overnight.) Yield: 1 gallon.

Toasted Coconut Ice Cream

2 cups flaked coconut
4 cups milk
1 cup sugar
6 egg yolks
2 cups half-and-half
1 (16-ounce) can cream of coconut
2 teaspoons vanilla extract
Garnish: toasted coconut

Bake 2 cups flaked coconut in a shallow pan at 350°, stirring occasionally, 10 minutes or until toasted.

Whisk together milk, sugar, and egg yolks in a heavy saucepan. Cook over medium heat, whisking constantly, 20 minutes or until mixture thickens and coats a spoon. (Do not boil.) Remove from heat; whisk in coconut, half-and-half, cream of coconut, and vanilla. Cover and chill 3 hours.

Pour custard into freezer container of a 4-quart hand-turned or electric freezer. Freeze according to manufacturer's instructions.

Pack freezer with additional ice and rock salt, and let stand 1 hour before serving. Garnish, if desired. Yield: 2½ quarts.

Blackberry Ice Cream

3 cups sugar
3 tablespoons all-purpose flour
½ teaspoon salt
10 cups half-and-half
8 egg yolks, beaten
1 teaspoon vanilla extract
4½ cups fresh or 1 (1-pound) package frozen blackberries
1½ cups sugar
1 tablespoon fresh lemon juice
Garnishes: fresh mint, fresh blackberries

Combine first 3 ingredients in a large Dutch oven. Whisk in half-and-half. Bring to a boil, stirring constantly, over medium-high heat.

Slowly whisk about 4 cups of hot mixture into egg yolks. Add egg mixture to remaining hot mixture, whisking constantly, until mixture reaches 160°. Immediately remove from heat. Let custard cool completely, stirring occasionally. Stir in vanilla; chill 8 hours or overnight.

Blackberry Ice Cream

Combine blackberries and 1½ cups sugar in a separate bowl; stir well. Cover and chill 8 hours, stirring occasionally to dissolve sugar. Stir in lemon juice.

Stir berry mixture into custard. Pour custard into freezer container of a 5- or 6-quart electric freezer. Freeze according to manufacturer's instructions. Pack freezer with additional ice and rock salt, and let stand 1 hour before serving. Scoop into serving bowls. Garnish, if desired. Yield: 1 gallon.

Note: *To hasten cooling of custard, partially fill sink with ice water to about halfway up sides of Dutch oven. Let pan remain in ice water, stirring often until custard reaches room temperature; chill.*

—*Food Writer Marcelle Bienvenu*
New Iberia, Louisiana

Plum Ice Cream

3   cups diced purple or black plums
    (about 6 plums)
1   cup sugar
3   cups whipping cream
¼   cup slivered almonds, toasted (optional)

Cook plums and sugar in a saucepan over medium heat 5 minutes or until plums are tender and sugar is dissolved.

Process plum mixture in a food processor until smooth; strain and discard skins.

Stir together plum puree and whipping cream in container of a 2- or 4-quart electric freezer. Freeze according to manufacturer's instructions.

Pack freezer with additional ice and rock salt, and let stand 1 hour before serving. Serve with almonds, if desired. Yield: 5 cups.

Blueberry-Peach Ice Cream

(shown on page 268)

3   medium peaches, peeled and sliced
2   cups milk
1   (14-ounce) can sweetened condensed milk
1   (12-ounce) can evaporated milk
3   large eggs, lightly beaten
1   cup sugar
3   cups whipping cream
1   pint fresh or frozen blueberries
Garnishes: peach slices, blueberries, fresh
    mint sprigs

Process peach slices in a blender until smooth.

Whisk together 2 cups milk and next 4 ingredients in a large heavy saucepan. Cook over medium heat, whisking constantly, until mixture reaches 160° (about 10 minutes). Remove from heat; cool 30 minutes.

Beat whipping cream at high speed with an electric mixer until soft peaks form. Let whipped cream stand 30 minutes. Stir whipped cream, pureed peach, and blueberries into custard.

Pour into freezer container of a 4-quart electric freezer. Freeze according to manufacturer's instructions.

Pack freezer with additional ice and rock salt, and let stand 1 hour before serving. Garnish, if desired. Yield: 3 quarts.

Plum Ice Cream

Sorbet can be savory or sweet and is typically served as dessert or as a palate cleanser between courses.

Watermelon Sorbet

Watermelon Sorbet

4   cups water
2   cups sugar
8   cups seeded, chopped watermelon
1   (12-ounce) can frozen pink lemonade
      concentrate, thawed and undiluted
Garnish: fresh mint sprigs

Bring 4 cups water and sugar just to a boil in a medium saucepan over high heat, stirring until sugar dissolves. Remove from heat. Cool.

Process sugar syrup and watermelon in batches in a blender until smooth. Stir in lemonade concentrate. Chill 2 hours.

Pour mixture into freezer container of a 4-quart electric freezer. Freeze according to manufacturer's instructions. Garnish, if desired. Yield: 2½ quarts.

Fresh Mango Sorbet

Mango season is from May to September. Store ripe mangoes in a plastic bag in the refrigerator up to 5 days.

2   large ripe mangoes, chopped
1   cup mango nectar
¾   cup sugar
1   tablespoon grated lime rind
½   cup fresh lime juice

Process all ingredients in a food processor until smooth. Pour mixture into freezer container of a 2-quart hand-turned or electric freezer. Freeze according to manufacturer's instructions. Yield: 1 quart.

serving suggestion

Fill two metal tubs with ice, and nestle one tub down into the other. Stick Sangría Pops down into the ice for serving.

Sangría Pops, White Sangría Pops

Sangría Pops put a frosty dessert spin on the popular party drink.

Sangría Pops

1   (12-ounce) can frozen lemonade
    concentrate, thawed and undiluted
1½ cups Burgundy wine
½   cup orange juice
½   cup water
½   cup sugar
3   tablespoons fresh lime juice
14 wooden craft sticks

Stir together first 6 ingredients until sugar dissolves. Pour into 14 (¼-cup) molds; freeze 1 hour or until firm. Insert wooden sticks. Freeze at least 8 hours. Yield: 14 pops.
White Sangría Pops: Substitute white wine for red wine. We tested with Sauvignon Blanc.

Wild Raspberry Tea Granita

6   cups cranberry juice drink
⅔   cup sugar
10 regular-size raspberry tea bags

Bring cranberry juice drink and sugar to a boil, stirring until sugar dissolves; pour over tea bags. Cover and steep 20 minutes; discard tea bags. Pour into a 13- x 9-inch pan. Cover and freeze 8 hours. Remove from freezer 20 minutes before serving. Break into pieces. Spoon into glasses, and serve immediately. Yield: 6 cups.

Grand Marnier Milk Shake

2   cups vanilla ice cream
½   cup Grand Marnier or other orange-
    flavored liqueur

Process vanilla ice cream and Grand Marnier in a blender just until blended, stopping once to scrape down sides. Serve immediately. Yield: 2¼ cups.

—*Chef Louis Osteen*
Louis's at Pawleys
Pawleys Island, South Carolina

{ pop molds

What could be more fun or appropriate than making frozen pops at the beach? Try our Sangría Pops for starters, but don't forget they're for adults only. You can freeze juice or soft drinks in plastic pop molds, too. The molds are inexpensive, lightweight, and easy to pack.

Above, left to right: These double pop molds, ice pop makers with straws, and pop-up molds are available at kitchen shops or even your local pharmacy.

Margarita Granita

3   cups water
1   cup sugar
½   cup fresh lime juice
⅓   cup fresh lemon juice
6   tablespoons orange liqueur
6   tablespoons gold tequila
2   teaspoons grated lime rind
Sugar

Bring 3 cups water and 1 cup sugar to a boil in a saucepan, stirring mixture constantly. Pour into a large bowl; add lime juice and next 4 ingredients. Cover and freeze 8 hours.

Process frozen mixture in a blender or food processor until slushy. Dip margarita glass rims into water; dip rims into sugar. Spoon granita into glasses. Yield: 5 cups.
Note: For a nonalcoholic version, omit liquors, and add ½ cup fresh orange juice.

Peanut Butter and Chocolate Chunk Cookies

Add eggs and vanilla; beat until blended.

Combine oats, baking soda, and salt. Add to butter mixture, beating until blended. Stir in chocolate chunks and pecans. Cover and chill dough 2 hours.

Drop dough by ¼ cupfuls 3 inches apart onto ungreased baking sheets; press to ¾-inch thickness.

Bake at 350° for 14 to 15 minutes or until edges are browned. Cool on baking sheets 3 minutes; remove to wire racks to cool completely. Yield: 3½ dozen.

Chocolate-Chocolate Chip Cookies

These double chocolate cookies are similar in texture to a brownie. For jumbo cookies, drop dough by ¼-cup measures and bake slightly longer.

½ cup butter
4 (1-ounce) unsweetened chocolate baking squares, chopped
3 cups (18 ounces) semisweet chocolate morsels, divided
1½ cups all-purpose flour
½ teaspoon baking powder
½ teaspoon salt
4 large eggs
1½ cups sugar
2 teaspoons vanilla extract
2 cups chopped pecans, toasted

Combine butter, unsweetened chocolate, and 1½ cups chocolate morsels in a large heavy saucepan. Cook over low heat, stirring constantly, until butter and chocolate melt; cool.

Combine flour, baking powder, and salt in a small bowl.

Beat eggs, sugar, and vanilla in a medium mixing bowl at medium speed with an electric mixer. Gradually add dry ingredients to egg mixture, beating well. Add chocolate mixture; beat well. Stir in remaining 1½ cups chocolate morsels and pecans.

Drop dough by 2 tablespoonfuls 1 inch apart onto parchment paper-lined baking sheets.

Bake at 350° for 10 minutes. Cool slightly on baking sheets; remove to wire racks to cool completely. Yield: about 2½ dozen.

Seven-Minute Chocolate Cookies

¼ cup butter or margarine
1 (12-ounce) package semisweet chocolate morsels
1 (14-ounce) can sweetened condensed milk
1 cup all-purpose flour
1 cup chopped pecans
1 teaspoon vanilla extract

Combine butter, chocolate morsels, and condensed milk in a heavy saucepan. Cook over low heat, stirring constantly, until blended. Remove from heat. Stir in remaining ingredients.

Drop by teaspoonfuls onto lightly greased baking sheets.

Bake at 350° for 7 minutes. Cool slightly on baking sheets; remove to wire racks to cool completely. Yield: 4½ dozen.
Recipe adapted from Cape Fear...Still Cooking.

Peanut Butter and Chocolate Chunk Cookies

2 cups creamy peanut butter
¾ cup butter or margarine, softened
1 cup sugar
1 cup firmly packed light brown sugar
3 large eggs
1 teaspoon vanilla extract
3 cups uncooked regular oats
2 teaspoons baking soda
¼ teaspoon salt
1 (11.5-ounce) package semisweet chocolate chunks or 3 (4-ounce) semisweet chocolate baking bars, chopped
1½ cups coarsely chopped pecans, toasted

Beat peanut butter, butter, and sugars at medium speed with an electric mixer until fluffy.

Chocolate Chip Supreme Cookies

½	cup shortening
½	cup butter or margarine, softened
¾	cup firmly packed dark brown sugar
¾	cup sugar
2	large eggs
1	(3.4-ounce) package vanilla instant pudding mix
1	tablespoon vanilla extract
2¼	cups all-purpose flour
1	tablespoon baking soda
1	teaspoon ground cinnamon
½	teaspoon salt
½	teaspoon ground nutmeg
2	cups (12 ounces) semisweet chocolate morsels
1½	cups chopped pecans
1	cup uncooked quick-cooking oats

Beat shortening and butter at medium speed with an electric mixer until creamy; add sugars, beating well. Add eggs, beating until blended. Add pudding mix and vanilla; beat until blended. Combine flour and next 4 ingredients. Gradually add to butter mixture, beating until blended. Stir in morsels, pecans, and oats.

Shape dough into 1½-inch balls; place on lightly greased baking sheets, and press to 1-inch thickness.

Bake at 375° for 10 to 12 minutes. Cool slightly on baking sheets; remove to wire racks to cool completely. Yield: 3 dozen.

White Chocolate-Macadamia Nut Cookies

½	cup butter or margarine, softened
½	cup shortening
¾	cup firmly packed light brown sugar
½	cup sugar
1	large egg
1½	teaspoons vanilla extract
2	cups all-purpose flour
1	teaspoon baking soda
½	teaspoon salt
1	(6-ounce) package white chocolate baking bars, cut into chunks
1	(6.85-ounce) jar macadamia nuts, chopped

Beat butter and shortening at medium speed with an electric mixer until creamy; gradually add sugars, beating well. Add egg and vanilla; beat well. Combine flour, soda, and salt; gradually add to butter mixture, beating well. Stir in white chocolate and nuts.

Drop dough by rounded teaspoonfuls 2 inches apart onto lightly greased baking sheets.

Bake at 350° for 8 to 10 minutes or until lightly browned. Cool slightly on baking sheets; remove to wire racks to cool completely. Yield: 5 dozen.

Chunky Hazelnut-Toffee Cookies

1	cup unsalted butter, softened
¾	cup firmly packed light brown sugar
½	cup sugar
2	large eggs
1	tablespoon vanilla extract
2¾	cups all-purpose flour
1½	teaspoons baking powder
½	teaspoon baking soda
½	teaspoon salt
4	(1.4-ounce) English toffee candy bars, chopped
2	(11.5-ounce) packages semisweet chocolate chunks
1	cup toasted, chopped hazelnuts or pecans

Beat butter at medium speed with an electric mixer until creamy. Gradually add sugars, beating well. Add eggs and vanilla, beating well.

Combine flour and next 3 ingredients, stirring well. Add to butter mixture, beating at low speed just until blended. Stir in chopped candy, chocolate, and nuts. Drop dough by heaping tablespoonfuls 1½ inches apart onto ungreased baking sheets.

Bake at 350° for 10 minutes or until lightly browned. Let cool on baking sheets; remove to wire racks to cool completely. Yield: 4½ dozen.

Cinnamon Chip Icebox Cookies

1	cup butter or margarine, softened
2	cups sugar
2	large eggs
2	teaspoons vanilla extract
4	cups all-purpose flour
1	(10-ounce) package cinnamon morsels
1	cup chopped pecans, toasted

Beat butter at medium speed with an electric mixer until creamy. Gradually add sugar, beating well. Add eggs and vanilla, beating until blended. Gradually add flour, beating at low speed just until blended. Stir in cinnamon morsels and pecans.

Divide dough into 3 (2-cup) portions; roll each portion into a 12-inch log. Wrap logs in wax paper. Chill 8 hours, or freeze in an airtight container up to 3 months.

Cut each log into 24 (½-inch-thick) slices, and place slices on ungreased baking sheets.

Bake at 350° for 13 to 15 minutes or until edges are lightly browned. Cool on baking sheets 5 minutes. Remove cookies to wire racks to cool completely. Yield: 6 dozen.

Note: Cookie dough may be dropped by rounded tablespoonfuls 2 inches apart onto ungreased baking sheets, and then baked.

Backpack Cookies

1	cup butter or margarine, softened
1	cup sugar
1	cup firmly packed light brown sugar
2	large eggs
1	teaspoon vanilla extract
2	cups all-purpose flour
1	teaspoon baking soda
½	teaspoon baking powder
⅛	teaspoon salt
1	cup uncooked regular oats
2	cups crisp rice cereal
2	cups candy-coated chocolate pieces
1	cup chopped unsalted roasted peanuts
1	cup (6 ounces) semisweet chocolate morsels
½	cup flaked coconut

Beat butter at medium speed with an electric mixer until creamy; gradually add sugars, beating well. Add eggs and vanilla; beat well.

Combine flour and next 3 ingredients; gradually add to butter mixture, mixing well. Stir in oats and remaining ingredients.

Drop dough by rounded tablespoonfuls 2 inches apart onto ungreased baking sheets.

Bake at 350° for 10 to 12 minutes or until cookies are lightly browned. Remove to wire racks to cool completely. Yield: 6 dozen.

Chunky White Chocolate S'mores

Chunky White Chocolate S'mores

½ cup shortening
½ cup sugar
½ cup firmly packed light brown sugar
1 large egg
1 cup all-purpose flour
½ teaspoon baking powder
½ teaspoon baking soda
½ teaspoon salt
¾ cup uncooked regular oats
¾ cup crisp rice cereal
½ teaspoon vanilla extract
2 (4-ounce) white chocolate baking bars, broken into chunks, or 1½ cups white chocolate morsels
12 large marshmallows

Beat shortening at medium speed with an electric mixer until fluffy; add sugars, beating well. Add egg, beating until blended.

Combine flour and next 4 ingredients in a separate bowl; gradually add to sugar mixture, beating after each addition.

Stir cereal, vanilla, and white chocolate into dough.

Drop by tablespoonfuls onto ungreased baking sheets; flatten slightly with fingertips.

Bake at 350° for 10 minutes or until lightly golden. Cool slightly on baking sheets; remove to wire racks to cool completely. Store in tins until ready to serve.

Place marshmallows on a long stick or skewer; toast (over a gas flame or campfire) over low heat (below 300°), 3 to 5 minutes or until golden. Place 1 marshmallow on a cookie, and top with a second cookie. Yield: 1 dozen sandwich cookies.

S'mores are a gooey union between graham crackers, toasted marshmallows, and chocolate. They're so good, you'll always want "some more."

Giant Oatmeal-Spice Cookies

1½ cups all-purpose flour
1 teaspoon ground cinnamon
½ teaspoon salt
½ teaspoon baking soda
½ teaspoon ground ginger
¼ teaspoon ground allspice
⅛ teaspoon ground cloves
1 cup butter or margarine, softened
1 (16-ounce) package dark brown sugar
2 large eggs
1 teaspoon vanilla extract
3 cups quick-cooking oats
1 cup chopped pecans, toasted
½ cup raisins (optional)

Stir together first 7 ingredients.

Beat butter and sugar at medium speed with an electric mixer until fluffy. Add eggs and vanilla, beating until blended. Gradually add flour mixture, beating at low speed until blended.

Stir in oats, chopped pecans, and, if desired, raisins.

Drop dough by ¼ cupfuls onto lightly greased baking sheets; lightly press down dough.

Bake at 350° for 12 to 14 minutes. (Cookies should not be brown around the edges, and centers will not look quite done.) Cool slightly on baking sheets. Remove to wire racks to cool completely. Yield: 2½ dozen.

Coconut Macaroons

4 egg whites
½ cup sugar
3 cups dry unsweetened grated coconut
1 vanilla bean
1 teaspoon grated lemon rind
¼ cup sour cream

Combine egg whites and sugar in top of a double boiler; cook, stirring constantly, over hot (not boiling) water until sugar dissolves and egg whites are warm.

Pour egg mixture into a large bowl; beat at medium speed with an electric mixer until stiff peaks form.

Place coconut in a separate large bowl. Cut vanilla bean in half lengthwise; scrape seeds and add to coconut. Stir until blended. Discard bean pod. Stir in lemon rind and sour cream.

Fold egg white mixture into coconut mixture. Shape into small mounds (1½ inches in diameter), and place on a parchment paper-lined baking sheet.

Bake at 350° for 10 to 12 minutes or until cookies begin to brown. Cool macaroons completely on wire racks. Yield: 32 macaroons.
Note: Use a small ice cream scoop to make evenly shaped cookies.

Italian Cinnamon Sticks

¾ cup sugar
½ cup walnuts, ground
1 teaspoon ground cinnamon
1 cup butter or margarine, softened
1 (8-ounce) package cream cheese, softened
2½ cups all-purpose flour
1 large egg, lightly beaten

Combine first 3 ingredients; set aside.

Beat butter and cream cheese at medium speed with an electric mixer until creamy; gradually add flour, mixing until well blended.

Shape dough into a ball; wrap in plastic wrap, and chill 30 minutes.

Divide dough in half; place 1 portion between two sheets of lightly floured wax paper, and roll into a 10-inch square (about ⅛ inch thick). Brush with egg; sprinkle with half of sugar mixture. Cut into 5- x ½-inch strips; twist strips, and place on ungreased baking sheets. Repeat procedure with remaining dough, egg, and sugar mixture.

Bake at 350° for 10 to 12 minutes or until golden. Transfer to wire racks to cool completely. Yield: about 6½ dozen.

Bay Brownies

1 cup butter
4 (1-ounce) unsweetened chocolate baking squares
4 large eggs
2 cups sugar
1 cup all-purpose flour
1 cup (6 ounces) semisweet chocolate morsels
Garnish: powdered sugar

Melt butter and chocolate squares in a heavy saucepan over low heat.

Beat eggs and sugar at medium-high speed with an electric mixer 8 minutes. Gradually add chocolate mixture, beating at low speed until blended. Gradually add flour, beating until blended. Stir in chocolate morsels. Pour into a lightly greased 13- x 9-inch pan.

Bake at 350° for 30 to 35 minutes. Cool in pan on a wire rack. Cut into squares. Garnish, if desired. Yield: 35 brownies.

Blonde Brownies

1 (16-ounce) package light brown sugar
¾ cup butter or margarine
3 large eggs
2¾ cups all-purpose flour
2½ teaspoons baking powder
½ teaspoon salt
1 cup chopped pecans
2 teaspoons vanilla extract

Heat sugar and butter in a saucepan over medium heat until butter melts and mixture is smooth. Remove from heat. Cool slightly. Add eggs, one at a time, beating after each addition.

Combine flour, baking powder, and salt; add to sugar mixture, stirring well. Stir in pecans and vanilla. Pour batter into a greased and floured 13- x 9-inch pan.

Bake at 350° for 25 to 26 minutes. Cool completely in pan on a wire rack. Cut into bars. Yield: 2 dozen.

Rosemary Shortbread

Fresh rosemary updates this basic but timeless shortbread.

1   cup butter, softened
¾   cup sifted powdered sugar
¼   cup cornstarch
1¾ cups all-purpose flour
1   tablespoon minced fresh rosemary

Beat butter at medium speed with an electric mixer until creamy; gradually add powdered sugar and cornstarch, beating well. Stir in flour and rosemary. (Dough will be stiff.)

Divide dough in half. Shape 1 portion of dough into a 6½" circle on an ungreased baking sheet. Crimp edges with a fork. Cut dough into 8 wedges (do not separate). Repeat procedure with remaining dough. Cover and chill 1 hour.

Bake at 300° for 30 minutes or until edges are barely browned. Cool 5 minutes on baking sheet; remove shortbread wedges to a wire rack to cool completely. Yield: 16 shortbread wedges.

Mint Julep Brownies

1   cup butter or margarine
4   (1-ounce) unsweetened chocolate baking
    squares
4   large eggs
2   cups sugar
1½ cups all-purpose flour
2   tablespoons bourbon
1   teaspoon peppermint extract
½   teaspoon salt
1   tablespoon powdered sugar

Melt butter and chocolate in a heavy saucepan over low heat, stirring until smooth; cool slightly.

Beat eggs at medium speed with an electric mixer 2 minutes. Gradually add 2 cups sugar, beating well. Add chocolate mixture, flour, and next 3 ingredients; beat well. Pour batter into a greased and floured 13- x 9-inch pan.

Bake at 350° for 25 to 30 minutes. Cool completely in pan on a wire rack. Cut into bars, and sprinkle with powdered sugar. Yield: 2 dozen.

Winnie's White Chocolate Drops

4   (4-ounce) packages white chocolate
    baking bars, broken
½   cup creamy peanut butter
1½ cups crisp rice cereal
1½ cups miniature marshmallows
1   cup unsalted dry-roasted peanuts
½   cup semisweet chocolate morsels

Cook white chocolate and peanut butter in a large heavy saucepan over low heat, stirring constantly, 5 to 6 minutes or until smooth; remove from heat.

Stir in cereal, marshmallows, and peanuts.

Drop mixture by rounded tablespoonfuls onto plastic wrap-lined baking sheets. Chill 10 minutes or until set.

Place chocolate morsels in a small heavy-duty zip-top plastic bag; seal. Submerge in hot water until chocolate melts. Snip a tiny hole in one corner of bag, and drizzle chocolate over candies. Chill 10 minutes or until set. Store in an airtight container. Yield: 2 dozen.

—Food Stylist Susan Brown Draudt
La Canada, California

Texas Millionaires

1   (14-ounce) package caramels,
    unwrapped
2   tablespoons butter or margarine
2   tablespoons water
3   cups pecan halves
1   cup (6 ounces) semisweet chocolate
    morsels
8   (2-ounce) vanilla candy coating
    squares

Cook first 3 ingredients in a heavy saucepan over low heat, stirring constantly, until smooth. Stir in pecan halves. Cool in pan 5 minutes.

Drop by tablespoonfuls onto lightly greased wax paper. Chill 1 hour, or freeze 20 minutes until firm.

Melt morsels and vanilla coating in a heavy saucepan over low heat, stirring until smooth. Dip caramel candies into chocolate mixture, allowing excess to drip; place on lightly greased wax paper. Let stand until firm. Store in refrigerator. Yield: 4 dozen.

Here are two versions of a summertime strawberry classic.
One sports the traditional biscuit base and is smothered with balsamic-splashed
berries; the other uses circles cut from a rich yellow cake that are
topped with berries and a minty custard sauce.

Strawberry Shortcake

(shown on page 10)

5   cups sliced fresh strawberries
½   cup sugar
1   teaspoon balsamic vinegar
3   cups all-purpose flour
½   cup sugar
2½ tablespoons baking powder
½   teaspoon salt
½   cup cold unsalted butter,
      cut into pieces
3   large eggs
2¼ cups whipping cream, divided
¼   cup sugar
¾   teaspoon vanilla extract
2   tablespoons powdered sugar

Stir together first 3 ingredients; let stand 1 hour, stirring occasionally.

Combine flour, ½ cup sugar, baking powder, and salt in a large bowl. Cut butter into flour mixture with a pastry blender until mixture is crumbly.

Stir together eggs and ¾ cup whipping cream; add to dry ingredients, stirring just until moistened.

Turn dough out onto a floured surface, and knead 3 or 4 times. Pat dough to ½-inch thickness; cut with a 3-inch biscuit cutter. Place shortcakes on an ungreased baking sheet.

Bake at 425° for 10 to 12 minutes or until golden. Remove to wire racks to cool.

Beat remaining 1½ cups whipping cream at medium speed with an electric mixer until foamy; gradually add ¼ cup sugar, beating until soft peaks form. Stir in vanilla.

Split shortcakes. Place 1 cake bottom on each of 8 individual serving plates. Spoon half of whipped cream mixture over shortcakes. Top with strawberry mixture, and dollop with remaining whipped cream. Add cake tops, and sprinkle

evenly with powdered sugar. Yield: 8 servings.
Note: To make 1 large shortcake, pat dough into 2 lightly greased 9-inch cakepans. Bake at 425° for 10 minutes or until golden. Remove to wire racks to cool. Place one cake on a serving plate; top with half each of strawberries and whipped cream. Top with second cake and remaining berries and cream.
—Ralph Brennan/Chef Haley Gabel
Bacco
New Orleans, Louisiana

Strawberry Shortcakes with Mint Cream

4   cups sliced fresh strawberries
2   cups granulated sugar, divided
1   cup vegetable oil
2   large eggs
2   cups self-rising flour
1   cup milk
1   teaspoon vanilla extract
1½ cups whipping cream
¼   cup sifted powdered sugar
Mint Cream
Garnishes: whole fresh strawberries, fresh
      mint sprigs

Stir together sliced strawberries and ½ cup granulated sugar in a bowl; let stand, stirring occasionally, 1 hour.

Beat remaining 1½ cups granulated sugar and oil at medium speed with an electric mixer until blended. Add eggs, 1 at a time, beating until blended after each addition.

Add flour to oil mixture alternately with milk, beginning and ending with flour. Beat at medium speed 4 minutes; stir in vanilla.

Grease a 15- x 10-inch jellyroll pan; line with wax paper. Grease and flour wax paper; pour batter into pan.

Bake at 350° for 28 to 30 minutes or until a wooden pick inserted in center comes out

clean. Cool in pan on a wire rack 10 minutes; remove from pan. Remove wax paper, and cool completely on wire rack.

Cut cake into 8 rounds with a 3-inch round cutter, and set rounds aside. Reserve remaining cake for other uses.

Beat whipping cream at high speed until foamy; gradually add powdered sugar, beating until soft peaks form.

Place 1 cake round on each of 4 individual serving plates, and top with sliced strawberries. Drizzle evenly with half of Mint Cream; dollop with whipped cream. Top with another cake round; drizzle evenly with remaining Mint Cream. Garnish, if desired, and serve immediately. Yield: 4 servings.

Mint Cream

1½ cups whipping cream
¼   cup fresh mint leaves
¾   cup sugar
3   egg yolks

Heat whipping cream and mint in a heavy saucepan over low heat, stirring often. (Do not boil.) Remove from heat; cool. Pour through a wire-mesh strainer into a small bowl, discarding mint. Return cream to saucepan.

Stir sugar into cream, and cook over medium heat, stirring constantly, until sugar dissolves.

Beat egg yolks until thick and pale. Gradually stir one-fourth of hot mixture into yolks; add to remaining hot mixture, stirring constantly. Cook over medium heat, stirring constantly, 5 minutes or until mixture thickens and coats a spoon. Remove from heat; cool. Yield: about 2 cups.

Strawberry Shortcake
with Mint Cream

Lemon-Scented Geranium Cake

9 lemon geranium leaves
1 cup unsalted butter, softened
1¾ cups sugar
4 large eggs, separated
1 tablespoon fresh lemon juice
1 cup milk
3 cups unbleached all-purpose flour
1 tablespoon baking powder
1 tablespoon freshly grated lemon zest
Powdered sugar
Garnishes: geranium leaves, lemon rind strips

Coat a 9-inch round cakepan with vegetable cooking spray. Place 6 or 7 geranium leaves, dull side up, in bottom of pan; set aside.

Mince remaining 2 or 3 leaves; set aside.

Beat butter and sugar at medium speed with an electric mixer until fluffy. Add egg yolks, 1 at a time, beating until blended after each addition. Stir in lemon juice. Add milk, and beat at low speed until blended. (Batter will look curdled.)

Combine flour and baking powder. Gradually add flour mixture to butter mixture, beating at low speed until blended. Stir in lemon zest and minced leaves.

Beat egg whites until soft peaks form; gently fold into batter. Pour batter into prepared pan.

Bake at 350° for 1 hour and 20 minutes or until a wooden pick inserted in center comes out clean. Cool in pan on a wire rack 30 minutes. Invert to remove cake; cool completely on wire rack. Dust with powdered sugar. Garnish, if desired. Yield: 1 (9-inch) cake.

—Mary Ann Esposito
Durham, New Hampshire

Lemon-Scented Geranium Cake

Piña Colada Cake

4 large eggs, separated
2 egg whites
1½ cups sugar, divided
½ cup vegetable oil
½ cup water
2 teaspoons vanilla extract, divided
1½ cups all-purpose flour
1 tablespoon baking powder
⅛ teaspoon salt
¼ cup pineapple juice
¼ cup cream of coconut
2 tablespoons light rum
6 tablespoons butter or margarine, softened
1 (16-ounce) package powdered sugar
⅓ cup whipping cream
¼ cup drained crushed pineapple
1 tablespoon dark rum
2 cups flaked coconut, toasted
Garnishes: fresh strawberries, mango slices, red grapes

Beat 6 egg whites at high speed with an electric mixer until foamy. Add ½ cup sugar, 1 tablespoon at a time, beating until stiff peaks form and sugar dissolves (2 to 4 minutes). Set aside.

Whisk together 4 egg yolks, oil, ½ cup water, and 1 teaspoon vanilla; set aside.

Stir together remaining 1 cup sugar, flour, baking powder, and salt in a large bowl. Fold in egg yolk mixture until blended; fold in egg white mixture. Pour batter into 2 lightly greased wax paper-lined 9-inch round cakepans.

Bake at 350° for 25 to 30 minutes or until a wooden pick inserted in center comes out clean. Cool in pans on wire racks 10 minutes; remove from pans, and cool on wire racks.

Stir together pineapple juice, cream of coconut, and light rum; brush over cake layers.

Beat butter at medium speed with an electric mixer until creamy. Gradually beat in powdered sugar and whipping cream until smooth. Stir in remaining 1 teaspoon vanilla. Remove ½ cup frosting; reserve remaining frosting.

Stir pineapple into ½ cup frosting. Spread pineapple frosting between layers.

Stir dark rum into remaining frosting; reserve ½ cup rum frosting. Spread remaining rum frosting on top and sides of cake. Press coconut onto top and sides of cake.

Spoon reserved ½ cup rum frosting into a decorator bag with a star tip; pipe around top edge. Garnish, if desired. Yield: 1 (2-layer) cake.

From the book The Sugar Mill Caribbean Cookbook, *by Jinx and Jefferson Morgan © 1999. Reprinted with permission from The Harvard Common Press.*

Grandma Gallo's Cream Sherry Cake

1   (18.25-ounce) package yellow cake mix
1   (3.4-ounce) package vanilla instant
     pudding mix
4   large eggs
¾   cup cream sherry
½   cup vegetable oil
Powdered sugar
Berries and Wine

Beat cake mix and next 4 ingredients at medium speed with an electric mixer 2 minutes. Pour batter into a greased and floured 10-inch tube pan.

Bake at 350° for 45 to 50 minutes or until a wooden pick inserted in center comes out clean. Cool in pan on a wire rack 10 minutes. Remove from pan; cool on wire rack. Sprinkle with powdered sugar, and serve with Berries and Wine. Yield: 1 (10-inch) cake.

Berries and Wine

2   cups dry red wine (we tested with Zinfandel)
¼   cup sugar
1   teaspoon fresh lemon juice
2   cups fresh strawberries
1   cup fresh raspberries
1   cup fresh blueberries
1   cup fresh blackberries

Stir together first 3 ingredients. Add remaining ingredients; let stand at room temperature 1 hour. Chill 30 minutes before serving. Serve with Grandma Gallo's Cream Sherry Cake. Yield: 12 servings.

—Caroline Coleman Bailey
Tiburon, California

Gingerbread with Molasses Whipped Cream

Gingerbread with Molasses Whipped Cream

Sweetening with molasses rather than sugar gives this fluffy cream topping a distinct flavor.

1½ cups molasses
⅓   cup firmly packed dark brown sugar
6   tablespoons butter, melted
¾   cup boiling water
3⅓ cups all-purpose flour
2¼ teaspoons ground ginger
1½ teaspoons baking soda
¾   teaspoon salt
¾   teaspoon ground cinnamon
Molasses Whipped Cream
Garnishes: chopped fresh pineapple, fresh
     blueberries

Combine first 4 ingredients in a large bowl. Combine flour and next 4 ingredients in a separate bowl; stir into molasses mixture until smooth. Spoon batter into a buttered 9-inch square pan.

Bake at 350° for 40 minutes or until a wooden pick inserted in center comes out clean. Cool completely in pan on a wire rack.

Cut gingerbread into squares. Serve with a dollop of Molasses Whipped Cream. Garnish, if desired. Yield: 8 servings.

Molasses Whipped Cream

2   cups heavy whipping cream
⅓   cup molasses

Beat whipping cream until foamy; gradually add molasses, beating until soft peaks form. Serve immediately. Yield: 4¾ cups.

—Food Historian Jessica B. Harris
New York, New York

Blackberry Jam Cake

Blackberry Jam Cake

This is a delicious and sturdy cake, perfect for transporting to a picnic.

1	cup unsalted butter, softened
1¼	cups sugar
4	large eggs
1	teaspoon vanilla extract
3	cups all-purpose flour
1½	teaspoons ground cinnamon
1	teaspoon baking soda
1	teaspoon ground nutmeg
1	teaspoon ground ginger
1	cup buttermilk
1	cup blackberry jam
2	cups fresh blackberries
	Crème Fraîche

Beat butter and sugar at medium speed with an electric mixer until fluffy. Add eggs, 1 at a time, beating until blended after each addition. Stir in vanilla.

Combine flour and next 4 ingredients; add to butter mixture alternately with buttermilk, beginning and ending with flour mixture. Beat at low speed until blended after each addition. Fold in jam. (Do not overmix.) Pour batter into a greased 10-inch Bundt pan.

Bake at 350° for 45 minutes to 1 hour or until a wooden pick inserted in center comes out clean. Cool in pan on a wire rack 20 minutes; remove from pan, and cool completely on a wire rack. Serve with blackberries and Crème Fraîche. Yield: 1 (10-inch) cake.

Crème Fraîche

1	(8-ounce) container sour cream
½	cup whipping cream
¼	cup powdered sugar

Stir together all ingredients; cover and chill 8 hours. Yield: 1⅓ cups.

—Caterer Sarah Aley
Tenants Harbor, Maine

Dad's Favorite Chocolate Angel Food Cake

Nell Newman created this recipe for her father, Paul. "I use organic ingredients whenever possible, but this cake is great with regular ingredients," says Nell. "It's light as air, low in fat, and very easy to make."

1¼	cups sugar, divided
1	cup all-purpose flour
½	teaspoon salt
12	egg whites
1	tablespoon fresh lemon juice
1	tablespoon vanilla extract
1	tablespoon grated orange rind
1½	(3-ounce) bars Newman's Own Organics Sweet Dark Chocolate with Orange Oil, finely grated*

Sift ¼ cup sugar, flour, and salt together into a bowl; set aside.

Beat egg whites in a large mixing bowl at high speed with an electric mixer until foamy. Add lemon juice, and beat until soft peaks form. Gradually sprinkle remaining 1 cup sugar onto whites, beating at medium speed until stiff peaks form and sugar dissolves.

Sift ¼ cup flour mixture over whites, and gently fold in by hand, with fingers spread. Add vanilla and orange rind. Fold in remaining flour mixture, alternating with grated chocolate.

Pour batter into an ungreased 10-inch tube pan. (Do not grease pan or use a nonstick pan, as the batter will not rise.) Cut through batter with a knife to remove air bubbles.

Bake at 350° for 40 to 45 minutes or until cake springs back when lightly touched.

Invert pan and cool 30 to 45 minutes. Gently loosen cake from sides of pan, using a narrow metal spatula; remove cake from pan.

Serve with strawberries and lightly sweetened whipped cream flavored with a small amount of vanilla, to taste. Yield: 1 (10-inch) cake.

*You can use 3 (1.2-ounce) bars Newman's Own Organics Sweet Dark Chocolate with Orange Oil; the slightly less amount of chocolate is negligible. You also may substitute other brands of orange-dark chocolate bars, if desired.

Key Lime Cheesecake with Strawberry Sauce

2   cups graham cracker crumbs
½   cup butter or margarine, melted
¼   cup sugar
3   (8-ounce) packages cream cheese, softened
1¼ cups sugar
3   large eggs
1   (8-ounce) container sour cream
1½ teaspoons grated lime rind
½   cup Key lime juice
Garnishes: strawberry halves, lime slices, lime zest
Strawberry Sauce

Stir together first 3 ingredients, and firmly press into bottom and 1 inch up sides of a greased 9-inch springform pan. Bake at 350° for 8 minutes; cool.

Beat cream cheese at medium speed with an electric mixer until fluffy; gradually add 1¼ cups sugar, beating until blended. Add eggs, 1 at a time, beating well after each addition. Stir in sour cream, lime rind, and juice. Pour batter into crust.

Bake at 325° for 1 hour and 5 minutes; turn oven off. Partially open oven door; let stand in oven 15 minutes.

Remove from oven, and immediately run a knife around edge of pan, releasing sides.

Cool completely in pan on a wire rack; cover and chill 8 hours. Garnish, if desired, and serve with Strawberry Sauce. Yield: 10 to 12 servings.

Strawberry Sauce

1¼ cups fresh strawberries
¼   cup sugar
1½ teaspoons grated lime rind

Process all ingredients in a food processor until smooth, stopping to scrape down sides. Yield: 1 cup.

Blueberry Cheesecake

1½ cups finely ground almonds
¼   cup sugar
3   tablespoons butter or margarine, softened
1   tablespoon all-purpose flour
3   (8-ounce) packages cream cheese, softened
1¼ cups sugar
3   tablespoons all-purpose flour
½   teaspoon salt
4   large eggs
1   (8-ounce) container sour cream
1   teaspoon vanilla extract
1   tablespoon grated lemon rind
1½ cups fresh or frozen blueberries
1   cup whipping cream
2   teaspoons sugar
2   tablespoons sour cream
Garnishes: blueberries, lemon rind strips

Stir together first 4 ingredients in a small bowl. Press mixture into bottom and 1½ inches up sides of a lightly greased 9-inch springform pan; set aside.

Beat cream cheese at medium speed with an electric mixer until smooth. Combine 1¼ cups sugar, 3 tablespoons flour, and salt. Add to cream cheese, beating until blended.

Add eggs, 1 at a time, beating well after each addition. Add 8-ounce container sour cream, vanilla, and lemon rind, beating just until blended. Gently stir in 1½ cups blueberries. Pour batter into prepared pan.

Bake at 300° for 1 hour and 10 minutes or until center is firm; turn oven off. Partially open oven door; let cheesecake stand in oven 30 minutes.

Remove cheesecake from oven; cool in pan on a wire rack 30 minutes. Cover and chill 8 hours. Release sides of pan.

Beat whipping cream at high speed until foamy; gradually add 2 teaspoons sugar, beating until stiff peaks form. Fold in 2 tablespoons sour cream. Spread over cheesecake. Garnish, if desired. Yield: 12 servings.

Blueberry Cheesecake;
Blueberry-Peach Ice Cream, page 252

Ambrosia Cheesecake

1½ cups almond shortbread cookie crumbs
    (about 12 cookies) (we tested with
    Keebler Sandies Almond Shortbread)
3 tablespoons sugar
3 tablespoons butter or margarine, melted
4 (8-ounce) packages cream cheese,
    softened
3 large eggs
1 cup sugar
1 (14-ounce) package sweetened flaked
    coconut
2 teaspoons vanilla extract
2 cups Fresh Orange Curd
1 cup sweetened flaked coconut, lightly
    toasted (optional)

Stir together first 3 ingredients; press mixture into bottom of a 10-inch springform pan. Bake at 350° for 8 minutes. Cool.

Beat cream cheese, eggs, and 1 cup sugar at medium speed with an electric mixer until fluffy. Stir in 14-ounce package coconut and vanilla. Pour into prepared crust.

Bake at 350° for 1 hour. Cool completely in pan on a wire rack.

Cover and chill 8 hours. Release sides of springform pan, and place cheesecake on serving platter or cake stand.

Spread Fresh Orange Curd evenly over top of cheesecake. Sprinkle 1 cup toasted coconut around outer edge of top, if desired. Yield: 12 servings.

Fresh Orange Curd

You can substitute reconstituted orange juice for fresh; however, squeezing navel oranges only takes a few minutes and can make all the difference in this cake's fresh flavor.

1 cup sugar
¼ cup cornstarch
2 cups fresh orange juice (4 to 6 navel
    oranges)
3 large eggs, lightly beaten
¼ cup butter
1 tablespoon grated orange rind

Combine sugar and cornstarch in a 3-quart saucepan; gradually whisk in fresh orange juice. Whisk in lightly beaten eggs. Bring to a boil (5 to 6 minutes) over medium heat, whisking constantly.

Cook, whisking constantly, 1 to 2 minutes or until a puddinglike thickness. Remove from heat, and whisk in butter and grated orange rind. Cover, placing plastic wrap directly on curd, and chill 8 hours. Yield: about 3 cups.

Bananas Foster Cheesecake

All the flavors of bananas Foster, the quintessential New Orleans dessert, are incorporated into this creamy delight of a cheesecake.

¾ cup all-purpose flour
¾ cup finely chopped pecans
3 tablespoons brown sugar
2 tablespoons sugar
¼ cup unsalted butter, melted
1½ tablespoons vanilla extract, divided
2 (8-ounce) packages cream cheese,
    softened
1½ cups sugar, divided
2 tablespoons cornstarch
3 large eggs
2 cups mashed very ripe banana (about
    4 large)
1 (16-ounce) container sour cream, divided
2 tablespoons fresh lemon juice
1½ teaspoons ground cinnamon, divided
⅛ teaspoon salt
½ teaspoon sugar
2 bananas
1 (12-ounce) jar caramel sauce
¼ cup dark rum

Stir together first 5 ingredients in a bowl. Stir in 2 teaspoons vanilla. Press into bottom of a 10-inch springform pan; set aside.

Beat cream cheese at medium speed with an electric mixer until creamy. Gradually add 1¼ cups sugar and cornstarch, beating well. Add eggs, 1 at a time, beating after each addition. Stir in mashed banana, half the sour cream, lemon juice, 2 teaspoons vanilla, 1 teaspoon cinnamon, and salt. Pour batter into prepared pan.

Bake at 350° for 1 hour or until center is set. Remove from oven, and set aside.

Combine remaining sour cream, ¼ cup sugar, and ½ teaspoon vanilla in a small bowl, stirring well. Spread over warm cheesecake; return to oven, and bake 10 more minutes. Turn oven off; let cheesecake cool in oven 2 hours or until room temperature. Cover and chill 8 hours.

Carefully remove sides of springform pan. Combine ½ teaspoon sugar and remaining ½ teaspoon cinnamon in a small bowl; sprinkle over cheesecake. Peel and slice 2 bananas; arrange slices on top of cheesecake.

Combine caramel sauce and rum in a small saucepan; cook over medium heat until warm. Drizzle some warm sauce over cheesecake, and serve with remaining sauce. Yield: 12 servings.

New York-Style Cheesecake

1¾ cups graham cracker crumbs
⅓ cup butter, melted
¼ cup sugar
5 (8-ounce) packages cream cheese,
    softened
1 cup sugar
3 tablespoons all-purpose flour
1 tablespoon vanilla extract
3 large eggs
1 (8-ounce) container sour cream
Garnishes: fresh strawberries

Stir together first 3 ingredients. Press crumb mixture into bottom and 1½ inches up sides of a lightly greased 9-inch springform pan. Bake at 350° for 10 minutes. Cool on a wire rack.

Beat cream cheese at medium speed with an electric mixer until smooth. Gradually add 1 cup sugar, flour, and vanilla, beating until blended. Add eggs, 1 at a time, beating until blended after each addition. Add sour cream, and beat just until blended. Pour mixture into prepared crust.

Bake at 350° for 1 hour and 5 minutes or until center is almost set. Remove cheesecake from oven; cool completely in pan on a wire rack. Cover and chill 8 hours. Gently run a knife around edge of cheesecake, and release sides. Garnish, if desired. Yield: 1 (9-inch) cheesecake.

Key Lime Pie

Key Lime Pie

1¼ cups graham cracker crumbs
¼ cup firmly packed light brown sugar
⅓ cup butter or margarine, melted
2 (14-ounce) cans sweetened condensed milk
1 cup fresh Key lime juice
2 egg whites
¼ teaspoon cream of tartar
2 tablespoons sugar
Garnish: lime slices

Combine first 3 ingredients. Press into a 9-inch pieplate. Bake at 350° for 10 minutes; cool.

Stir together milk and lime juice until blended. Pour into crust.

Beat egg whites and cream of tartar at high speed with an electric mixer just until foamy. Add sugar, 1 tablespoon at a time, beating until soft peaks form and sugar dissolves (2 to 4 minutes). Spread meringue over filling.

Bake at 325° for 25 minutes. Cool pie completely. Chill 8 hours. Garnish, if desired. Yield: 1 (9-inch) pie.

Chocolate-Peanut Butter Ice Cream Pie

21 cream-filled chocolate sandwich cookies
½ cup unsalted dry-roasted peanuts
¼ cup butter or margarine, melted
3 pints chocolate ice cream, softened
8 (1.5-ounce) packages peanut butter cup candies, coarsely chopped
1 (8-ounce) jar fudge topping
¼ cup strong brewed coffee
2 tablespoons coffee liqueur (optional)

Process cookies and peanuts in a food processor until finely crumbled. Add melted butter, and process until blended.

Press crumb mixture into a 9-inch deep-dish pieplate, and freeze 15 minutes.

Stir together chocolate ice cream and chopped candies; spoon into piecrust. Freeze at least 6 hours. Remove from freezer, and let stand 15 minutes before serving.

Heat fudge sauce in a small saucepan over low heat, stirring constantly. Remove from heat; stir in coffee and, if desired, coffee liqueur. Drizzle over pie. Yield: 1 (9-inch) deep-dish pie.

that famous Floridian pie

Key lime pie is perhaps the perfect ending to a great seafood dinner. Known as the pie with a high pucker factor, it's detected by a pastry or graham cracker crust filled with sweetened condensed milk, egg yolks (sometimes), and freshly squeezed juice from Key limes. The golf ball-size yellow fruits that were once shipped from the Florida Keys (thus the name) now come primarily from Mexico. The familiar green Persian limes come close, but they are less acidic and have a milder flavor. Key limes have 2 to 3 times the acidity of other limes. It's this high acid level that "cooks" the pie's filling and thickens it.

Why sweetened condensed milk? Anyone who loves to dip a sampling finger into the can while cooking may ask "why not?", but there is a reason. In the mid-1800s, before refrigeration, tropical weather in the Keys ruined any hopes of storing fresh milk. Canned milk's long shelf life beat the heat and, paired with abundant Key limes, spawned this classic, meringue-topped dessert.

Our version features a crisp graham cracker crust with a rich filling that is doubly deep compared to most Key lime pies. (And our version is sans egg yolks so the threat of uncooked egg is not even an issue.) And it's all captured under just the right amount of toasty meringue.

Cookie-Pecan Mud Pie

1¼ cups cream-filled chocolate sandwich
    cookie crumbs (14 cookies)
3   tablespoons butter or margarine,
    melted
1¼ cups chopped pecans
1   tablespoon sugar
1   pint coffee ice cream, softened
1   pint chocolate ice cream, softened
10 cream-filled chocolate sandwich cookies,
    coarsely chopped
1   (11.75-ounce) jar fudge topping

Stir together cookie crumbs and butter. Press into a 9-inch pieplate. Bake at 350° for 8 minutes. Cool.

Place pecans on a lightly greased baking sheet; sprinkle with sugar.

Bake at 350° for 8 to 10 minutes. Cool.

Stir together ice creams, 1 cup cookie chunks, and 1 cup pecans; spoon into crust. Freeze 10 minutes. Press remaining cookie chunks and pecans on top. Cover and freeze pie 8 hours. Serve with fudge sauce. Yield: 1 (9-inch) pie.

Black-Bottom Pie

2   tablespoons water
2   tablespoons rum
1   envelope unflavored gelatin
⅔   cup sugar
1   tablespoon cornstarch
2   cups milk
4   egg yolks
1   cup (6 ounces) semisweet chocolate
    morsels
Gingersnap Crust
2   cups whipping cream
3   tablespoons powdered sugar
Garnish: chocolate curls

Stir together 2 tablespoons water and rum in a small bowl. Sprinkle gelatin over mixture. Stir mixture, and set aside.

Combine sugar and cornstarch in a heavy saucepan; gradually whisk in milk and egg yolks. Bring to a boil over medium heat, whisking constantly; boil 1 minute. Stir in gelatin mixture until dissolved.

Stir together 1 cup custard mixture and morsels until smooth. Pour into Gingersnap Crust. Chill 30 minutes or until set. Set aside remaining custard mixture.

Beat whipping cream at high speed with an electric mixer until foamy; gradually add powdered sugar, beating until soft peaks form.

Fold 1 cup whipped cream into remaining custard mixture. Spoon over chocolate mixture. Chill pie and remaining whipped cream 2 hours or until pie is set. Spread remaining whipped cream over pie. Garnish, if desired. Yield: 1 (9-inch) deep-dish pie.

Gingersnap Crust

1½ cups gingersnap crumbs (about
    26 cookies)
⅓   cup butter or margarine,
    melted
2   tablespoons sugar

Stir together all ingredients. Press into bottom and up sides of a 9-inch deep-dish pieplate.

Bake at 350° for 8 to 10 minutes. Cool on a wire rack. Yield: 1 (9-inch) crust.

Cookie-Pecan Mud Pie

Coconut Cream Cheese Pie

Look for cream of coconut near the piña colada and margarita mixes.

1⅔ cups graham cracker crumbs
⅓   cup butter or margarine, melted
¼   cup sugar
1   (8-ounce) package cream cheese, softened
1   cup cream of coconut
1   (3.4-ounce) package cheesecake instant pudding mix (we tested with Jell-O Instant Pudding Cheesecake Flavor)
1   (6-ounce) package frozen sweetened flaked coconut, thawed
1   (8-ounce) container frozen whipped topping, thawed
1   cup whipping cream
Garnish: sweetened flaked coconut

Stir together first 3 ingredients; press mixture evenly in bottom and up sides of a 9-inch pieplate.

Bake at 350° for 8 minutes; remove to a wire rack, and cool completely.

Beat cheese and cream of coconut at medium speed with an electric mixer until smooth. Add pudding mix, beating until blended.

Stir in coconut; fold in whipped topping. Spread cheese mixture evenly into prepared crust; cover and chill 2 hours or until set.

Beat whipping cream with an electric mixer until soft peaks form; spread evenly over top of pie. Garnish, if desired. Yield: 1 (9-inch) pie.

Coconut-Macadamia Nut Pie

½   (15-ounce) package refrigerated piecrusts
1   cup sugar
3   large eggs
1   cup light corn syrup
¼   cup whipping cream
1   tablespoon butter or margarine, melted
1   teaspoon vanilla extract
¾   cup coarsely chopped macadamia nuts
1   cup flaked coconut
Garnishes: whipped cream, chopped macadamia nuts, toasted flaked coconut

Fit piecrust into a 9-inch pieplate according to package directions; fold edges under, and crimp. Freeze 15 minutes.

Bake at 425° for 6 to 8 minutes or until golden. Cool on a wire rack.

Whisk together sugar and next 5 ingredients; stir in nuts and coconut. Pour into prepared piecrust.

Bake at 350° for 55 to 60 minutes; cool completely on wire rack. Garnish, if desired. Yield: 1 (9-inch) pie.

Tiramisù Toffee Trifle Pie

1½ tablespoons instant coffee granules
¾   cup warm water
1   (10.75-ounce) loaf frozen pound cake, thawed
1   (8-ounce) package mascarpone or cream cheese, softened
½   cup powdered sugar
½   cup chocolate syrup
1   (12-ounce) container frozen whipped topping, thawed and divided
2   (1.4-ounce) English toffee candy bars, coarsely chopped

Stir together coffee and ¾ cup warm water until coffee is dissolved. Cool.

Cut cake into 14 slices. Cut each slice in half diagonally. Place triangles in bottom and up sides of a 9-inch deep-dish pieplate. Drizzle coffee mixture over cake.

Beat mascarpone cheese, sugar, and chocolate syrup at medium speed with an electric mixer until smooth. Add 2½ cups whipped topping, and beat until light and fluffy.

Spread cheese mixture evenly over cake. Dollop remaining whipped topping around edges of pie. Sprinkle with candy. Chill 8 hours. Yield: 8 to 10 servings.

Chocolate Pudding

Straining this smooth pudding gives it an even silkier texture.

2   ounces unsweetened chocolate, coarsely chopped
2   (3-ounce) bars dark chocolate, coarsely broken
1   (4-ounce) bar semisweet chocolate, coarsely broken
2   tablespoons cornstarch
⅔   cup sugar
2   tablespoons cocoa
⅛   teaspoon salt
2   cups milk
1   cup whipping cream
3   egg yolks
1   tablespoon butter
2   teaspoons vanilla extract

Place first 3 ingredients in a medium bowl. Microwave at HIGH 1 minute. Stir and microwave 1 more minute or until melted. Stir well.

Combine cornstarch and next 3 ingredients in a medium saucepan. Gradually whisk in milk, cream, and egg yolks. Stir in melted chocolate. Place over medium heat. Cook, stirring constantly, 18 minutes or until mixture begins to thicken. Cook, stirring constantly, 2 more minutes.

Remove from heat, and add butter, stirring until it melts; stir in vanilla. Strain pudding into a bowl. To prevent a skin from forming atop pudding, cover with plastic wrap, gently pressing directly on pudding. Cool 30 minutes. Chill thoroughly. Yield: 4⅔ cups.

Chocolate Mousse au Grand Marnier

1   (4-ounce) package sweet baking chocolate
4   (1-ounce) semisweet chocolate baking squares
¼   cup Grand Marnier or other orange liqueur
2   cups whipping cream
½   cup sifted powdered sugar

Combine 8 ounces chocolate and Grand Marnier in a heavy saucepan; cook, stirring constantly, over low heat until chocolate melts. Remove from heat, and cool to lukewarm.

Beat whipping cream until foamy; gradually add powdered sugar, beating until soft peaks form. Gently fold about ½ cup of whipped cream into chocolate; fold in remaining whipped cream. Spoon into individual serving dishes. Chill until ready to serve. Yield: 6 servings.

Frozen Key Lime Soufflés with Raspberry Sauce

Kay Kahle, caretaker of the Willey house in Naples, Florida, shares her recipe for a dessert that's sure to please. It's now a Coastal Living *staff favorite.*

½   cup unsalted butter
1   teaspoon grated lime rind
1½ cups sugar
1   cup Key lime juice
¼   teaspoon salt
3   egg yolks
3   large eggs
2   cups heavy whipping cream
1   (10-ounce) package frozen raspberries
      in light syrup, thawed
½   cup honey
1   pint fresh raspberries

Fold wax paper to create a 1½-inch-wide collar for each of 6 (4-ounce) ramekins. Wrap paper collars around the outside of ramekins, allowing 1 inch or more to extend above the rim; tape to secure. Set ramekins aside.

Melt butter in top of a double boiler; stir in rind and next 3 ingredients. Whisk together yolks and whole eggs; stir into juice mixture. Cook over medium heat 10 minutes, stirring constantly, until mixture thickens and coats the back of a spoon. Cool completely. Chill. (Mixture will be thick.)

Beat whipping cream with an electric mixer until stiff peaks form. Gently fold lime mixture into whipped cream. Spoon 1 cup mixture into each prepared ramekin. (Mixture will extend up sides of collars.) Freeze 8 hours or until firm.

Puree thawed raspberries with honey in a blender; strain to remove seeds.

Let soufflés stand 10 minutes at room

temperature before serving; remove paper collars. Top each soufflé with fresh raspberries and drizzle with raspberry sauce. Yield: 6 servings.

Chilled Lemon Soufflé

The tricky timing and advanced skills required for a baked soufflé are eliminated in this show-stopping chilled soufflé.

1   tablespoon butter or margarine
2   tablespoons sugar
2   envelopes unflavored gelatin
½   cup cold water
1   teaspoon sugar
1   tablespoon grated lemon rind
¾   cup lemon juice
⅓   cup meringue powder*
1½ cups sugar
1   cup water
2   cups whipping cream
1   (2-ounce) package slivered almonds,
      toasted and chopped
Candied Lemon Peel (optional)
Garnish: lemon slices

Cut a piece of wax paper long enough to fit around a 2-quart soufflé dish, allowing a 1-inch

overlap; fold paper lengthwise into thirds. Lightly butter one side of paper and soufflé dish. Wrap paper around outside of dish, buttered side against dish, allowing it to extend 3 inches above rim; secure with cellophane or masking tape. Sprinkle sides of dish with 2 tablespoons sugar.

Sprinkle gelatin over ½ cup cold water in a saucepan; let stand 1 minute. Add 1 teaspoon sugar; cook over low heat, stirring until gelatin dissolves. Stir in lemon rind and juice.

Beat meringue powder, 1 cup sugar, and 1 cup water in a large bowl at high speed with an electric mixer 5 minutes. Gradually add remaining ½ cup sugar, and beat at high speed 5 minutes or until stiff peaks form. Fold in gelatin mixture.

Beat whipping cream at medium speed until soft peaks form. Fold into gelatin mixture.

Pour into prepared dish, and chill 8 hours. Remove collar, and pat chopped almonds around sides. Top with Candied Lemon Peel, if desired. Garnish, if desired. Yield: 8 to 10 servings.
We used Wilton meringue powder in this soufflé. Look for it in the cake decorating section of crafts stores or at Wal-Mart.

Candied Lemon Peel

1   large lemon
2   tablespoons light corn syrup
1   tablespoon sugar

Peel lemon; cut rind into ¼-inch-wide strips. Reserve lemon for other uses.

Combine lemon rind and corn syrup in a small saucepan; bring to a boil over medium heat; reduce heat, and cook 3 to 4 minutes.

Toss lemon rind with sugar, and spread on wax paper to dry. Yield: about ⅓ cup.

Blackberry Custard

Key Lime and Mango Yogurt Parfaits

2   cups milk

2   tablespoons butter or margarine

½   cup sugar, divided

2   large eggs

1   egg yolk

1   tablespoon cornstarch

2   cups plain low-fat yogurt

2   ripe mangoes, peeled and seeded

2   tablespoons Key lime juice

1   (10.75-ounce) package frozen pound
    cake

⅓   cup strawberry jam

12   fresh strawberries, sliced

1   cup whipping cream

¼   cup sugar

*Garnishes: fresh strawberries, toasted
    coconut, grated lime rind*

Combine milk, butter, and ¼ cup sugar in
a heavy saucepan; bring to a simmer over
medium heat.

Beat remaining ¼ cup sugar, eggs, egg yolk,
and cornstarch at medium-low speed until
blended. Gradually stir about one-fourth of hot
milk mixture into egg mixture; add to remaining
hot mixture, stirring constantly. Cook over medium heat about 4 minutes or until mixture thickens, stirring constantly. (Do not boil.)

Remove from heat, and stir in yogurt. Divide
custard into 2 portions. Process 1 mango in a
blender until smooth, stopping to scrape down
sides. Stir into 1 portion of yogurt custard; cover
and chill. Stir lime juice into remaining yogurt
custard; cover and chill.

To assemble, cut pound cake into 12 slices,
and spread jam on 1 side of each slice. Slice
remaining mango.

Place 2 tablespoons mango custard and 2
tablespoons lime custard into each of 6 (1½-
cup) parfait or balloon wine glasses. Top each
with 1 cake slice, jam side up, cutting cake to
fit in glass, if needed.

Arrange strawberry slices around inside of
glasses. Add 3 tablespoons mango custard and
remaining cake slices. Arrange mango slices
around glasses, and top with 3 tablespoons lime
custard.

Beat whipping cream at high speed until
foamy; gradually add ¼ cup sugar, beating until

Blackberry Custard

¾   cup sugar

⅓   cup all-purpose flour

Dash of salt

4   egg yolks

2   cups milk

½   teaspoon vanilla extract

1   cup whipping cream

2   tablespoons sugar

2   cups fresh blackberries

Garnish: fresh mint sprigs

Combine first 3 ingredients in a heavy saucepan;
whisk in egg yolks and milk. Cook over medium
heat, whisking constantly, 5 to 7 minutes or until
thickened. Remove from heat; stir in vanilla. Pour
into a serving dish; cool. Cover and chill 2 hours.

Beat whipping cream at medium speed
with an electric mixer until foamy; gradually
add 2 tablespoons sugar, beating until soft
peaks form. Spread over custard. Top with
fresh blackberries. Garnish, if desired. Yield:
4 servings.

soft peaks form. Pipe or dollop whipped cream on top of parfaits. Chill parfaits 2 to 4 hours. Garnish, if desired. Yield: 6 servings.

Old-Fashioned Bread Pudding

1   (16-ounce) day-old French bread loaf, cubed
2   (12-ounce) cans evaporated milk
1   cup water
6   large eggs, lightly beaten
1   (8-ounce) can crushed pineapple, drained
1   large Red Delicious apple, grated
1½ cups sugar
1   cup raisins
5   tablespoons vanilla extract
¼   cup butter or margarine, cut into pieces and softened
Bourbon Sauce

Combine first 3 ingredients; stir in eggs, blending well. Stir in pineapple and next 4 ingredients. Stir in butter, blending well. Pour mixture into a greased 13- x 9-inch baking dish.

Bake at 350° for 35 to 45 minutes or until set. Serve with Bourbon Sauce. Yield: 8 servings.

Bourbon Sauce

3   tablespoons butter or margarine
1   tablespoon all-purpose flour
½   cup sugar
1   cup whipping cream
2   tablespoons bourbon
1   tablespoon vanilla extract
1   teaspoon grated nutmeg

Melt butter in a small saucepan; whisk in flour, and cook 5 minutes. Stir in sugar and whipping cream; cook 3 minutes. Stir in bourbon, vanilla, and nutmeg; simmer 5 minutes. Yield: 1½ cups.

Baklava

1   (16-ounce) package frozen phyllo pastry, thawed overnight in refrigerator
1¼ cups butter, melted
1   cup finely chopped pecans
1   cup finely chopped walnuts
1   cup finely chopped almonds
½   cup finely crushed zwieback (about 6 pieces)
½   cup sugar
1   teaspoon ground cinnamon
Honey Syrup

Lightly grease a 13- x 9-inch pan with butter. Cut phyllo into 13- x 9-inch sheets, covering with plastic wrap and a slightly damp towel. Layer 10 sheets of phyllo in pan, brushing each sheet with melted butter.

Combine pecans and next 5 ingredients; stir well. Sprinkle one-fourth of nut mixture over phyllo in pan; lightly drizzle with melted butter. Top nut mixture with 7 sheets of phyllo, brushing each sheet with melted butter. Repeat procedure 3 times with remaining nut mixture, phyllo, and butter, ending with 10 sheets of buttered phyllo. Cut into triangles, using a sharp knife.

Bake at 350° for 45 minutes or until golden. Drizzle 2 cups Honey Syrup over Baklava. Cool completely on a wire rack. Serve with remaining Honey Syrup. Yield: 3 dozen.

Honey Syrup

2½ cups sugar
1¼ cups water
½   cup honey
2   tablespoons fresh lemon juice

Combine all ingredients in a medium saucepan; bring to a boil. Reduce heat, and simmer, uncovered, 1 minute or until sugar dissolves. Yield: 3 cups.

Louis Pappas Market Cafe
Tampa, Florida

Baklava

Berry and Melon Napoleon

Poached Pears

Berry and Melon Napoleon

2 cups whipping cream
3 tablespoons powdered sugar
½ teaspoon vanilla extract
2 large honeydew melons
20 fresh strawberries
½ pint fresh raspberries
½ pint fresh blackberries
Powdered sugar
Garnishes: fresh mint leaves, whipped cream,
    fresh blueberries
Cantaloupe Sauce

Beat whipping cream until foamy; gradually add powdered sugar and vanilla, beating until soft peaks form. Set aside.

Cut 3 (¾-inch-thick) slices from outer edges of each honeydew without cutting into cavities. Peel slices. Cut 1 round from each slice with a 2½-inch round cutter. Cut rounds in half horizontally. Set aside. Reserve remaining honeydew for other uses.

Cut 8 strawberries in half lengthwise; slice remaining strawberries.

Spoon a whipped cream mound in center of each serving dish. Arrange 4 strawberry halves, cut side down, around each whipped cream mound. Top each whipped cream mound with a honeydew round, raspberries, and a dollop of whipped cream. Top with a honeydew round, blackberries, and a dollop of whipped cream. Top with a honeydew round, sliced strawberries, and a dollop of whipped cream. Sprinkle with sugar. Garnish, if desired, and serve with Cantaloupe Sauce. Yield: 4 servings.

Note: *For a less formal presentation, toss bite-size sliced fruit with the sweetened whipped cream and Cantaloupe Sauce.*

Cantaloupe Sauce

2 cups chopped fresh cantaloupe
1 tablespoon sugar
2 tablespoons orange juice
2 tablespoons melon liqueur (optional)

Process all ingredients in a blender until smooth, stopping once to scrape down sides. Chill, if desired. Yield: about 2 cups.

Poached Pears

10 firm Bosc pears
1 (750-milliliter) bottle cream sherry
½ cup honey
1 cinnamon stick
Garnish: 6-inch cinnamon sticks

Peel pears, leaving stems intact. Cut a thin slice from bottom of each pear, allowing pears to stand.

Combine sherry, honey, and cinnamon stick in a Dutch oven. Add pears and water to cover. Bring to a simmer over medium heat. Simmer 45 to 50 minutes, or until pears are tender. Remove pears from Dutch oven with a slotted spoon. Chill.

Bring sherry mixture to a boil, and boil until mixture is reduced to 1 cup (about 20 minutes). Chill. Serve sauce with pears. Garnish, if desired. Yield: 10 servings.

—Steve Winston
The Spanish Table
Seattle, Washington

Baked Pear Caramel with Berry Sauce

Berry Sauce

1 cup fresh or thawed frozen raspberries
1 tablespoon sugar
1 teaspoon lemon juice

Process raspberries in a blender or food processor 10 seconds or until pureed. Pour mixture through a wire-mesh strainer into a bowl, pressing with back of a spoon against sides of strainer to squeeze out juice; discard solids. Add sugar and lemon juice, stirring until sugar dissolves. Yield: ½ cup.

—*Judy Hawkins*
Seattle, Washington

spun sugar

Make spun sugar by cooking 1 cup sugar, 3 tablespoons water, and a pinch of cream of tartar to hard crack stage (300°) on a candy thermometer, without stirring. Carefully dip a fork or whisk into sugar syrup and spin it into fine threads on wax paper. Allow spun sugar to cool; then transfer to dessert.

French Toast with Poached Pears, Walnut Ice Cream, and Caramel Sauce

½ cup sugar
2 cups dry white wine
3 firm Bartlett pears
4 large eggs
2 cups milk
2 tablespoons sugar
¼ teaspoon salt
¼ teaspoon ground cinnamon
¼ teaspoon ground nutmeg
12 (¾-inch-thick) French baguette
    slices
2 tablespoons butter or margarine
Walnut Ice Cream
Caramel Sauce
Garnishes: fresh mint sprigs, pesticide-free
    pansies

Bring ½ cup sugar and wine to a boil in a Dutch oven over medium-high heat, stirring until sugar dissolves. Reduce heat, and simmer 5 minutes.

Baked Pear Caramel with Berry Sauce

1½ cups sugar, divided
4 Bosc pears
½ teaspoon vanilla extract
2 teaspoons grated lemon rind
¼ teaspoon salt
½ cup unsalted butter, softened
1 tablespoon all-purpose flour
2 large eggs, lightly beaten
Berry Sauce
Garnishes: fresh raspberries, spun sugar

Sprinkle 1 cup sugar in a large heavy skillet. Cook over medium heat, stirring constantly with a wooden spoon, until sugar melts and turns light brown. Quickly pour hot caramel evenly into 6 (4-ounce) ramekins or custard cups, tilting to coat bottom of each ramekin; set aside. (As it cools, caramel syrup will harden and crack.)

Peel, core, and chop pears. Combine pear, remaining ½ cup sugar, vanilla, lemon rind, and salt in a medium saucepan. Cook over medium heat 40 minutes or until pear is very tender. Remove from heat, and let cool 5 minutes. Stir in butter, flour, and eggs.

Spoon pear mixture evenly into ramekins, pressing down lightly. Place ramekins in a 13- x 9-inch pan. Add hot water to depth of 1 inch around ramekins. Bake at 350° for 30 to 35 minutes or until a knife inserted in center comes out clean.

Drizzle Berry Sauce onto individual dessert plates; loosen edges of pear caramels with a knife, and invert onto plates. Garnish, if desired. Yield: 6 servings.

Note: *To make ahead, cool ramekins to room temperature; cover and chill. Remove from refrigerator; let stand 30 minutes. Bake at 350° for 10 minutes. Invert onto dessert plates.*

Peel and core pears; cut in half. Add to wine mixture. Bring to a boil; cover, reduce heat, and simmer 10 to 15 minutes or until pears are crisp-tender. Transfer pears and poaching liquid to a bowl; cool completely. Cut each pear half into 6 wedges; return to liquid. Cover and chill.

Whisk together eggs, milk, and next 4 ingredients. Dip each bread slice into egg mixture.

Melt 1 tablespoon butter in a large nonstick skillet over medium heat; add half of the bread slices, and cook 2 to 3 minutes on each side or until lightly browned. Remove from skillet, and keep warm. Repeat procedure with remaining 1 tablespoon butter and bread slices.

Drain pears. Serve French toast slices with pears and Walnut Ice Cream. Drizzle with Caramel Sauce. Garnish, if desired. Yield: 6 servings.

Walnut Ice Cream

1   quart milk
1   quart whipping cream
2   cups sugar, divided
2   vanilla beans, cut in half lengthwise
2   dozen egg yolks
2   cups coarsely chopped walnuts, toasted

Bring milk, cream, 1 cup sugar, and vanilla beans to a boil in a large, heavy saucepan over medium heat, whisking constantly. Remove from heat.

Whisk together egg yolks and remaining 1 cup sugar in a large bowl. Gradually add one-fourth hot mixture into yolk mixture; whisk into remaining hot mixture.

Cook over low heat, whisking constantly, 10 to 15 minutes or until mixture thickens.

Pour mixture through a fine wire-mesh strainer into a large bowl, discarding vanilla beans. Immediately set bowl in ice, and let stand, stirring constantly, until cool. Stir in walnuts.

Pour mixture into freezer container of a 1-gallon electric freezer. Freeze according to manufacturer's instructions.

Pack freezer with additional ice and rock salt, and let stand 1 hour before serving. Yield: 1 gallon.

French Toast with Poached Pears, Walnut Ice Cream, and Caramel Sauce

Caramel Sauce

3   cups whipping cream
2   cups sugar
1   tablespoon water
¼   cup butter or margarine

Cook whipping cream in a heavy saucepan over medium heat, stirring occasionally, until almost boiling. Remove from heat; set aside.

Sprinkle sugar in a heavy saucepan; drizzle with water. Place over medium heat, and cook, shaking pan constantly, until sugar melts and turns light golden brown. Gradually add hot whipping cream to caramelized sugar, stirring constantly. Cook over low heat, stirring constantly, until blended. Stir in butter. Yield: 4 cups.

—Chef Christopher Freeman
Toppers at the Wauwinet
Nantucket, Massachusetts

Pineapple Tarte Tatin

Pineapple Tarte Tatin

2   medium-size fresh pineapples
1⅓ cups unsalted butter, softened
1   cup firmly packed light brown sugar
1   cup sugar
3   tablespoons dark rum
¼   teaspoon ground cinnamon
⅛   teaspoon salt
3   vanilla beans, split lengthwise
     (optional)
1   (17.3-ounce) package frozen puff pastry
     sheets, thawed
Vanilla ice cream (optional)

Peel and core pineapples. Cut pineapples into
6 (1½-inch-thick) rings. Set aside.

Beat butter and sugars at medium speed
with an electric mixer until creamy. Add rum,
cinnamon, and salt; beat well.

Divide butter mixture into 6 (6-inch) cast-
iron skillets. Place over medium-high heat until
butter melts. Add 1 slice of pineapple and, if
desired, half of a vanilla bean to each skillet.
Cook until pineapple caramelizes on bottom;
flip and repeat procedure. Keep warm.

Roll out puff pastry to ¼-inch thickness.
Cut 3 (7½-inch) circles out of each sheet.
Place 1 circle over each pineapple slice, and
tuck in edges. Repeat procedure with remaining
pastry sheet.

Bake at 400° for 20 minutes or until golden.

Remove from oven, and let stand 5 minutes.
Place plate upside down over top of pan, and
carefully invert tart onto plate. Repeat process
with remaining skillets. Top each with a scoop
of ice cream, if desired. Serve immediately.
Yield: 6 servings.

Note: If substituting 1 (12-inch) skillet, use
only 4 pineapple slices, ¾ cup butter, and half
amounts of the remaining ingredients. Use 1
pastry sheet to cover all slices. After baking,
invert tart onto platter. Cut into wedges.

—Chef Bob Kinkead
Kinkead's
Washington, D.C.

Wine-Pepper Strawberries

Wine-Pepper Strawberries

*We cut store-bought pound cake into little
sticks to serve as a garnish.*

¼   cup butter or margarine
3   tablespoons sugar
½   cup dry red wine (we tested with Red
     Zinfandel)
½   teaspoon coarsely ground pepper
1   quart fresh strawberries, halved
Vanilla ice cream and pound cake

Melt butter and sugar in a large skillet over
medium heat 5 minutes or until mixture is
lightly browned. Stir in wine and pepper
(mixture will clump). Cook 6 minutes or until
syrupy. Stir in strawberries; cook 1 minute or
just until thoroughly heated.

Serve warm over ice cream along with
pound cake. Yield: 4 servings.

Blueberry-Apricot Tart

1½ cups all-purpose flour
¼ cup sugar
¼ teaspoon salt
½ cup butter or margarine
1 large egg
6 fresh apricots, halved and seeded*
1½ cups fresh blueberries
1 cup buttermilk
3 egg yolks
½ cup sugar
2 tablespoons all-purpose flour
1 tablespoon grated lemon rind
1 tablespoon fresh lemon juice
1 teaspoon vanilla extract
½ teaspoon salt

Pulse first 3 ingredients in a food processor until blended. Add butter; pulse until mixture is crumbly. Add whole egg; process until mixture forms a ball. Cover and chill 30 minutes.

Roll pastry to ⅛-inch thickness on a lightly floured surface. Fit into a 10-inch tart pan with removable bottom; trim edges. Arrange apricot halves, cut side down, in tart pan. Sprinkle berries around apricots. Process buttermilk and remaining ingredients in a food processor until smooth. Pour buttermilk mixture over fruit.

Bake at 375° for 1 hour or until set. Cool in pan on a wire rack. Yield: 1 (9-inch) tart.
*Dried apricots may be substituted.
—Caterer Sarah Aley
Tenants Harbor, Maine

Island Rhubarb Crisp

3½ cups sliced fresh rhubarb
2 tablespoons sugar
3 cups berries (any combination of
   blackberries, blueberries, and
   gooseberries)
1 apple, cored and sliced
1½ cups uncooked regular oats
¾ cup firmly packed light brown sugar
¼ cup all-purpose flour
1 teaspoon ground cinnamon
⅓ cup butter, cut into pieces
Cream (optional)

Spoon rhubarb evenly into a lightly greased 11- x 7-inch baking dish; sprinkle with 2 tablespoons sugar. Top with berries and apple. Set aside.

Combine oats and next 3 ingredients; cut in butter with a pastry blender until crumbly. Sprinkle over fruit mixture.

Bake at 375° for 25 minutes or until topping is browned and fruit is bubbling. Serve warm with cream, if desired. Yield: 8 servings.

Tropical Pineapple Crisp

This flaky pastry can be made without the coconut rum if you don't have it on hand.

1 fresh pineapple, peeled, cored, and
   cubed (about 4 cups)*
2 tablespoons coconut rum or 1 teaspoon
   coconut extract
⅓ cup all-purpose flour
⅓ cup firmly packed dark brown sugar
⅓ cup cold butter or margarine, cut into
   pieces
1 cup crumbled white chocolate and
   macadamia nut cookies (we tested with
   Pepperidge Farm Tahoe White Chocolate
   Macadamia Big Cookies)
½ cup flaked coconut
Simple Coconut Ice Cream (optional)

Combine pineapple and rum; spoon into a 9-inch baking dish or 6 (5-inch) individual ramekins or custard cups.

Combine flour and sugar; cut in butter with a pastry blender or fork until mixture is crumbly. Stir in cookie crumbs and coconut; sprinkle over pineapple.

Bake at 400° for 30 minutes or until golden. Serve with Simple Coconut Ice Cream, if desired. Yield: 6 servings.
*2 (20-ounce) cans pineapple chunks in juice, drained, may be substituted.
Simple Coconut Ice Cream: Stir together ½ gallon softened vanilla ice cream, 1 (16-ounce) can cream of coconut, and ½ to 1 cup flaked coconut in a large bowl. Cover and freeze 8 hours or until firm.

Blueberry Crisp

9 cups fresh blueberries
⅓ cup sugar
⅓ cup firmly packed light brown sugar
⅓ cup all-purpose flour
½ teaspoon ground cinnamon
¼ teaspoon ground nutmeg
Streusel Topping

Stir together first 6 ingredients in a large mixing bowl; toss until berries are coated.

Spoon berry mixture into a lightly greased 13- x 9-inch baking dish. Spoon Streusel Topping over berry mixture.

Bake at 375° for 40 minutes or until golden. Yield: 12 servings.

Streusel Topping

1½ cups all-purpose flour
1½ cups uncooked regular oats
1 cup firmly packed light brown sugar
½ cup butter, melted

Combine flour, oats, and brown sugar; stir in butter until mixture is crumbly. Yield: 4 cups.

Blueberry Crostata

4 cups fresh blueberries
1 cup sugar
⅛ teaspoon ground cinnamon
1¾ cups all-purpose flour
½ cup stone-ground yellow cornmeal
½ cup sugar
1 teaspoon baking powder
1 teaspoon grated lemon rind
½ teaspoon kosher salt
¾ cup unsalted butter, cut into pieces
1 large egg
1 egg yolk
2 teaspoons ice water
Sweetened whipped cream (optional)

Combine first 3 ingredients in a large heavy saucepan over medium-high heat. Cover and cook, without stirring, 5 minutes or until blueberries begin to release some liquid. Uncover, and simmer until sugar dissolves, stirring constantly. Reduce heat and simmer 25 minutes or until mixture thickens, stirring occasionally.

Remove from heat; cool completely. Cover and chill. (Jam will continue to thicken as it cools.)

Stir together flour and next 5 ingredients; cut in butter with a pastry blender until mixture is crumbly. Combine egg and egg yolk; beat lightly with a wire whisk. Add egg mixture to crumb mixture, stirring lightly with a fork. Sprinkle water, 1 teaspoon at a time, evenly over surface, stirring with a fork until dough is moist enough to hold together. Pat dough into a round-shaped disk; cover and chill 1 hour.

Divide dough into 2 portions (about two-thirds and one-third of the total). Place larger piece on a lightly floured surface. (Cover remaining portion, and store in refrigerator.)

Roll pastry into an 11-inch circle (about ⅛ inch thick). Transfer dough to a 9-inch tart pan with a removable bottom. Carefully fit dough into pan (do not stretch dough). Remove excess dough by rolling back and forth over top of pan with a rolling pin. Spoon blueberry jam into pastry.

Roll remaining one-third of pastry into a 9-inch circle (about ⅛ inch thick). Cut circle into 8 (¾-inch-wide) strips, using a knife or pastry wheel. Lightly brush rim of dough with water. Place 4 strips diagonally across top of tart. Place remaining 4 strips diagonally in opposite direction across top of tart, removing excess dough. Press edges of strips against pastry shell edges. Place tart on baking sheet lined with aluminum foil.

Bake at 350° for 40 to 43 minutes or until golden brown. Cool on a wire rack 15 minutes. Remove rim of pan; cool completely on wire rack. Cut tart into wedges, and serve with whipped cream, if desired. Yield: 8 servings.
Recipe from Tom's Big Dinners *by Tom Douglas. © 2003 by Tom Douglas. Reprinted by permission of HarperCollins Publishers Inc.*

Blackberry Cobbler

1⅓ *cups sugar*
½   *cup all-purpose flour*
½   *cup butter or margarine, melted*
2   *teaspoons vanilla extract*
2   *(14-ounce) packages frozen blackberries, unthawed*
½   *(15-ounce) package refrigerated piecrusts*
1   *tablespoon sugar*
Vanilla ice cream (optional)
Sugared Piecrust Sticks (optional)

Stir together first 4 ingredients in a large bowl. Gently stir in blackberries until sugar mixture is crumbly. Spoon fruit mixture into a lightly greased 11- x 7-inch baking dish.

Cut 1 piecrust into ½-inch-wide strips. Arrange strips diagonally over blackberry mixture. Sprinkle top with 1 tablespoon sugar.

Bake at 425° for 45 minutes or until crust is golden brown and center is bubbly. Serve with ice cream and Sugared Piecrust Sticks, if desired. Yield: 6 to 8 servings.

Sugared Piecrust Sticks: *Cut 1 refrigerated piecrust into ½-inch-thick strips. Sprinkle strips with 1 tablespoon sugar; place on a lightly greased baking sheet. Bake at 425° for 6 to 8 minutes or until golden brown.*

Blackberry Cobbler

from the grill

grilling

Grilled Grouper with Plantains and Salsa Verde

Olive oil-flavored cooking spray
1   underripe plantain
¼   teaspoon salt, divided
2   (6-ounce) grouper fillets (about ½ inch thick)
1   tablespoon fresh lime juice
1   tablespoon minced fresh cilantro
½   cup bottled green salsa
2   tablespoons sour cream
Garnish: chopped fresh cilantro

Heat a large grill pan coated with cooking spray over medium-high heat.

Cut plantain in half lengthwise; cut each half crosswise into 2 pieces. Spray plantain pieces with cooking spray; grill 4 minutes on each side or until golden and slightly soft. Sprinkle with ⅛ teaspoon salt.

Drizzle fish with lime juice; sprinkle with ⅛ teaspoon salt and minced cilantro. Grill 4 minutes on each side or until fish flakes with a fork. Top fish with salsa and sour cream, and serve with plantain pieces. Garnish, if desired. Yield: 2 servings.

Mahimahi Kabobs with Tropical Salsa

2   cups diced mango
1   cup diced pineapple
1   red bell pepper, chopped
½   to 1 jalapeño, seeded and minced
½   cup chopped red onion
2   tablespoons chopped fresh cilantro
3   tablespoons fresh lime juice
¼   cup soy sauce
2   tablespoons honey
1   teaspoon grated fresh ginger
¼   teaspoon freshly ground pepper
2   pounds mahimahi steaks, cut into 1½-inch cubes

Combine first 7 ingredients; cover and chill. Stir together soy sauce and next 3 ingredients

in a shallow dish. Add mahimahi; cover and chill 30 minutes.

Thread fish onto 8 (12-inch) skewers. Grill kabobs, covered with grill lid, over medium-high heat (350° to 400°) 5 minutes on each side or until done. Serve with salsa. Yield: 4 servings.

Monkfish Provençal Kabobs

Monkfish has a lobsterlike flavor and is easy to cut into chunks.

¼   cup minced dried tomatoes in oil
3   tablespoons chopped fresh basil
1   tablespoon chopped fresh thyme
1   tablespoon chopped fresh or 1 teaspoon dried marjoram
2   garlic cloves, minced
1   teaspoon salt
½   teaspoon freshly ground pepper
2   tablespoons white wine vinegar
⅓   cup extra-virgin olive oil
1½   pounds monkfish, cut into pieces
1   small eggplant, cubed
1   (8-ounce) package fresh mushrooms

Stir together first 8 ingredients in a large bowl. Gradually whisk in olive oil in a slow, steady stream until blended.

Alternately thread monkfish, eggplant, and mushrooms onto 8 (8-inch) skewers; brush with sauce. Cover and chill 30 minutes.

Grill kabobs, covered with grill lid, over medium-high heat (350° to 400°) 5 to 6 minutes on each side or until done. Yield: 4 servings.

BBQ Grilled Salmon

Mesquite or hickory wood chips
4   (6-ounce) salmon fillets
2   tablespoons Sweet BBQ Rub

Soak wood chips in water to cover at least 30 minutes; drain well. Wrap chips in heavy-duty aluminum foil; pierce several holes in foil.

Coat salmon with Sweet BBQ Rub; cover and chill 30 minutes.

Place foil-wrapped chips on left side of grill grate over medium-high heat (350° to 400°); cover with grill lid, and heat 10 to 15 minutes or until chips begin to smoke. Coat right side of grill grate with vegetable cooking spray. Place salmon on grate.

Grill fish, covered with grill lid, 5 to 7 minutes on each side or until fish flakes with a fork. Yield: 4 servings.

Sweet BBQ Rub

⅓   cup paprika
⅓   cup firmly packed dark brown sugar
3   tablespoons kosher salt*
2   tablespoons sugar
1   tablespoon ground coriander
2   teaspoons garlic powder
1   teaspoon celery seeds
¾   teaspoon ground red pepper
½   teaspoon coarsely ground black pepper

Combine all ingredients. Store in an airtight container. Yield: 1 cup.
*If substituting regular salt, use 1½ tablespoons.

Here are over 50 of our favorite recipes for the grill, smoker, and wood plank.

Citrus-Marinated Smoked Shrimp,
page 306

Grilled Salmon Quesadillas with Cucumber Salsa

1   (8-ounce) salmon fillet (about ¾ inch thick)
8   (6-inch) flour tortillas
1   cup (4 ounces) shredded Monterey Jack cheese
½   cup (2 ounces) goat cheese, crumbled
2   fresh jalapeño peppers, seeded and thinly sliced
Cucumber Salsa
Garnish: fresh cilantro sprigs

Grill salmon, covered with grill lid, over medium-high heat (350° to 400°) 5 minutes on each side or until fish flakes with fork. Cool and flake.

Spoon salmon evenly over 4 tortillas; top evenly with cheeses and pepper slices, and cover with remaining tortillas.

Cook tortillas in a large nonstick skillet over high heat 1 minute on each side or until tortillas are lightly browned and cheese melts. Cut each quesadilla into 4 triangles, and top with Cucumber Salsa. Garnish, if desired. Yield: 4 servings.

Cucumber Salsa

3   small cucumbers, chopped
1   garlic clove, minced
1   jalapeño pepper, seeded and diced
½   small red onion, chopped
½   small yellow bell pepper, seeded and chopped
2   tablespoons minced fresh cilantro
2   teaspoons red wine vinegar
1   teaspoon olive oil
½   teaspoon sugar
¼   teaspoon salt
⅛   teaspoon freshly ground pepper

Combine all ingredients; cover and chill. Yield: 1¼ cups.

grilling 101

With a few helpful hints and a little practice, you'll be a grillmaster in no time.

• **Wash hands thoroughly with hot soapy water** before and after handling raw seafood, meat, and poultry.

• **Start with a clean grill.** Dip a paper towel in oil and rub it over grill grates before preheating or lighting charcoal. Use a light touch because dripping oil causes flare-ups.

• **Start cooking with a hot surface.** Preheat the grill before adding food to ensure even cooking and reduce sticking.

• **For charcoal grills, use chimney-type starters** to help coals heat quickly with a match and a few pieces of newspaper. Or use an electric charcoal lighter with a heating element.

• **Fire needs oxygen to burn,** so be sure vents are open enough to keep it burning. The wider the vent, the hotter the fire. Cleaning out old ashes will also allow better air flow, which equals more oxygen.

• **Cook whole fish, fish steaks, or fillets in a grill basket** to ease turning. Coat the hinged wire basket with vegetable cooking spray before placing the seafood inside. If a grill basket isn't available, place seafood pieces on aluminum foil or directly on the grill grate perpendicular to the grill bars to minimize sticking and keep pieces from falling through the grate. Don't flip a thin, tender fillet such as flounder—it may end up in pieces.

• **Basting brushes made of natural bristles** (rather than nylon) are handy for dabbing on marinades and sauces.

• **Long-handled tongs and spatulas** are great for turning hot foods on the grill. Tongs won't pierce the flesh and will keep juices inside.

• **Keep a spray bottle filled with water nearby** to control flare-ups or stray sparks. Be careful not to douse the fire.

• **Test for doneness.** Instant-read and digital thermometers with forklike prongs are available at kitchen and home supply stores. Best used on cuts at least 1 inch thick, they should be inserted into the thickest portion of the food. Cook chicken breasts to 170°, thighs to 180°, beef to 145° (medium rare) to 160° (medium), and pork to 160° (medium). Fish should flake at its thickest part. Chicken should have no pink areas, and juices should run clear. Overcooking seafood makes it dry and tasteless, so check fish often for doneness.

• **Fish is done when it turns from translucent to opaque.** It's OK to use a small sharp knife to take a peek. Many people prefer salmon and tuna less cooked.

• **Clean the grill grate with a wire brush after every use.** A hot grate is easier to scrape than a cold one.

grilling guide for seafood

Fillets, Steaks, and Boneless Cubes

Place firm fish directly on greased grill grate and more delicate fillets on heavy-duty aluminum foil. Cook for time given in chart or until fish is opaque but still moist in thickest part; turn once halfway through cooking time (unless fish is on foil).

	size	cooking time
Fillets	½ inch	6 to 8 minutes
	¾ inch	8 to 10 minutes
Fillets and Steaks	1 inch	10 minutes
Boneless Cubes (Kabobs)	1 inch	8 to 10 minutes

Whole Fillets and Whole Fish

Place whole fillets and whole fish, skin side down, on greased grill grate. Support more delicate fish on heavy-duty aluminum foil. Cook for time given in chart or until fish is opaque but still moist in thickest part.

	size	cooking time
Whole Fish	1 inch	10 minutes
	1½ inches	10 to 15 minutes
	2 to 2½ inches	20 to 30 minutes
	3 inches	30 to 40 minutes

Shellfish

Place shellfish on grill grate. Cook crab, lobster, shrimp, and scallops for time given in chart or until opaque in thickest part; turn once halfway through cooking time. Scrub and rinse live clams, mussels, and oysters; cook until shells open. Discard any that do not open.

	size	cooking time
Crab, whole	About 2½ pounds	10 to 12 minutes
Lobster, whole	About 2 pounds	18 to 20 minutes
Lobster Tails	8 to 10 ounces	8 to 10 minutes
Shrimp	Medium (21 to 25 per pound)	4 to 5 minutes
	Large (10 to 15 per pound)	5 to 6 minutes
	Extra large (under 10 per pound)	6 to 8 minutes
Scallops, shell off	1 to 2 inches in diameter	4 to 6 minutes
Clams, hard-shell	Medium	5 to 8 minutes
Mussels, in shell	Under 12 per pound	4 to 5 minutes
Oysters, in shell	Small	8 minutes

Chart courtesy of Weber Grills.

Yankee Creek Ranch Salmon

Pear, apple, or mesquite wood chips
6 (8-ounce) king salmon fillets
2 teaspoons salt
2 teaspoons pepper
Beurre Rouge

Soak wood chips in water to cover at least 30 minutes; drain well. Wrap chips in heavy-duty aluminum foil; pierce several holes in foil.

Sprinkle salmon with salt and pepper; cover and set aside.

Prepare grill, placing foil-wrapped chips on hot coals. Place salmon, skin side down, on grill grate coated with vegetable cooking spray.

Grill salmon, covered with grill lid, over medium-high heat (350° to 400°) 5 to 7 minutes on each side or until fish flakes with a fork. Serve with Beurre Rouge. Yield: 6 servings.

Beurre Rouge

2 cups Pinot Noir or other dry red wine
2 shallots, quartered
1 (½-ounce) package dried assorted mushrooms
½ medium beet, finely chopped
½ cup unsalted butter, cut into pieces
¼ teaspoon salt

Combine first 4 ingredients in a saucepan; bring to a boil over medium-high heat. Reduce heat, and simmer until reduced to 1 cup. Strain mixture through sieve into a bowl, discarding solids.

Return wine mixture to saucepan; cook until mixture is reduced to ½ cup. Reduce heat to low; add unsalted butter, 1 piece at a time, stirring with a whisk. (Do not overheat or sauce will separate.) Add salt. Yield: about 1 cup.

—Chef Jens Haagen Hansen
Jens' Restaurant
Anchorage, Alaska

Spice-Crusted Salmon Fillets with Cucumber Raita

1   tablespoon cumin seeds
1½ teaspoons coriander seeds
1   teaspoon black peppercorns
½   teaspoon fennel seeds
⅛   teaspoon ground red pepper
¼   teaspoon kosher salt
2   tablespoons olive oil
6   (8-ounce) salmon fillets (about 1 inch thick), skin on
Cucumber Raita

Cook first 5 ingredients in a small skillet over medium-high heat, shaking pan occasionally, until spices begin to smoke. Cool. Transfer mixture to a coffee grinder or a mortar; grind.

Combine ground spices, salt, and olive oil in a small bowl; spread over salmon fillets. Cover and chill 1½ to 2 hours.

Cut 6 (10-inch) lengths of heavy-duty aluminum foil. Fold each 2 or 3 times to fit the size of the fillet. Place each fillet, skin side down, on foil sheet.

Prepare a hot fire by piling charcoal on one side of grill, leaving other side empty. (For gas grills, light only one side.) Place grate on grill. Arrange food over unlit side.

Grill fillets, covered with grill lid, 15 minutes or until fish flakes with a fork. Slide spatula between skin and flesh of fillet; transfer fillet to plate, leaving skin behind. Top with Cucumber Raita. Serve immediately. Yield: 6 servings.

Cucumber Raita

¾   cup fat-free yogurt
½   cup grated English cucumber, drained
2   teaspoons chopped fresh mint
¼   teaspoon ground cumin
¼   teaspoon kosher salt
¼   teaspoon freshly ground pepper
Dash hot sauce

Combine all ingredients, stirring until blended. Chill up to 6 hours. Yield: 1 cup.

Grilled Sardines with Salsa Verde

½   slice day-old bread
2   tablespoons red wine vinegar
2   bunches fresh Italian parsley, divided
¼   cup capers, rinsed and drained
6   canned anchovy fillets, drained
6   garlic cloves, minced and divided
1½ cups extra-virgin olive oil
4   hard-cooked eggs, finely chopped
½   teaspoon freshly ground black pepper, divided
12 fresh sardines, dressed
1   tablespoon olive oil
¼   teaspoon salt
Garnish: fresh lemon wedges
Crusty Italian bread

Place day-old bread in a food processor. Add vinegar, and let stand 5 minutes. Add 1½ bunches parsley, capers, anchovies, and half of garlic. Pulse until coarsely chopped. With processor running, slowly add 1½ cups oil through food chute. Process until combined. Transfer mixture to a bowl, and fold in chopped egg. Add ¼ teaspoon pepper, and set aside. Chop reserved parsley.

Place sardines in a single layer on a baking sheet. Brush with 1 tablespoon oil, and sprinkle with chopped parsley, remaining garlic and ¼ teaspoon pepper, and salt.

Place sardines on grill grate; grill sardines, uncovered, over medium-high heat (350° to 400°) 3 to 4 minutes on each side or until done.

Transfer sardines to a platter; drizzle with small amount of sauce. Garnish, if desired. Serve with bread and remaining sauce. Yield: 6 servings.

Reprinted with permission from San Francisco Seafood *by Michelle Anna Jordan. © 1993 by Michelle Anna Jordan, Ten Speed Press, Berkeley, CA. Available from your local bookseller, by calling Ten Speed Press at 800-841-2665, or by visiting us online at www.tenspeed.com*

Grilled Apple-Smoked Striped Bass

The key to this simple dish is high-quality fresh fish. You can substitute red snapper, which cooks in about 8 minutes. A fish basket works great, but a perforated sheet of aluminum foil will also let you easily remove fish from the grill.

¼   cup apple wood chips
2   dried habanero chiles
1   tablespoon peanut or vegetable oil
1   teaspoon salt
½   teaspoon freshly ground pepper
1   (3-pound) striped bass fillet (about 1 inch thick)
1   lemon, thinly sliced

Soak wood chips in water to cover 1 hour. Drain.

Place chiles in a spice or coffee grinder; process until finely ground. Place ⅛ teaspoon ground chile in a small bowl (reserve remaining ground chile for another use). Add oil, salt, and pepper, stirring to combine. Rub spice mixture over fish; refrigerate 30 minutes.

Prepare grill. Place wood chips on hot coals. Coat a large piece of heavy-duty aluminum foil with vegetable cooking spray; pierce several holes in foil. Place foil on grill grate coated with cooking spray. Place fish on foil; arrange lemon slices over fish. Grill fish, covered with grill lid, 20 minutes or until fish flakes with a fork. Serve immediately. Yield: 8 servings.

—*Jessica B. Harris*
New York, New York

Whole Grilled Red Snapper Provençal

2   garlic bulbs, unpeeled
1⅔ cups extra-virgin olive oil, divided
2   medium tomatoes
½   cup slivered fresh basil leaves
¾   teaspoon fine-grained sea salt, divided
¾   teaspoon freshly ground pepper, divided
2   (2½- to 3-pound) whole red snapper, dressed, skin on
6   sprigs fresh rosemary

Cut off pointed end of garlic; place bulbs on a piece of aluminum foil, and drizzle with 1 tablespoon olive oil. Fold to seal.

Bake at 425° for 30 minutes; cool. Squeeze pulp from garlic cloves into a small saucepan.

Cook tomatoes in boiling water for 30 seconds; drain. Peel, seed, and dice tomatoes; add to garlic. Stir in 1½ cups olive oil, basil, ¼ teaspoon sea salt, and ¼ teaspoon pepper. Set aside.

Sprinkle snapper cavities with remaining ½ teaspoon salt and ½ teaspoon pepper; insert rosemary sprigs. Brush skins lightly with remaining olive oil. Place fish in 2 lightly greased grill baskets.

Grill snapper, covered with grill lid, over high heat (400° to 500°) 10 to 12 minutes on each side or until fish flakes with a fork.

Cook tomato sauce over low heat until warm. Spoon 1 cup sauce over fish. Serve immediately with remaining sauce. Yield: 4 to 6 servings.

—Cookbook Author Sarah Leah Chase
Barnstable, Massachusetts

Grilled Snapper with Orange-Almond Sauce

6   (8-ounce) snapper or grouper fillets
2   tablespoons olive oil
1   teaspoon coarse-grained sea salt
1   teaspoon freshly ground pepper
4   fresh thyme sprigs
½   cup butter
½   cup sliced almonds
½   to 1 tablespoon grated orange rind

Rub fish fillets with oil. Sprinkle evenly with 1 teaspoon salt and 1 teaspoon pepper.

Arrange thyme sprigs on hot charcoal or hot lava rocks on grill. Coat grill grate with vegetable cooking spray; place on grill over high heat (400° to 500°). Place fish on grate, and grill, without grill lid, 5 to 6 minutes on each side or until fish flakes with a fork.

Melt butter in a saucepan over medium-high heat; add almonds, and sauté 5 minutes or until butter is brown. Remove from heat. Stir in orange rind. Pour sauce over fish. Yield: 6 servings.

Grilled Sturgeon with Roasted Poblano Salad

3   tablespoons fresh lime juice
3   tablespoons olive oil
1   teaspoon ground cumin
1   teaspoon kosher salt
½   teaspoon freshly ground pepper
6   (6- to 8-ounce) sturgeon steaks
Roasted Poblano Salad

Combine first 5 ingredients in a small bowl; brush mixture on both sides of sturgeon steaks. Cover with plastic wrap; chill 1 to 2 hours.

Grill steaks, without grill lid, over medium heat (300° to 350°) 10 to 12 minutes or until fish flakes with a fork, turning once. Serve warm with Roasted Poblano Salad. Yield: 6 servings.

Roasted Poblano Salad

1   medium white onion, cut into ½-inch slices
1   tablespoon olive oil
2   poblano chile peppers
1   red bell pepper
1   teaspoon olive oil
1   tablespoon chopped fresh cilantro
½   teaspoon kosher salt
⅛   teaspoon freshly ground pepper
⅛   teaspoon ground cumin

Brush onion slices with 1 tablespoon olive oil. Grill onion, without grill lid, over high heat (400° to 500°) 6 to 8 minutes or until tender. Cut each slice in half; set aside.

Grill poblano chile peppers and red bell pepper, without grill lid, over medium-high heat (350° to 400°) 5 to 7 minutes, turning often, until peppers look blistered.

Place peppers in a heavy-duty zip-top plastic bag; seal, and let stand 10 minutes to loosen skins. Peel peppers; remove and discard seeds. Cut peppers into ½-inch strips.

Combine onion, peppers, 1 teaspoon oil, and remaining ingredients; toss gently. Yield: 2½ cups.

Grilled Swordfish with Rosemary

½   cup dry white wine
5   garlic cloves, minced
2   teaspoons chopped fresh rosemary, divided
4   (4-ounce) swordfish steaks
¼   teaspoon salt
¼   teaspoon pepper
2   tablespoons lemon juice
1   tablespoon extra-virgin olive oil
Lemon wedges (optional)
Garnish: fresh rosemary

Combine wine, garlic, and 1 teaspoon rosemary in an 8-inch square baking dish.

Sprinkle fish with salt and pepper; place fish in baking dish, turning to coat. Cover and chill at least 1 hour. Remove fish from marinade, discarding marinade.

Coat grill grate with vegetable cooking spray; place grate on grill over high heat (400° to 500°). Grill fish, covered with grill lid, over high heat 4 to 5 minutes on each side.

Combine remaining 1 teaspoon rosemary, lemon juice, and olive oil. Spoon over fish, and serve immediately with lemon wedges, if desired. Garnish, if desired. Yield: 4 servings.

Grilled Tuna

¼   cup soy sauce
1   tablespoon maple syrup
1   tablespoon prepared horseradish
4   (¾-inch-thick) tuna steaks (about 1½ pounds)

Combine first 3 ingredients in a heavy-duty zip-top plastic bag; add tuna. Seal and chill 1 hour, turning occasionally. Remove tuna from plastic bag; discard marinade.

Grill tuna, covered with grill lid, over high heat (400° to 500°) 2 minutes on each side or to desired degree of doneness. Yield: 4 servings.

fish sticks

Get a handle on seafood kabobs.

• **Select thick, firm-textured fish** for kabobs. Here are a few ideal choices: halibut, kingfish, mahimahi, monkfish, salmon, yellowtail snapper, striped bass, swordfish, and tuna. Let local availability, personal taste, and recommendations from your grocer dictate substitutions. Purchase fish steaks so it's easy to cut cubes. If you have a thin piece, leave the skin on; it keeps the meat from falling off the skewer and peels off easily after cooking. Many fish, such as flounder and sole, are too thin and delicate for skewering. Unless prepared whole in a grill basket, they'll fall apart.

• **To bathe fish in flavor,** brush a marinade on the kabobs. With few exceptions, fish and shellfish are low in fat and can dry out when cooked, so the addition of butter or olive oil in the marinade keeps seafood moist and prevents flesh from sticking to grill grates. Fatty fish such as salmon or mackerel will baste in their own natural oils to offer juicy, flavorful meat.

• **Use skewers 6 inches or shorter** for cooking appetizers, 10 inches and longer for entrées. Of course wood burns, so soak wooden skewers in water for at least 30 minutes before grilling. The natural texture of wood actually helps hold food on, but to avoid having the food spin heaviest side down when you're flipping it, simply use two skewers.

• **Mix different fish on a skewer** for variety, but make sure all pieces are the same size for even cooking. And leave space between the fish pieces when threading ingredients.

• **To keep kabobs from sticking,** spray the grill grate with vegetable cooking spray or brush with oil before heating. Be sure to preheat the grill; fish is more likely to stick to a cold grate. And don't forget that loaded kabobs are unwieldy. Use tongs to turn or remove them, being careful not to crush tender seafood. If the kabobs do stick, use a metal spatula to loosen them gently.

• **Finally, fish kabobs are done** when the flesh turns from translucent to opaque.

Sesame-Hoisin Tuna Kabobs

2   pounds tuna steaks, cut into 2-inch cubes
1   large onion, cut into wedges
1   (8-ounce) package fresh mushrooms
½   cup hoisin sauce
1   tablespoon sesame seeds
1   tablespoon sesame oil
1   tablespoon dry sherry
Hot cooked rice

Alternately thread tuna, onion, and mushrooms onto 8 (12-inch) skewers. Place skewers in a 13- x 9-inch baking dish.

Stir together hoisin sauce and next 3 ingredients; brush over skewers. Cover and chill 30 minutes.

Grill skewers, covered with grill lid, over medium-high heat (350° to 400°) 5 to 6 minutes on each side or to desired degree of doneness. Serve with rice. Yield: 4 servings.

Grilled Tuna and Pearl Barley Niçoise

½   cup lemon juice
1   tablespoon thinly sliced fresh basil
2   tablespoons extra-virgin olive oil
2   tablespoons anchovy paste
2   teaspoons herbes de Provence
¼   teaspoon ground pepper
4   garlic cloves, minced
4   cups water
1   cup uncooked pearl barley
½   teaspoon salt
1   pound green beans
2   tablespoons cracked pepper
6   (¾-inch-thick) tuna steaks (about 2 pounds)
2   hard-cooked eggs, sliced
1   fennel bulb, cut into ¼-inch strips
½   red onion, cut in half and thinly sliced
6   plum tomatoes, cut into wedges (about ¾ pound)
30 niçoise olives
Bibb lettuce leaves

Whisk together first 7 ingredients in a small bowl. Set dressing aside.

Bring 4 cups water to a boil in a large saucepan. Add barley and salt; cover, reduce heat, and simmer 45 minutes. Remove from heat; let stand 5 minutes. Drain, if necessary. Stir in ⅓ cup dressing, reserving remaining dressing.

Cook beans in boiling water until crisp-tender; drain. Plunge into ice water to stop the cooking process; drain and set aside.

Press cracked pepper over tuna. Grill tuna, covered with grill lid, over high heat (400° to 500°) 3 minutes on each side or to desired degree of doneness.

Arrange tuna, barley, green beans, egg slices, and next 4 ingredients on lettuce-lined plates. Drizzle with reserved dressing. Yield: 6 servings.

Easy Roasted Oysters

A sheet of tin cut 1 inch smaller than the size of the grill
5   dozen fresh oysters in the shell
A double thickness of burlap (large enough to cover oysters)
A spray bottle (to mist burlap)
Kane Island Cocktail Sauce
Melted butter
Hot sauce
Saltine crackers

Place sheet of tin on grill over a hot fire. Arrange oysters in the shell on the sheet of tin, and cover with burlap. Mist burlap with water, and cook 7 to 9 minutes.

Uncover oysters, and remove from grill with long-handled tongs. Open oysters and serve with Kane Island Cocktail Sauce, melted butter, hot sauce, and saltine crackers. Yield: 5 servings.

Kane Island Cocktail Sauce

2   cups ketchup
¾   cup chili sauce
½   cup prepared horseradish
¼   cup red wine vinegar
2   tablespoons minced onion
2   tablespoons minced celery
2   tablespoons Worcestershire sauce
1   tablespoon fresh lemon juice
1   teaspoon freshly ground pepper

Combine all ingredients in a small bowl, stirring until blended; cover and chill. Yield: 4 cups.

**Grilled Scallops with
Creole Tomato Sauce**

Grilled Scallops with Creole Tomato Sauce

24 large sea scallops (about 2¼ pounds)
2 tablespoons olive oil
¾ teaspoon kosher salt
½ teaspoon freshly ground pepper
Creole Tomato Sauce
Garnish: fresh thyme sprigs

Brush scallops with olive oil; sprinkle with salt and pepper.

Grill scallops, without grill lid, over high heat (400° to 500°) 4 to 5 minutes or just until scallops are opaque, turning once. Serve warm with Creole Tomato Sauce. Garnish, if desired. Yield: 8 appetizer servings.

Creole Tomato Sauce

¾ cup finely chopped onion
¾ cup finely chopped red bell pepper
1 tablespoon minced garlic
1 teaspoon dried thyme
½ teaspoon dried oregano
⅛ teaspoon ground red pepper
1 tablespoon olive oil
⅓ cup dry white wine
1 (14½-ounce) can diced tomatoes, undrained
¼ teaspoon kosher salt
¼ teaspoon freshly ground black pepper

Sauté first 6 ingredients in hot oil in a large skillet over medium-high heat 5 minutes or until vegetables are tender. Add wine, and cook until most of the liquid evaporates. Stir in tomatoes, salt, and black pepper; cook 5 to 7 minutes or until mixture thickens, stirring occasionally. Cool slightly.

Process tomato mixture in a blender or food processor until blended. Return sauce to skillet; keep warm. Yield: 1¾ cups.

Maple-Glazed Scallops

To prevent scallops from rotating on the skewer, use 2 skewers for each kabob.

12 bacon slices, cut in half
24 large sea scallops (2 pounds)
1   cup maple syrup
2   tablespoons butter, melted
1   teaspoon grated orange rind
3   tablespoons fresh orange juice
⅛   teaspoon salt
Garnish: orange wedges

Partially cook bacon in a large skillet. Wrap each scallop with 1 half slice bacon. Set aside.

Bring syrup to a boil in a medium saucepan over medium-high heat. Cook, uncovered, until reduced to ⅔ cup (about 5 minutes). Remove from heat; stir in butter and next 3 ingredients.

Thread bacon-wrapped scallops onto 12 (10- to 12-inch) skewers; brush syrup mixture over kabobs. Coat grill grate with vegetable cooking spray; place on grill over medium-high heat (350° to 400°). Place kabobs on grate.

Grill kabobs, covered with grill lid, 3 to 4 minutes on each side or just until scallops are opaque, basting often. Garnish, if desired. Yield: 6 servings.

Shrimp Skewers with Curried Mango Sauce

30 unpeeled, large fresh shrimp (2 pounds)
2   to 3 teaspoons chili powder
½   teaspoon kosher salt
1   tablespoon olive oil
Curried Mango Sauce
Garnish: lime wedges

Peel shrimp, leaving tails intact. Devein shrimp, if desired.

Toss together shrimp, chili powder, salt, and olive oil in a large bowl. Thread 5 shrimp onto each of 6 (10-inch) skewers, bending each shrimp to pass through skewer twice.

Grill shrimp, without grill lid, over high heat (400° to 500°) 4 to 5 minutes or just until shrimp turn pink, turning once. Serve warm with Curried Mango Sauce. Garnish, if desired. Yield: 6 servings.

Curried Mango Sauce

1   medium mango, chopped
⅓   cup peeled and chopped English cucumber
2   tablespoons olive oil
1   tablespoon fresh lime juice
1   teaspoon balsamic vinegar
¼   teaspoon curry powder
¼   teaspoon kosher salt
⅛   teaspoon freshly ground pepper

Process all ingredients in a blender until smooth, stopping once to scrape down sides. Yield: 1 cup.

Shrimp Saté with Peanut Sauce

24 unpeeled, large fresh shrimp (about 2 pounds)
2   teaspoons minced fresh ginger
4   garlic cloves, quartered
1   cup loosely packed fresh cilantro leaves
½   cup creamy peanut butter
⅓   cup lite soy sauce
2   tablespoons dark sesame oil
2   tablespoons water
2   tablespoons honey
1½ tablespoons fresh lemon juice
½   teaspoon dried crushed red pepper
Garnishes: fresh cilantro, lemon wedges

Peel shrimp, leaving tails intact, and devein, if desired; set aside. Combine ginger and next 9 ingredients in a food processor. Process until well blended, stopping to scrape down sides.

Thread 2 shrimp onto each of 12 (6-inch) skewers. Measure ¼ cup peanut sauce, and brush on shrimp. Reserve remaining sauce.

Grill shrimp, covered with grill lid, over medium-high heat (350° to 400°) 3 minutes on each side or until shrimp turn pink. Serve with reserved sauce. Garnish, if desired. Yield: 6 appetizer servings.

Maple-Glazed Scallops

Garlic-Skewered Grilled Shrimp

24   unpeeled, jumbo fresh shrimp
3   large garlic cloves, minced
1/3 cup olive oil
1/4 cup tomato sauce
2   tablespoons chopped fresh basil
2   tablespoons red wine vinegar
1/2 teaspoon ground red pepper
18   large garlic cloves, peeled

Peel shrimp, and devein, if desired. Combine minced garlic and next 5 ingredients in a medium bowl. Add shrimp; stirring well. Cover and marinate in refrigerator 30 minutes.

Place 18 garlic cloves in a small saucepan; add water to cover, and bring to a boil. Boil 3 minutes; drain well, and set aside.

Remove shrimp from marinade, reserving marinade. Bring marinade to a boil in a small saucepan; set aside.

Thread shrimp and garlic cloves evenly onto 6 (10-inch) metal skewers.

Grill shrimp, covered with grill lid, over medium-high heat (350° to 400°) 3 to 4 minutes on each side or until shrimp turn pink, basting with reserved marinade. Yield: 6 servings.

Grilled Rib-Eye Steak with Crispy Gorgonzola Crust and Grilled Scallions

1 tablespoon minced garlic
1 tablespoon minced shallot
1 tablespoon olive oil
1 teaspoon kosher salt
1/4 teaspoon ground white pepper
4 (8-ounce) rib-eye steaks
8 ounces Gorgonzola cheese
1/4 cup fine, dry breadcrumbs
8 large green onions
1 tablespoon olive oil
1/2 teaspoon kosher salt
1/4 teaspoon ground white pepper

Combine first 5 ingredients; stir well. Brush mixture evenly on both sides of steaks. Grill steaks, covered with grill lid, over medium-high heat (350° to 400°) 6 to 8 minutes on each side or to desired degree of doneness.

Remove steaks from grill, and place on a lightly greased rack in a broiler pan. Crumble cheese evenly over steaks; sprinkle breadcrumbs evenly over cheese. Place green onions around steaks on rack. Combine olive oil, 1/2 teaspoon kosher salt, and 1/4 teaspoon white pepper; brush over green onions.

Broil 5 1/2 inches from heat 3 minutes or until cheese is lightly browned and green onions are heated. Yield: 4 servings.

Grilled Sirloin Steak with Stilton Sauce

1/2 cup butter or margarine, melted
1/3 cup Worcestershire sauce
8 ounces Stilton cheese, crumbled
1 garlic clove, crushed
1/2 teaspoon salt
1/4 teaspoon pepper
2 pounds lean boneless top sirloin steak (3 inches thick)

Combine first 4 ingredients in a medium saucepan. Cook over low heat until cheese melts, stirring constantly. Set aside 2/3 cup sauce; keep remaining sauce warm.

Sprinkle salt and pepper over steak. Grill steak, covered with grill lid, over medium-high heat (350° to 400°) 18 minutes on each side or to desired degree of doneness, basting often with 2/3 cup sauce.

To serve, cut steak diagonally across the grain. Serve steak with remaining sauce. Yield: 6 servings.

Acapulco Fillet

1 medium onion
1 small tomato
2 (6-ounce) beef tenderloin steaks
1 yellow bell pepper, halved
3 jalapeño peppers, halved and seeded
2 (6-inch) corn tortillas
Burgundy Mole Sauce
Sweet Salsa
Pico de Gallo
Garnish: fresh cilantro sprigs

Cut a thin slice from top and bottom of onion and tomato; discard. Cut onion and tomato into 2 slices.

Grill onion, steaks, and peppers, covered with grill lid, over medium-high heat (350° to 400°) 10 minutes, turning after 7 minutes. Add tomato, and grill 3 minutes, turning occasionally. Add tortillas, and grill 1 minute on each side or until crisp. Remove vegetables and tortillas; remove steaks (medium rare), or continue grilling to desired degree of doneness.

Place tortillas on individual serving plates; top evenly with peppers, tomato, Burgundy Mole Sauce, steaks, and onion. Serve with Sweet Salsa and Pico de Gallo. Garnish, if desired. Yield: 2 servings.

Burgundy Mole Sauce

1 cup sliced fresh shiitake or portobello mushrooms
8 garlic cloves, chopped
2 tablespoons olive oil
1/2 cup dry red wine
1 (10 1/2-ounce) can condensed beef broth, undiluted
1/3 cup soy sauce
1 tablespoon semisweet chocolate morsels

Sauté sliced mushrooms and chopped garlic in hot oil until crisp-tender; drain. Stir in red wine

and remaining ingredients. Bring mixture to a boil. Reduce heat, and simmer, stirring occasionally, 30 minutes. Yield: 2/3 cup.

Sweet Salsa

1 green onion, chopped
1 small jalapeño pepper, diced
1/2 cup chopped avocado
1/3 cup salsa
1/4 cup ketchup
2 tablespoons chopped fresh cilantro
2 tablespoons fresh lime juice

Stir together all ingredients in a small bowl. Cover and chill. Yield: 1 cup.

Pico de Gallo

You may be more familiar with a tomato version of this condiment. Here is the traditional Mexican recipe. Pico de gallo seasoning is a blend of ground mixed hot peppers and salt. Find it on the spice aisle.

1/2 cup diced jicama
1/2 small cucumber, peeled and thinly sliced
2 small oranges, sectioned
1/4 teaspoon pico de gallo seasoning
2 tablespoons lemon juice
1 green bell pepper, halved

Stir together first 5 ingredients. Cover and chill at least 2 hours; spoon into pepper halves. Yield: 2 servings.

Garlic-Herb Steaks

4 (4-ounce) beef tenderloin steaks
1/4 teaspoon salt
1/4 teaspoon freshly ground pepper
1/4 cup minced garlic
1 tablespoon minced fresh rosemary

Sprinkle steaks with salt and pepper; coat with garlic and rosemary. Chill 1 hour.

Prepare fire by piling charcoal or lava rocks on one side of grill, leaving other side empty; place grate on grill. Arrange steaks over empty side, and grill, covered with grill lid, over high heat (400° to 500°) 10 minutes on each side or to desired degree of doneness. Yield: 4 servings.

grilling guide for beef, chicken, and pork

type of meat	grilling time	°F	notes
Beef			
Steaks, 1 inch thick	**Medium rare:** 10 minutes **Medium:** 12 minutes **Well:** 14 minutes	145	Medium fire, direct heat
Steaks, 2 inches thick	**Medium rare:** 17 minutes **Medium:** 19 minutes **Well:** 22 minutes	145	Sear over direct high heat; then move to indirect.
Flank steak, 1 inch thick	**Medium rare:** 8 minutes **Medium:** 10 minutes	145	Medium fire, direct heat
Ground beef patties, ½ inch thick	**Medium:** 8 minutes **Well:** 10 minutes	160	Medium fire, direct heat
Ground beef patties, 1 inch thick	**Medium:** 12 minutes **Well:** 14 minutes	160	Medium fire, direct heat
Kabobs, 1- to 1½-inch cubes	**Medium rare:** 11 minutes **Medium:** 13 minutes **Well:** 15 minutes	145	Medium fire, direct heat
Tenderloin, whole (3½ to 4 pounds)	35 to 50 minutes	145	Sear over direct medium heat; then move to indirect.
Chicken			
Breast, boneless (4 ounces each)	12 to 15 minutes	170	Medium fire, direct heat. Grill until there are no traces of pink at center.
Whole (3½ to 5 pounds) indirect heat	1 to 1½ hours	180	Medium fire, indirect heat. Grill until there are no traces of pink at center.
Drumsticks	14 to 16 minutes	180	Medium fire, indirect heat. Grill until there are no traces of pink at center.
Pork			
Chops, ¾ inch thick	8 to 10 minutes	160	Medium-hot fire, direct heat. Grill until light pink at center.
Ground patties, ½ inch thick	8 to 10 minutes	160	Medium-hot fire, direct heat
Tenderloin (½ to 1½ pounds)	15 to 25 minutes	160	Medium-hot fire, indirect heat
Ribs (2 to 4 pounds)	1½ to 2 hours	160	Low fire, indirect heat

- °F is the USDA recommended minimum doneness temperature.
- Cooking times are meant to be guidelines. Times include turning once, just past the halfway point in the grilling time.
- Judging a fire's temperature: Red meats are usually cooked over a medium or medium-hot fire, while fish, poultry, and vegetables usually do best over a medium fire. Wait until the coals are covered in ash. Hold your hand about 5 inches above grilling surface. If you can hold your hand there for 2 to 3 seconds, it's a hot fire; 4 to 5 seconds, a medium fire; and 6 to 7 seconds, a low fire.

know your grill

- **Shop around and ask questions.** Find out the difference between one model and the next upgrade: Is it more expensive because it's bigger and has an added work surface, or has the frame been welded as opposed to bolted, and the firebox upgraded from painted aluminum to porcelain-coated or stainless steel?
- **Pay attention to materials.** Find out what the frame is made of as well as vulnerable components such as grates, burners, and heating media.
- **Investigate the warranty.** Many manufacturers' warranties cover the firebox for 10 years or a lifetime but protect lids, burners, cooking grates, and other parts for a significantly reduced period, such as three or five years.
- **Ask about safety devices for new gas grills.** Models built after October 1995 contain gas-flow regulators and heat-sensitive shut-down devices that automatically stop gas flow if the hose leaks or catches fire. Gas grills manufactured after October 1997 incorporate protection devices that prevent a propane tank from being overfilled.
- **Some gas grills can be attached to a permanent gas line,** just like a gas stove or other inside appliance. The advantage is that you don't need propane tanks. If you want a permanent setup on the grill, ask before you buy.
- **If you don't plan to use your grill during the winter months,** store it in a garage or shed to help protect it from inclement weather and salt air. If it's a gas grill, make sure you first remove the propane tank, which should never be kept in an enclosed space. If you don't have garage or shed space, protect the grill with a grill cover or tarp.

charcoal, gas, or electric?

charcoal grills

cooking method: Use pure, lump hardwood charcoal or charcoal briquettes. Fire starters, such as lighter fluid, and metal charcoal chimneys hasten ignition.
advantages: Low cost, portability, and authentic smoky flavor.
disadvantages: Coals can be difficult to light and take a while to warm up. Cleanup is not as easy as with gas, and it can be more difficult to regulate heat.

gas grills

cooking method: Use flame and typically utilize steel plates, ceramic briquettes, or lava rocks to increase and retain heat.
advantages: Easily started with a push-button or rotary igniter. Optional accessories include smokers, steamers, and electric rotisseries. Cleanup is simple.
disadvantages: Significantly more expensive than charcoal grills. Food doesn't have the smoky intensity or charcoal-grilled flavor.

electric grills

cooking method: Require an outlet and cook food over electric coals.
advantages: Easy starts and precisely controlled temperatures.
disadvantages: Take a while to heat up and are difficult to clean. The absence of an open flame can be disappointing.

Grilled Prime Aged Sirloin with Garlic-Scallion Skillet Potatoes and Béarnaise Sauce

6	large garlic cloves, minced
1	tablespoon salt
2	tablespoons freshly ground pepper
2	tablespoons olive oil
1	(5- to 5½-pound) prime aged sirloin roast

Garlic-Scallion Skillet Potatoes
Béarnaise Sauce

Combine first 4 ingredients in a small bowl; stir into a paste. Rub garlic paste over roast; cover and let stand up to 2 hours.

Grill roast, covered with grill lid, over medium-high heat (350° to 400°) 15 minutes, turning every 5 minutes. Turn off one side of grill. Place roast on unlit side of grill. Turn lit side of grill to high (400° to 500°). Grill roast 20 minutes; turn roast, and grill 20 more minutes or until a meat thermometer inserted into thickest portion registers 150°. Remove from heat; cover with aluminum foil. Let stand 10 minutes before carving. Serve with Garlic-Scallion Skillet Potatoes and Béarnaise Sauce. Yield: 6 servings.

Garlic-Scallion Skillet Potatoes

3	pounds baking potatoes, scrubbed
6	large garlic cloves, minced
4	large green onions, chopped (about 1 cup)
1½	teaspoons salt
¾	teaspoon freshly ground pepper
1	tablespoon olive oil
6	tablespoons butter

Cook potatoes in boiling, salted water to cover 15 minutes or until tender. Drain, cool, and peel potatoes. Coarsely chop potato.

Heat a 12-inch cast-iron skillet in a 450° oven for 10 minutes. Meanwhile, toss together potato, garlic, green onions, salt, and pepper.

Pour olive oil into hot skillet. Add 2 tablespoons butter, stirring until butter melts. Add potato mixture, pressing lightly with the back of a spoon. Dot with ¼ cup butter. Cook over medium-high heat 5 minutes or until golden on bottom.

Bake at 450° for 20 minutes or until golden on top. Let stand 10 minutes; invert onto a large serving plate, and cut into 6 wedges. Yield: 6 servings.

Béarnaise Sauce

1   tablespoon chopped fresh tarragon, divided
3   tablespoons white wine vinegar
3   tablespoons dry white wine
10 black peppercorns, crushed
3   shallots, minced
1   tablespoon water
¼   teaspoon salt
⅛   teaspoon ground red pepper
3   egg yolks
¾   cup butter, cut into 12 pieces
1   teaspoon minced green onions

Bring 1½ teaspoons tarragon and next 4 ingredients to a boil in a small saucepan. Cook over medium-high heat 5 minutes or until liquid is reduced to 1 tablespoon, stirring occasionally.

Pour mixture through a wire-mesh strainer into top of a double boiler, discarding solids. Add 1 tablespoon water, salt, and red pepper. Whisk in egg yolks. Cook over hot, not boiling, water, whisking constantly until slightly thickened. Add butter, 4 pieces at a time, whisking until butter melts and sauce thickens. Stir in remaining 1½ teaspoons tarragon and green onions; remove sauce from double boiler. Serve warm. Yield: 1 cup.

—Chef Bob Kinkead
Kinkead's
Washington, D.C.

Grilled Prime Aged Sirloin with Garlic-Scallion Skillet Potatoes and Béarnaise Sauce

Grilled Garlic-Lime Pork with Jalapeño-Onion Marmalade

½ cup olive oil
⅓ cup fresh lime juice
6 large garlic cloves, chopped
2 tablespoons soy sauce
2 tablespoons grated fresh ginger
2 teaspoons Dijon mustard
½ teaspoon salt
¼ teaspoon ground red pepper
4 (¾-pound) pork tenderloins, trimmed
Jalapeño-Onion Marmalade

Process first 8 ingredients in a food processor until well blended, stopping once to scrape down sides. Pour marinade into a large heavy-duty zip-top plastic bag; add pork. Seal bag securely, and turn to coat pork. Marinate in refrigerator 8 hours, turning bag occasionally. Remove pork from marinade, discarding marinade.

let it soak in

Working with marinades can be a bit tricky. You don't want to overmarinate or under-marinate your fare. Here's what to know:
• **Marinate seafood for 15 to 30 minutes.** Poultry and beef can marinate overnight in the refrigerator.
• **When using a sauce to marinate raw meat** and serve with cooked meat, avoid contamination by first dividing the mixture; keep half refrigerated until serving time.
• **Marinate in a heavy-duty zip-top plastic bag** or nonreactive container such as a glass baking dish. Turn items occasionally for even absorption.
• **Always marinate in the refrigerator** and never at room temperature, which can be warmer than you think. Always follow the time recommended in the recipe to avoid overmarinating.
• **Pierce foods with a fork** to allow more flavor penetration.
• **Turn meat while it's marinating,** and baste frequently during cooking for added flavor.
• **To use a marinade for basting,** bring it to a full boil. Boiling kills bacteria from raw meat.

Coat grill grate with vegetable cooking spray; place on grill over medium-high heat (350° to 400°). Place pork on grate; grill pork, covered with grill lid, 22 minutes or until a meat thermometer inserted into thickest portion of each tenderloin registers 160°, turning once. Let stand 5 minutes before slicing. Serve with Jalapeño-Onion Marmalade. Yield: 9 servings.

Jalapeño-Onion Marmalade

3 tablespoons olive oil
1¼ pounds red or yellow onions, finely chopped
¼ teaspoon salt
¼ teaspoon pepper
2 jalapeño peppers, seeded and minced
2 tablespoons sugar or honey
¼ cup red wine vinegar
¼ cup water

Heat oil in a large skillet over medium-high heat. Add onion, salt, and pepper; cook until tender, stirring occasionally. Add jalapeño; cook 1 minute. Add sugar; cook 1 minute. Stir in vinegar; simmer, stirring constantly, until most of liquid evaporates. Stir in water; simmer 10 minutes or until mixture is slightly thickened and onion is very soft, stirring often. Yield: 1¾ cups.

Grilled Pork Chops

½ cup chopped fresh Italian parsley
¼ cup chopped fresh basil
4 garlic cloves, minced
¼ cup balsamic vinegar
1 cup olive oil
8 (8-ounce) pork or veal loin chops

Combine first 5 ingredients in a large shallow dish or heavy-duty zip-top plastic bag; add pork chops. Cover or seal, and chill 4 to 6 hours, turning chops occasionally. Remove chops from marinade, discarding marinade.

Grill chops, covered with grill lid, over medium-high heat (350° to 400°) 6 to 8 minutes on each side or until done. Yield: 8 servings.

Garlic-Grilled Lamb Chops

Be sure to purchase lamb sirloin chops, which are about twice the size of loin chops, for this savory entrée.

6 (1-inch-thick) lamb sirloin chops
½ cup soy sauce
½ cup cider vinegar
3 garlic cloves, minced
3 tablespoons honey
2 teaspoons ground ginger
¼ teaspoon dry mustard
¼ teaspoon pepper

Place lamb chops in a heavy-duty zip-top plastic bag or shallow dish.

Combine soy sauce and remaining ingredients; stir well. Pour over chops. Seal or cover, and marinate in refrigerator at least 8 hours.

Remove chops from marinade, reserving marinade. Bring marinade to a boil in a small saucepan; set aside.

Grill chops, covered with grill lid, over medium heat (300° to 350°) 8 to 10 minutes on each side or to desired degree of doneness, basting often with marinade. Yield: 6 servings.

Jerked Ribs

6 pounds baby pork spareribs
1 medium onion, quartered
2 cloves
1 bay leaf
6 celery leaves
1 teaspoon dried thyme
¼ teaspoon freshly ground black pepper
3 tablespoons vegetable oil, divided
Jerk Seasoning
1 cup water
2 tablespoons lemon juice

Cut ribs into 2- to 3-rib sections.

Bring ribs, next 6 ingredients, and water to cover to a boil in a large Dutch oven over high heat. Reduce heat, simmer 30 minutes or until ribs are tender. Drain.

Rub ribs with 1 tablespoon oil. Set aside 1 tablespoon Jerk Seasoning; rub ribs evenly with remaining Jerk Seasoning, and place in a large pan. Cover and chill 1 hour.

grilling over direct and indirect heat

Grilling directly over high heat results in quick cooking with more surface browning. It's best for small cuts of meat such as chops, kabobs, and burgers. Large cuts such as whole chickens, bone-in chicken pieces, tenderloins, ribs, and roasts require slow cooking over indirect heat.

Stir together 1 cup water, remaining 2 tablespoons oil, lemon juice, and 2 teaspoons reserved Jerk Seasoning. Set aside.

Prepare fire by piling charcoal or lava rocks on one side of grill, leaving the other side empty. Coat grill grate with vegetable cooking spray, and place grate on grill. Arrange food over empty side, and grill ribs, covered with grill lid, over medium-high heat (350° to 400°) 1 hour, turning once and basting occasionally with lemon juice mixture. Sprinkle with remaining 1 teaspoon Jerk Seasoning before serving. Yield: 6 servings.

Jerk Seasoning

2   bunches green onions, chopped
1   Scotch bonnet or habanero chile pepper, seeded and chopped*
1   tablespoon salt
1   teaspoon freshly ground black pepper
1   teaspoon ground cinnamon
1/4 teaspoon ground nutmeg
2   tablespoons jerk seasoning blend (we tested with Johnny's "Jamaica Me Crazy" Jerk Seasoning)
1/3 cup red wine vinegar
2   tablespoons vegetable oil
2   tablespoons soy sauce

Stir together all ingredients. Yield: 1 1/2 cups.
*6 jalapeño peppers, chopped but not seeded, may be substituted for 1 Scotch bonnet or habanero chile pepper.
From the book The Sugar Mill Caribbean Cookbook, by Jinx and Jefferson Morgan © 1999. Reprinted with permission from The Harvard Common Press.

Grilled Chicken and Pesto Clubs

4   skinned and boned chicken breast halves
1/2 teaspoon salt
1/2 teaspoon pepper
Homemade Pesto*
12 large whole wheat bread slices, lightly toasted
1   (3-ounce) package goat cheese, crumbled
1   (5.2-ounce) jar roasted red bell peppers, drained and thinly sliced
4   plum tomatoes, sliced
8   bacon slices, cooked and cut in half
2   cups mixed salad greens

Sprinkle chicken evenly with salt and pepper.

Grill chicken, covered with grill lid, over medium-high heat (350° to 400°) 8 to 10 minutes on each side or until done. Let stand 10 minutes; cut into 1/4-inch-thick slices.

Spread Homemade Pesto evenly on 1 side of each bread slice.

Layer 4 bread slices, pesto side up, with chicken, goat cheese, and roasted bell pepper slices. Top with 4 bread slices, pesto side up; layer with tomato, bacon, and greens. Top with remaining 4 bread slices, pesto side down. Cut into quarters, and secure with wooden picks. Yield: 4 servings.
*3/4 cup prepared pesto may be substituted for homemade.

Homemade Pesto

1   cup firmly packed fresh basil leaves
1   cup shredded Parmesan cheese
1/2 cup pine nuts, toasted
1/2 cup olive oil
3   garlic cloves

Process all ingredients in a blender or food processor until smooth, stopping occasionally to scrape down sides. Yield: 3/4 cup.

Lemon-Garlic Grilled Chicken

3   bone-in chicken breast halves
3   chicken thighs
4   garlic cloves, peeled
1   cup fresh parsley sprigs
1   teaspoon grated lemon rind
3   tablespoons fresh lemon juice
1/2 teaspoon salt
1/4 teaspoon pepper
Garlic-flavored cooking spray

Rinse chicken under cold water, and pat dry. Loosen skin from chicken by inserting fingers under skin and gently pushing fingers between skin and meat.

With food processor running, drop garlic through food chute; process until minced. Add parsley and next 4 ingredients; process until finely minced. Rub parsley mixture over chicken under loosened skin. Coat chicken with cooking spray.

Prepare grill. Grill chicken, covered with grill lid, over medium heat (300° to 350°) 30 minutes or until done, turning occasionally. Yield: 3 servings.

Grilled Chicken with Basting Sauce

1/4 cup butter or margarine
1   tablespoon sugar
2   tablespoons red wine vinegar
2   tablespoons Worcestershire sauce
1 1/2 teaspoons lemon juice
1   garlic clove, chopped
1/2 teaspoon dried crushed red pepper
1/2 teaspoon coarsely ground black pepper
8   bone-in chicken breast halves
1   teaspoon salt
1/2 teaspoon black pepper

Cook first 8 ingredients in a saucepan over medium-low heat, stirring occasionally, until butter melts; set aside.

Sprinkle chicken evenly with salt and pepper. Grill chicken, covered with grill lid, over medium-high heat (350° to 400°) 40 to 45 minutes or until done, turning occasionally and basting with sauce during the last 10 minutes. Yield: 8 servings.

Chicken and Shrimp Saté

1   pound unpeeled, jumbo fresh shrimp
4   skinned and boned chicken breast
    halves, cut into 3/4-inch strips
3   garlic cloves, minced
1/2 cup soy sauce
1/2 cup fresh lemon juice
3   tablespoons water
2   teaspoons curry powder
1/2 teaspoon freshly ground pepper
Peanut Dipping Sauce

Peel shrimp, leaving tails on; devein, if desired.
Place in a heavy-duty zip-top plastic bag. Place
chicken strips in a separate heavy-duty zip-top
plastic bag. Stir together garlic and next 5
ingredients; pour half of marinade over shrimp
and half over chicken. Seal bags, and marinate
in refrigerator 30 minutes.

Soak 6-inch wooden skewers in water 30
minutes. Remove shrimp from marinade, discarding marinade. Thread shrimp onto skewers.
Repeat with chicken.

Grill chicken, covered with grill lid, over
medium-high heat (350° to 400°) 5 minutes
on each side or until done. Add shrimp; cook
2 minutes on each side or until shrimp and
chicken are done. Serve with Peanut Dipping
Sauce. Yield: 8 servings.

Peanut Dipping Sauce

1   small garlic clove
1   (1/8-inch-thick) slice fresh ginger
1   small onion, quartered
2/3 cup creamy peanut butter
1/2 cup water
2   tablespoons soy sauce
1   tablespoon fresh lemon juice
1   tablespoon honey

With food processor running, drop garlic
through food chute; process until minced. Drop
ginger through food chute; process until
minced. Add onion to food processor bowl;
pulse twice or until chopped. Add remaining
ingredients; process until smooth, stopping to
scrape down sides. Yield: 1 3/4 cups.

Chicken and Fruit Salad

3/4 cup orange marmalade
3   tablespoons soy sauce
3   tablespoons lemon juice
1 1/2 tablespoons chopped fresh ginger
6   skinned and boned chicken breast halves
1   cored fresh pineapple
1   large jicama (optional)
2   cups fresh strawberry halves
1   cup fresh raspberries
Orange-Raspberry Vinaigrette
Lettuce leaves

Combine first 4 ingredients; remove 1/4 cup
marmalade mixture, and chill.

Place chicken in a shallow dish or heavy-
duty zip-top plastic bag; pour remaining
marmalade mixture over chicken. Cover or
seal, and chill 8 hours, turning occasionally.

Cut pineapple into spears or chunks; peel
jicama and cut into 1/2-inch slices.

Place pineapple and jicama in a shallow
dish or heavy-duty zip-top plastic bag; pour
1/4 cup reserved marmalade mixture over
pineapple mixture. Cover or seal, and chill
8 hours.

Remove chicken from marinade, discarding
marinade; drain pineapple mixture. Coat
chicken and pineapple mixture with vegetable
cooking spray.

Grill chicken, covered with grill lid, over
medium-high heat (350° to 400°) 5 to 6 minutes on each side or until done. Grill pineapple
and jicama 2 to 3 minutes on each side.

Chicken and Fruit Salad

Cut chicken and jicama into thin strips; cut pineapple into bite-size pieces. Combine chicken, jicama, pineapple, strawberry halves, and raspberries; toss gently with Orange-Raspberry Vinaigrette. Serve over lettuce leaves. Yield: 6 servings.

Orange-Raspberry Vinaigrette

½   cup orange marmalade
¼   cup raspberry vinegar
1   medium jalapeño pepper, seeded and minced
2   tablespoons finely chopped fresh cilantro
2   tablespoons olive oil

Whisk together all ingredients in a small bowl. Yield: 1 cup.

Chicken-Pineapple Kabobs

¼   cup firmly packed light brown sugar
¼   cup soy sauce
1   tablespoon chopped fresh cilantro
1   tablespoon vegetable oil
1   teaspoon minced fresh ginger
½   teaspoon dried crushed red pepper
2   garlic cloves, minced
4   skinned and boned chicken breast halves, cut into strips
1   small cored fresh pineapple, cut into 2-inch pieces
Hot cooked rice
Garnishes: chopped green onions, fresh cilantro

Combine first 7 ingredients in a shallow dish or large heavy-duty zip-top plastic bag; add chicken. Cover or seal; chill 2 hours, turning chicken occasionally.

Remove chicken from marinade, discarding marinade. Thread chicken onto 3 (6-inch) skewers and pineapple onto 3 (6-inch) skewers.

Grill chicken, covered with grill lid, over medium-high heat (350° to 400°) 15 to 20 minutes or until done, turning occasionally. Grill pineapple 5 to 7 minutes or until thoroughly heated. Serve over rice. Garnish, if desired. Yield: 6 servings.

Grilled Chicken Tortas

4   large skinned and boned chicken breast halves
1   (16-ounce) container refrigerated hot chile salsa
¼   cup tequila
2   tablespoons chopped fresh cilantro
2   tablespoons lime juice
3   poblano chile peppers
¼   teaspoon salt
1   (16-ounce) can refried beans or black beans, drained
1   tablespoon olive oil
8   (6-inch) crusty sandwich rolls, split
3   avocados, peeled and mashed
2   cups (8 ounces) shredded Monterey Jack cheese

Place chicken between 2 sheets of heavy-duty plastic wrap, and flatten to ¼-inch thickness using a meat mallet or rolling pin.

Stir together salsa and next 3 ingredients. Remove 1 cup mixture, and set aside remaining mixture.

Place chicken in a shallow dish or heavy-duty zip-top plastic bag; pour 1 cup salsa mixture over chicken. Cover or seal, and chill 1 hour, turning occasionally. Remove chicken from marinade, discarding marinade.

Grill peppers, covered with grill lid, over medium-high heat (350° to 400°) 5 to 7 minutes, turning often, until peppers look blistered.

Place peppers in a heavy-duty zip-top plastic bag; seal and let stand 10 minutes to loosen skins. Peel peppers; remove and discard seeds. Cut peppers into thin strips; set aside.

Grill chicken, covered with grill lid, over medium-high heat (350° to 400°) 5 minutes on each side or until done. Cool slightly. Cut chicken into thin slices, and sprinkle evenly with salt.

Stir together beans and olive oil in a 1-quart glass bowl, and microwave at HIGH 2 minutes or until thoroughly heated, stirring once.

Spread beans evenly over bottom halves of rolls. Spread avocado over top halves of rolls. Top bottom halves evenly with chicken, pepper strips, cheese, and top halves of rolls. Serve with reserved salsa mixture. Yield: 8 servings.

Grilled Honey Chicken Wings

10   chicken wings
½   cup soy sauce
¼   cup dry sherry
¼   cup honey
¼   teaspoon garlic powder
¼   teaspoon ground ginger
3   tablespoons butter

Cut off wingtips, and discard; cut wings in half at joint.

Combine soy sauce and remaining ingredients in a small saucepan; cook over medium heat, stirring constantly, until thoroughly heated. Reserve ¼ cup marinade, and chill.

Pour remaining marinade into a large heavy-duty zip-top plastic bag; add chicken, and seal. Chill 2 hours, turning occasionally.

Remove chicken from marinade, discarding marinade. Cook chicken, covered with grill lid, over medium-high heat (350° to 400°) 20 minutes, turning once and basting with reserved ¼ cup marinade. Yield: 20 appetizers or 2 to 3 main-dish servings.

Grilled Portobello Steaks

4   large portobello mushrooms (3 to 4 ounces each)
½   cup olive oil
2   garlic cloves, minced
1   teaspoon salt
2   teaspoons Worcestershire sauce
½   teaspoon freshly ground pepper

Cut stems off mushrooms near cap. Reserve stems for other uses. Place mushroom caps, gill side up, on a plate. Combine olive oil and remaining ingredients. Spoon oil mixture evenly into gills of each mushroom. Cover and chill until ready to grill. Place mushrooms, gill side up, on grill grate.

Grill mushrooms, covered with grill lid, over medium heat (300° to 350°) 4 minutes. Turn mushrooms; grill, covered, 4 minutes or just until tender. Yield: 4 servings.

Grilled Corn with Jalapeño-Lime Butter

Grilled Corn with Jalapeño-Lime Butter

$\frac{1}{2}$ cup butter, softened

2   jalapeño peppers, seeded and minced

2   tablespoons grated lime rind

1   teaspoon fresh lime juice

6   ears fresh corn

1   tablespoon olive oil

2   teaspoons kosher salt

1   teaspoon freshly ground pepper

Combine first 4 ingredients, and shape into a 6-inch log; wrap in wax paper, and chill 1 hour.

Remove and discard husks and silks from corn. Rub corn with olive oil; sprinkle evenly with salt and pepper.

Grill corn, covered with grill lid, over high heat (400° to 500°) 10 to 15 minutes or until tender, turning often. Serve with flavored butter. Yield: 6 servings.

Grilled Corn on the Cob

If you purchase young, tender ears of corn, be sure to cook the lesser time.

6   ears fresh corn

$\frac{1}{4}$ cup butter or margarine, melted

1   teaspoon salt

1   teaspoon pepper

Remove and discard husks and silks from corn. Brush corn with butter; sprinkle with salt and pepper. Wrap each ear tightly in aluminum foil.

Grill corn, covered with grill lid, over medium heat (300° to 350°) 15 to 20 minutes or until tender, turning often. Yield: 6 servings.

The flavor of fresh corn is greatly enhanced on the grill.

Grilled Fennel and Radicchio Salad

4   fennel bulbs

1   head radicchio, separated into leaves

$\frac{1}{2}$ cup orange juice

$\frac{1}{4}$ cup orange marmalade

2   tablespoons olive oil

1   tablespoon white wine vinegar

2   garlic cloves, minced

$\frac{1}{2}$ teaspoon salt

$\frac{1}{4}$ teaspoon freshly ground pepper

Garnish: fennel sprigs

Cut fennel bulbs vertically into ½-inch slices. Blanch fennel in boiling water 3 minutes or just until crisp-tender; drain. Combine fennel and radicchio in a large bowl; set aside.

Combine orange juice and next 6 ingredients in a jar. Cover tightly, and shake vigorously. Chill ¼ cup vinaigrette; pour remaining vinaigrette over fennel and radicchio, tossing gently to coat. Let fennel mixture stand 15 minutes; drain.

Grill fennel, covered with grill lid, over medium-high heat (350° to 400°) 15 minutes, turning once. Remove fennel from grill, and set aside. Grill radicchio, covered with grill lid, 2 minutes or until crisp-tender. Toss fennel and radicchio with reserved vinaigrette. Garnish, if desired. Serve immediately. Yield: 5 servings.

Note: *Don't core fennel before grilling. The core will hold the slices of fennel together so they won't fall through the grill grate.*

Grilled Onion Salad

4   large Vidalia onions

$\frac{1}{3}$ cup balsamic vinegar

2   tablespoons walnut oil

2   tablespoons honey

1   teaspoon salt

8   cups mixed salad greens

$\frac{1}{4}$ cup chopped fresh parsley

$\frac{1}{4}$ cup chopped pecans, toasted

Peel onions, leaving root ends intact. Cut each onion vertically into quarters, cutting to within

½ inch of root ends. Cut each quarter vertically into thirds. Place in a shallow dish.

Whisk together vinegar and next 3 ingredients. Pour over onions; cover and chill 2 hours.

Drain onions, reserving vinaigrette mixture.

Grill onions, covered with grill lid, over medium-high heat (350° to 400°) 10 to 15 minutes or until tender. Place each onion on 2 cups salad greens; drizzle with reserved vinaigrette. Sprinkle with parsley and pecans. Yield: 4 servings.

Grilled Summer Squash and Tomatoes

This little ditty of a recipe received our top votes for ease and flavor.

¼ cup olive oil
2 tablespoons balsamic vinegar
1 teaspoon salt
½ teaspoon pepper
4 garlic cloves, minced
4 medium-size green tomatoes, cut into ¼-inch-thick slices
1 pound yellow squash, cut diagonally into ½-inch-thick slices

Combine first 5 ingredients in a shallow dish or heavy-duty zip-top plastic bag; add tomato and squash. Cover or seal; chill 30 minutes.

Remove vegetables from marinade, reserving marinade.

Grill vegetables, covered with grill lid, over medium-high heat (350° to 400°) 10 minutes, turning occasionally. Before serving, toss with reserved marinade. Yield: 6 servings.

Dr. Bosker's Boogie-Woogie Brown-Sugared Barbecued Bananas

6 unpeeled ripe bananas
6 tablespoons light brown sugar
6 tablespoons orange liqueur
Ice cream or whipped cream

Cut a lengthwise slit in each banana, being careful not to cut all the way through; spread open slightly. Gently pack 1 tablespoon brown sugar inside each. Drizzle liqueur over brown sugar.

Grill bananas, without lid, over medium heat (300° to 350°) 4 minutes on each side. Top each grilled banana with ice cream or a dollop of whipped cream. Serve immediately. Yield: 6 servings.

From Patio Daddy-O © *1996 by Gideon Bosker, Karen Brooks, and Leland and Crystal Payton. Used with permission of Chronicle Books LLC, San Francisco. Visit ChronicleBooks.com*

Grilled Pineapple with Vanilla-Cinnamon Ice Cream

1 pineapple
3 tablespoons light brown sugar
½ teaspoon ground cinnamon
1 tablespoon grated fresh ginger
Vanilla-Cinnamon Ice Cream

Peel pineapple; remove and discard pineapple core. Cut pineapple lengthwise into halves.

Combine brown sugar, cinnamon, and ginger; rub evenly over pineapple.

Coat grill grate with vegetable cooking spray; place on grill over medium-high heat (350° to 400°). Place pineapple on grate.

Grill pineapple, covered with grill lid, 5 to 7 minutes on each side. Remove pineapple from grill; cut into ¼-inch-thick slices. Serve with Vanilla-Cinnamon Ice Cream. Yield: 6 servings.

Vanilla-Cinnamon Ice Cream

1 quart vanilla ice cream, softened
¼ cup milk
2 tablespoons brown sugar
¼ teaspoon ground cinnamon

Stir together all ingredients. Freeze 1 hour. Yield: about 4 cups.

Dr. Bosker's Boogie-Woogie Brown-Sugared Barbecued Bananas

smoking

Smoked King Crab Legs and Lobster Tails

Apple or alder wood chunks

1   cup butter or margarine, melted
¼   cup fresh lemon juice
1   tablespoon minced fresh parsley
½   teaspoon grated lemon rind
Pinch salt
5   pounds frozen king crab legs, thawed
4   frozen lobster tails, thawed (2 pounds)

Soak wood chunks in water to cover at least 1 hour.

Prepare charcoal fire in smoker; let burn 15 to 20 minutes. Drain chunks, and place on coals. Place water pan in smoker; add hot water to fill line.

Stir together butter and next 4 ingredients. Divide lemon-butter mixture in half. Crack crab legs, and split lobster tails. Brush lobster and crab with half of butter mixture; set aside remaining mixture.

Coat rack with vegetable cooking spray; place in smoker. Arrange crab legs and lobster tails on rack; cover with smoker lid. Smoke crab about 20 minutes and lobster about 45 minutes to 1 hour or until flesh is white and firm.

Serve with reserved lemon-butter mixture. Yield: 4 servings.

Smoked Sea Scallops

Mesquite wood chips

6   cups water
⅓   cup kosher salt
¼   cup sugar
36 sea scallops
⅔   pound thinly sliced prosciutto
6   green onions, sliced

Soak wood chips in water to cover at least 30 minutes.

Combine 6 cups water, salt, and sugar in a bowl, stirring to dissolve. Rinse scallops, and stir into brine. Cover and chill 1 hour; drain.

Arrange scallops in a single layer on a wire rack; chill 1 hour.

Prepare charcoal fire in smoker; let burn 15 to 20 minutes. Drain chips, and place on coals. Place water pan in smoker; add hot water to fill line.

Wrap strips of prosciutto around scallops, securing with wooden picks. Place scallops on upper rack. Place rack in smoker. Sprinkle green onions over scallops (most will drop into water); cover with smoker lid. Smoke 20 minutes or until done. Yield: 6 servings.

Citrus-Marinated Smoked Shrimp

(shown on page 287)

Maple or cherry wood chunks

2   pounds unpeeled, jumbo fresh shrimp
1   cup fresh orange juice
¼   cup honey
1   tablespoon chopped fresh basil
1   tablespoon chopped fresh thyme
1   teaspoon grated orange rind
2   oranges, sliced
Garnishes: orange slices, fresh thyme sprigs

Soak wood chunks in water to cover at least 1 hour.

Place shrimp in a shallow dish or large heavy-duty zip-top plastic bag. Stir together orange juice and next 4 ingredients; pour over shrimp, stirring to coat. Cover or seal, and chill 1 hour. Drain, reserving marinade.

Prepare charcoal fire in smoker; let burn 15 to 20 minutes. Drain chunks, and place on coals. Place water pan in smoker; add orange slices. Add hot water to fill line. Coat rack with vegetable cooking spray; place in smoker.

Place shrimp on upper rack; cover with smoker lid. Smoke 45 minutes.

Bring marinade to a boil. Reduce heat, and simmer, uncovered, 5 to 7 minutes or until reduced by half. Serve with shrimp. Garnish, if desired. Yield: 8 appetizer servings.

Smoked Rosemary-Scented Salmon

Hickory or alder wood chips

1   (3-pound) salmon fillet, halved
    crosswise
¾   cup fresh lime juice
3   tablespoons minced fresh rosemary
2   tablespoons olive oil
1½ teaspoons prepared horseradish
¾   teaspoon salt
1½ teaspoons cracked pepper
Garnish: fresh rosemary sprig

Soak wood chips in water to cover at least 30 minutes.

Place salmon fillet in a shallow dish or large heavy-duty zip-top plastic bag. Stir together lime juice and next 3 ingredients; pour over fish. Cover or seal, and chill 3 hours, turning occasionally. Remove fish, reserving marinade. Sprinkle fish with salt and pepper; set aside.

Prepare charcoal fire in smoker; let burn 15 to 20 minutes. Drain chips, and place on coals. Place water pan in smoker; add reserved marinade. Add hot water to fill line. Coat rack with vegetable cooking spray; place in smoker.

Arrange fish, skin side down, on rack; cover with smoker lid. Smoke 50 minutes or until fish flakes with a fork. Garnish, if desired. Yield: 6 servings.

A smoker or grill and a handful of wet wood chips will infuse your favorite seafood with a wonderfully woodsy aroma and flavor.

Smoked Trout

Pecan shell chips or hickory wood chips

3   (8-ounce) trout fillets, each halved
      lengthwise
1¼ cups water
⅓ cup firmly packed dark brown
      sugar
¼ cup lemon juice
¼ teaspoon ground red pepper
¼ teaspoon salt

Soak shell or wood chips in water to cover at least 30 minutes.

Place fillets in a large heavy-duty zip-top plastic bag. Stir together 1¼ cups water and next 3 ingredients; pour over fillets. Seal and chill 2 hours, turning plastic bag occasionally. Remove fish from bag, reserving marinade.

Prepare charcoal fire in smoker; let burn 15 to 20 minutes. Drain chips, and place on coals. Place water pan in smoker; add reserved marinade. Add hot water to fill line. Coat rack with vegetable cooking spray; place in smoker.

Arrange fish, skin side down, on rack; cover with smoker lid. Smoke 1 hour or until fish flakes with a fork. Sprinkle with salt. Yield: 4 servings.

Smoked Tuna

Cherry wood chunks

4   (10-ounce) tuna steaks
2   quarts water
⅔ cup kosher salt
½ cup firmly packed light brown
      sugar
5   bay leaves, crumbled
2   tablespoons fresh lemon juice
Vegetable oil
2   tablespoons coarsely ground black
      peppercorns
4   cups dry white wine

Soak wood chunks in water to cover at least 1 hour.

Place tuna steaks in a large heavy-duty zip-top plastic bag. Stir together 2 quarts water and next 4 ingredients; pour over steaks. Seal bag; chill steaks 3 hours, turning bag occasionally.

Remove steaks from brine. Wash and pat dry. Place on a rack; let dry 30 minutes. Brush with vegetable oil. Pat pepper on both sides of steaks.

Prepare charcoal fire in smoker; let burn 15 to 20 minutes. Drain chunks, and place on coals. Place water pan in smoker; add wine. Coat rack with vegetable cooking spray; place in smoker. Place steaks on upper rack; cover with smoker lid. Smoke 3 to 4 hours or to desired degree of doneness. Yield: 4 servings.

smoke signals

- **Just about any seafood can be smoked,** but this is one culinary case where fat works in your favor. Smoke penetrates high-fat fish more evenly and completely than lean fish, and fish types high in fat maintain better texture than lean ones, which tend to dry out. Prime picks include catfish, mackerel, mullet, salmon, shark, striped bass, swordfish, trout, sardines, tuna, and shellfish—including shrimp, lobster, crabs, clams, oysters, mussels, and scallops.

- **Smoke the freshest fish available.** Even the richest smoky essence can't save a poor piece of fish.

- **Herbs, spices, salt, and sugar all contribute to the taste,** but it's the wood that gives smoked seafood its signature flavor.

- **Alder, apple, beech, cherry, grapevine, hickory, maple, mesquite, and oak each have their own characteristics.** Hickory and mesquite impart the strongest smoke flavor; alder is the wood of choice when smoking salmon. Some devout fish smokers blend woods, so keep in mind that smoking can be a savory experiment. Find what pleases your palate.

- **Soaking wood chips in water ensures that they'll smoke slowly** and impart their fragrance to fish before burning down to ashes. A short soak is usually sufficient because most types of fish cook quickly. Soak chips at least 30 minutes and chunks 1 to 24 hours. If you're after an abundance of smoke flavor, be sure the wood is waterlogged.

- **A lot of wood isn't necessary to gain good flavor.** Two handfuls of chips or three or four chunks should be plenty, but experiment by using more wood for a stronger smoke flavor or less for milder results.

- **Start your fire and let coals burn down until they're covered with gray ash.** Cover coals with soaked chips, and set smoker vents to produce a smooth, even draft. Add herbs, citrus peel, or spices to the fire for more complex flavor.

- **Lightly oil smoker racks to prevent fish from sticking.** If only one rack is needed, use the upper level. Arrange fish on rack, skin side down, with enough room between pieces for air to circulate.

- **Get creative when it comes to filling the smoker's water pan.** Why not add beer, wine, cola, fruit juice, or a marinade instead of hot water? The liquid bestows even more flavor to the fish as it steams and smokes.

- **For best results, smoke only one type of fish at a time** and use fish pieces that are the same size and weight.

- **Butterfly small fish and spread them open for smoking.** Cut larger fish into fillets or steaks. Smoke oysters on the half shell, and leave shrimp in the shell.

- **Resist the temptation to lift the lid to check fish before the minimum recommended cooking time.** If the lid is lifted, heat and moisture escape and 15 minutes should be added to the cook time.

- **Fully cooked smoked seafood should be firm to the touch,** but not tough. Smoked fillets should flake with a fork. A smoky flavor and aroma should be evident but not overpowering.

planking

Potlatch Salmon

1   alder plank
4   coriander seeds
2   small whole dried red peppers
4   teaspoons kosher salt
2   teaspoons dried basil
2   teaspoons dried oregano
2   teaspoons paprika
1   teaspoon ground red pepper
1   (3-pound) salmon fillet

Soak plank in water to cover 3 hours; drain.

Process coriander seeds and whole red peppers in a food processor 1 minute or until finely crushed. Add kosher salt and next 4 ingredients; process 5 seconds. Rub seasoning mixture on flesh side of salmon. Wrap salmon in heavy-duty plastic wrap, and chill 3 hours.

Place seasoned salmon on plank. Grill salmon, covered with grill lid, over medium-high heat (350° to 400°) 27 minutes or until fish flakes with a fork. Yield: 8 servings.

—*Executive Chef Emmanuel Afentoulis*
Dolce Skamania Lodge
Stevenson, Washington

Chinook Salmon on Alderwood with Vidalia Onion and Mustard Crust

Serve your entrée on the plank for an impressive restaurant-style presentation.

1   alder plank
1   (3-pound) salmon fillet
Sea salt
Freshly ground pepper
2   small Vidalia onions, thinly sliced
3   garlic cloves, minced
2   tablespoons mustard seeds
2   green onions, finely chopped
2   tablespoons chopped fresh rosemary
2   tablespoons rice wine vinegar
2   tablespoons olive oil
1   large lemon, cut into wedges
Garnish: rosemary sprig

Soak plank in water to cover 1 hour; drain.

Season salmon with sea salt and pepper. Place fish on plank.

Stir together onion and next 6 ingredients. Spoon onion mixture over salmon, pressing firmly. Cover with grill lid; grill salmon over medium-high heat (350° to 400°) 15 to 20 minutes or until fish flakes with a fork. Squeeze lemon over fish. Garnish, if desired. Yield: 8 servings.

Reprinted by permission of Willow Creek Press, Inc.

Chinook Salmon on Alderwood with Vidalia Onion and Mustard Crust

From the first bite, you'll be hooked. Planked fish has it all—flavor, ease, and flair.

plank history

Unlike grilled foods, which can dry out quickly when left on the grill too long, food cooked on a plank stays moist and tender because of the damp smoke that wafts from the wood plank. The smoldering plank adds a smoky essence that complements other flavors without overpowering them.

The technique of cooking on planks is not new. Developed by native Americans along the Pacific Northwest, cooking on cedar and alder has been a tradition for centuries. Chef Emmanuel Afentoulis of the Skamania Lodge in Stevenson, Washington, prepares 35 to 40 pounds of salmon a day this way. He uses 1-inch-thick alder boards designed with holes drilled on the diagonal. The 3- to 5-pound salmon fillets are secured with soaked wooden skewers; then the planks are hung vertically around a cone-shaped, slow-burning fire pit where the whole salmon fillets roast slowly, basting in their own oil as they absorb the scents of the wood and smoke.

At least three hours before grilling, Emmanuel coats each fillet with potlatch seasoning, a spice rub named after the ceremonial feast of the native Americans of the Northwest coast. Made by pulverizing hot peppers and dry spices, this recipe has been used for years at the lodge, but Emmanuel adds his own touch to each batch. (See recipe, opposite page.)

plank grilling tips

- **Planks for grilling** are sized to fit standard grills and are available seasonally from barbecue and gourmet stores (like Williams-Sonoma) and from seafood markets year-round. You can also order planks online from www.barbecuewood.com
- **Always soak the plank before using** to help keep the fish moist. A soaked plank produces maximum smoke and is less likely to burn. Submerge it in water at least an hour (see photo 1, at right). Weigh it down with a can.
- **If the fillet is skinless,** lightly coat the plank with cooking spray.
- **After placing the plank** on the grill, immediately cover the grill so that the smoke quickly surrounds the food.
- **Food that touches the wood** takes on more flavor, so arrange it on the wood plank in a single layer (see photo 2, at right).
- **Cedar planks burn more easily than some woods,** so keep a spray bottle handy to douse flare-ups.
- **Use oven mitts** to remove the plank and place it on a heatproof serving platter or baking sheet. The edges may be charred and smoldering.
- **If you're serving fillets,** cut them into serving-size portions; then serve directly from the plank, carefully sliding a thin spatula between the skin and meat.

Alder-Planked Salmon in an
Asian-Style Marinade

Alder-Planked Salmon in an Asian-Style Marinade

Grilling over indirect heat allows the fish to stay moist and to take on a subtle smokiness from the plank.

1   (15- x 6½- x ⅜-inch) alder plank
½   cup rice vinegar
½   cup soy sauce
2   tablespoons honey
1   teaspoon ground ginger
½   teaspoon freshly ground pepper
3   garlic cloves, minced
1   lemon, thinly sliced
1   (3½-pound) salmon fillet
¼   cup chopped green onions
1   tablespoon sesame seeds, toasted

Soak plank in water to cover 1 hour; drain.

To prepare grill for indirect grilling, heat one side of the grill to high heat (400° to 500°).

Combine vinegar and next 6 ingredients in a large zip-top plastic bag; seal. Shake to combine. Add fish; seal. Marinate in refrigerator 30 minutes, turning once.

Place plank on grill grate over high heat; grill 5 minutes or until lightly charred. Carefully turn plank over; move to cool side of grill. Remove fish from marinade; discard marinade.

Place fish, skin side down, on charred side of plank. Grill salmon, covered with grill lid, 15 minutes or until fish flakes with a fork. Sprinkle with green onions and sesame seeds. Yield: 9 servings.

—Judith Fertig
Shawnee Mission, Kansas

Halibut with Dried Tomato-Basil Pesto

1   (15- x 6½- x ⅜-inch) cedar plank
4   (6-ounce) halibut fillets
½   teaspoon salt
¼   teaspoon freshly ground pepper
Dried Tomato-Basil Pesto

Soak plank in water to cover 1 hour; drain.

Place fillets on plank; sprinkle evenly with salt and pepper. Coat each fillet with Dried Tomato-Basil Pesto. Place plank on grill grate.

Grill halibut, covered with grill lid, over medium-high heat (350° to 400°) 15 minutes or until fish flakes with a fork. Yield: 4 servings.

Dried Tomato-Basil Pesto

¼   cup dried tomatoes in oil, drained and minced
1   tablespoon minced fresh basil
3   tablespoons olive oil
2   teaspoons fresh minced garlic

Place all ingredients in a food processor. Process until smooth. Yield: ½ cup.

—Executive Chef John Howie
Seastar Restaurant and Raw Bar
Bellevue, Washington

Cedar-Planked Halibut Tacos with Citrus Slaw

If you can't find fresh halibut, use catfish, mahimahi, or snapper. Serve this dish with gazpacho or chilled cucumber soup.

1   (15- x 6½- x ⅜-inch) cedar plank
½   teaspoon salt
2   cups shredded napa (Chinese) cabbage
1   cup gourmet mixed salad greens
⅔   cup chopped green onions
¼   cup sour cream
2   tablespoons fresh lime juice
2   teaspoons chili powder
½   teaspoon freshly ground pepper
¼   teaspoon salt
1   (1½-pound) halibut fillet
12 (8-inch) flour tortillas

Soak plank in water to cover 1 hour; drain.

Prepare grill, heating one side to medium heat (300° to 350°) and one side to high heat (400° to 500°).

To prepare slaw, combine ½ teaspoon salt, shredded cabbage, salad greens, green onions, sour cream, and lime juice; toss well to coat. Chill.

To prepare tacos, combine chili powder, pepper, and ¼ teaspoon salt in a small bowl. Sprinkle chili powder mixture over fish.

Place plank on grill grate over high heat; grill 5 minutes or until lightly charred.

Carefully turn plank over; move to medium heat. Place fish on charred side of plank. Grill halibut, covered with grill lid, 18 minutes or until fish flakes with a fork.

Warm tortillas according to package directions. Break fish into chunks, and place about 2 ounces fish on each tortilla. Top each taco with ¼ cup slaw; fold tortillas in half. Yield: 6 servings.

—Judith Fertig
Shawnee Mission, Kansas

Oak-Planked Peppercorn Tuna Steaks with Orange Mayonnaise

The citrus-flavored mayonnaise, which you can make ahead, takes the heat off the spicy peppercorn-crusted tuna. Serve over couscous.

1   (15- x 6½- x ⅜-inch) oak plank
¼   cup mayonnaise
¼   teaspoon grated orange rind
2   tablespoons fresh orange juice
2   teaspoons chopped fresh chives
4   (6-ounce) Bluefin tuna steaks (about 1 inch thick)
½   teaspoon salt
2   tablespoons mixed peppercorns, crushed

Soak plank in water to cover 1 hour; drain.

Prepare grill, heating one side to medium heat (300° to 350°) and one side to high heat (400° to 500°).

Combine mayonnaise, orange rind, juice, and chives; stir well with a whisk. Chill.

Lightly coat top of tuna with vegetable cooking spray. Sprinkle tuna with salt; firmly press peppercorns into tuna.

Place plank on grill grate over high heat; grill 5 minutes or until lightly charred. Carefully turn plank over; move to medium heat. Place tuna on charred side of plank. Grill tuna, covered with grill lid, 10 minutes or to desired degree of doneness. Serve tuna with orange mayonnaise. Yield: 4 servings.

—Judith Fertig
Shawnee Mission, Kansas

Everything from tuna to tenderloin can be cooked and served on a wood plank.

woods that work

- **Each of our recipes specifies a certain type of aromatic wood plank,** but the subtle flavors of different woods are difficult to distinguish, especially when sassy sauces and side dishes accompany the entrée. Alder and cedar planks are the easiest to find. Resinous woods, such as birch, pine, and poplar, impart a bitter flavor, so avoid them. Consider these fine options:
- **Alder produces a delicate flavor that works well with mild foods.** Alder and seafood—especially salmon—are a perfect match.
- **Cedar, the most aromatic wood, lends a deep but gentle flavor that resembles its familiar aroma.** Pair cedar with hearty foods, such as pork. It also stands up nicely to spicy dishes.
- **Hickory gives an intense smoky flavor** that works well with beef and chicken (think of barbecue and spicy rubs and sauces).
- **Maple imparts a mild smoky flavor with subtle sweetness.** It works nicely with fish, chicken, and pork. Bacon and hams are often smoked with maple.
- **Oak offers a medium aroma.** Expect a pleasantly acidic note similar to the essence oak barrels give Chardonnay. Pair oak with most any food, especially chicken, fish, and pork.

Hickory-Planked Pork Tenderloin with Rosemary-Dijon Potatoes

The mustard glaze does double duty on the pork and potatoes. Jump-start the potatoes in the microwave, so they'll come off the grill with the pork.

1	(15- x 6½- x ⅜-inch) hickory plank
¼	cup Dijon mustard
1	tablespoon honey
½	teaspoon freshly ground pepper
½	teaspoon chopped fresh rosemary
2	garlic cloves, minced
1	(1-pound) pork tenderloin, trimmed
2	cups (¼-inch-thick) slices red potato (about 8 ounces)
1	tablespoon fresh lemon juice

Soak plank in water to cover 1 hour; drain.

To prepare grill for indirect grilling, heat one side of grill to high heat (400° to 500°).

Combine mustard, honey, pepper, rosemary, and garlic, stirring well with a whisk. Brush half of mustard mixture over pork.

Place the potato in a microwave-safe bowl, and cover with plastic wrap. Microwave at HIGH 1 minute. Add remaining mustard mixture and juice; toss gently to coat.

Place plank on grill grate over high heat; grill 5 minutes or until lightly charred. Carefully turn plank over; move to cool side of grill. Place pork in middle of charred side of plank; arrange potato mixture around pork in a single layer. Grill pork, covered with grill lid, 20 minutes or until a meat thermometer inserted into thickest portion of pork registers 160° (slightly pink). Yield: 4 servings.

—Judith Fertig
Shawnee Mission, Kansas

Argentinean Oak-Planked Beef Tenderloin with Chimichurri Sauce

This recipe is reminiscent of churrasco, a spicy grilled beef dish. Made from fresh herbs, the sauce is a robust accompaniment to the simple tenderloin.

1	(15- x 6½- x ⅜-inch) oak plank
4	(4-ounce) beef tenderloin steaks, trimmed (¾ inch thick)
½	teaspoon salt
¼	teaspoon freshly ground black pepper
¾	cup fresh Italian parsley leaves
¼	cup fresh cilantro leaves
¼	cup fresh mint leaves
¼	cup chopped onion
¼	cup chicken broth
3	tablespoons sherry vinegar
2	tablespoons fresh oregano leaves
1	teaspoon olive oil
½	teaspoon salt
½	teaspoon freshly ground black pepper
½	teaspoon crushed red pepper
3	garlic cloves

Soak plank in water to cover 1 hour; drain.

Prepare grill, heating one side to medium heat (300° to 350°) and one side to high heat (400° to 500°).

To prepare steak, sprinkle steaks with ½ teaspoon salt and ¼ teaspoon black pepper.

Place plank on grill grate over high heat; grill 5 minutes or until lightly charred. Carefully turn plank over; move to medium heat. Place steaks on charred side of plank. Grill steaks, covered with grill lid, 12 minutes or to desired degree of doneness.

To prepare sauce, combine parsley and remaining ingredients in a food processor, and process until smooth. Serve with steaks. Yield: 4 servings.

—Judith Fertig
Shawnee Mission, Kansas

Argentinean Oak-Planked Beef Tenderloin
with Chimichurri Sauce

the coastal kitchen

Coastal Living test kitchens secrets

We may be biased, but we think food just tastes better in a coastal setting. For entertaining or preparing meals for simple family gatherings, you'll find everything you need here, plus our best secrets for seaside cooking and dining.

The Coastal Pantry

The right ingredients and seasonings are key when cooking seafood. Here's advice and a handy list of ingredients we routinely use in the *Coastal Living* Test Kitchens.

A Word About Herbs

• **Herbs are flavoring agents** from the leafy part of a plant. Examples include basil, dill, oregano, marjoram, bay leaf, thyme, rosemary, cilantro, and parsley.

• **Wrap fresh herbs in a damp paper towel,** place in an airtight plastic bag, and refrigerate up to five days. For longer storage in the refrigerator, place herbs, stem end down, in a cup filled with an inch of water. Cover cup with plastic wrap.

• **Store dried herbs in a cool, dark place** for up to six months. If kept longer, place in the freezer to preserve flavor and aroma. Heat robs herbs (and spices, too) of pungency, so keep them away from stoves and dishwashers.

• **Dried herbs have concentrated flavor,** so use a 1:3 ratio when substituting for fresh. For example, use 1 tablespoon dried herb for every 3 tablespoons fresh. Rosemary is the one exception. Use it in the same amount whether fresh or dried.

The Spice Shelf

• **Spices are aromatic seasonings** from seeds (caraway, cardamom); flower buds (cloves); stamens (saffron); bulbs (garlic); fruit or berries (coriander, allspice, vanilla bean); bark (cinnamon); or roots (ginger, turmeric).

• **Store ground spices up to six months in a cool, dry place.** If kept longer, store in the freezer. Whole spices last up to two years in the freezer because of the protective seed coatings and hulls.

• **Volatile oils in ground spices dissipate after a few months,** leaving them less aromatic (75 to 80 percent of perceived flavor is actually smell—think fresh-baked bread or apple pie). For maximum aroma and flavor, grind whole spices with a small coffee grinder or mortar and pestle.

• **Toasting spices intensifies aroma and flavor.** Place a dry skillet over medium heat. When hot, add whole or ground spices and roast for 30 to 60 seconds until you detect their scent.

• **Cold temperatures dull aroma and taste,** so chilled foods may need more seasoning than warm items.

• **For even distribution,** stir ground spices into dry ingredients before adding to the rest of a recipe.

Salt of the Sea

People want a variety of everything these days, from wine to coffee to peppers. So naturally, they want a variety of salt, too. Enter gourmet sea salt. Aficionados prefer the lighter taste of natural sea salt as well as its crunchy texture. Try it and you'll be hooked.

• **All salt is from the sea.** Processing and the amount of additives and natural minerals determine the difference between table salt and sea salt. The quantity and type of trace minerals create subtle flavor variations.

• **Regular table salt,** mined from underground deposits formed by ancient seas, has minerals (called impurities) removed and anticaking agents added. "Natural" sea salts may be mined, but they aren't processed to remove color and don't include additives.

• **Gourmet sea salt is harvested, or "farmed,"** by channeling seawater into clay ponds. Wind and sun evaporate the water while salt crystals form. Natural minerals color the crystals from ivory to red.

• **Use expensive sea salts as finishing salts** sprinkled on cooked foods. Since all salts dissolve in liquid, the nuances of sea salt are lost when mixed with food that's still cooking.

• **Moister than table salt, sea salt** may clump slightly. If it's exposed to excessive humidity, a crust can form on the surface and should be broken up. Store sea salts in earthenware crocks.

• **As a mineral, salt can never go stale,** so it doesn't need to be ground in a mill just before serving to remain fresh. For a finer texture, grind large dry salt crystals in a salt mill. Salt is corrosive to metal, so the mill should have a ceramic or hard plastic mechanism.

• **Many of the recipes in this book** call for coarse-grained or kosher salt. You can substitute regular table salt; just use half the amount.

Coastal Pantry Favorites

Condiments
- Chili sauce
- Cocktail sauce
- Dijon/coarse-grained mustard
- Fish sauce
- Hoisin sauce
- Hot sauce
- Kalamata and green olives
- Ketchup
- Mayonnaise
- Oyster sauce
- Prepared horseradish
- Soy sauce
- Tartar sauce
- Worcestershire sauce

Dried Herbs/Spices
- Bay leaves
- Cajun/Creole seasoning
- Crushed red pepper flakes
- Curry powder
- Dried basil
- Dried dill
- Dried mustard
- Dried thyme
- Ground cumin
- Ground red pepper
- Kosher salt
- Old Bay seasoning
- Paprika
- Peppercorns (for grinding)
- Rock salt (for bedding oysters and packing ice cream)
- Saffron

Dry Items
- All-purpose flour
- Brown sugar, light and dark
- Cornflakes cereal
- Cornstarch
- Fish bouillon cubes
- Grits
- Panko breadcrumbs
- Powdered sugar
- Sesame seeds
- Stone-ground cornmeal

Nuts
- Pecans
- Pine nuts
- Walnuts

Wines/Spirits
- Dry Sherry
- Red wine
- Rum
- Tequila
- White wine

Oils/Vinegars
- Good-quality vinegars: balsamic, red wine, rice wine, and white wine
- Olive oil, extra virgin and pure
- Peanut oil
- Sesame oil, dark and regular

Canned/Bottled Items
- Black beans
- Capers
- Chicken broth
- Chipotle peppers in adobo sauce
- Clam juice
- Coconut milk
- Diced tomatoes
- Dried tomatoes in oil
- Honey
- Key lime juice
- Roasted red peppers
- Salsa

Pasta/Rice
- Basmati rice
- Couscous, plain and flavored
- Long-grain and wild rice
- Orzo

Dairy
- Blue cheese
- Butter
- Cream cheese
- Eggs
- Feta cheese
- Half-and-half
- Milk
- Parmesan cheese
- Sour cream
- Whipping cream

Fresh Herbs/Produce
- Basil
- Celery
- Cilantro
- Garlic
- Ginger
- Green onions
- Italian parsley
- Jalapeño peppers
- Lemon grass
- Lemons, limes, oranges
- Mint
- Plum tomatoes
- Red onions
- Rosemary
- Shallots
- Sweet onion
- Tomatillos

Other
- Bacon
- French bread
- Good-quality party crackers
- Wood chips (such as hickory, alder, and mesquite)

Tips and Shortcuts from the Test Kitchens

The key to preparing great coastal meals is no secret: It's all about keeping things simple and casual. Our Test Kitchens staff share their best tips and shortcuts for no-stress seafood.

When Buying Fresh Fish

• **What you see:** Clear, protruding eyes with black pupils. Shiny, intact, tightly adhering scales. Bright red gills. Flesh that looks moist and translucent, not milky white.
• **What you smell:** A mild, almost sweet and faintly marine smell. "Fishy" odor is a sign of a fish past its prime.
• **What you feel:** Firm, elastic flesh that bounces back when pressed.
• **Take a small cooler along to the fish market.** Most reputable fishmongers will not only wrap your fish for you, but also fill your cooler with ice to go.

How Much Is Enough?

• **For whole fish,** allow ¾ to 1 pound per serving.
• **For fish fillets or steaks,** count on ⅓ to ½ pound per serving.
• **One-half to ¾ pound raw shrimp in shells,** or ⅓ to ½ pound peeled raw shrimp, or ¼ to ⅓ pound cooked peeled shrimp serves one.
• **One pound raw shrimp in the shell** yields about ½ pound cooked and peeled shrimp.
• **One whole lobster** or 1 (8-ounce) lobster tail serves one.
• **One-third to ½ pound shucked raw scallops** serves one.
• **One pound live crawfish** serves one.

Storing Fish

• **Fresh is best,** so try to cook fish the same day you buy or catch it.
• **If you must store fresh fish,** keep it in the coldest part of your refrigerator and, if possible, on ice. Fish stored at 32° (which is its temperature if covered with ice) keeps almost twice as long as fish stored at 40° (which is the temperature of most refrigerators).
• **For easy ice storage,** place fish or shellfish in a colander, cover with ice, and store over a drip pan in the refrigerator.
• **Keep an opened box of baking soda** nearby in the refrigerator.
• **Use refrigerated fish** within 1 or 2 days.

Checking for Doneness

• **It's about time:** A rule of thumb for cooking fish is 7 to 10 minutes per 1 inch of thickness.
• **Fork in the fish:** Insert a fork into the thickest flesh and twist it slightly to check for doneness. It's ready when the fish flakes easily.
• **The eyes have it:** Visually, fish becomes opaque and the juices milky white when it's done.
• **Open sesame:** When cooking oysters, clams, or mussels in the shells, the shells open when done. If not, discard them. If cooked out of the shells, they become plump and opaque.

• **Blushing beauties:** Shrimp turn pink when done, while lobster and crawfish turn red.

Grilling

• **Select fish** at least 1 inch thick for grilling.
• **Grill fish fillets skin side up first.** When turned to grill skin side down, the skin will stick to the grill. Lift off cooked fish carefully with a wide spatula, leaving skin on the grill.
• **If cooking directly on the grill grate,** spray the grate with vegetable cooking spray before placing it over a hot fire.

Frying

• **Reduce splatters** by patting fish dry before lowering it into hot oil.
• **Use heavy-duty zip-top plastic bags** for dredging fish in flour and seasonings. This keeps your hands dry and smelling clean.
• **Fry in peanut oil** for the crispiest crust.
• **Keep the oil frying temperature** consistently around 365° to 375° to maximize crispness and minimize greasiness.

Poaching

• **Start poaching whole fish in cold liquid** so the outside doesn't overcook before the interior is done; start fillets in simmering liquid.
• **To add flavor, use wine, beer, or broth** instead of water as the poaching liquid, and add herbs, spices, or citrus to the pot.

Pan-Frying

• **Make sure the fat is hot before adding the fish;** a strong sizzle when the fish hits the skillet encourages nice browning.
• **When pan-frying fish,** you should turn the fish only once, so put the best looking side down in the pan first.

Microwaving

• **Cover fish with wax paper** and microwave at HIGH for 3 to 4 minutes per pound. Let stand 3 minutes to complete cooking.
• **Arrange thicker portions of fish to the outside** so they get done without overcooking thinner portions.

Blot It Out

• **To remove the white coagulated protein** that sometimes surfaces on cooked fish, simply blot fish with paper towels.

Wine at Work

• **White wine's not the only pairing for fish**—if it's a spicy dish, light red wines are a nice complement. If it's grilled salmon, Pinot Noir is perfect. Experiment with your favorite wines. See our Wine & Food Pairing chart on page 329 for more suggestions.

Citrus Splash

• **Squeezing citrus over fish brings out flavor.** A little spritz of lemon just before serving brings the simplest fish recipe to life.

Opening Shellfish

• **Place oysters or clams in shells on a jellyroll pan** and bake at 350° for about 15 minutes. This step helps the shells open slightly and makes them easier to shuck.
• **Wear heavy rubber gloves** for shucking shellfish to avoid nicked knuckles.

Seafood Kabobs

• **Thread fish and veggies onto 2 skewers instead of 1** so food can lie flat on the grill.
• **Thread same-sized pieces of fish and shellfish** onto skewers to ensure that they cook in the same amount of time.

Tools and Secrets

• **Tweezers or needle-nose pliers** are handy for removing small fish bones.
• **Picking shells from fresh crabmeat** comes easy when you have a colander set up over the sink and a bowl handy for the discards.
• **Get rid of lingering fish odor** by grinding leftover lemon pieces in the garbage disposal.
• **A grill basket keeps delicate fish intact** and holds shellfish in a batch on the grill for easier turning. Be sure to grease the basket before adding the seafood.

To Devein or Not

• **Deveining shrimp is an aesthetic choice rather than a necessity.** In small shrimp, it's really not noticeable, but in larger shrimp, it's unappealing and can add a gritty, muddy taste.
• **To devein shrimp,** just slit the shrimp lengthwise down its back, and pull away the vein with the tip of a knife or a deveiner tool.

Fish Tales

• Save the heads and skeletons of fish as well as the heads and shells of shrimp—they make great stock for soups. Keep them tightly wrapped in the freezer up to one month.

fish substitutions

Can't find a particular fish? Use this substitution list, selecting the same form as called for in the recipe—whole, fillets, or steaks.

• **Catfish:** haddock, pollock, flounder
• **Flounder:** ocean perch, orange roughy, sole, turbot
• **Grouper:** halibut, sea bass, snapper
• **Haddock:** cod, ocean catfish, flounder
• **Halibut:** sea bass, snapper, monkfish

• **Mackerel:** bluefish, lake trout
• **Perch:** walleyed pike, orange roughy, flounder, turbot, sole
• **Pompano:** snapper, sea bass, yellowtail, redfish
• **Salmon:** swordfish, halibut, lake trout

• **Sea Bass:** grouper, halibut, snapper
• **Snapper:** sea bass, grouper, redfish, pompano
• **Sole:** flounder, turbot, orange roughy, ocean perch
• **Swordfish:** halibut, shark, marlin, tuna

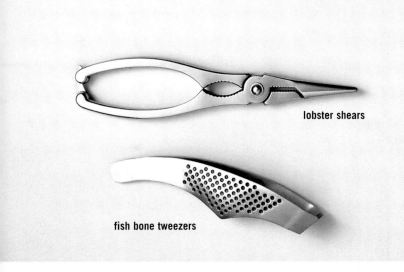

lobster shears

fish bone tweezers

Coastal Kitchen Tools

The Basics

Whether you're packing up to spend the summer at your beach cottage or just driving down to the coast for a weeklong vacation, here are some basic pieces of equipment you'll need for cooking seafood meals. Use this as a checklist for stocking your place, or, if you're renting, call and ask the owners if any of these are available.

- Skillet
- Large saucepan
- Medium saucepan
- Heavy-gauge baking sheet
- Sharp knives (chef's, paring, and boning)
- Broiler pan
- Stockpot
- Wooden spoons
- Grill
- Blender
- Baking dish
- Several spatulas
- Liquid and dry measuring cups

Seafood Tools

Preparing and eating seafood have their challenges. While it's worth the effort, you may find yourself fumbling with the slippery delicacies. Add these top tools to your kitchen drawer and you won't know what you ever did without them.

◀ **Crack into tough shellfish with wooden mallets.** Before blasting into the shell, spread black-and-white newspaper on a table. (Colored ink may contain toxins.) Add lemon halves and a wooden mallet to each setting, and don't skimp on paper towels.

- Easy to grasp and safer than a sharp knife, **a slender shrimp deveiner and peeler** does the dirty work for you.

- **Grab a pair of fish bone tweezers** (see photo, above left) and you'll have no trouble removing pin bones from fresh salmon or other selections.

- **Slice into shellfish with stainless steel lobster shears** (see photo, above left). Use the ridged crackers in the center for legs and claws, or safely lock the handles and pry open stubborn shells with the plier-like nose.

- **Simple-to-use oyster/clam knives** shuck without damaging dinner—or your hands.

- **The slender lobster and crab fork** offers tines at one end and a narrow spoon at the other to get hard-to-reach meat that's far too good to leave behind.

◀ Scoop seafood from the grill or skillet with ease. The offset handle on **a stainless steel fish turner or large slotted spatula** allows you to get flaky fish to the plate in one piece.

wooden mallet

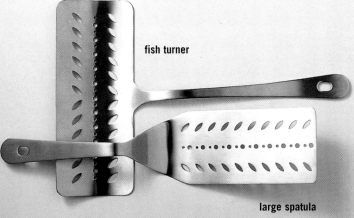

fish turner

large spatula

Don't Leave Home Without These

There are some things you never forget when packing for the beach: a swimsuit, SPF protection, and a good book. Here's the culinary gear that some of us at *Coastal Living* can't leave home without.

- a fishing pole and a seasoned cast-iron skillet for cooking over an open fire
- a pair of kitchen tongs for turning food on the grill or serving ice or pasta
- a corkscrew for wine
- good wine glasses
- a colander for draining shellfish after rinsing off sand and barnacles. Plus, it makes a great sand toy. ▶
- a beer bottle opener
- grilling tools
- a Microplane® grater
- a coffee grinder
- a reliable coffee maker
- a sharp knife
- paddleball (to play while you're grilling)
- a good-quality nonstick skillet
- a large cutting board
- disposable gloves for handling raw seafood
- a cordless blender for mixing frozen drinks in a flash. You can even take it out on the boat with you.
- wood planks for grilling seafood and meats
- vegetable cooking spray for the grill
- zip-top plastic bags for bringing beach treasures home
- just-picked corn from a farmers' market and a big stockpot for making a Lowcountry shrimp boil
- a good salad spinner ▶
- a couple of favorite cookbooks, especially ones with lots of great seafood recipes to take advantage of the catch of the day
- omelet pans for a leisurely beach brunch
- extra coolers to bring back fresh seafood when you return home
- ▼ salt and pepper mills

graduated colanders

salad spinner

salt and pepper mills

Our Best Picnic Pointers
When it comes to planning the perfect picnic, surrender to simplicity. Here's how:

First, stop at your favorite market for ingredients. But think beyond the tired standbys of dips and chips. Instead, select cheeses, deli meats, pâtés, cold roasted chicken, fresh or dried fruit, and a loaf of bread. And don't forget an assortment of cookies and a bottle of wine. Now all you need are some stylish satchels to put it all in.

Head for the beach with a smart-looking basket or tote. Whether you choose a fishing creel, a cooler disguised as a handsome basket, or a canvas bag, fill it with supplies that suit your needs. Consider including a throw or tablecloth, a corkscrew, a bottle opener, salt and pepper shakers, a paring knife, and a small cutting board. Add acrylic or enamel plates to your mix, or buy paper plates and add rattan holders for stability.

Napkins, flatware, and acrylic glasses finish off the packing list, unless you're a wine connoisseur who opts for finer stemware. If that's the case, use terry towels for napkins and wrap them around the glasses for protection en route. Add food and good friends, and you're ready to go.

Tips for Take-Alongs:

• **Shop for lightweight, sealable serving containers.** In the photo at right, we show a bowl with a lid that sports a built-in ice ring to keep food fresh for hours. Shallow containers provide more surface area to keep food cold and make packing easier.

• **Place heavier items on the bottom of your basket** and lighter, more fragile items on top. Begin by packing items that you will need last, ending with the tablecloth.

• **Take along folding chairs for added comfort.**

• **Pick a bunch of daisies for the centerpiece,** or tie a few blossoms onto your basket. Better yet, make a simple arrangement with fresh fruit.

• **Pack a cooler for perishable food.** Use frozen gel packs or ice sealed in heavy-duty zip-top plastic bags to avoid soggy food. Also, try freezing water or fruit juice in plastic bottles to help keep food cold; you can drink it later with your meal.

• **Know your perishables.** Milk products, eggs, poultry, meats, fish, shellfish, cream pies, custards, and creamy salads should be kept at 40° or below. Chill the food before placing it in the cooler.

• **On warm days, don't leave food out for more than an hour.** Be safe. When in doubt, throw it out.

• **Use a thermos designed to keep hot foods hot.** Don't forget to rinse it with boiling water just before filling it, and heat the food to a high temperature before pouring it into the thermos.

• **Include entertainment,** such as games, a portable CD player, and a beach ball or Frisbee. Add a telescope for stargazing.

• **Tuck in a disposable camera** and a small journal to record the memories.

• **For evening picnics,** pack breezeproof torches, a hurricane lantern, or citronella candles, which provide both light and bug repellent. To create your own luminarias, fill paper bags with sand from the beach and place votive candles inside.

• **Provide bug spray for guests,** and keep insects away from the food with mesh domes.

• **Prepare for cleanup** by having wet wipes, paper towels, and two garbage bags: one for trash and one for dirty dishes. You want to leave the beach at least as clean as you found it.

coastal entertaining ideas

Entertaining at the coast has but one rule: casual. Plan ahead for a relaxed atmosphere of fun and fine food. See how you can maximize your style of beach entertaining. From setting up a bar to just getting the plates on the table, we'll show you how.

Warm Welcomes

The Invitation

A clever invitation sets the mood for a great party, so be creative from start to finish. Give your friends a party invitation that stands out in the crowd. Then sit back and wait for "We'll be there." Here are some pointers:

- **Add a personal touch with handwritten invitations.** Use standard wording or try your luck with poetry or prose. Your tone should match the design of the invitation.
- **Include the necessary facts—who, what, when, where, why—and the how-tos:** how to dress, how to respond, how to get there, and perhaps how to help (what to bring).
- **Use unexpected materials in creative ways** for invitations, such as beach balls, sandpaper, fabric, craft paper, fish netting, photo note cards, button-and-string envelopes, floral marbles, plastic bags, luggage tags, and coffee bags.
- **Forget "regrets only" and include "R.S.V.P." or "please reply."** You need to know how many people will be attending.
- **"Save-the-date" notices are popular for large parties** where people will be traveling to attend; make this compatible with the invitation that will follow.
- **Package your invitation to make a statement.** The appearance, the handwriting, and the stamp all factor in having your envelope opened first. Visit your post office, or go to **usps.com** to order designer stamps on-line.

Thoughtful Hostess Gifts

Whether you're invited for a meal or a week at a friend's coastal retreat, go prepared with a thank-you gift in tow. These clever ideas will help you show your gratitude.

- **Look for a treasure the host probably doesn't already have.** It should be thoughtful and useful, but not necessarily expensive.

Everyone appreciates something home-made that doesn't require immediate attention—such as a pound cake or cheese wafers—but let the host know you don't expect it to be served right away.

- **Wine is a safe bet,** but again, chances are the host has made a selection for the gathering, so include a note suggesting it be saved for another occasion. Wine glasses or cocktail napkins are great ideas, as well.
- **Select mementos that don't collect dust:** Look for something that can be read, played with, written on, or consumed. Welcome items include games, non-perishable gourmet goodies, books, note cards, scented soaps, and candles.
- **Always package your present to make a statement.** A clever wrap lets your friend know you put time and thought into the gift. Tuck a seashell, a coastal ornament, a flower, or an herb into the ribbon, and write a few kind words to convey your thoughts.
- **Blank journals** can serve as guest books for signatures and special memories at the shore.
- **Pretty stationery inspires beautiful letters** and elevates even the shortest message. Look for nautical designs or seascapes. Better yet, make your own cards using a sketch or photograph of your host's retreat.
- **Paper cocktail napkins and dinner napkins** always come in handy. Buy ones with coastal scenes, or have plain napkins personalized with the host's initials or the name of the beach house.
- **A large bowl or platter** that can double as a decorative accessory will be a lasting reminder of your visit.
- **Colorful kitchen, beach, or bath towels are always appreciated.** Present them in a fashionable beach tote.
- **Fill photo albums with images** that capture your last visit, or give one with blank pages for the recipient's discretion.

Planned or impromptu, buffets are a blessing for coastal hosts. You can invite more friends than you have seating for, and set up ahead so guests can dine at their leisure. Everyone—including you—will have more time to mingle. Consider these tips for easy buffet entertaining.

Beach Buffet Basics

Strategizing

- **Let guests eat with plates on their laps at large, casual parties,** but serve food that doesn't require a knife. (It's awkward, if not dangerous, to cut while balancing a plate on two knees.)
- **When serving messy or difficult-to-eat foods,** such as barbecued shrimp or whole lobster, have a seated buffet. Each place setting can include flatware, a napkin, a beverage glass—even the dessert. Place desired condiments down the center of the table.
- **People expect to eat while standing at a cocktail or appetizer buffet.** However, allow plenty of surface area for them to temporarily place plates and drinks.
- **When dining alfresco,** consider setting up the buffet table inside. This keeps bugs away and prevents seagulls from dive-bombing your dip. (Out on the dining tables, keep bugs at bay with citronella candles.)
- **Have a separate table for dessert.** Also, put out extra forks and napkins, as guests may have disposed of their first set with the main course. Not enough forks? Serve cookies, petit fours, and tartlets.

Housekeeping

- **In a pinch, clean only the parts of the house the guests will see.** Give special attention to bathrooms, where you should set out extra tissue.
- **Consider hiring someone to help you.** Save your time and energy for cooking and socializing.

Hardware

- **Mix and match plates and napkins.** Stacked plates and napkins of different hues add a colorful element to the buffet table. Just select plates of similar size so they'll stack well without falling.
- **Use separate dinner, salad, and dessert plates** for small seated buffets. At large parties, guests should be able to put all their food on one plate. Cocktail parties require additional plates per person, as guests return to the table.
- **It's OK to skip the flatware,** but be sure all foods can be picked up with fingers. Keep spoons available at the beverage table if serving coffee or tea.

- **Help traffic flow by placing beverage glasses on a separate table.** Offer a variety of sizes, but reserve the largest ones for water. (A 16-ounce cup for wine is just as awkward as a 4-ounce glass for water.)
- **Set out colorful acrylic cups for little ones' beverages.** You don't want anyone mistaking a Tom Collins for lemonade.
- **Designate a tray for dirty plates and glasses,** and frequently move dirty dishware out of sight—but not necessarily to the kitchen, where guests tend to congregate. Instead, stack it in a large galvanized or plastic tub tucked away elsewhere. Cover it with a towel and return to your guests.

Menu

- **Have finger foods**—spiced nuts, chips, crackers, cheese—available for light noshing before the meal.
- **Choose recipes that use a variety of cooking techniques.** For space and time reasons, you won't want all recipes to be prepared on the cooktop or in the oven. Opt for dishes similar to what you've prepared before so there are no surprises. Include easy recipes that can be made ahead.
- **Select dishes with a variety of colors** that balance taste with texture. (Go for opposites: crunchy/smooth, spicy/mild, soft/firm.)
- **Serve foods that are tasty warm or at room temperature.** Foods that should be kept hot or cold shouldn't enter "the danger zone" (temperatures between 40° and 140°) for more than two hours. Use small platters and replenish as needed. (This also keeps the food from looking picked over.) For extended parties, serve cold foods such as shrimp salad in a bowl over ice; get creative and place lemon slices or flower petals in the ice. For hot foods, try a chafing dish or electric warming tray.
- **Select recipes that are easy to serve.** Slice meats and vegetables into individual servings. Avoid thin, messy sauces.

Table

- **Go with the flow.** For large parties, set out a double-sided buffet to avoid bottlenecks. Sideboards and circular tables are fine for small parties. Ask a friend to be first in line in case guests are hesitant to begin.
- **Set up the buffet table in logical order.** Keep flatware and napkins together at the end for guests to pick up after getting

their food. Place the least expensive foods first. Why? Some people push their all-you-can-eat limits, and if you want the rest of your guests to sample the stone crab claws or imported smoked caviar, you'll need to position the good stuff at the end of the line.

• **Use varying heights for visual appeal.** Place food on pedestals or over sturdy cloth-covered containers. Fill vertical space with flowers or breadsticks.

• **Fill additional trays of food** so that you can replenish the table by exchanging a full tray for an empty one.

• **Fill serving bowls at least three-fourths full for a sumptuous spread.** Bread and rolls can spill over to give the look of abundance. Use simple, uncontrived garnishes.

• **Enhance the buffet table with one or more centerpieces.** Use votives or lanterns to avoid open flames around guests' sleeves as they reach for food.

Raising the Bar

Bone Up on Your Bartending Basics

Buy a guide and polish your bartending skills. Serve old standbys, or even better, try a new creation—and don't forget to give the drink a name. Start with fresh juice; bottled and dried mixes are no match. A juicer makes it easy.

For lighter drink endeavors, keep a supply of sparkling and mineral waters, fruit and vegetable juices, and nonalcoholic beer. And there are plenty of refreshing "mocktails."

bar necessities

When entertaining, check your supply of bar equipment ahead of time. Before you pour on the charm, gather these:

- Bar towels
- Bar glasses
- Jiggers
- Blender. Purchase an extra canister to handle a large party.
- Cocktail shaker
- Coiled-rimmed strainer
- Long-handled spoon or muddler (a rounded hardwood stick used for stirring, crushing mint, and cracking ice cubes)
- Mixing/serving pitcher
- Martini pitcher
- Ice bucket and scoop
- Lemon zester
- Corkscrews
- Bottle opener, stoppers
- Wine thermometer
- Swizzle sticks
- Measuring spoons
- Sharp knife and small cutting board
- Olive or pickle fork

- Party tub
- Coasters
- Cocktail napkins

Classic Condiments
- Grenadine syrup
- Superfine sugar
- Angostura and orange bitters
- Hot sauce
- Worcestershire sauce
- Margarita salt
- Maraschino cherries
- Green olives
- Cocktail onions

Fresh Additions
- Lemons, limes, oranges, pineapple, strawberries
- Mint sprigs
- Celery stalks
- Prepared horseradish
- Whipping cream

Drink Details

The gracious host will offer guests something to drink upon their arrival—iced tea, soft drink, wine, or spirited beverage. However, an elaborate, prominently displayed bar is not necessary for a small party. You may want to offer a limited selection of beverages, perhaps wine or champagne, fruit juice, and one special mixed drink. For a large party, you will want to offer a wider variety of mixed drinks.

There are a number of ways to make the bar area look inviting. For small gatherings, set beverage supplies on an attractive cart, tray, table, or counter; you or one of the guests can serve as bartender. For larger parties, a more formal, organized bar and a professional bartender will be helpful.

Do the Math

The amount of liquor you should plan on per person depends on several factors—the type of party, how long the party will last, and the type of food to be served. Plan on approximately two drinks per hour per guest. To help in planning, count on these figures:
- There are four 6-ounce servings in each 750-milliliter bottle of wine.
- There are about 17 drinks per 750-milliliter bottle of liquor when 1½ ounces are used per drink.
- One 10-ounce bottle of mixer per person is usually sufficient.
- One case of champagne will serve about 50 people; you

should be able to get 4 to 6 glasses per bottle, depending on the size of your glasses.

• For large casual parties, a keg of beer is perfectly acceptable and makes for easy serving. A keg will adequately serve 30 to 40 guests.

the well-stocked bar

If you entertain on a regular basis and you want to build a well-stocked home bar, have the following on hand:

Liquor
• Vodka - 2 (750-milliliter) bottles
• Scotch - 2 (750-milliliter) bottles
• Light rum - 1 (750-milliliter) bottle
• Dark rum - 1 (750-milliliter) bottle
• Gin - 2 (750-milliliter) bottles
• Bourbon - 2 (750-milliliter) bottles
• Blended whiskey - 2 (750-milliliter) bottles

Liqueur
• Amaretto (almond-flavored) - 1 (750-milliliter) bottle
• Benedictine (cognac-based) - 1 (750-milliliter) bottle
• Cointreau, Grand Marnier, or Triple Sec (orange-flavored) - 1 (750-milliliter) bottle
• Crème de Menthe (mint-flavored) - 1 (750-milliliter) bottle
• Kahlúa (coffee-flavored) - 1 (750-milliliter) bottle

Wine
• White wine - 4 (750-milliliter) bottles
• Red wine - 4 (750-milliliter) bottles
• Rosé wine - 2 (750-milliliter) bottles
• Sherry - 2 (750-milliliter) bottles
• Dry vermouth - 1 (750-milliliter) bottle
• Sweet vermouth - 1 (750-milliliter) bottle
• Sparkling wine or champagne - 2 (750-milliliter) bottles

Beer
• Light beer - 2 six-packs
• Dark beer - 1 six-pack
• Imported beer - 2 six-packs

Mixers
• Sparkling water
• Club soda
• Tonic water
• Ginger ale
• Soft drinks
• Tomato juice
• Orange juice

wine & food pairing

There are no hard-and-fast rules for pairing wine and food. Follow some of our guidelines below or experiment on your own. (Wines listed by grape variety are in regular type; regional varieties are in italics.)

food	wines
Hot, spicy foods **Ingredients like:** chiles, ginger, and pepper **Common cuisines:** Chinese, Indian, Mexican, and Thai	**Slightly sweet, fruity, light wines** such as *Beaujolais, Burgundy,* Chenin Blanc, Gewürztraminer, Pinot Noir, Riesling, *Rhône* wines, Sauvignon Blanc, and light Zinfandels
Acidic, tart foods **Ingredients like:** citrus, feta cheese, garlic, lemon, tomatoes, and vinegar **Common cuisines:** Creole, Greek, Italian, and Japanese	**Highly acidic wines** such as Chardonnay, *Chianti,* Sauvignon Blanc, and sparkling whites
Rich foods **Ingredients like:** butter, cheese, lobster, red meats, and salmon **Common cuisines:** French, German, Italian, and Southern	**Acidic, citrusy wines** such as Sauvignon Blanc **Oaky, toasty, buttery wines** such as Chardonnay **Tannic (tart), darker red wines** such as Cabernet Sauvignon, Merlot, and dark Zinfandel
Salty or smoked foods **Ingredients like:** olives, salt-cured or smoked meats, and soy sauce **Common cuisines:** Japanese, German, Greek, and Southern	**Slightly sweet, fruity light wines** such as *Beaujolais,* Chenin Blanc, Gewürztraminer, Pinot Noir, Riesling, sparkling wines, and light Zinfandels
Sweet foods **Ingredients like:** coconut, corn, fruits, mint, and thyme **Common cuisines:** Chinese, French, Indian, and Thai	**For foods other than desserts: slightly sweet wines** such as Chenin Blanc, Gewürztraminer, and Riesling **For desserts: sweet wines** such as Madeira, Ruby Port, *Sauternes,* Sherry, and sparkling wines such as *Asti* (formerly Asti Spumante) ***Note:*** Pair sweet foods with sweet wines, but the food should never be sweeter than the wine.

Stacked plates and napkins of different shades add a colorful element to a buffet table.

Stock a Party Closet

Before gathering your party necessities and accessories, figure out how many guests you and your home can accommodate; then prepare in case more people unexpectedly turn up. At the beach, a party of 12 can quickly turn into 24. No problem—seating is the least of your worries. If you have everything you need—forks, plates, glasses, serving pieces—you'll relax and enjoy the crowd.

First, find the perfect place to stash your wares. If your kitchen pantry is full, enlist an armoire, a guest room closet, or a covered space in your garage.

Next comes the fun part: **gathering the goods.**

• **Treat your friends to real plates;** balancing a paper plate is no fun for guests. Save paper and plastic goods for picnics or children's parties. Search for bargains on dinnerware at a restaurant supply store or the closest outlet mall. White plates are versatile and never go out of style. Oversize plates, while fashionable, are difficult to store and fit into the dishwasher.

◄ **Provide easy-care fabric napkins with the meal,** but keep an assortment of paper cocktail napkins to use before dinner and with pickup desserts.

• **Select plenty of bowls** that can be used for stews, salads, pastas, or desserts. Buy mugs for soup and coffee. Be creative and mix complementary colors or patterns, or just stick to basic white.

◄ **Buy a case of all-purpose wineglasses** that you can also use for iced tea, water, and even desserts. Make sure the stems will fit in your dishwasher. Simple bistro glasses are even more versatile, and they also stack well.

• **Stock up on inexpensive stainless steel forks, knives, and spoons.** No need for matching patterns. Antique shops and flea markets offer inexpensive finds. Spring for steak knives, too, if you like to serve grilled meats.

• **Collect large bowls, oversize platters and trays, large casseroles, and pitchers** to accessorize your home and add flair to your table. Opt for a variety of patterns, colors, shapes, and textures. A brightly colored enamel Dutch oven or a well-seasoned cast-iron pan goes from the cooktop to the table to keep the food hot. Don't forget the trivets.

• **Stock a bounty of baskets**—large ones, small ones, and sizes in between. They're perfect for serving breads, crackers, and cookies.

• **Line baskets with large, colorful tea towels for a bright, casual touch on the table;** after the party, simply shake the towels out—the cleanup is speedier than washing dishes.

- **Look for long-handled serving spoons, forks, ladles, and tongs.** Smaller sauce ladles, spoons, pickle forks, and spreaders are good to have on hand, too.
- **Search for breezeproof lanterns or candleholders for evening dining.** While you're at it, buy extra boxes of tapered, votive, and birthday candles, and keep fireplace matches or a butane lighter handy. Remember to store candles at comfortable room temperature or colder; the attic is too hot.
- **Equip the bar with a large ice bucket and scoop.** Have on hand a party-size barrel, acrylic or galvanized tub, or large planter to fill with ice for keeping beverages cold.
- **Accumulate fabrics to use as table coverings.** Hemming isn't necessary—just tuck the ends under and anchor with a centerpiece.

Flower Power

On the dining table or all through the house, flowers add a touch of flair you won't want to be without. But flowers needn't be fussy, and you can collect a few key containers to keep on hand that will simplify arranging the blooms. Here's advice for containers and flowers:

- **Collect containers suitable for instant flower arranging;** simple vases or bottles work well, as does a planter to corral a few bedding plants from a garden shop.
- **Browse through cabinets and closets** for out-of-the-ordinary containers. Don't hesitate to use items not traditionally used for floral arranging. If a container will not hold water or is very large, place a jar or cup inside to hold the flowers.
- **Keep centerpieces at a height** that allows good eye contact among guests. Tall arrangements command attention and work better on buffets than on the dining table.
- **A bowl full of fruit** with a hint of flowers and greenery looks great on a sideboard or a chest. Candlesticks ringed with flowers and fruit add height to the grouping.
- **A grouping of candles** makes a quaint display in the center of a small table. Place them on a decorative tile to serve as a base and tie the candles together. Place a few flowers on the side to add a soft touch.
- **Simple bouquets are the most appealing.** Interest comes from varying flower shapes and colors. Bouquets need not be large, but cut flowers should be of similar size.
- **Feel free to supplement garden flowers** with blooms purchased from the florist for variety.
- **Arrange the tallest stems first** so they set an outline for the bouquet. Insert taller flowers in the center, and fill in with flowers that become progressively shorter as you near the edges of the container.
- **To keep an arrangement from wilting,** place it away from direct sunlight.

Seaside Flair

Simple Centerpieces

A table without a centerpiece is like a little black dress without pearls. Even casual meals have a bit more polish when you add a simple bouquet of flowers like the two shown here.

Seashells and lilies say summer at the beach. Here's what you'll need: calla lilies, wheat shafts, bear grass, seashells, and cockscomb (which resembles coral). First, fill a glass cylinder with water; put it in the center of a glass bell jar. Place lilies, wheat, and grass in the cylinder. Fill in around cylinder with seashells. Then arrange cockscomb around edge of cylinder to cover base of arrangement. Place candles in two other jars, and fill in around base with seashells. ▶
Lilacs in a coffeepot make a breezy table topper. Since coffeepots are typically watertight, just fill one with water and add lilacs to fill the pot.▼

Tin Soldiers

From beach to garden to table, there's a galvanized pail for every purpose.

There are many uses for galvanized products. Here are a few ideas from our *Coastal* crew.

• **Galvanized metals are fine for food display** when another container (or ice) is used between the metal and the food. Construct a crustacean tower, for example, by stacking two different-size trash can lids (brand-new, of course) and elevating one with a small pail. Place the tower in a low dish for stability. Fill the tiers with cracked ice and mounds of chilled steamed shellfish (still in the shell). Your bountiful plateau will be impressive and cost-efficient. ▶

• **Arrange bouquets** in classic galvanized French flower buckets.

• **Keep catalogs,** beach towels, hand towels, paperback books, children's toys, and garden tools neat in small trash cans, washtubs, or oval tubs.

• **Stock large tubs** with wine, beer, and soft drinks; top with plenty of ice.

• **To create a table,** balance plywood atop a large sand-filled trash can (or two, if you prefer a long table for a beach banquet).

• **Stack firewood** in a large tub or trash can and kindling in a small pail for a fire that's ready when you are.

• **Purchase pails for gift giving.** Fill with items that reflect the interests of the recipient, such as toys for a young friend; cleaning supplies for the student moving into an apartment; sunscreen, sunglasses, and a pair of flip-flops for the beachcomber; or grilling tools for a new neighbor.

• **Celebrate a special occasion** by filling a pail with ice and a bottle of champagne; then complete the package with two flutes tied to the side.

• **Turn a galvanized tote into a tool caddy.**

• **Pour sand into miniature pails;** anchor a votive candle or taper in the sand. Better yet, tie several small pails together with thin wire to make a hanging lantern. Add sand and candles.

• **Pack a large washtub** as a carryall to take

to the beach. Invert the tub to make a cocktail table for your picnic.

Note: Galvanizing, the process of coating

iron metal with zinc, protects metal from rusting. Galvanized containers are not recommended for cooking or serving.

seafood primer

all about fish

Expand your coastal savvy with our facts about fish and A-to-Z seafood dictionary that defines the most popular kinds of fish.

Fish Class

Fat and Lean Fish

Fish are classified as *fat* or *lean*. Fat fish have an oil content of more than 5 percent and tend to be higher in calories and stronger in flavor than lean fish. The color of fat fish is usually darker, due to oil distributed throughout the flesh. The oil produces a pronounced flavor, as well as more of a meatlike texture than in lean fish. Fat fish require less basting during cooking than lean fish to keep flesh moist and tender. Dry-heat methods of cooking, such as grilling, broiling, and smoking, are ideal for fat fish.

Lean fish have an oil content of less than 5 percent. The oil is concentrated in the liver, which is removed when fish are cleaned. Lean fish are generally milder in flavor and whiter in appearance than fat fish because the oil is not distributed throughout the body of the fish.

Among our favorite lean fish are black sea bass, cod, flounder, grouper, mahimahi, and snapper. These are available fresh year-round, though they're more abundant during the warmer months. We've chosen to feature those that can be bought whole, but these and larger lean fish, such as halibut, can be purchased as fillets or steaks.

Lean fish tend to dry out during cooking because of their low fat content; therefore, moist-heat methods, such as poaching and baking, are best. Lean fish can be grilled or broiled successfully if basted often. A good rule of thumb for cooking time is to measure the thickest part of the fish and cook 7 to 10 minutes per inch. When done, the fish should still be moist and tender but flake easily with a fork.

When substituting one fish for another in a recipe, it's best to choose a substitute from the same classification. Use the chart below as a guide.

Selecting Fish

When shopping for fish, deal with a reputable fish and seafood market. Purchase fish from a store that has quick turnover, regularly replenishes its stock, and uses refrigerated cases to store fish. Get to know the seafood market manager, and before purchasing, ask where and when the fish was caught.

If you know the characteristics of high-quality fish, you can easily judge its freshness. The eyes of a fresh fish should be clear, clean, and full, almost bulging. The gills should be pinkish red and not slippery. The flesh of the fish should be firm and elastic (that means it should spring back when lightly touched). The skin should have no faded markings; it should be shiny, with scales firmly attached. Perhaps, though, the best indicator of freshness is odor: A fresh fish should have a clean, mild smell, not an offensive "fishy" odor.

Use some of the same pointers to judge freshness in fish that's dressed and cut. The flesh should be firm to the touch. Cut surfaces of fish steaks and fillets should be moist, not dried out. There should be no signs of yellowing or browning edges. The fish should have a mild, fresh odor.

fish classifications

Fat Fish	Lean Fish	
Amberjack	Cod	Scamp
Freshwater Catfish	Flounder	Scrod
Herring	Grouper	Sea Bass
Lake Trout or Rainbow Trout	Haddock	Snapper
Mackerel	Halibut	Sole
Mullet	Mahimahi	Swordfish
Pompano	Orange Roughy	Tilapia
Salmon	Perch	Tilefish
Sardine	Pike	Triggerfish
Tuna	Pollock	Turbot
Whitefish	Redfish	Walleye
	Rockfish	Whiting

Fish is highly perishable, so it's important to follow some basic guidelines for buying and storing it properly.

The eyes of a fresh fish should be clear, clean, and full, almost bulging.
The gills should be pinkish red and not slippery. The flesh of the fish should
be firm and elastic, and the skin should be shiny, with scales firmly attached.
Perhaps, though, the best indicator of freshness is odor:
A fresh fish should have a clean, mild smell.

Know What You're Buying

You can purchase fresh fish in a variety of market forms. Knowing the following terms will help you select the right type and amount of fish for your needs.

- **A whole or round fish** is marketed just as it comes from the water. When cooked, a whole fish makes a dramatic presentation on the plate. Count on 1 pound per serving.
- **A drawn fish** is a whole fish that has been eviscerated (internal organs removed) and scaled. Allow 1 pound per serving.
- **A dressed fish** is one that has been eviscerated and scaled, and has head and fins removed. The tail may or may not be removed as well. Smaller fish that have been dressed are referred to as *pan-dressed*. Allow ½ pound per serving.
- **Fish steaks** are crosscut slices of large dressed fish. They're usually cut about 1 inch thick. The only bone is a cross section of the backbone and ribs. Plan on about ⅓ to ½ pound per serving.
- **Fillets** are the sides of fish cut lengthwise away from the backbone. They're often skinned and are practically boneless (though small pin bones may be present). For *butterfly fillets,* the fillets are held together by the uncut belly skin. Skinless fillets tend to dry out quickly during cooking, so watch them carefully. Allow ⅓ to ½ pound per serving for fillets.

Handling Fish

Fresh fish is best if cooked the day of purchase but may be stored in the original wrapping in the coldest part of the refrigerator up to 2 days if the wrapping is moisture- and vapor-resistant. If it's not, wrap the fish carefully before storing. Place a damp cloth over the fish, inside the wrapping, to prevent fish from drying out. Fresh fish should be frozen within

2 days of purchase. Freeze it up to 3 months. Some fish sold in the unfrozen state have been flash-frozen or blast-frozen. Once fish have thawed, do not refreeze. If you intend to freeze a fish, ask if it was previously frozen.

If you're not going directly home after purchasing fish, have the wrapped fish placed in a plastic bag filled with ice. When you arrive home, remove fish from its wrapper, rinse in cold water, and pat dry with paper towels. Then repackage fish in wax paper and an airtight plastic bag. Place the bag directly on ice in a colander set in a large bowl in the refrigerator.

When buying frozen fish, make sure the package is tightly wrapped and sealed. There should be little or no air within the wrapping. Be sure that there's no blood visible inside or outside of the package and that the fish is solidly frozen and free of ice crystals. Thaw frozen fish in the refrigerator. If you need to thaw it quickly, place the frozen fish wrapped in plastic wrap under cold running water until thawed. Drain and blot thawed fish with paper towels before cooking.

Frozen breaded fish products should not be thawed before cooking; prepare these according to package directions. Leftover cooked fish will keep 2 days in the refrigerator.

be savvy about seafood

Stay up-to-date about seafood conservation and food safety issues with these Web sites that monitor the latest findings:

- www.seafoodchoices.com is sponsored by the Seafood Choices Alliance.
- www.foodsafety.gov is sponsored by the FDA.
- www.aboutseafood.com is sponsored by the National Fisheries Institute.

Amberjack

Also known as yellowtail, this lean, mild-flavored fish swims the waters of the Gulf of Mexico and the West Indies. Cook it shortly after catching, or freeze for later use. It's best prepared as fillets or steaks, and baked or coated with breadcrumbs or cornmeal and then fried.

Anchovy

There are many species of anchovy available, but in North America, the primary source is the anchoa family. They're sold fresh as bait (other fish know a good thing when they taste it, too) or canned with salt and oil.

These little guys are supremely powerful in condensed fish flavor. Smoked anchovies often add depth of flavor to thick pastes or thin sauces in Mediterranean or Vietnamese fare, respectively.

Anchovies should have a pleasantly strong aroma; if they actually stink, it's a sure sign they've gone bad. Choose anchovies packed in olive oil for the best flavor; the ones in glass jars tend to taste better than canned. If you find them too salty, soak them in cold water for up to 20 minutes, and pat them dry with paper towels. Note that ½ teaspoon anchovy paste equals one anchovy fillet. Never put anchovies into oil that is too hot; they'll quickly burn.

Multitined anchovy and sardine forks are highly collectible and make fine accoutrements for these classy little fish.

Bass

A general name given to a variety of fresh and saltwater fish, bass have spiny fins and rough scales. They are lean fish with a delicate to mild flavor. Bass are excellent fried, broiled, baked, and grilled.

Black Sea Bass

These small, black-scaled fish are native to the Atlantic Coast, from Cape Cod all the way to Florida. They're usually sold at 1 to 3 pounds, though they can sometimes weigh a couple of pounds more. Their flesh is firm and flavorful. When cleaning black sea bass, be careful with the spiny dorsal fin, or ask the seller to clean the fish. Black sea bass are true bass.

Catfish

Long whiskers give this fish its name. Catfish are generally thought of as a freshwater fish, though they are also plentiful in saltwater. However, the majority of catfish sold at market are farm raised, and only these and freshwater catfish are recommended for eating.

Catfish don't have scales; instead, they have a tough skin that must be removed before the fish are cooked. The flesh is firm to the touch and mild in flavor, making catfish good for frying, poaching, steaming, baking, or grilling.

Caviar

Better known as fish eggs, the prospect of eating them may sound decidedly unappealing to some, but the salted roe of the female sturgeon is one of the world's most renowned delicacies.

The best way to learn about caviar is to find a good supplier and take the plunge. Don't hesitate to sample many types. You'll not only find your favorite, but you'll develop your palate, too.

The Basics of Caviar

There's no need to be intimidated by caviar. Here's the scoop: The exotic names usually denote the type of sturgeon the eggs come from. It's a bit like comparing Chardonnay to Sauvignon Blanc.

• **Beluga** is traditionally considered the best (and certainly the most expensive) caviar. It comes from the beluga sturgeon found in the Caspian Sea. The largest of all sturgeon, beluga can take up to 20 years to sexually mature, making theirs the rarest kind of sturgeon roe. Beluga caviar is steel to dark gray

Blini with caviar

in color, and eggs are large—just smaller than allspice berries. They are rather sturdy and give a distinctive burst when pressed against the roof of the mouth.

• **Osetra** comes from smaller osetra sturgeon. About the size of white peppercorns, the eggs are brownish gray, with a delicate texture and a nutty or fruity flavor. Some harder to find versions may be golden. Europeans often prefer osetra to beluga because of its good taste and average price.

• **Sevruga** caviar has an intense, almost lemony flavor. Of these three roe varieties, sevruga eggs are the darkest and smallest; each is only slightly larger than a mustard seed. The eggs' texture is almost crisp, but not tough. Quite small, sevruga sturgeon mature in 7 years, so their roe is most plentiful.

• **Malossol** simply means "little salt." While all caviar is salted, malossol is considered the highest grade of caviar because it has less than 5-percent salt. The term *malossol* can describe the roe of beluga, osetra, or sevruga sturgeon.

• **Pressed caviar** is made from damaged eggs, which are pressed to remove the liquid. It has a strong flavor and "jammy" texture that some aficionados love. Significantly less expensive than whole eggs, pressed caviar is a bargain for those who love its intensity.

• **Pasteurized caviar** has been heat treated to make it shelf stable. The caviar's taste, consistency, and especially texture suffer greatly from the cooking process. Use it only in recipes in which other flavors will play an important role in the dish.

• **Domestic caviars** are creating a buzz in the industry since Russian imports have suffered from the breakup of the Soviet Union, overfishing, and pollution. American companies now produce caviar from the roe of wild and farm-raised sturgeon, salmon, whitefish, and paddlefish or spoonfish. The United States at one time was a major exporter of caviar to Europe, mainly Germany, before American sturgeon became endangered, due to industrial pollution and overfishing. But now the hackleback sturgeon is thriving in the Mississippi and Missouri river systems, and its roe's taste and texture are acclaimed. Spoonfish, a freshwater cousin of sturgeon, yields a fine-quality caviar similar to sevruga—at a third of the price.

Savvy Spoons Contact with metal, especially silver, can affect caviar's taste, so serve it from spoons made of horn or mother-of-pearl.

Caviar Caveats

Handling and serving caviar properly are just as important as buying good quality product. Here are a few tips from the experts.

Serving

Fine caviar is best served with plain or buttered toast points. To make toast points, cut good-quality, thin-sliced white bread into triangles. Bake at 350° for 8 to 10 minutes. Cool and store in zip-top plastic bags or other airtight containers.

When serving guests, provide the traditional accompaniments—onions, chives, and chopped eggs—as a courtesy for those who may still be developing a taste for this exotic hors d'oeuvre.

Another classic way to serve caviar is with blini—tiny buckwheat pancakes—topped with a dollop of sour cream and crowned with pearly roe (see photo, far left).

When serving caviar, plan on 1 ounce per person. Opt for ½ ounce if other appetizers are served.

Beverages

What should you drink with caviar? Champagne, vodka, or sparkling water.

Purchasing

Since most caviar is sold in jars or tins, checking for freshness is something of a moot point. But the eggs should be shiny, not cloudy, and should not have a strong smell. Mail-order products are generally shipped in coolers with several chill packs to assure freshness. Unopened caviar can be held for about 10 days; once opened, it should be refrigerated and consumed within 3 days.

Cod

Cod is a widely relished fish, sporting a mild, delicate flavor. The fish has a large head and a deep slit of a mouth. Most cod caught today weigh between 4 and 9 pounds, and are 16 to 32 inches long. Haddock, a related fish, is often substituted for cod in recipes. Haddock resembles a small cod, with a thin, black stripe down its body. Experts generally don't recommend grilling cod because the soft and flaky flesh can fall apart on the grill.

Flounder

Flounders are part of a group called flatfish, and sometimes the term *flounder* is used to describe all flatfish. Flounders are indeed flat, with asymmetrical bodies and both eyes on one side of the head (the fish lives at the bottom of the sea, and both of its eyes look up). The eyed side of the fish is usually dark, and the sightless side is pale white.

Most members of the flounder family—such as sole, turbot, and halibut—are excellent for eating. They cook up delicate, sweet, and flaky, with the exception of halibut, which is firm fleshed.

Who's Who?

Trying to learn all the flounders can make you, well, flounder. Some are true flounders; others are flatfish that are commonly considered flounders. Here's a rundown of some popular varieties.

Atlantic Species

- **Atlantic halibut** is a large fish that can weigh up to several hundred pounds, but it averages around 50 pounds. It has a firm texture and delicate flavor, and is most often sold as steaks.
- **Southern flounder** is found from North Carolina to Texas, where it is a popular sport fish, as well as a commercially harvested species. Good flavor and moderately firm flesh are its hallmarks. It's usually sold as 1½- to 2-pound whole fish or as fillets.
- **Summer flounder** is found from the Carolinas to New England and typically weighs between 2 and 5 pounds. Summer flounder is gray-brown to olive green in color and is plentiful inshore during the summer, as its name indicates. It is the most abundant flatfish on the East Coast, and because of its size, fillets are thicker.
- **Winter flounder,** found from the Chesapeake Bay to southern Canada, is also known as lemon sole or blackback. These fish weigh 1 to 2 pounds and have very tender flesh that falls apart easily when cooked. Winter flounder has a rust-brown or black color and is plentiful from fall through spring.

Pacific Species

- **Pacific halibut** is a large, flavorful fish usually sold frozen. Like Atlantic halibut, it is mostly steaked because of its large size.
- **Petrale sole,** prized for its flavor, is the most popular flatfish in the Pacific Northwest. Due to its small size (about a pound) and delicate flesh, it is best cooked and eaten "on the bone."
- **Rex sole** is an even smaller species that is just as delicious as the petrale and also best when cooked whole.
- **Sand dab** ranges the West Coast from California to Alaska and is a very small fish that tops out at about a pound. It is generally fried or grilled whole.

face-to-face with a flatfish

If you serve flounder whole, show your guests how to remove the top layer of the meat and take out the bones:

- Serve the fish with the dark side up.
- Cut down the middle of the dark side to the tail.
- Slide the knife into the opening and under half of the fillet, lifting it away from the bone. Set aside.
- Repeat with the other half. Lift out the bones and discard.

Handle with Care

Because of their lean, tender flesh, flounders cook quickly and require close attention to prevent them from drying out. Baking, broiling, sautéing, frying, even poaching work well, but grilling fillets is not recommended. Whatever method you choose, cook flounder with the skin on to keep the meat intact, and be careful not to overcook. (If you poach, carefully remove the skin before serving.) Most flounders have thin, edible skin that complements the fish's flesh. Have your fishmonger scale the fish; then rub your fingers over it at home to find any stray scales, which you can scrape off with a knife.

Pan-dressed fish—those with their heads, scales, and internal organs removed—will stay fresh longer and are more practical for cooking than whole fish. (Also, you won't have two eyes gazing up at you as you cook.)

Grouper

A name given to a great many varieties of fish, grouper can grow to hundreds of pounds. It's the smaller ones—between 5 and 10 pounds—that are sold whole. Members of the sea bass family, grouper are caught on both coasts, as well as the Gulf. Though they can vary widely in appearance, they are generally thick-bodied fish. Extrafirm flesh and distinctive taste are the grouper's hallmarks.

Haddock

Haddock is a low-fat, firm-textured, mild-flavored white saltwater fish related to the cod, but smaller. Haddock are found in the north Atlantic Ocean, from Cape Cod to Newfoundland. They can be baked, poached, sautéed, or grilled, and are sold as whole fish, fillets, or steaks. Frozen and smoked haddock also are available.

Halibut

A very large, low-fat, firm-textured, mild-flavored, white salt-water fish, halibut is a member of the flatfish family. Halibut are abundant in northern Pacific and Atlantic waters. They can be baked, grilled, poached, and broiled. Fresh and frozen halibut are sold as fillets and steaks.

Mackerel

Mackerel is a family of saltwater fish that has a firm, high-fat flesh and a strong, but pleasant flavor. Common types include Spanish, Atlantic, Pacific, and king mackerel. Purchase mackerel fresh, frozen, smoked, canned, or salted. Because of its high-fat content, fresh mackerel doesn't keep well; cook it the same day it's purchased.

Mahimahi

This fish is easy to recognize with its high, blunt forehead. Mahimahi usually appears at market between 5 and 15 pounds. It has dense flesh and a mild, sweet flavor. Not many people wanted this fish under its most common previous name, which was dolphin or dolphinfish, although it's not related to the mammal. Fisherfolk found it much easier to market under its Hawaiian name.

Mullet

A silvery gray, moderate- to high-fat fish with a firm, white flesh and mild, nutty flavor, mullet can be found in the waters of the southern Atlantic Ocean and in the Gulf of Mexico. They can be fried, baked, broiled, or poached. They are most popular on the Gulf Coast and especially in the Florida Panhandle, where they are fried or smoked.

Orange Roughy

A low-fat fish found in the coastal waters of New Zealand and Australia, orange roughy has a firm, white flesh and a mild flavor, which lends itself to poaching, baking, broiling, or sautéing. Flounder or other lean white fish make good substitutes for orange roughy.

Perch

Perch include various freshwater fish with spiny fins found in North America and Europe. The most familiar variety in the United States is the yellow perch, with an olive green back, dark vertical bands, and red-orange fins. They have firm flesh, with a delicate, mild flavor, and are best pan-fried, broiled, sautéed, baked, or used in soups and stews. There are several saltwater fish that are incorrectly identified as perch, including the white perch (a member of the bass family) and ocean perch (a member of the rockfish family).

Pike

A family of freshwater fish that includes the muskellunge and pickerel, pike are sometimes referred to as the shark of fresh water because of their long body, large mouth, and fierce-looking teeth. The pike has lean, firm, low-fat flesh, with a mild flavor, but does contain many small bones. Pike is the traditional fish used in quenelles and gefilte fish.

Pompano

Pompano is a saltwater fish found in the waters off the coast of Florida. It has a firm, white, mild-flavored flesh, with a moderate amount of fat. Pompano is sold whole and in fillets, both fresh and frozen. Though this versatile fish can be prepared by most any classic cooking method, it is often served *en papillote.*

Redfish

A member of the drum family, with reddish orange skin, redfish has a black-spotted tail and firm, ivory-colored flesh, with a mild flavor. This is the lean fish that originally catapulted blackened dishes to popularity and has become much more scarce as a result.

Rockfish

Rockfish is one of the largest families of fish found in the Pacific Ocean. This low-fat, firm-fleshed fish generally has black or olive to bright orange or crimson skin with yellow fins, and is sometimes spotted or striped. Significant varieties include bocaccio, ocean perch, orange rockfish, and yellowtail. They're suitable for most cooking methods.

Salmon

Salmon is an oily fish. This oil gives it its distinctive taste and makes it an excellent source of omega-3 fatty acids—linked to the prevention of heart attacks, strokes, depression, and more. King salmon has the highest amount of omega-3s compared with other wild salmon species. Wild salmon's red flesh is due to their diet, including such crustaceans as shrimp. If frozen immediately, salmon retains its fresh-caught flavor and texture. Don't refreeze salmon, or its flavor and texture will deteriorate.

Salmon's high fat content helps keep it from drying out. The fish is well suited for a variety of cooking techniques, such as baking, braising, broiling, grilling, poaching, sautéing, and steaming.

Salmon fillets have pin bones running along the side of the meat; you will need to remove them if the fish market hasn't already. Using needle-nose pliers or tweezers, pull out the bones at the same angle to avoid tearing the flesh. Skinning the fillet first makes this task easier.

Who's Who?
Farm-Raised Atlantic Salmon

Farm-raised Atlantic salmon accounts for much of the salmon consumed in this country and is available year-round. Atlantic salmon has a fat content of about 6 percent, which gives it a rich flavor.

Atlantic salmon, not surprisingly, used to come from the Atlantic Ocean, where it was the only salmon species. Sadly, after a century of dam construction and pollution on the Eastern Seaboard, the fish's numbers are dwindling. As a result, nearly all Atlantic salmon is now farm raised. Somewhat confusingly, Atlantic salmon can be farm-raised anywhere—from Washington to Chile to Maine. It's the species that makes it Atlantic, not the place where it was raised.

Pacific Wild Salmon

All the salmon that come from the Pacific Ocean are wild. Pacific salmon live most of their lives at sea; then they instinctively return to their freshwater natal streams to spawn and die.

Depending on the species, Pacific salmon can have a very high fat content, especially if the fish traveled great distances (as much as 2,500 miles) up glacially cold rivers to lay its eggs. To make the journey, wild salmon store a reservoir of fat that gives certain species an opulent flavor. Following are descriptions of the Pacific species.

• **King or chinook** is the most prized of wild salmon species. Its high fat content, rich flavor, and silky texture ensure that king salmon commands some of the highest prices. King are also the biggest salmon, weighing up to 50 pounds, and are usually troll-caught (individually hooked on a fishing line) off Northwest coasts. By comparison, fish caught in huge nets are more easily bruised.

The most legendary king salmon are caught in Alaska's Copper River from mid-May to mid-June. Copper River king salmon are very rich and well marbled—much like a fine steak. Each year, most of the Copper River king catch is snapped up by top chefs, though you can sometimes find it at fish markets. During the off-season, consumers can find frozen king salmon at seafood markets or order it online.

• **Coho or silver** salmon is smaller and much leaner than king salmon. As a result, it's not as rich and has a lighter, more delicate texture and flavor. For this reason, part of the coho catch ends up as canned salmon.

• **Sockeye or red** salmon is abundant, especially in Alaska, and is often a bright orange-red color. Nicely textured and with a hearty flavor, it shows up in markets more than it used to and is great for grilling. Sockeye that is canned is often called "blueback."

• **Chum** salmon is somewhat coarse and quite lean. Chum can be very pale in color, almost more gray than red. Historically, chum was often smoked, but today it's more commonly sold both fresh and frozen in grocery stores. The small roe of the female chum is highly regarded as salmon caviar.

• **Pink** salmon is the smallest salmon and has a delicate, mild flavor. It is frequently used in salmon salads. Well over half of all canned salmon is pink.

Sardine

The name derives from the isle of Sardinia, where the small fish—a species of pilchard—were originally cured and preserved. Now, canned sardines from the United States (mostly Maine) and Canada (Nova Scotia) are actually Atlantic herring. The classic American canning sardine, the Pacific or California sardine, seems to be nearly extinct.

Fresh sardines, which have a nutty, slightly sweet taste, are available seasonally at fish markets. Although canned sardines last indefinitely, fresh ones are highly perishable—immediately store them on ice, and cook the same day. When shopping for fresh fish, look for clear eyes and a uniformly silver skin, free of yellow blotches. The flesh should be firm, not mushy; the smell, clean.

To uphold their shape, prepare them quickly by roasting, chargrilling, or frying. Canned sardines are available whole packed in oil or mustard sauce, fried, or smoked. They also come skinned and boned as fillets.

The Well-Dressed Sardine

Fresh sardines should be dressed before being cooked. Ask your local fish merchant to perform this messy task. (If you'd like them to remain bone-in, however, say so.) If you clean them yourself, here's what to do:

To scale a sardine, run a fish scaler (or back of a chef's knife) along the skin from tail to head. (To keep the scales from flying everywhere, do this in your sink under running water.)

To de-head and gut a sardine, grab the head, twist it off, and pull it down (the innards should follow). To remove the bones, gently pull out the backbone using a small knife or your fingers. Note that the bones, which are edible, keep the fish from falling apart during the cooking process.

Shark

Shark is a type of saltwater fish that ranges in taste, color, and texture according to the variety. For example, the dogfish and blacktip sharks have white, mild-tasting meat, while the mako shark, similar to swordfish, is firmer textured and has a stronger flavor.

Shark can be broiled, grilled, baked, poached, or fried. Because it has a firm flesh, shark is good for cutting into cubes and threading onto kabobs; it can also be simmered in soups, or cooked and chilled and added to salads.

Snapper

Hundreds of species of snapper swim the world over. The fish is often confused with less tasty cousins or with fish bearing similar names, such as redfish.

Ways of the Wild Salmon

• Wild salmon begin life in freshwater streams and rivers, then follow the rivers' flow and begin adulthood in salt water. They return to spawn in the same river in which they were hatched. This migration is called a "run." A salmon run does not necessarily include all species, and the dates vary.

• Wild Alaskan salmon is one of the most environmentally friendly buys. Karen Tarica of the Marine Stewardship Council says, "It is the only U.S. seafood to earn the MSC seal of approval, showing it hasn't been overfished or harvested in ways that harm the ocean."

Snapper, particularly red snapper, is favored in fine restaurants, as well as in home kitchens. Its fine white flesh has a fresh, sweet taste and is adaptable to many styles of cooking. True red snapper is actually white fleshed, but its skin and the irises of its eyes are red. Because lower quality fish is often passed off under its name, red snapper should always be purchased with its reddish skin attached. The skin offers proof of snapper authenticity, and if skinless fillets are labeled red snapper, many times they're impostors. Most snappers sold are already filleted; they usually weigh 5 to 10 pounds whole, but they can grow as large as 35 pounds. Smaller snappers are also sold whole and are good for stuffing and grilling.

Red snapper's rosy hue is so spectacular, the best way to serve the famous fish is whole. Because the head makes up half the weight of the fish, a 2- to 3-pound snapper serves two plentifully.

Broiling, grilling, and pan-frying are popular ways to cook whole snapper.

Sole

A saltwater flatfish, sole is related to the flounder family, with a white underside and brown to gray top skin. The flesh is lean, pearly white, and mild flavored. The best known type is Dover sole, which is harvested in coastal waters from Denmark to the Mediterranean Sea. True Dover sole is imported frozen. Much of what is sold in the United States as sole is actually flounder. Sole can be prepared in a variety of ways, including poaching, steaming, baking, and broiling.

Swordfish

A very large saltwater sport fish, the swordfish has a dorsal fin and an upper jawbone that projects to a bladelike point. Found in waters throughout the world, swordfish can weigh up to several hundred pounds and are difficult to catch, which makes them one of the more pricey fish on the market.

Swordfish meat varies from off-white to orange and is mild-flavored, moderately fat, firm, and dense. Enjoy swordfish by sautéing, broiling, baking, or poaching.

Enjoy the splendor of red snapper by serving it in its rosy-hued entirety.

Tilapia

Tilapia, a freshwater fish native to Africa, increasingly is farm raised in the United States and other countries. All American-raised tilapia goes to the market line, while imported tilapia arrives frozen. Tilapia generally has gray skin, lean white flesh, a firm texture, and a sweet, mild flavor. It's suitable for almost any cooking method.

Tilefish

A saltwater fish found in the Atlantic Ocean from the Mid-Atlantic States to New England, tilefish has multicolored skin with distinctive yellow dots and low-fat, firm flesh.

Trout

These are a large group of fish, related to the salmon family. They're found primarily in freshwater lakes and streams, though they are sometimes farm raised. Trout generally have a firm white, orange, or pink flesh with a medium to high fat content. There are many different species, but some of the most common are rainbow trout, brook or speckled trout, steelhead trout, and brown trout. They can be purchased fresh or frozen, whole, or in fillets. They can be pan-fried, poached, baked, grilled, or broiled. Canned, smoked, and kippered trout are also available in some supermarkets.

Tuna

Tuna is a member of the mackerel family and can be as large as 1,500 pounds or as small as 6 pounds. There are six species, all very migratory and all quite different in flavor and texture. Increasingly, restaurants as well as supermarkets are indicating which species are featured on their menus or in their seafood departments.

A Guide to the Four Most Popular Tunas

• **Albacore** is found in both the Atlantic and Pacific oceans in temperate and tropical waters. It is the most valuable tuna for canning, although albacore is also beginning to show up in fresh markets. The pinkish white flesh is delicate and flavorful, making the steaks perfect for poaching and grilling.

• **Yellowfin,** found throughout the world in tropical and subtropical waters, is prized in Hawaii. It's known there as *ahi,* a name now adopted by many restaurants and markets. Its English name comes from the yellow stripe found on its side and the color of its fins. Because of its delicacy and flavor, ahi is often quickly seared and served virtually raw inside.

• **Bluefin,** which gets its name from the steel blue color of its skin, is the largest of all tunas. A record-setting bluefin weighing almost 1,500 pounds was landed off Nova Scotia in 1976. Until recently, this tuna had very little commercial value in the United States, although it has long been prized in the Mediterranean as well as Japan, where it is sliced into sashimi. Prepared in this manner, it is soft-textured, meaty, and not at all "fishlike" in flavor. In fact, when served raw, its flavor has been compared to roast beef. Once cooked (as it's prepared in the Mediterranean), bluefin becomes firm and is a bit of an acquired taste. It is, therefore, often brined before cooking.

• **Skipjack,** one of the smallest tunas, sometimes weighing a mere 6 pounds, is found in all tropical and semitropical waters. It's an important species in Japan, where it's called *katsuo* and served as sashimi, as well as in Hawaii, where it is known as *aku.* Not as common on American restaurant menus as yellowfin or albacore, the skipjack is often used in canned "light meat" tuna.

Turbot

A flatfish found in waters off Iceland to the Mediterranean, turbot has a firm, lean, white flesh and mild flavor. Many think turbot rivals the quality of Dover sole. True turbot is usually imported frozen to the United States. It can be poached, baked, broiled, or fried.

Whiting

Whiting is a saltwater fish found in the Atlantic Ocean, from New England to Virginia, which is sometimes called silver hake or silver perch. It's a member of the cod family and has a low-fat, firm, delicate-flavored flesh. It can be salted, smoked, poached, broiled, pan-fried, or baked.

More than two-thirds of our country's tuna catch ends up canned, making it the most common canned fish on the market. Canned "light meat" tuna has a stronger taste than the prized "white meat" tuna, which comes from only albacore.

all about shellfish

Clams

Though there are many types of clams, they are often roughly divided into two groups: soft-shells and hard-shells. Soft-shell clams grow in muddy coastal areas; hard-shells grow in sandier bays and along the beach. Varieties of soft- and hard-shell clams can be found on both coasts.

Clam size varies tremendously, from tiny clams no bigger than a thumbnail to giant sea clams that can weigh hundreds of pounds. Generally, the smaller the clam, the more tender it is.

Most small clams are terrific to cook with and are nearly effortless to prepare. All that's needed is a quick scrubbing of their shells or a good rinsing in cold water. Once clean, they can be tossed with abandon—shell and all—into soups, stews, and pasta dishes.

Common Edible Clams

- **Cockles** are heart shaped, with a scalloped rim. They are found off both the Pacific and Atlantic coasts, although smaller Pacific cockles are often preferred for their tender texture and mild flavor. Tougher, larger, boldly flavored Eastern cockles are more commonly used in chowders.
- **Steamers** are primarily East Coast clams. Though any number of small clams can be steamed, the ones we commonly call steamers come from flats in New England and the Chesapeake. For a time, steamers were also known as Ipswich clams after Massachusetts's Ipswich Bay. Steamers, the classic clambake clam, are very tasty and perfect for eating raw, fried, or—of course—steamed.
- **Aquagems** are small farm-raised clams from Florida. They are available year-round and, because they are farm raised, are free from sand and grit. Plump, sweet tasting, and about an inch in diameter, Aquagems are often the first choice of chefs.
- **Quahogs** (pronounced CO-hogs) are Eastern U.S. clams that come in three different sizes:

The smallest quahogs are often called **little necks** (spelled as two words). These succulent clams are frequently served raw on the half shell. There are also two species of native West Coast littlenecks (spelled as one word). These are not quahogs, however, and are too tough and tasteless for eating raw.

The next larger quahog—about 2 inches in diameter—is commonly called a **cherrystone.** Cherrystones are very tender and perfect either on the half shell or in any recipe.

Very large quahogs—shells 3 inches or more in diameter—are also called **bay quahogs, chowders,** or **surf clams.** Eat them in chowders or fritters.

- **Manila clams** are Japanese little necks, which are believed to have hitchhiked their way to the Pacific Coast with Japanese oyster seeds. They are a bit smaller than the native West Coast littleneck and have a bright purple adductor scar. Manilas are the most tender of all clams and are delicious however you prepare them.
- **Razor clams** have long shells that look rather like an old-fashioned straight razor. They're too chewy to be eaten raw; instead, they're generally chopped into fritters or used in soups and chowders.
- **Geoduck** (pronounced GOOEY-duck) is the largest American soft-shell clam. Its remarkable gray-brown neck never completely hides within the shell and can, in fact, protrude up to several feet. Only the neck is used in cooking and usually must be parboiled before being minced, ground, or sliced into cutlets and fried.

How to Buy and Store Clams

Without exception, clams in the shell should be bought alive. Dead clams smell bad and are unsafe to eat. Luckily, it's easy to tell if a clam is feeling feisty: Live soft-shell clams will retract further into their shells if you poke inside them. If a soft-shell doesn't retract and try to close, then be sure to discard it—the clam is dead.

Live hard-shells will be clamped so tight it's nearly impossible to pry their shells apart, even using an oyster knife. If you can move the shells of a hard-shell clam, discard it—the clam has died.

Store clams in an open bowl in the refrigerator, and use promptly. Do not put clams in a sealed plastic bag or on ice; they will die.

How to Clean Clams

Because soft-shell clams have a shell that is slightly open, they can contain unpleasant grains of sand. To remove the sand from commercial, store-bought clams, rinse them thoroughly in cold running water.

If you dig clams yourself, soak them for a few hours in salted water to which you've added a handful of cornmeal—the cornmeal cleans their stomachs—and be sure to change the water at least once. Drain and then rinse again, and the clams will be ready for cooking. Hard-shell clams are not sandy. All they require is a quick rinse under cold water to remove anything that might be on the outside of the shell.

Crabs

Though there are more than 4,000 species of crab in the world—and more of these live off the coasts of North America than anyplace else—there are only four that serious eaters need to know about: Dungeness crab, king crab, stone crab, and blue crab.

Dungeness Crabs

The scrumptious Pacific crab is a real West Coast specialty. In fact, in San Francisco and Seattle, it's often eaten at New Year's with nothing more than a spicy dipping sauce, some crusty sourdough bread, and a bottle of white wine.

Dungeness crabs are fairly big and meaty, generally weighing 2 to 4 pounds. During their season—December 1 through July 1—you can sometimes buy them live, which means you'll need to boil them. But most markets sell them already cooked. You can tell the cooked ones by their bright red shells. Most markets will also crack and clean cooked crabs, making the meat easy to extract with a small pick and a nutcracker.

Cooked Dungeness crab is often eaten cold, but you can use the meat in cioppino, a San Francisco–style fisherman's stew, or roast the crab (still in its shell) in the oven and serve it warm.

King Crabs

King crab, also called Alaskan crab because Alaskan waters are its home, is one of the sea's most magnificent crustaceans. Weighing up to 20 pounds and with a leg span of 6 feet or more, king crabs are rarely shipped live. Instead, they're immediately cooked, separated into parts, and frozen aboard the large vessels that fish them. Midwinter is their peak season.

The most commonly eaten part of a king crab is the meaty, delicious legs, which are sold frozen. These can simply be steamed for 5 minutes, or for an unusual twist, throw them on a hot grill for a few minutes, just until the shell turns hot. To open the shells, crack with a nutcracker, then pull out the meat and serve with melted butter and lemon.

Stone Crabs

This famous Florida crab, with its beautiful, plump, orange-and-black-tipped claws, is the inspiration behind one of America's oldest and most popular restaurants: Joe's Stone Crab Restaurant in Miami Beach. As tradition dictates, this crab is typically eaten chilled with nothing more than a simple mustard dipping sauce on the side.

The rich, firm claw meat is, in fact, the only part of the stone crab that is eaten—or can be. It's against the law for fishermen to harvest the whole crab; instead they must break off a claw and throw the crab back into the sea where it will regenerate a new one. The season runs from November to May.

SOFT SHE[...]

crabbing 101

- **Crabbing is a warm-weather activity,** possible year-round in mild climates. Crabs hibernate in cold Northern regions, but when water temperatures reach 60°, they become active.
- **A simple method for crabbing, handlining** is the most interactive. The only tools you need are a small piece of wood, string, and bait. Attach wood to one end of the string and bait to the other. Drop the bait into the water. Wait for a tug, then wind the string around the wood. Use a long-handled net to snare the crabs near the surface.
- **Any calm location less than 12 feet deep is ideal.** Water currents make crabbing tricky: It's hard to keep bait on the line, and you can't feel the crab's tug as easily. If there is a slight current, place a lead weight near the bait so it remains on the bottom, where crabs feed.
- **Bait? Chicken's a safe bet.** Crabs love any part, so use the cheapest: backs, wings, necks. Cleaned fish carcasses or heads work well, too.
- **Local fishing regulations vary,** but blue-crab bodies should measure at least 5 inches from tip to tip. Keeping sponge (egg-laden female) crabs is generally prohibited.
- **As with other shellfish, cook only live crabs.** Dead ones should be discarded to prevent foodborne illnesses. Prepare crabs easily by immersing them in seasoned, boiling water to cover. Cook 10 minutes, drain, and rinse in cool water.

Blue Crabs

Most of the crabs sold in America are blue crabs, and conveniently, the meat has already been picked from the shell. And for good reason. Extracting the meat from this small crab (4 to 6 inches across) can be either maddening or enchanting, depending on your point of view. But in either case, it's never quick.

Not surprisingly, blue crabs have blue-green shells and bluish claws that, on females, can be tipped with orange. They are found in bays and estuaries from Cape Cod south to all along the Gulf Coast. Blue crabs are in season when the waters are warm, which in some places can be as early as February.

If instead of buying lump crabmeat you buy or harvest whole blue crabs live, watch your fingers, and be sure to use tongs. These guys pinch. You'll need to give them a 5-minute boil before icing them down to cool. After you crack them and remove the meat, the crab is ready to be eaten or used in a crab recipe.

• **Soft-Shell Crabs** The blue crab is abundant from New Jersey to Texas. But it is the 180-mile-long Chesapeake Bay that is the center for catching soft crabs, the stage the blue crab enters when it sheds its hard shell for a day or two in order to grow, usually beginning in mid-May.

To become a 6-inch adult in its lifespan of a few years, the blue crab must shed some 20 times, briefly turning soft on each molt. It is a fact of crustacean life that translates to one of the sublimest tastes our coastal waters afford.

For several hours after it backs out of its old shell, a shedding blue crab, whose pincers normally could severely lacerate a finger, is silken to the touch and can be consumed with just a light crunch. Live soft-shells are so popular that they are flown all over the world when in season. You can find them on menus year-round; out-of-season, know that they've been frozen in the molting stage.

Harvesting

It is one thing to know shoals are rich in crabs and quite another to work them. A crab scrape, or type of dredge about 4 feet wide, is towed through vast, shallow grass beds, where shedding crabs seek cover. Skilled crabbers maneuver their boats in water where a few inches are all the difference between floating and sticking, all the time working furiously, heads down, to sort the crabs from the grass.

Peelers

Few soft crabs are actually caught soft; rather they are taken as "peelers," still hard but, to the experienced eye of a crabber, showing a tinge of color no larger than a fingernail clipping along the edge of the rear swim fins. The color, darkening from white to red, means a crab is within hours or a day of shedding its shell. It need be held only briefly in wooden trays, through which seawater is pumped, before the market value is transformed from a few cents as a hard crab to as much as $1.50 commanded by big spring softies.

The crabber sorts the harvest in his cramped boat. Into one tub go "green peelers." Held in tanks at the shedding shanty, these will emerge soft in several days. "Rank peelers," which will shed sooner, go to another tub. "Buckrams," which have shed but are turning just a little too hard to market as soft, go back overboard or in a basket destined for home consumption.

Buying Live Crabs

Buy from a market known for the freshness and quality of its fish. As for the crabs themselves, they should be lively and active. If a crab doesn't move, don't buy it.

Buying Fresh Crabmeat

Many markets carry fresh crabmeat—usually blue crab—that has already been cooked, shelled, and cleaned. It can be dressed with a little mayonnaise, heaped into a salad, and eaten as is. It also can be molded into crab cakes and sautéed, or used in just about any crab dish you have in mind.

Fresh crabmeat comes in three forms: lump, flake, and claw. Lump crabmeat is made up of solid morsels of white meat from the body of the crab. It's used in crabmeat cocktails and salads in which the appearance of dishes is important. Flake crabmeat is made up of smaller pieces of meat from the rest of the body. Claw meat is also small, and because it isn't as snow white as body meat, it's often used in soups and other dishes in which color is not as important.

When buying fresh crabmeat, avoid any that is gray or yellowish in color—a sign that it's old. Truly fresh crabmeat should smell clean and fresh, and should not have even a whiff of ammonia.

Crawfish

Also called crawdads or mudbugs—and outside the South, crayfish—these crustaceans resemble tiny lobsters. In fact, crawfish are prepared by most of the same methods as lobster, and like lobster, they turn bright red when cooked. Crawfish are sold live or boiled. Cooked, peeled tails are also available either fresh (from March to June) or frozen. Real crawfish fans know boiled crawfish are generally peeled and eaten with the juices and the sweet meat sucked from the heads.

As the self-proclaimed crawfish capital of the world, Louisiana harvests most of the nation's supply.

Lobsters

How to Pick Out a Lobster

Live lobsters are greenish brown to black; it's when they're cooked that they turn bright red. You'll find them in water tanks at seafood markets and some larger supermarkets. When you buy, look for medium-size lobsters that are lively in water. The most tender meat comes from lobsters that weigh 2 pounds or less. Generally, a 1½- to 2-pound lobster is considered a single serving.

How to Cook It, Claws and All

The secret to great lobster cookery is freshness: The sooner the lobster is cooked after being taken from the sea, the better. So buy it fresh the same day you plan to cook it.

The most common methods of cooking whole lobster are boiling and steaming. These methods allow lobster to retain the most juices, with the most tender results.

The claws will be banded when you buy a lobster. Leave the bands on until just before you cook it; then carefully remove them with scissors. To cook, bring about 4 quarts water to a rolling boil in a large kettle or Dutch oven. Hold the lobster by the tail and plunge it, headfirst, into the pot of boiling water. Cover the pot; boil the lobster 10 minutes for the first pound and 3 more minutes for each additional pound.

To steam the lobster, set a rack or steamer basket in the bottom of a large covered kettle or roaster. Pour in 1½ inches of water and boil. Add the live lobster; tightly cover the kettle or roaster to keep in the steam. Steam the lobster 13 minutes for the first pound and 3 more minutes for each additional pound.

You can also roast lobster. Place the live lobster on a large jelly-roll pan, and brush with oil. Bake at 450° for 15 to 20 minutes.

And for an outdoor dinner, add your lobsters to the grill. Place live lobsters on a baking sheet, and freeze for 20 minutes. Then place them on the grill, backside down, close the grill lid, and grill over high heat (400° to 500°) for 15 to 20 minutes or until they're done.

How to Get to the Meat

Eating a lobster is a little bit of work and more than a little messy. It's also very much worth the effort. Just make sure to give everyone a large bib and plenty of napkins.

For the best flavor and texture, you must prepare lobsters live, and that makes the process a little more exotic than many culinary experiences. We can assure you of three things. One: It can be a thoroughly delightful experience. Two: You can successfully pull off a lobster feast even as a novice. Three: It takes lots of practice to look like you know what you're doing. Fortunately, the practice is anything but a chore.

First, twist off the large claws. Crack each claw with a lobster cracker, or use a nutcracker, pliers, hammer, or even a rock. Separate the tail from the body by arching the back until the shell cracks. Break off the tail flippers, insert a fork, and push the tail meat out in one piece. Remove and discard the black vein that runs along the tail, if you want. A common alternative is to cut through the translucent underside of the shell with kitchen shears and pull the tail meat out whole. Break away the small walking legs from the body. The easiest way to get to the excellent meat in the legs is to suck it out.

Mussels

Mussels are exceptionally healthful. They have especially high amounts of protein and omega-3 fatty acids and are low in cholesterol and saturated fats. New Zealanders even use Lyprinol, an extract from mussels, to treat arthritis and asthma. No wonder aficionados consider mussels the ideal melding of taste and nutrition.

Surprisingly, although mussels have a delicate taste, they hold their own when served with strong seasonings, such as the hot chili peppers used by Thai cooks. When you savor a batch of freshly harvested mussels, you'll experience the salty taste of the sea overlaid with a touch of sweetness.

Along the East Coast, the blue mussel is found from Canada to the Carolinas. On the West Coast, the most common edible mussel is the Mediterranean mussel, said to have hitchhiked to these shores on the hulls of Spanish ships. Importers also offer New Zealand's huge Greenshell mussel, particularly good for stuffing, but more bland than the homegrown species.

Although Europeans have been cultivating mussels for centuries, North American mussel farming began only in recent years, particularly in Atlantic Canada, New England, and Washington State.

Depending upon how carefully they're raised, cultivated mussels grow faster, are freer from grit, and usually lack the calcified pearls sometimes found in their wild counterparts. Most grow on posts, on ropes suspended in tidal waters, or at the bottoms of protected coves. If you can find a reliable source of cultivated mussels, sample them.

Before buying mussels, ask to see the obligatory inspection tag—coded with the harvest date—that guarantees they were collected from pollution-free waters. Once harvested, mussels have a shelf life of about 7 to 10 days.

Knowing the water conditions is critical because mussels are stationary feeders that eat by filtering plankton and diatoms out of the water they ingest. (A mature mussel can filter between 10 and 15 gallons of water a day.) They can become contaminated by pollutants and toxins—one reason mussels are off-limits during red tide.

Each mussel attaches itself to a surface with its byssus—a fiberlike growth, known as a beard. If you're foraging them yourself, the easiest way to harvest mussels is to pull them off in bunches, put them in a plastic laundry basket, and keep them submerged in seawater until you've finished.

Once home, bury them in ice in an open container with good drainage. Do not seal in plastic, since mussels need to breathe. Kept cool, harvested mussels will usually stay closed (keeping seawater inside). To clean, discard any mussels that seem exceptionally heavy or light, and scrub the rest with a stiff brush under running water. Often, mud-filled mussel shells mimic the real thing. Hold suspect mussels between your thumb and forefinger, press on the bias, and the mud-filled shells will slide open. A slightly open mussel can be alive, but it should close when you press down on its hinge or tap its shell.

Debeard each mussel at the last minute, since this process may damage the mussel's inner tissue. Hold each mussel in one hand and the beard in the other, and yank down with a quick motion. Rinse again, put the mussels in a pot, cover with your ingredients, and steam just until the mussels open. Shake the pan occasionally. Serve immediately.

Because both the mussel shells and meat are so attractive, French chefs use mussels as garnishes for cooked fish or on salads. They also strain and save the liquor exuded during cooking, using cheesecloth or a coffee filter to remove grit. Any leftover liquor adds flavor to fish sauces or soups. Boil the liquid to concentrate its flavor, freeze in ice-cube trays, and use the cubes within two months.

Most people can easily go through 1¼ to 1½ pounds of mussels at a sitting. Count on about 3 ounces of meat for each pound of mussels.

Stretch your mussels In France, where more than 10,000 tons of *moules* are consumed yearly, steamed mussels serve as both meal and utensil. Stretch your own mussels a bit, and try this new approach to eating them: Use a utensil to remove the meat from the first mussel shell; then use that hinged shell to pluck the meat from the remaining bivalves. You'll find it to be an efficient—yet disposable—set of tongs.

Oysters

An oyster is a bivalve mollusk found in saltwater regions throughout the world. Oysters usually have a rough, gray shell that contains gray, soft, slippery-textured flesh that can be eaten raw or cooked.

There are three main species of oysters sold in the United States: Pacific or Japanese, Atlantic or Eastern, and Olympia. Pacific oysters are found along the Pacific seaboard and can reach up to a foot long. Atlantic oysters come in various sizes, have a briny flavor, and are known for their place of origin, such as Apalachicola or Chesapeake Bay. Olympia oysters are usually very small and are harvested from Washington's Puget Sound.

Fresh oysters are available year-round; however, they are at their peak during fall and winter months. Oysters in the shell can be served raw, baked, steamed, or in special recipes, such as oysters Rockefeller. Shucked oysters can be fried, sautéed, used in soups or stews, in dressings or stuffings, or made into appetizers, such as angels on horseback. For the best flavor, oysters should be served within 5 minutes of shucking. The flavorful, clear liquor that fresh, shucked oysters are packed in can also be used in soups and stews. Oysters are also available canned and smoked.

The past 10 years have seen somewhat of an oyster renaissance. Oyster farming, private ownership of tidelands, better refrigeration techniques, quicker delivery systems, and strict water quality protection and inspection help guarantee fresher and safer oysters, especially good news for the many fans of raw oysters.

Oyster farmers grow 5 different species, and when you order oysters from many menus or fish markets, you can specify a favorite variety by its water of origin. An oyster takes on unique flavor and shell formations from the minerals, nutrients, and salinity of its home waters, so the market name helps maintain consistency. It also stirs debates about which waters grow the best oysters.

Storage

Live oysters are best eaten as fresh as possible; reject those that do not have tightly closed shells or that don't snap shut when tapped. Live oysters can be covered with a damp towel

and refrigerated up to 3 days; however, the sooner they're used, the better they'll taste. If you must, refrigerate shucked oysters, covered in their liquor, up to 2 days, or freeze up to 3 months. Canned oysters can be kept in a cool, dry place up to 2 years.

Scallops

Though technically there are many varieties, scallops are generally classified as bay scallops or sea scallops. Bay scallops are smaller and are found in saltwater ponds close to shore, with the shucked meat ranging from 40 to 100 per pound. Because they are sweeter and in shorter supply, the little guys are more prized and more expensive than the chunkier deep-water sea scallops, which usually come 20 to 30 per pound.

Sea scallops are dredged by offshore trawlers in deeper waters. Like bay scallops, they come to American consumers primarily from the Atlantic waters of Canada, New England, and the Mid-Atlantic States. They're harvested year-round, but bays are taken in the fall and winter, which is when they taste best.

The key to selecting scallops is to note their color and smell. They should have a moist sheen and a sweet smell, and their color can range between pinkish and beige. When shopping for bays, take note: If they are a bright white color, the scallops may have been soaked in water to increase their weight. And seafood wholesalers outside the scalloping territories of New England and the Mid-Atlantic States are sometimes tempted to chop sea scallops to satisfy demand for the smaller, more delicate bays.

Don't overcook scallops. They can become rubbery and change flavor after just a few minutes of direct heat, so cook them just until they turn opaque.

Shrimp

Americans eat more shrimp than do citizens of any other country—about 2½ pounds per person per year. Hundreds of millions of pounds of shrimp are harvested each year from U.S. waters, but production can't keep pace with our appetite: 70 percent of the shrimp we eat is imported from other countries.

The majority of shrimp are frozen, often while still at sea. Fortunately, the fast-freezing method used preserves much of the freshness.

Though fresh shrimp that have never been frozen can be found in coastal communities during harvest season, the fresh

shrimp in your local market most likely have been frozen.

Shrimp in the United States are divided into two categories: cold-water shrimp and warm-water shrimp. They're harvested in federally regulated seasons: cold-water shrimp off the West Coast from April through October and in the Northeast from December through mid-April; brown warm-water shrimp in the Gulf from May through July; white warm-water shrimp in bays and estuaries along the Gulf in August.

Whether you're buying in or out of season, make sure the shrimp smell only slightly fishy; avoid any with an odor of ammonia. High-quality shrimp will be firm, not soft or sticky; their shells will be firmly intact and gray to pale pink in color. Though tiny shrimp (sometimes labeled popcorn shrimp) are frequently sold cooked, most shrimp are sold raw, in their shells, with the heads removed.

Shrimp with heads are more difficult to find. Though the heads are typically removed before cooking, you can use them to flavor sauces, stocks, and soups.

Shrimp are sold according to the number per pound, which varies from region to region. See the chart below for examples.

Different types vary in color and flavor, but are interchangeable in recipes. A shrimp's body is nearly 80-percent water; the remaining 20 percent is a rich source of protein, vitamins, and minerals.

Shrimp are easy to prepare, and many seafood chefs believe they taste best when cooked simply. Avoid overcooking them. Even a few extra seconds of cooking will make them tough. Cook just until they turn pink. Small shrimp will cook in just 1 to 3 minutes; larger shrimp will take only moments longer.

You can cook shrimp peeled or unpeeled, deveined or with the vein still intact. See page 319 for more tips on deveining.

shrimp statistics

- **1 pound raw, unpeeled shrimp**
    = 12 ounces raw, peeled, deveined shrimp
    = 8 to 9 ounces cooked shrimp
- **colossal** = 11 shrimp per pound
- **jumbo** = 15 to 18 shrimp per pound
- **large** = 26 to 29 shrimp per pound
- **medium** = 37 to 40 shrimp per pound
- **small** = 45+ shrimp per pound

metric equivalents

The recipes that appear in this cookbook use the standard United States method for measuring liquid and dry or solid ingredients (teaspoons, tablespoons, and cups). The information in the following chart is provided to help cooks outside the U.S. successfully use these recipes. All equivalents are approximate.

Equivalents for Different Types of Ingredients

A standard cup measure of a dry or solid ingredient will vary in weight depending on the type of ingredient. A standard cup of liquid is the same volume for any type of liquid. Use the following chart when converting standard cup measures to grams (weight) or milliliters (volume).

Standard Cup	Fine Powder	Grain	Granular	Liquid Solids	Liquid
	(ex. flour)	(ex. rice)	(ex. sugar)	(ex. butter)	(ex. milk)
1	140 g	150 g	190 g	200 g	240 ml
¾	105 g	113 g	143 g	150 g	180 ml
⅔	93 g	100 g	125 g	133 g	160 ml
½	70 g	75 g	95 g	100 g	120 ml
⅓	47 g	50 g	63 g	67 g	80 ml
¼	35 g	38 g	48 g	50 g	60 ml
⅛	18 g	19 g	24 g	25 g	30 ml

Liquid Ingredients by Volume

¼ tsp						=	1 ml	
½ tsp						=	2 ml	
1 tsp						=	5 ml	
3 tsp	=	1 tbls			= ½ fl oz	=	15 ml	
		2 tbls	=	⅛ cup	= 1 fl oz	=	30 ml	
		4 tbls	=	¼ cup	= 2 fl oz	=	60 ml	
		5⅓ tbls	=	⅓ cup	= 3 fl oz	=	80 ml	
		8 tbls	=	½ cup	= 4 fl oz	=	120 ml	
		10⅔ tbls	=	⅔ cup	= 5 fl oz	=	160 ml	
		12 tbls	=	¾ cup	= 6 fl oz	=	180 ml	
		16 tbls	=	1 cup	= 8 fl oz	=	240 ml	
		1 pt	=	2 cups	= 16 fl oz	=	480 ml	
		1 qt	=	4 cups	= 32 fl oz	=	960 ml	
					33 fl oz	=	1000 ml	= 1 liter

Dry Ingredients by Weight

(To convert ounces to grams, multiply the number of ounces by 30.)

1 oz	=	¹⁄₁₆ lb	=	30 g	
4 oz	=	¼ lb	=	120 g	
8 oz	=	½ lb	=	240 g	
12 oz	=	¾ lb	=	360 g	
16 oz	=	1 lb	=	480 g	

Length

(To convert inches to centimeters, multiply the number of inches by 2.5.)

1 in			=	2.5 cm			
6 in	=	½ ft	=	15 cm			
12 in	=	1 ft	=	30 cm			
36 in	=	3 ft	= 1 yd	=	90 cm		
40 in			=	100 cm	=	1 meter	

Cooking/Oven Temperatures

	Fahrenheit	Celsius	Gas Mark
Freeze Water	32° F	0° C	
Room Temperature	68° F	20° C	
Boil Water	212° F	100° C	
Bake	325° F	160° C	3
	350° F	180° C	4
	375° F	190° C	5
	400° F	200° C	6
	425° F	220° C	7
	450° F	230° C	8
Broil			Grill

recipe index

● chef recipe   ● for kids   ● from the grill   ● make ahead   ● naturally healthy   ● quick & easy

● chef recipe   ● for kids   ● from the grill   ● make ahead   ● naturally healthy   ● quick & easy

● chef recipe　　● for kids　　● from the grill　　● make ahead　　● naturally healthy　　● quick & easy

● chef recipe　　　● for kids　　　● from the grill　　　● make ahead　　　● naturally healthy　　　● quick & easy

● chef recipe ● for kids ● from the grill ● make ahead ● naturally healthy ● quick & easy

● **chef recipe**   ● **for kids**   ● **from the grill**   ● **make ahead**   ● **naturally healthy**   ● **quick & easy**

● *These recipes contain good-for-you ingredients and are low in fat, sugar, and/or sodium.*

subject index

credits

Photographers:

Ralph Anderson: pages 104, 107, 120, 139, 166, 167, 183, 209, 274, 320 (all)

Jim Bathie: pages 11 (bottom left, top right), 103, 125, 130, 141, 176, 188, 193, 196, 199, 204, 206, 207, 223, 271, 302, 308, 321 (all), 332 (top and bottom)

Matt Brown: page 187

Bruce Buck: pages 118, 129, 179, 279

Langdon Clay: pages 56, 57, 58, 59, 60, 61, 95

Tina Cornett: left back cover, pages 121, 133, 192, 195, 217, 252, 263, 265, 270, 283

Wyatt Counts: pages 50, 51, 52, 53, 54, 55, 134, 164, 276

William Dickey: pages 222, 232 (left), 268, 338, 339

Fran Gealer: right front cover, pages 109, 128

J. Savage Gibson: pages 30, 31, 32, 33, 34, 35, 36, 37, 38, 39, 40, 41, 174, 216

David Harp/Chesapeake Photos: pages 6, 100, 148, 154, 171, 200, 226, 242, 243, 261, 352

Brit Huckabay: right back cover, pages 11 (middle top), 97 (top), 102, 110, 111, 114, 115, 116, 117, 119, 131, 140, 142, 153, 160, 161, 168, 173, 180, 210, 224, 233 (right), 236, 237, 239, 241, 244, 249, 253, 254, 255, 256, 258, 260, 266, 281, 287, 293, 294, 295, 304, 305, 330, 337, 344, 345, 347, 351, 353

Michael Jensen: pages 22, 23, 24, 25, 26, 27, 28, 29, 68, 69, 70, 71, 72, 73, 113, 124, 126, 137, 184, 277, 278

Deborah Whitlaw Llewellyn: pages 9, 94

Becky Luigart-Stayner: pages 2, 5, 97 (bottom), 162, 163, 203, 250, 284, 309 (right top and bottom), 310, 313, 317, 319, 342, 349, 350

Sylvia Martin: page 324

Randy Mayor: pages 285, 288

Art Meripol: pages 225, 238

Gary Moss: pages 11 (bottom right), 74, 75, 76, 77, 78, 79, 170

Howard Lee Puckett: left and middle front cover, middle back cover, pages 4, 7 (top and bottom), 10, 11 (top left, middle bottom), 12, 13, 14, 15, 16, 17, 18, 19, 20, 21, 42, 43, 44, 45, 46, 47, 48, 49, 62, 63, 64, 65, 66, 80, 81, 82, 83, 84, 85, 98, 99, 105, 108, 122, 123, 145, 147, 150, 155, 156, 157, 169, 172, 177, 181, 197, 208, 229, 231, 232 (right), 233 (left), 234, 245, 246, 251, 264, 275, 280, 299, 314, 315, 322, 323, 325, 327, 329 (bottom), 334, 335

Allen Rokach: page 228

Barth Tillotson: page 212

Ben Van Hook: background back cover, page 247

Charles Walton IV: background front cover, pages 1, 86, 87, 88, 89, 90, 91, 92, 93, 112, 127, 175, 191, 218, 219, 220, 227, 235, 273, 328 (top and bottom), 329 (top), 333

Special thanks to Sexton's Seafood of Birmingham, Inc.

Special thanks to Judy Feagin, the original Coastal Living *Food and Entertaining Editor*

favorite recipes journal

Jot down your family's and your favorite recipes for quick and handy reference. And don't forget to include the dishes that drew rave reviews when friends came for dinner.

Recipe	Source/Page	Remarks